Lessons from Good Language Learners

CAMBRIDGE LANGUAGE TEACHING LIBRARY

A series covering central issues in language teaching and learning, by authors who have expert knowledge in their field.

Lessons from Good Language Learners

Edited by

Carol Griffiths

CAMBRIDGE
UNIVERSITY PRESS

CAMBRIDGE UNIVERSITY PRESS
Cambridge, New York, Melbourne, Madrid, Cape Town, Singapore, São Paulo,
Delhi

Cambridge University Press
The Edinburgh Building, Cambridge CB2 8RU, UK

www.cambridge.org
Information on this title: www.cambridge.org/9780521718141

First published 2008

Printed in the United Kingdom at the University Press, Cambridge

A catalogue record for this publication is available from the British Library

Library of Congress Cataloging-in-Publication Data

ISBN 978-0-521-71814-1   paperback
ISBN 978-0-521-88963-6   hardback

Library of Congress Cataloging-in-Publication Data

Lessons from good language learners / edited by Carol Griffiths.
     p. cm. — (Cambridge language teaching library)
   Includes bibliographical references and index.
   ISBN 978-0-521-71814-1 (pbk. : alk. paper) — ISBN 978-0-521-88963-6 (hard-
back : alk. paper)
   1. Language and languages—Study and teaching. I. Griffiths, Carol. II. Title.
III. Series.

P51.L4975 2008
418.007—dc22

2008000624

Contents

Contents

To commemorate the publication of Joan Rubin's seminal article in *TESOL Quarterly* (1975) and to acknowledge those who have contributed to the field since then

Contributors

Neil J. Anderson, Humanities Professor of Linguistics and English Language and Coordinator of the English Language Center, Brigham Young University, Provo, Utah, USA

Margaret Bade, Lecturer in ESOL, UNITEC, New Zealand

Adam Brown, Senior Lecturer, AIS St Helens, Auckland, New Zealand

Anna Uhl Chamot, Professor, George Washington University, USA

Andrew D. Cohen, Professor of Applied Linguistics and Chair of ESL Program, University of Minnesota, Minneapolis, USA

Sara Cotterall, Associate Professor, Akita International University, Akita, Japan

Madeline Ehrman, Consultant and Trainer, Arlington Virginia, USA

Claudia Finkbeiner, Professor of Applied Linguistics, University of Kassel, Germany; Chair of the Association for Language Awareness

Louise Gordon, Freelance, Auckland, New Zealand

Carol Griffiths, Teacher Trainer, Min Zu Da Xue (CUN), Beijing, China; Research Associate, AIS St Helens, Auckland, New Zealand

Yasushi Kawai, Associate Professor, Hokkaido University, Sapporo, Hokkaido, Japan

Patricia McCoy, Asuntos Internacionales, Universidad de las Americas, Cholula, Mexico

Jo Moir, Freelance, Wellington, New Zealand

Paul Nation, Professor, LALS, Victoria University of Wellington, New Zealand

Carisma Nel, Professor, Faculty of Education Sciences, School for Education North-West University, Potchefstroom, South Africa

Martha Nyikos, Associate Professor, University of Indiana, USA

Rebecca Oxford, Distinguished Scholar-Teacher, University of Maryland, USA

Kyoung Rang Lee, Postdoc, Yongsei University, Seoul, Korea

Leila Ranta, Department of Educational Psychology, University of Alberta, Edmonton, Canada

Michael Roberts, Academic Director, AIS St Helens, Auckland, New Zealand

Joan Rubin, Consultant, Teacher Trainer, Researcher; Joan Rubin Associates, Wheaton, Maryland, USA

Karen Schramm, Professor of German as a Foreign Language, Herder Institute, University of Leipzig, Germany

Zia Tajeddin, Assistant Professor of TEFL, Allameh Tabatabai University, Tehran, Iran

Ema Ushioda, Associate Professor, Centre for English Language Teacher Education, University of Warwick, Coventry, UK

Cynthia White, Professor of Applied Linguistics, School of Language Studies, Massey University, Palmerston North, New Zealand

Goodith White, Senior Lecturer, School of Education, University of Leeds, UK

To my father

Acknowledgements

This book was begun in about March 2005, which was, in fact, the year of the 30th anniversary of the publication of Joan Rubin's (1975) article "What the 'Good Language Learner' can teach us." Naively, I planned to have it finished before the end of the year . . .

When it comes to acknowledgements for this book, it is hard to know where to start. I guess we have to start with a tribute to Joan herself. I did not know Joan when I began this project, but, of course, almost everybody in the field knows her landmark article. When I did finally meet her, in Auckland New Zealand in early 2007, I understood what Andrew Cohen in his Prologue to this volume means by describing her as someone with "an impressive abundance of energy".

And, of course, I am deeply indebted to the numerous contributors to the book. Frankly, keeping track of so many, checking that they are all kept informed, and so on, has at times been, to put it somewhat euphemistically, a challenge. However, the variety of authors, representing many of the "big names" as well as the "new blood" in the field certainly adds to both the depth and the breadth of the volume.

On a personal level, I am also deeply grateful to Rebecca Oxford. My relationship with Rebecca goes back to when I wrote to her asking for permission to use her questionnaire in my own research, permission which she unhesitatingly gave. Another on whose help and advice I have often depended is Andrew Cohen, whom I got to know well during the year he spent with his wife in New Zealand. It is wonderful to know someone like Andrew who is so fast on the reply button! Yet another is Zoltán Dörnyei. Although I was disappointed that Zoltán was not able to contribute to the volume himself, he recommended two people who did contribute, and his encouragement and support have been much appreciated throughout. Rod Ellis, whom I know from Auckland University, was also unable to contribute. But Rod's personal example of unrelenting and focused hard work has been more of an inspiration than he may well realize.

When I started the project in 2005 I was working at Auckland Institute of Studies in New Zealand. Although I have moved on since to gain professional experience in China, I would like to acknowledge with gratitude the support I received from AIS St Helens in Auckland, New

Zealand in the early stages. Also very supportive was my first institution in China, Beijing Ti Yu Da Xue (Beijing Sports University), and, likewise, my current university, Min Zu Da Xue (Central University of Nationalities).

In addition, there have been many colleagues who have given advice and contributed ideas. There have been students who have uncomplainingly acted as "guinea pigs" for research projects. And there are those who have nobly agreed, or even volunteered(!) to proof read piles of pages – a tedious but essential part of the process of producing a book. Reviewers have also contributed to polishing the book into its final form.

It was, of course, a great joy to have our manuscript accepted by Cambridge Univerity Press, and I would like to thank especially Jane Walsh and Laila Friese who have been our main points of contact. They have been consistently patient, thorough and professional in a manner which befits a publishing house of Cambridge's status.

And finally, last but absolutely not least, I would like to thank my friends and family. What is the definition of a friend? A friend is someone who is still there when you emerge from turning down all their invitations to dinner and such since this is almost the only way you can ever get enough time to get a large project like this one finished. I am especially grateful for the support of my daughters ("Go for it, Mum"), my siblings ("If you need anything, Sis, just let us know") and their families.

I consider myself singularly fortunate to have had the kind of support I have received from so many. Thanks so much to all.

The authors and publishers are grateful to the following for permission to use copyright material. While every effort has been made, it has not been possible to identify the sources to all of the material used and in such cases the publishers would welcome information from the copyright owners. Apologies are expressed for any omissions.

For pp. 159–173 for text adapted from *Prospect 17*, 1, 2002, 15–35, by Jo Moir and Paul Nation, with permission from the The National Centre for English Teaching and Research. © Macquarie University, Australia.

For the examples on pp. 236–238 from: Karen Schramm, L2-Leser in Aktion. Der fremdsprachliche Leseprozeß als mentales Handeln (From L2 readers in action. The foreign language reading process as mental action). © Waxmann, Münster 2001, with permission from Waxmann, Münster.

Editor's overview

Carol Griffiths

Key questions

In her seminal article Rubin (1975, p. 42), suggested that "if we knew more about what the 'successful learners' did, we might be able to teach these strategies to poorer learners to enhance their success record." Aptitude, motivation, and opportunity, she argued, are essential characteristics of good language learners who either have or can develop these characteristics. Rubin constructed a list of strategies typical of good language learners, who, according to her observations, are willing and able to use clues (for instance non-verbal, word association, and general knowledge) in order to guess meaning; use a variety of techniques (such as circumlocution, paraphrase, or gestures) in order to communicate or learn from communication; manage inhibitions (such as the fear of appearing foolish or of making mistakes); attend to form (for instance by analyzing, categorizing, and synthesizing); practice the language they are trying to learn (for instance by seeking out native speakers and initiating conversations); monitor both their own and others' speech (for instance by learning from mistakes); and attend to meaning (for instance by interpreting mood and intonation). These strategies, as Rubin pointed out, will vary according to a number of factors including the task, the learning stage, the learner's age, the learning context, learning style, and cultural differences. Rubin concluded by suggesting that knowledge about good language learners "will lessen the difference between the good learner and the poorer one" (p. 50).

When Rubin published her article on good language learners in 1975, she probably did not expect that she would sow the seeds of a controversy which would still be unresolved more than 30 years later. This volume traces various aspects of the controversy, tries to draw the threads of consensus together, and points to the future for the critical questions:

- What is it that makes for a good language learner?
- Why are some learners more successful than others?
- How do learner characteristics such as motivation, beliefs, aptitude, age, gender, style, personality and culture, and learner behavior such

as strategy use, metacognition, or autonomy relate to effective language learning?

- How can learners manage aspects of the learning situation such as teaching/learning method, strategy instruction, error correction, or task, in order to effectively reach learning goals such as building vocabulary, expanding grammatical knowledge and functional competence, improving pronunciation, and developing their listening, speaking, reading, and writing skills?
- What have we already found out and what do we still need to know?
- What can educators do to help?

Although Rubin focussed mainly on language learning strategies, this book approaches the question of how good language learners learn from a broader perspective. It pursues some of the areas Rubin identified as requiring further research, and includes yet others which she did not mention, at least directly (for instance gender, personality, and autonomy). These variables have also been identified as potentially important contributors to success or otherwise in language learning.

Aims of this book

In the 30 years since Rubin's famous article was published, debate has raged and continues to this day. Failure to reach consensus over even basic definitions has inhibited research initiatives (O'Malley, Chamot, Stewner-Manzanares, Kupper, and Russo, 1985) and contributed to a "theoretical muddle" which is overdue for "clearing away" (Dornyei and Skehan, 2003, p. 610). This book attempts to contribute to this clearing away process by looking at a wide range of variables in relation to good language learners and their learning. However, given the "veritable plethora" (Ellis, 1994, p. 471) of such variables which have been identified, it has not been possible to include them all in this volume; as many as possible of those most commonly researched are represented. Given such breadth, it has not been possible to go into any of the topics in depth. The aim has been to:

- provide a comprehensive overview of learner/learning issues
- review the literature and research to date
- provide a reference base
- address theoretical issues
- consider pedagogical implications
- identify gaps in our current understanding
- suggest useful research initiatives
- consider how all of these relate to successful language learning by unique individuals in a variety of situations.

In other words, this book looks at language learning from research, literature, theoretical, pedagogical, and human perspectives.

Organisation of the book

The book is divided into two parts:

Part I is about learner variables, which include motivation, aptitude, age, style, personality, gender, culture, beliefs, strategies, metacognition, and autonomy. Although some of these variables may be influenced to a greater or lesser extent by external factors, they are individual characteristics or behaviors which make each learner unique.

Part II is about learning variables, including vocabulary, grammar, pronunciation, function, listening, speaking, reading, and writing, the learning of which is influenced by factors in the learning situation such as the teaching/learning method, strategy instruction, error correction practices, or task requirements. These variables have their origin externally, but must be managed by the learners if successful learning is to take place.

In order to provide a variety of perspectives, each part contains both state-of-the-art articles and research-based articles. Within each of these divisions, specialists in their various fields have written on specific topics (such as motivation, strategies, instruction, or vocabulary). Each topic is defined, the literature reviewed, and related issues discussed before implications for the teaching/learning situation and questions for further research are suggested.

The list of variables dealt with in this volume is, of course, not exhaustive. Indeed, as indicated previously, it is almost certainly impossible to include every conceivable variable in any one volume. Furthermore, new research initiatives are adding to the existing body of knowledge all the time. Especially fertile at the moment are the areas of situational variables, identity, volition, the development of pragmatic competence and self-regulation, as well as affective variables including self-efficacy and anxiety. Nevertheless, this book covers a wide range of topics related to how good language learners develop a target language, and aims to provide a basic core of information on the subject areas and to act as a springboard for those who want to pursue a particular topic in greater depth.

Terminology

The lack of consensus to which O'Malley *et al.* (1985) refer extends beyond definition to the even more basic level of terminology. A review of the literature reveals a bewildering array of terms used in the field of language development: ESL, EFL, SLA, ESOL, L1, L2, and so on. Sometimes these terms seem to be used to refer to much the same concept, other times their meanings appear to be quite different.

When talking about learners, many writers (for instance Cook, 1991; Ellis, 1994; Larsen-Freeman and Long, 1991; Sharwood Smith, 1994) opt for the terms *second language* or *L2* to describe the students, even though it may be used "somewhat confusingly" (Ellis, 1994, p. 12). The term is confusing because it does not allow for the many students who may already be multilingual and who may be in the process of learning a third, fourth, or subsequent language. There is also frequent confusion between the terms *second language* or *ESL* (to describe a language being studied in the environment where the language is spoken, for instance Somalis studying English in New Zealand), and *foreign language* or *EFL* (to describe a language being studied in an environment other than where it is spoken, for instance French as it is taught in England or New Zealand, or English as it is taught in China). Although some writers use the *ESL/EFL* terms with more or less the same meaning, others regard them as quite distinct from each other. The term *SOL* (speakers of other languages), as favored by publications such as *TESOL Quarterly, TESOL Matters* and *TESOLANZ Journal*, has arisen partly to avoid this confusion. However, it is rather long and clumsy. Other terms such as *non-native, non-primary, non-English-speaking-background* have been used, but the intrinsically negative perspective of these terms makes them less than universally acceptable.

Because of the sometimes uncomfortable distinctions noted above, the question arises of what to call the language being studied. Options such as *additional language* or *additive language* tend to make the language sound either marginalised or like a brand of food or petrol! The increasingly common term *target language* tends to sound a little aggressive and militaristic, but does at least denote the goal at which the student is aiming.

And, of course, the gulf established by Krashen (for instance Krashen, 1981) between acquisition (the development of language in a naturalistic environment) and learning (the development of language by means of conscious study) has never been entirely bridged in a universally acceptable manner. Although the field has moved on considerably in the more than 20 years since Krashen hypothesised a nil interface position regarding the learning–acquisition constructs, and although contemporary writers often use these two terms more or less interchangeably, the dichotomous view regarding the development of language established more than 20 years ago continues to create an area of uncertainty and potential misunderstanding.

Unfortunately, universally acceptable terms in the field of language development by students who already speak other languages and who are aiming to learn a new language have yet to be coined, or at least agreed upon. For the purposes of the present work, the term *speakers of other languages* (SOL) will be favored, since it at least avoids the confusion between second language and foreign language, it allows for the possibility that the student may speak any number of other languages, and it avoids negative implications. The language a student is aiming at will be termed the *target* or *new* language, and the term *language development* will be used to include both *acquisition* and *learning* unless some clear distinction is being drawn between the two.

Who is this book for?

Although Rubin's 1975 article focused especially on strategies, she suggested that many other variables need to be considered when looking at good language learners. This volume attempts to take Rubin's initiative further by investigating a wide range of variables, any one of which has the potential to affect how students learn, and which, in combination, present an extremely complex picture.

This book is intended for and will be especially useful to:

- those studying for degrees or diplomas in language development; they will find that this volume contains a wealth of information and references which can be used as the basis for completing assignments focusing on learners and how they go about learning language successfully;
- trainee teachers to help prepare them for the realities of life in the classroom;
- practicing teachers who want to be better informed, to clarify their insights into what may be happening in their classrooms day by day and to obtain inspiration;
- teacher educators who can use this volume as a means of augmenting their knowledge and as a base of information from which lectures can be developed;
- course designers who could use the volume as the basis for a number of interesting and useful learner-centered courses or programs;
- researchers, for whom a multitude of areas still needing investigation is suggested.

Finally, not least, it is for those who have been involved in the field of language education over the last 30 years. We owe a tribute to Joan for her insight and her perseverance in getting her seminal article published. We also owe a debt to the many who have toiled in the field since then. Two people whom I would especially like to mention and who have had a major influence on my own thinking and work, and on whose advice and support I have depended while compiling this volume are Andrew Cohen and Rebecca Oxford. The fact that they are referred to in almost every chapter in this book testifies to the breadth of their influence and the debt owed to them by those of us who have come later to the field.

As editor, I have tried to ensure that all the chapters in this book, though inevitably having their own style, are highly readable, with a consistency of structure that provides coherence to the book as a whole. To all of you, our readers, I hope you find this book informative and enjoyable. And, perhaps most importantly, I hope it inspires you to continue with the work which remains to be done investigating how successful language development can be promoted. Good language learners have much to teach us, and, even after 30 years, many lessons remain to be learnt.

References

Cook, V. (1991) *Second Language Learning and Language Teaching*. London: Edward Arnold.

Dörnyei, Z. and Skehan, P. (2003) Individual differences in second language learning. In C. Doughty and M. Long (eds.), *Handbook of Second Language Acquisition*. Oxford: Blackwell, 589–630.

Ellis, R. (1994) *The Study of Second Language Acquisition*. Oxford: Oxford University Press.

Krashen, S. (1981) *Second Language Acquisition and Second Language Learning*. Oxford: Pergamon Press.

Larsen-Freeman, D. and Long, M. (1991) *An Introduction to Second Language Acquisition Research*. London and New York: Longman.

O'Malley, J.M., Chamot, A.U., Stewner-Manzanares, G., Kupper, L., and Russo, R. (1985) Learning strategies used by beginning and intermediate ESL students. *Language Learning*, 35(1), 21–46.

Rubin, J. (1975) What the "good language learner" can teach us. *TESOL Quarterly*, 9(1), 41–51.

Sharwood Smith, M. (1994) *Second Language Learning: Theoretical Foundations*. London and New York: Longman.

Prologue

Andrew D. Cohen

Since this volume is commemorating Joan Rubin's seminal work on the good language learner and acknowledging the initiatives that it inspired, I thought it fitting to offer a brief prologue that will serve as an historical note regarding Joan's initial contribution to the topic of the good language learner. It is written more as a narrative since it is now in vogue to tell our stories as a means of enriching our academic experiences.

I was three years into my doctoral studies in international development education at Stanford University when I first met Joan in the fall of 1970. I had already had the pleasure of reading her study of Spanish–Guaraní bilingualism in Paraguay (Rubin, 1968) so I knew of her as a trained anthropologist and as an experienced sociolinguist. My advisor at the Committee on Linguistics at Stanford, Charles Ferguson, had told me many fine things about her.

Joan arrived at Stanford with questionnaire data she had collected in Indonesia as part of a sociolinguistic survey being conducted in various parts of the world, and her main mission was to analyze and report on the findings. I expected her to pursue her interests drawing on her survey work to make statements about language planning. What was a surprise for me at the time was to experience first hand Joan's keen fascination with the language learner and with studying the language learning act up close and personal. She was determined to pursue an interest in better understanding how language learners did what they did and why.

For those of you who don't know Joan Rubin, you need to know that she is a person with an impressive abundance of energy. When she takes on tasks, she takes them on with gusto. She became determined to explore the nature of students' participation in language classes, and she used Stanford's language program as a convenient vehicle for this exploration. She started sitting in on French, German, and Spanish classes and following what learners were doing in class. She would watch them as they attended to class activities, she listened attentively when individual students spoke up in class, and she also observed what they wrote in their notebooks – even taking notes on what they took notes on. During the breaks, she would go up to the students she was observing and would ask them about things they had written down in their notebooks. She wanted to better understand their rationale for doing what she observed them to be doing.

In order to situate Joan's activities within the current instructional context at that time, it could be said that the field of instruction, and specifically language instruction, wasn't really interested then in the learner's side. What was considered important was for teachers to have their instructional act together. This was seen as the key to success. In fact, at Stanford's School of Education, the emphasis was not just on teaching, but on micro-level teaching. My wife obtained her degree in that program, where the emphasis was on videotaping of teachers engaged in what was referred to as "microteaching" (based on the work of Dwight Allen, who had been on the Stanford faculty until 1967). A typical unit, for example, would focus on teachers' questioning techniques. There was no focus at the time on what the learners were doing. It was assumed that good teaching automatically meant good learning.

The reason I knew about Joan's activities is that we would meet periodically for lunch and she would tell me a bit about what she was doing and what she was finding. I must admit that at first it seemed totally off the wall to me. Given the educational context at that time, it was like the Wright brothers telling people about their ideas for a "flying machine." Just as that seemed a bit misguided at best when these two brothers first broached the topic, so too the thrust that Joan was taking didn't seem so valuable to me at first. Some might even have branded her a "heretic" in some respects since, in her focus on students as a key part of the instructional process, she wasn't toeing the party line.

Still, probably due largely to Joan's strength of character, it didn't take her long to convince me, and it started me thinking about learners and their approaches to learning. In fact, it was from interacting with Joan that I first started looking at language learner strategies. Even though I had studied seven languages other than English, I hadn't conceived of the learner's act in the way Joan was dealing with it. But then I began to see that she was truly onto something.

The real challenge for Joan, however, was in getting her ideas published. She wrote up her insights in the form of a paper on what the good language learner can teach us and wasn't able to find a publisher for it for a few years. Her paper had been circulating for perhaps four years before the *TESOL Quarterly* published it in 1975 – a clear indication that the field wasn't ready for this new direction at that time.

I think that all of us who have benefited from this learner perspective over the years are thrilled that Joan Rubin pursued her goal to raise consciousness about the language learner. In retrospect, we can see that the publication of the article helped to mobilize a movement of concerned language educators. The appearance of the article helped give momentum to the launching of a series of TESOL conference colloquia that a number of us participated in along with Joan Rubin (for instance, Anita Wenden, Michael O'Malley, Anna Chamot, David Mendelsohn, Martha Nyikos, and others) at the end of the 1970s/beginning of the 1980s.

So, scroll ahead about 25 more years, and the focus on the language learner is clearly well-established, as witnessed by this robust collection of chapters by a cross-section of leading and upcoming specialists in the field. The issue is no longer whether to look at learners, but rather what to look at and how to do it. We have come a long way since 1970, when Joan was a voice in the wilderness. The field has come of age, thanks largely to Joan's initial pioneering efforts. It is inspiring to see that Joan Rubin has continued to be active in the field and that she herself shares her current work in this volume.

References

Rubin, J. (1968) *National Bilingualism in Paraguay*. The Hague: Mouton.

Reflections

Joan Rubin

Perhaps the most important change in the field of language research and teaching since my 1975 publication "What the 'Good Language Learner' Can Teach Us" is the clear recognition the field now gives to the role of learning as a critical component in the process of teaching, with an acceptance that the two are inseparable from one another and that teachers need to place importance not only on the target language but also on the learning process. In addition, there has been a radical change in research and teaching giving increased recognition and attention to the critical role of learners in shaping their own learning.

The teaching field did not always recognize the relationship of learning to teaching. This lacuna is perhaps best exemplified by an experience I had in the mid-1980s in a phone call from a Russian instructor, trained in the strong Russian pedagogical tradition, who called and asked "I understand you're interested in teaching?" "No," I replied, "I'm interested in learning." "Oh!" he said, "GOODBYE!!"

Clear recognition of the close relationship of teaching and learning can be found in current teacher training books. Examples include: Nunan (1988) *The Learner Centered Curriculum*, which presents curriculum as a collaborative effort between teachers and learners, and stresses the need for a differentiated curriculum for different learners; Cook and Cook (2001) *Second Language Learning and Teaching* and Brown (2000) *Principles of Language Learning and Teaching*, both of which put "learning" before "teaching" in their titles and encourage teachers to use techniques which approach learners as individuals.

Further evidence of this trend to involve learners in the process includes manuals for teachers to enable learners to begin to take charge of their learning. For instance: Willing (1989) *Teaching How to Learn*; Oxford (1990) *Language Learning Strategies: What Every Teacher Should Know*; Wenden (1991) *Learner Strategies for Learner Autonomy*; Chamot, Barnhardt, El-Dinary, and Robbins (1999) *The Learning Strategies Handbook*.

In addition, there are manuals that directly provide learners with the knowledge and skills to begin to take charge of their learning, such as: Rubin and Thompson (1994) *How to Be a More Successful Language Learner*; Ellis and Sinclair (1989) *Learning to Learn English*; Brown

(1991) *Breaking the Language Barrier: Creating Your Own Pathway to Success;* Peace Corps (2000) *Volunteer On-Going Language Learning Manual;* Paige, Cohen, Kappler, Chi, and Lassegard (2002) *Maximizing Study Abroad.*

Additional evidence of the focus on the learner can be seen in the research on style (Ehrman, 1996; Reid, 1995) and on individual differences (Skehan, 1989; Dörnyei, 2005). Clear evidence of the shift toward including the learner in both research and teaching and of how far the field has come since 1975 is the recent statement by Magnan (2005, p. 315) who observes that one of the basic issues in language acquisition is the need to consider: "Who are our learners? What are they learning? What do they wish to learn? Where and how are they learning? and What is our role in their learning process?"

Perhaps the most basic modification to thinking about good language learners since my 1975 article is the recognition that, although good learners use strategies, not all strategies are created equal. Starting in about 1990, in the writings of O'Malley and Chamot (1990), Oxford (1990), Wenden (1991) and Chamot (1994), the difference between cognitive and metacognitive strategies became clearer and more critical. Based on the work of Flavell, but applied to language learning by Wenden (1998), the cognitive/metacognitive distinction evolved into a clear separation of *knowledge* from *self-management* and eventually into what Rubin (2001), following the cognitive psychologist Butler (1997), called *knowledge and procedures.* Research has shown that *knowledge* (for instance, of strategies, self, or background) will vary by learner. *Procedures* do not vary by learner but are rather the overarching management process which all expert learners use to regulate/manage their learning and which do not vary by learner but rather by task, learner goal and learner purpose.

The ability to self-manage can perhaps explain why the "good language learner is [. . .] comfortable with uncertainty [. . .] and willing to try out his guesses" (Rubin, 1975, p. 45) since the learner knows/has experienced the fact that learning is dynamic and changing and accepts a certain level of uncertainty as part of the nature of the process. Hence, since expert learners recognize that change is an integral part of the learning process, they are more comfortable with uncertainty. There is increasing evidence that management of learning is critical to success. Evidence for this can be seen in the diary of Henze (Rubin and Henze, 1981), and the report of Huang (1984). Such management must attend both to the type of task (Vann and Abraham, 1990; Abraham and Vann, 1987) as well as the general culture used to learn a particular subject (Uhrig, 2004).

One other thing we have learned is that it is not the *presence* or *absence* of a strategy that leads to effective learning; rather it is *how* that strategy is used (or not used) to accomplish tasks and learner goals. Ehrman, Leaver, and Oxford (2003) acknowledge that in order to be useful a strategy must relate well to the task at hand, must fit the particular student's learning style preferences to one degree or another, and must be employed effectively and linked with other relevant strategies. As Dörnyei (2005) notes, it is the operationalization of the strategy that is critical, not the strategy, in and of itself.

Implications for the teaching/learning situation

My 1975 article pointed to the possibility of incorporating "learning to learn" into our teaching/learning methods in order to "lessen the difference between the good learner and the poorer one" (p. 50). Since then, several experiments have been carried out to show the impact of learner instruction on performance. Probably the most comprehensive review is that conducted by Macaro, Vanderplank, and Graham (2005). Teaching students how to learn has the potential to greatly enhance their learning ability if we can find ways of instructing them effectively.

A recent experiment reported by Rubin and McCoy (2005) demonstrated that providing instruction even to highly unmotivated learners can lead to a significant increase in learners' ability to do task analysis. Further, the experimental group outperformed the control group on the final exam. These results (reported later in this volume) appear to support the belief that effective procedural instruction can improve a student's performance.

Another area that is increasingly gaining attention, especially for those whose task is to enable learners to reach the most advanced levels of language competence, is providing learners with the ability to analyze genre in order to better plan for learning. Paltridge (2001), Byrnes (2002) and Ryshina-Pankova (2005) provide examples of how this is being incorporated into language learning curricula and classroom teaching.

Questions for ongoing research

An area only hinted at in my 1975 article, that there are different kinds of good language learners, needs more exploration. Much more research needs to be conducted to profile the range of variables, such as those considered in the present volume, that leads to good language learning. What are the combinations of factors which lead to success?

Also, we need to know more about how to develop teachers' abilities to promote learner self-management. Many teachers genuinely want to help their students to learn to regulate their own learning, but they simply do not know how to go about doing this. In the face of contradictory messages from the literature, possible opposition from their educational establishments, and, perhaps, reluctance from the very students they are trying to help, busy teachers are likely to simply give up and follow the traditional teacher-centred line of least resistance. They need training and support if they are to be willing and able to effectively develop their students' abilities to manage their own learning. How can this goal best be achieved?

Conclusion

Although many teachers and texts give a strong nod in the direction of learner-centered learning, changing the paradigm and providing the necessary knowledge and skills for teachers has proven to be quite daunting. Perhaps the task is larger and more complex than many of us realized 30 years ago. Focusing on a complex, dynamic, situated learning process, and providing the necessary knowledge and skills takes much more time for both learners and teachers to understand and be able to use than might have been predicted.

While more and more teachers are recognizing the importance of a variety of factors that affect learners, many still adhere to an older model that defines their job as providing information in a fixed fashion, regardless of learner differences. Recently, while giving a workshop on learner self-management, a teacher told me that if he did not give learners all the correct answers and all necessary information, he would be failing his responsibility as a teacher. Attitudes like this are not uncommon. So while many aspects of the field have come a long way, actual practice still has a way to go.

References

Abraham, R.G. and Vann, R.J. (1987) Strategies of two learners: a case study. In A.L. Wenden and J. Rubin (eds.), *Learner Strategies in Language Learning*. New York: Prentice-Hall, 85–102.

Brown, H.D. (1991) *Breaking the Language Barrier: Creating Your Own Path to Success*. Yarmouth, ME: Intercultural Press.

Brown, H.D. (2000) *Principles of Language Learning and Teaching* (fourth edition). White Plains, New York; Harlow: Longman.

Butler, D.L. (1997) The role of goal setting and self-monitoring in students' self-regulated engagement in tasks. Paper presented in Chicago at the American Education Research Association Meeting.

Byrnes, H. (2002) The role of task and task-based assessment in a content-oriented collegiate foreign language curriculum. *Language Testing*, 19(4), 419–437.

Chamot, A.U. (1994) A model for learning strategy instruction in the foreign language classroom. In J.E. Alatis (ed.), Georgetown University Round Table on Language and Linguistics 1994, Washington, DC: Georgetown University Press, 323–336.

Chamot, A.U., Barnhardt, S., El-Dinary, P.B., and Robbins, J. (1999) *The Learning Strategies Handbook*. White Plains, NY: Addison Wesley, Longman.

Cook, V.J. and Cook, V. (2001) *Second Language Learning and Teaching* (third edition). London and New York: Arnold Publishers.

Dörnyei, Z. (2005) *The Psychology of the Language Learner*. Mahwah, NJ: Lawrence Erlbaum Associates.

Ehrman, M.E. (1996) *Understanding Second Language Difficulties*. Thousand Oaks, CA: Sage.

Ehrman, M.E, Leaver, B.L., and Oxford, R.L. (2003.) A brief overview of individual differences in second language learning, *System*, 31, 313–330.

Ellis, G. and Sinclair, B. (1989) *Learning to Learn English*. Cambridge: Cambridge University Press.

Huang, X.H. (1984) *An investigation of learning strategies in oral communication that Chinese EFL learners in China employ*. Unpublished MA Thesis. Chinese University of Hong Kong.

Macaro, E., Vanderplank, R., and Graham, S. (2005) A systematic review of the role of prior knowledge in unidirectional listening comprehension. In *Research Evidence in Education Library*. London: EPPI Centre, Social Science Research Unit, Institute of Education, University of London. (Retrieved from: http//eppi.ioe.ac/uk/EPPIWebcontent/reel/review_groups? MFL/mfl_w2/MFL_vFv2.pdf)

Magnan, S.S. (2005) From the editor: presenting the special issue. *Modern Language Journal*, 89(3), 315.

Nunan, D. (1988) *The Learner-Centered Curriculum*. Cambridge: Cambridge University Press.

O'Malley, J.M. and Chamot, A.U. (1990) *Learner Strategies in Second Language Acquisition*. Cambridge: Cambridge University Press.

Oxford, R.L. (1990) *Language Learning Strategies: What Every Teacher Should Know*. New York: Newbury House Publishers.

Paige, R.M., Cohen, A.D., Kappler, B., Chi, J.C., and Lassegard, J.P. (2002) *Maximizing Study Abroad: a Student's Guide to Strategies for Language and Culture Learning and Use*. Minneapolis, MN: Center for Advanced Research on Language Acquisition.

Paltridge, B. (2001) *Genre and the Language Learning Classroom*. Ann Arbor, MI: University of Michigan Press.

Peace Corps. (2000) *Volunteer On-Going Language Learning Manual*. Washington, DC: Information Collection and Exchange.

Reid, J.M. (ed.) (1995) *Understanding Learning Styles in the ESL/EFL Classroom*. Boston, MA: Heinle & Heinle.

Rubin, J. (1975) What the "good language learner" can teach us. *TESOL Quarterly*, 9(1), 41–51.

Rubin, J. (2001) Language learner self-management. *Journal of Asian Pacific Communication*, 11(1), 25–27.

Rubin, J. and Henze, R. (1981) The foreign language requirement: a suggestion to enhance its educational role in teacher training. *TESOL Newsletter*, 2(81), 17, 19, 24.

Rubin, J. and McCoy, P. (2005) The role of task analysis in promoting learner self-management. Paper presented at AILA, Madison, Wisconsin.

Rubin, J. and Thompson, I. (1994 [1982]) *How to Be a More Successful Language Learner*. Boston, MA: Heinle & Heinle.

Ryshina-Pankova, M. (2005) Fostering syntactic complexity in curriculum-based L2 writing development. Paper presented at AILA, Madison, WI.

Skehan, P. (1989) *Individual Differences in Second Language Learning*. London and New York: Edward Arnold.

Uhrig, K. (2004) Context orientation in language learning strategy research. Paper presented at the TESOL Conference, April 3, Long Beach, California.

Vann, R.G. and Abraham, R.J. (1990) Strategies of unsuccessful language Learners. *TESOL Quarterly*, 24(2), 177–198.

Wenden, A.L. (1991) *Learner Strategies for Learner Autonomy*. Hemel Hempstead, UK: Prentice Hall International.

Wenden, A.L. (1998) Metacognitive knowledge and language learning. *Applied Linguistics*, 19(4), 515–537.

Willing, K. (1989) *Teaching How to Learn: Learning Strategies in ESL*. Sydney, Australia: National Centre for English Language Teaching and Research.

Part I: Learner variables

1 Motivation and good language learners

Ema Ushioda

It almost goes without saying that good language learners are motivated. Common sense and everyday experience suggest that the high
achievers of this world have motivation, a word which derives from
the Latin verb *movere* meaning to move. Thus, simply defined, we
might say that motivation concerns what moves a person to make
certain choices, to engage in action, and to persist in action. The need
for personal motivation is a message that resonates across so many
stories of major and minor human endeavor, whether in the single-
minded dedication of an athlete pursuing an Olympic dream, the drive
and ambition of a young executive aiming for the top of the corporate
ladder, or the willpower and self-discipline of someone determined to
lose weight or to give up smoking. Without motivation, success will be
hard to come by, and the case of learning a second or foreign language
is little different. Motivation is listed by Rubin (1975) among the three
essential variables on which good language learning depends. As
Corder (1967, p. 164) famously put it forty years ago, "Let us say that,
given motivation, it is inevitable that a human being will learn a second
language if he is exposed to the language data." Yet however com-
monsensical this general observation might be, the pursuit of its empirical verification has exercised language acquisition scholars for decades
and generated an enormous amount of research.

The social-psychological perspective

Led by the pioneering work of Canadian social psychologists Gardner
and Lambert (1972), research into motivation was for many years
shaped by social-psychological perspectives on learner attitudes to target
language cultures and people. Gardner and Lambert argued that language learning motivation was qualitatively different from other forms
of learning motivation, since language learning entails much more than
acquiring a body of knowledge and developing a set of skills. On top
of this, the language learner must also be willing "to identify with
members of another ethnolinguistic group and to take on very subtle
aspects of their behavior, including their distinctive style of speech and

19

their language" (Gardner and Lambert, 1972, p. 135). Gardner and Lambert speculated that learners' underlying attitudes to the target language culture and people would have a significant influence on their motivation and thus their success in learning the language.

This speculation gave rise to the now classic distinction between *integrative* and *instrumental* orientations, the former reflecting a sincere and personal interest in the target language, people, and culture and the latter its practical value and advantages (Gardner and Lambert, 1972). A substantial body of largely correlational research was generated to explore the hypothesis that integratively motivated learners are likely to be successful language learners in the long run. While findings have been to some extent mixed (for a recent meta-analysis, see Masgoret and Gardner, 2003), there is little doubt that the concept of integrative motivation and the social-psychological angle of inquiry powerfully shaped the way language learner motivation was theorized and empirically explored until the early 1990s. So much so that Skehan (1989, p. 61) suggested that "almost all other writing on motivation therefore seems to be a commentary, in one way or another, on the agenda established by Gardner."

At the risk of over-simplifying the social-psychological legacy of research on language learning motivation, however, I think it is true to say that the angle of inquiry it promoted yielded few genuinely useful insights for teachers and learners. Despite evolving from a social-psychological model (Gardner and Lambert, 1972) to a socio-educational model of language learning (Gardner, 1988), Gardner's theory and the research it generated came under sharp criticism for failing to take adequate account of the classroom context of learner motivation (see in particular Crookes and Schmidt, 1991). At bottom, this failure may simply be a reflection of the rather different concerns of researchers and teachers (Ushioda, 1996). It is only within the last decade or so that we have witnessed more productive interaction between the interests of researchers and teachers. Crookes and Schmidt's (1991) seminal critique of the social-psychological tradition and their call for a more practitioner-validated classroom-based concept of motivation marked the beginning of an unprecedented wave of discussion among motivation scholars during the 1990s (for a review, see Dörnyei, 1998). This "motivational renaissance" (Gardner and Tremblay, 1994, p. 526) led to a broadening of the research agenda and a move towards what Dörnyei (2001a, pp. 103–105) has called more "education-friendly" approaches to language learner motivation which provide potentially much richer insights for teachers and learners.

Motivation from within

With the move towards more education-friendly and classroom-based approaches to the study of motivation, research attention since the 1990s has increasingly turned to cognitive theories of learner motivation, thus bringing language learner motivation research more in line with the cognitive revolution in mainstream motivational psychology. Cognitive theories focus on the patterns of thinking that shape motivated engagement in learning. These patterns of thinking include, for example, goal setting, mastery versus performance goal-orientation, self-perceptions of competence, self-efficacy beliefs, perceived locus of control, and causal attributions for success or failure (for a comprehensive overview, see Pintrich and Schunk, 2002). From a pedagogical perspective, a key message emanating from research on cognitive theories of motivation in education and in language learning is the vital importance of learners having their own motivation "from within" (Deci and Flaste, 1996, p. 10).

Generally speaking, the optimal kind of motivation from within is identified as *intrinsic motivation* – that is, doing something as an end in itself, for its own self-sustaining pleasurable rewards of enjoyment, interest, challenge, or skill and knowledge development. Intrinsic motivation is contrasted with *extrinsic motivation* – that is, doing something as a means to some separable outcome, such as gaining a qualification, getting a job, pleasing the teacher, or avoiding punishment (Ryan and Deci, 2000). There is a considerable body of research evidence to suggest that intrinsic motivation not only promotes spontaneous learning behavior and has a powerful self-sustaining dynamic but also leads to a qualitatively different and more effective kind of learning than extrinsic forms of motivation. This may be because the rewards of learning are inherent in the learning process itself, in the shape of feelings of personal satisfaction and enhanced personal competence and skill deriving from and sustaining engagement in learning (Csikszentmihalyi, 1978). Thus, intrinsically motivated learning is not simply "learning for the sake of learning" (though many teachers would undoubtedly value such learner behavior in itself); nor is it simply learning for fun and enjoyment (though many teachers and learners, especially within primary and secondary school contexts, might regard "motivating" as synonymous with "fun" as opposed to "boring"). Rather, intrinsically motivated learners are deeply concerned to learn things well, in a manner that is intrinsically satisfying and that arouses a sense of optimal challenge appropriate to their current level of skill and competence (Deci and Ryan, 1980). Compared to their extrinsically motivated counterparts, research suggests that such learners are likely to display much

21

higher levels of involvement in learning, engage in more efficient and creative thinking processes, use a wider range of problem-solving strategies, and interact with and retain material more effectively (Condry and Chambers, 1978; see also Amabile and Hennessy, 1992; Fransson, 1984).

In the language learner motivation field, there has been a tendency to conflate the intrinsic/extrinsic distinction with the integrative/ instrumental distinction to some extent, since intrinsic motivation, like integrative motivation, is founded in deep-rooted personal interests and positive attitudes and feelings (for instance, Dickinson, 1995; Noels, 2001). However, as Gardner (1985) has made clear, both integrative and instrumental motivational orientations are defined with reference to ultimate purposes for learning a language (social-integrative or pragmatic purposes), and thus both constitute forms of extrinsic motivation since the language is learned as a means to an end. As Schmidt and Savage (1994) note, a language learner might have strong integrative motivation yet derive very little intrinsic pleasure from the learning process. This point is particularly pertinent to our discussion of good language learners' motivation, since it brings to our attention the positive value and effectiveness of some forms of extrinsic motivation. As noted earlier, after all, there is a wealth of research in the social-psychological tradition to indicate that learners with strong motivation, whether defined by integrative or instrumental goals, are likely to succeed in language learning. Thus, while its self-sustaining dynamic may make intrinsic motivation an optimal form of learning motivation, we should not lightly dismiss extrinsic motivation as inherently less effective and less desirable. In many educational contexts, certain types of extrinsic goal are indeed positively valued (for instance, examination success, academic, career, or life ambitions).

Rather, motivational factors intrinsic to the learning process (enjoyment, sense of challenge, skill development) and those extrinsic to the learning process (personal goals and aspirations) are best viewed as working in concert with one another in the good language learner (van Lier, 1996). At bottom, what seems crucially important is not whether these motivational factors are intrinsic or extrinsic to the learning process, but whether they are internalized and self-determined (emanating from within the learner), or externally imposed and regulated by others (teachers, peers, curricula, parents, educational, and societal expectations). The clear message is that externally regulated motivation (the traditional "carrot-and-stick" approach) can have short-term benefits only, and that our real aim as educators must be to foster learners' own motivation from within (Deci and Flaste, 1996).

The social context of motivation

Over the past decade or so there has been growing interest among moti-vation researchers in the socially situated context of motivation and in the significant role of social processes and influences in shaping individ-ual motivation. This growth of interest in the social dimension of moti-vation is reflected in recent important volumes of papers on motivation research in education that address a range of situational factors, such as societal and cultural influences, curricular and institutional context, classroom environment, peer relations, teaching style, and methods, materials, or task design (for instance, McInerney and Van Etten, 2004; Volet and Järvelä, 2001). In the study of language learner motivation, the move towards more education-friendly approaches has similarly prompted an increased interest in the social learning environment, as reflected in current influential models of language learner motivation. For example, Dörnyei's (1994) framework of motivation integrates language-related and learner-internal factors with learning situation factors, including teacher socialization of motivation and classroom group processes. Similarly, in their comprehensive cognitive model of language learner motivation, Williams and Burden (1997) combine learner-internal factors with external factors such as interaction with sig-nificant others (parents, teachers, peers) and influences from the broader social context (for instance, cultural norms, societal expectations and attitudes).

Where discussion of the good language learner is concerned, the social context of motivation has some important implications. In an illuminat-ing critique of good language learner research, Norton and Toohey (2001) discuss the limitations of a tradition of inquiry that has focused on the mental processes of internalizing language forms in interaction with available target language input, and on the influence of (good) lan-guage learner characteristics on these processes. They point out that the "situated experience" (p. 310) of learners has not been adequately taken into account in this research tradition, and argue the need for a dual focus on good language learners and on the social practices in the con-texts in which they learn language. They make the case that the success of good language learners depends very much on the degree and quality of access to a variety of conversations in their communities, and not just on processes of internalizing linguistic forms and meanings. The extent to which the surrounding social practices facilitate or constrain learners' access to the linguistic resources of their communities will affect the quality and level of language learning success.

According to Norton and Toohey (2001), good language learners are those who find ways of exercising agency to negotiate entry into the desired social networks. They illustrate this claim with two examples of Polish-speaking learners of English (an adult learner, Eva, and a kindergarten learner, Julie) both of whom succeed in commanding well-respected identities and valued social and intellectual resources for themselves, thus enhancing their opportunities to participate in the conversations around them. In Eva's case, although initially marginalized as an immigrant at her place of work, she achieves a more respected position among her co-workers and management when she brings her partner into the picture on social outings, as she becomes seen as someone in a desirable relationship with a partner who also provides transport for her colleagues in his car. In addition to these social resources, Eva is able to draw on intellectual resources and command respect for her knowledge of Italian and of European countries. In a similar vein but in the very different social context of a kindergarten community, five-year-old Julie comes to be regarded by her peers as a desirable playmate with access to valued information or "secrets," including knowledge of Polish, and with important grown-up and peer group allies, especially her cousin Agatha who is an experienced speaker of English and Polish.

Norton and Toohey's (2001) argument for a dual focus on good language learners and on the surrounding social practices is underpinned by a view of language learning as a struggle for identity, a view that is very much positioned within a poststructuralist critical perspective. At the heart of this critical perspective on language learning and use is recognition of inequitable power relations in language learners' struggle to participate in interactional settings in desired social, educational, or professional communities of practice. As Block (2002) wryly comments, for example, Gricean cooperative principles are often far from default conditions in interactional settings between native and non-native speakers. In relation to motivation in particular, Norton (2000, p. 10) has developed the concept of "investment," defined as the "socially and historically constructed relationship of learners to the target language, and their often ambivalent desire to learn and practise it" (see also Norton, 1995). When learners invest in learning a new language, they do so with the understanding that they will acquire a wider range of symbolic and material resources, which will enhance their cultural capital, their conception of themselves, and their desires for the future. A person's investment in a language may be mediated by other investments that may conflict with the desire to speak, such as fear of being marginalized as an immigrant, or resistance when one's professional status or cultural background is not valued or when access to desired symbolic and material resources is denied. For Norton and Toohey (2001), good language learners are people who exercise agency and succeed in setting up counter-discourses in which their identities are respected and their resources valued, and who thus succeed in negotiating entry. Yet, as they comment, Eva and Julie are both fortunate in that the communities to which they desire access are eventually receptive to their contributions. An important critical insight highlighted by this poststructuralist perspective on motivation is that good language learning is never simply in the hands of the motivated learner, since much will depend on the surrounding social practices. Good language learning and motivation are in this sense socially constructed or constrained, rather than simply influenced, positively or negatively, by the social context.

One theoretical tradition in particular that can illuminate this socially constructed nature of motivation is Vygotskian sociocultural theory. Though sociocultural theory broadly informs Norton and Toohey's (2001) work on motivation, its potential richness as a conceptual framework for analyzing language learner motivation remains rather underdeveloped (Ushioda, 2007). This is despite its increasing influence in other major domains of language teaching research, such as task-based language learning (for instance, Swain, Brooks and Tocalli-Beller, 2002) and the literature on autonomy (for instance, Little, 1999). One reason why the influence of sociocultural theory has not firmly penetrated the language learning motivation field may be that the motivational dimension of Vygotsky's theory itself remains relatively under-theorized (Ushioda, 2007) and it is only fairly recently that it has begun to attract significant attention among motivation researchers in education (for instance, Hickey and Granade, 2004). Central to Vygotsky's sociocultural theory of mind is the principle that higher-order cognitive functions are internalized from social interaction with more competent others (Vygotsky, 1978). Bronson (2000, p. 33) explains how this principle applies also to the socially constructed growth of motivation by highlighting the important distinction between the organismic impetus to learn and to regulate one's actions, and the socialization of motivation for culturally constructed goals and activities. This process of socialization takes place through the child's participation in activities in a particular sociocultural setting. Thinking, wanting and doing are shared and jointly constructed in the dialogic interactions between children (learners) and members of the surrounding culture or social learning environment. Gradually, children (good language learners) appropriate for themselves culturally valued patterns of planning, attending, thinking and remembering (Lantolf, 1994), and culturally valued goals and intentions (Ushioda, 2007). This Vygotskian perspective illuminates how motivation "from within" can be fostered through the formulation of shared intentions and purposes (rather than exclusively teacher-imposed goals). It also highlights the way in which motivation develops through social participation

25

and interaction. As Rueda and Moll (1994) explain, motivation is not located solely within the individual but is socially distributed, created within cultural systems of activities involving the mediation of others. Good language learners, including Norton and Toohey's (2001) Eva and Julie, know how to seek out and to exploit this social interdependence and the human need for relatedness or connectedness that is integral to internally driven motivation (Ryan, 1991).

Motivational self-regulation

Where the pursuit of any difficult and challenging personal goal is concerned, the long path towards success is never easy and is usually beset with obstacles of one kind or another. Motivation will suffer unless ways are found to regulate it. Aside from the inevitable detriments to motivation posed by institutionalized learning (for instance, coursework requirements, examination pressures, competing demands from other courses of study), steady increases in the cognitive burden of language learning may also have negative consequences. As language proficiency develops, the learning demands grow exponentially in terms of cognitive and linguistic complexity, and skill and activity range, while any pay-off for the learning effort expended in terms of increased mastery becomes less and less tangible. Sadly, research all too often points to a steady decline in levels of motivation, once the initial enthusiasm and novelty of learning a new language begin to wear off (for instance, Chambers, 1999; Little, Ridley and Ushioda, 2002; Williams, 2004; Williams, Burden and Lanvers, 2002). How many of us know people who eagerly take up a new language, only to drop out of evening classes after just a few weeks?

For motivation to be sustained through the vicissitudes of the learning process, it seems clear that learners need to develop certain skills and strategies to keep themselves on track. These might include setting themselves concrete short-term targets, engaging in positive self-talk, motivating themselves with incentives and self-rewards, or organizing their time effectively to cope with multiple tasks and demands. Such strategies are variously discussed in terms of self-motivating strategies (Dörnyei, 2001b), affective learning strategies (Oxford, 1990), efficacy management (Wolters, 2003), effective motivational thinking (Ushioda, 1996), anxiety management (Horwitz, 2001), self-regulatory skills (Dörnyei and Ottó, 1998), and motivational self-regulation (Ushioda, 2003, 2007). Good language learners, it seems, develop strategies for "getting your motivation on line again," as expressed by one successful and motivated language learner (Ushioda, 2001, p. 117). This might entail, for example, engaging in an intrinsically motivating activity, or "rediscovering your enjoyment as it were by doing something you know you like doing" (p. 117).

Unfortunately, research on how language learners might be brought to think positively and develop skills in motivational self-regulation is still scarce. In keeping with much of the literature on learning strategies, Dörnyei (2001b) stresses the importance of raising learners' awareness of self-motivating strategies through discussion and sharing of experiences. Ushioda (1996, 2003) emphasizes the role of teacher feedback in promoting positive and constructive thinking. According to McCombs (1994), our capacity for motivational self-regulation is a function of the degree to which we are aware of ourselves as agents in the construction of the thoughts, beliefs, goals, and expectations that shape our motivation. As McCombs argues, without an understanding of our role as agents in formulating goals, self-perceptions, and motivation, the stage cannot be set for the emergence of self-regulatory processes – that is, recognition of our potential to have control over what we think, and thus control over our motivation. Failure to recognize the self as agent in controlling thought and thus motivation can lead learners to become trapped in negative patterns of thinking and self-perceptions, with detrimental consequences for their motivation. This latter phenomenon is well documented in the field of education, reflected in particular in the maladaptive motivational pattern of "learned helplessness" among learners who experience repeated poor performance and see little point in exerting further effort (Dweck, 1999; Peterson, Maier and Seligman, 1993).

Implications for the teaching/learning situation

When we turn our attention to what teachers and learners might do to achieve and maintain motivation, we find that it becomes impossible to consider pedagogical approaches to fostering motivation from within without considering approaches to fostering self-determination. A fundamental pedagogical principle in promoting learner-regulated motivation rather than teacher-regulated motivation is that learning needs to be driven by learners' own personal needs, goals, and interests. This entails involving learners in making informed choices and decisions about their learning and in setting their own goals and learning targets, and thus fostering feelings of personal responsibility (Ushioda, 1996). This intimate connection between self-determination and motivation is vividly captured in Dam's (1995) account of her original reasons for giving her reluctant language learners more autonomy in the classroom.

Motivation and good language learners

a new insight

Thus, whereas motivation has traditionally been regarded as something that teachers "do" or "give" to learners through a variety of motivational tricks and strategies, current insights emphasize the importance of fostering learners' own motivation and sense of self-determination (for instance, Dickinson, 1995; Noels, 2001; Lamb, 2004). Yet, as Dam's (1995) full account of her classroom practice makes plain, the healthy growth of individual motivation depends very much on the quality and level of interpersonal support provided in the social learning environment.

In order to promote healthy interaction between social and individual processes of motivation, it seems clear that there must be close alignment between pedagogical goals and values, individual needs and interests, and peer-related interpersonal goals (Ushioda, 2003). As the literature on autonomy suggests, achieving such alignment entails involving learners in some of the decision-making processes that shape classroom learning. Important insights derive also from research on cooperative and collaborative language learning (for instance, Crandall, 1999; Dörnyei, 1997; Littlewood, 2002; Nunan, 1992). Incorporating classroom activities where learners work together in pairs or small groups to achieve common goals can help to foster cognitive and motivational interdependence among learners and a sense of shared responsibility. The powerful role of collaborative learning in mediating the growth of individual motivation is widely recognized in studies of child development (for instance, Bronson, 2000), theories of intrinsic motivation (Deci and Flaste, 1996; Ushioda, 1996), classroom studies (for instance, Good and Brophy, 1987), and research on peer tutoring in higher education (for instance, Falchikov, 2001).

Getting learners involved and motivated in learning is essential. For teachers and learners, however, the real challenge lies in finding ways of sustaining that motivation through the long and often arduous process of learning a language. This entails developing skills and strategies for regulating motivation. How can learners be brought to see themselves as agents of their own thinking and thus with the capacity to redirect their thinking in healthier ways? Once again, the social-interactive context of learning would seem to play a crucial role. As McCombs (1994) argues, by providing positive interpersonal support and appropriately structured feedback, teachers can prompt and scaffold learners' attempts to reflect constructively on their learning experience and to redirect their thinking in more positive ways. The teachers' task here is not so much to tell learners what *they* think, but to lead *learners* to reflect on and evaluate their own achievements and learning experience in a constructive manner (Ushioda, 1996). For example, faced with disappointment or frustration at their unsatisfactory performance in a task, learners might be prompted

28

to analyze the problems experienced and their underlying causes, and to identify positive steps they can take to address these areas. Recognizing that how they choose to think can affect how they feel is a vital step in the path towards motivational self-regulation. As Bruner (1996, p. 49) comments, once learners are brought to realize that they act not directly "on the world" but on beliefs they hold about the world, they can begin to "think about their thinking" and so take control of their learning.

Questions for further research

Despite the growing body of theorizing in the field, actual classroom-based studies of motivational events and processes and of good language learners in this situated framework remain surprisingly few in number. Undoubtedly, the key players who have potentially much to contribute here are teachers and learners themselves. Teachers are ideally positioned to undertake research on motivation in their own classrooms – research that is sensitive to local needs and conditions, that is shaped by clear ped-agogical aims and principles, and that can contribute to teachers' own professional development as well as to professional knowledge at large. There is growing recognition of the value of practitioner research in lan-guage education, whether framed as action research (Edge, 2001; Wallace, 1998), exploratory practice (Allwright, 2003), or teachers' nar-rative inquiry (Johnson and Golombek, 2004). More experience-based insights from teachers would greatly enrich our understanding of lan-guage learner motivation, and contribute to bringing theory and practice into much closer interaction.

Above all, research insights from learners themselves in a variety of learning contexts are much needed to substantiate and inform our theo-rizing, particularly in relation to the socially situated growth and regu-lation of motivation. Norton and Toohey's (2001) work is an important contribution in this regard, but perhaps the most promising line of inquiry lies in enabling language learners' own voices and stories to take centre stage, either in person (for instance, Lim, 2002) or minimally mediated by the researcher (for instance, Lamb, 2005). Good language learners have much to teach us about motivation.

Conclusion

Until relatively recently, research interest has focused primarily on describing, measuring, and classifying language learner motivation (inte-grative, instrumental, intrinsic, extrinsic), and examining its relationship

29

with achievement or behavioral outcomes such as classroom participation or persistence in learning. For researchers, motivation is an interesting issue because it is a significant variable in theoretical models of language learning by those who already speak other languages and implicated in learning success.

For teachers, on the other hand, motivation is an issue because it is usually a problem, and the learners they have to deal with are not theoretical abstractions but real people in actual learning situations with complex individual histories and personalities and a variety of conflicting goals and motives. Thus, for teachers, the distilled research finding that positive attitudes and motivation contribute to successful learning yields little useful insight into their day-to-day problems of how to motivate little Samantha in Class 2B and keep her motivated.

Fundamentally, two key principles seem crucial to the maintenance of motivation: first, motivation must emanate from the learner, rather than be externally regulated by the teacher; second, learners must see themselves as agents of the processes that shape their motivation. After all, as long as motivation is externally regulated and controlled by the teacher, learners cannot be expected to develop skills in regulating their own motivation on which good language learning depends.

References

Allwright, D. (2003) Exploratory practice: rethinking practioner research in language teaching. *Language Teaching Research*, 7(2), 113–141.

Amabile, T.M. and Hennessey, B.A. (1992) The motivation for creativity in children. In A. Boggiano and T.S. Pittman (eds.), *Achievement and Motivation: A Social-Developmental Perspective*. Cambridge: Cambridge University Press, 54–74.

Block, D. (2002) McCommunication: a problem in the frame for SLA. In D. Block and D. Cameron (eds.), *Globalization and Language Teaching*. London and New York: Routledge, 117–133.

Bronson, M. (2000) *Self-regulation in Early Childhood: Nature and Nurture*. New York: Guildford Press.

Bruner, J. (1996) *The Culture of Education*. Cambridge, MA: Harvard University Press.

Chambers, G.N. (1999) *Motivating Language Learners*. Clevedon: Multilingual Matters.

Condry, J. and Chambers, J. (1978) Intrinsic motivation and the process of learning. In M. Lepper and D. Greene (eds.), *The Hidden Costs of Reward: New Perspectives on the Psychology of Human Motivation*. Hillsdale, NJ: Lawrence Erlbaum, 61–84.

Corder, S.P. (1967) The significance of learners' errors. *International Review of Applied Linguistics*, 5(2–3), 161–169.

Crandall, J. (1999) Cooperative language learning and affective factors. In J. Arnold (ed.), *Affect in Language Learning*. Cambridge: Cambridge University Press, 226–245.

Crookes, G. and Schmidt, R.W. (1991) Motivation: re-opening the research agenda. *Language Learning*, 41, 469–512.

Csikszentmihalyi, M. (1978) Intrinsic rewards and emergent motivation. In M. Lepper and D. Greene (eds.), *The Hidden Costs of Reward: New Perspectives on the Psychology of Human Motivation*. Hillsdale, NJ: Lawrence Erlbaum, 205–216.

Dam, L. (1995) *Learner Autonomy 3: From Theory to Classroom Practice*. Dublin: Authentik.

Deci, E.L. and Flaste, R. (1996) *Why We Do What We Do: Understanding Self-Motivation*. New York: Penguin.

Deci, E.L. and Ryan, R.M. (1980) The empirical exploration of intrinsic motivational processes. In L. Berkowitz (ed.), *Advances in Experimental Social Psychology*, Vol. 13. New York: Academic Press, 39–80.

Dickinson, L. (1995) Autonomy and motivation: a literature review. *System*, 23(2), 165–174.

Dörnyei, Z. (1994) Motivation and motivating in the foreign language classroom. *Modern Language Journal*, 78, 273–284.

Dörnyei, Z. (1997) Psychological processes in cooperative language learning: group dynamics and motivation. *Modern Language Journal*, 81, 482–493.

Dörnyei, Z. (1998) Motivation in second and foreign language teaching. *Language Teaching*, 31, 117–135.

Dörnyei, Z. (2001a) *Teaching and Researching Motivation*. Harlow: Longman.

Dörnyei, Z. (2001b) *Motivational Strategies in the Language Classroom*. Cambridge: Cambridge University Press.

Dörnyei, Z. and Ottó, I. (1998) Motivation in action: a process model of L2 motivation. *Working Papers in Applied Linguistics (Thames Valley University)*, 4, 43–69.

Dweck, C.S. (1999) *Self-Theories: Their Role in Motivation, Personality, and Development*. Philadelphia, PA: Psychology Press.

Edge, J. (ed.) (2001) *Action Research*. Alexandria, VA: TESOL.

Falchikov, N. (2001) *Learning Together: Peer Tutoring in Higher Education*. London: RoutledgeFalmer.

Fransson, A. (1984) Cramming or understanding? Effects of intrinsic and extrinsic motivation on approach to learning and test performance. In J.C. Alderson and A.H. Urquhart (eds.), *Reading in a Foreign Language*. London and New York: Longman, 86–115.

Gardner, R.C. (1985) *Social Psychology and Second Language Learning: The Role of Attitudes and Motivation*. London: Edward Arnold.

Gardner, R.C. (1988) The socio-educational model of second-language learning: assumptions, findings, and issues. *Language Learning*, 38, 101–126.

Gardner, R.C. and Lambert, W.E. (1972) *Attitudes and Motivation in Second-Language Learning*. Rowley, MA: Newbury House.

Gardner, R.C. and Tremblay, P.F. (1994) On motivation: measurement and conceptual considerations. *Modern Language Journal*, 78, 524–527.

Good, T.L. and Brophy, J.E. (1987) *Looking in Classrooms.* New York: Longman.

Hickey, D.T. and Granade, J.B. (2004) The influence of sociocultural theory on our theories of engagement and motivation. In D.M. McInerney and S. Van Etten (eds.), *Big Theories Re-visited: Research on Sociocultural Influences on Motivation and Learning.* Greenwich, CO: Information Age Publishing, 223–247.

Horwitz, E. (2001) Language anxiety and achievement. *Annual Review of Applied Linguistics,* 21, 112–126.

Johnson, K.E. and Golombek, P.R. (eds.) (2004) *Teachers' Narrative Inquiry as Professional Development.* Cambridge: Cambridge University Press.

Lamb, M. (2004) "It depends on the students themselves": independent language learning at an Indonesian state school. *Language, Culture and Curriculum,* 17(3), 229–245.

Lamb, T.E. (2005) Listening to our learners' voices: pupils' constructions of language learning in an urban school. University of Nottingham. Unpublished doctoral dissertation.

Lantolf, J.A. (1994) Sociocultural theory and second language learning. Introduction to the special issue. *Modern Language Journal,* 78(4), 418–420.

Lim, H.-Y. (2002) The interaction of motivation, perception and environment: one EFL learner's experience. *Hong Kong Journal of Applied Linguistics,* 7(2), 91–106.

Little, D. (1999) Developing learner autonomy in the foreign language classroom: a social-interactive view of learning and three fundamental pedagogical principles. *Revista Canaria de Estudios Ingleses,* 38, 77–88.

Little, D., Ridley, J., and Ushioda, E. (2002) *Towards Greater Learner Autonomy in the Foreign Language Classroom.* Dublin: Authentik.

Littlewood, W. (2002) Cooperative and collaborative learning tasks as pathways towards autonomous independence. In P. Benson and S. Toogood (eds.), *Learner Autonomy 7: Challenges to Research and Practice.* Dublin: Authentik, 29–40.

McCombs, B. (1994) Strategies for assessing and enhancing motivation: keys to promoting self-regulated learning and perfomance. In H.F. O'Neil, Jr. and M. Drillings (eds.), *Motivation: Theory and Research.* Hillsdale, NJ: Lawrence Erlbaum, 49–69.

McInerney, D.M. and Van Etten, S. (eds.) (2004) *Big Theories Revisited: Research on Sociocultural Influences on Motivation and Learning.* Volume 4. Greenwich, CO: Information Age Publishing.

Masgoret, A.-M. and Gardner, R.C. (2003) Attitudes, motivation, and second language learning: a meta-analysis of studies conducted by Gardner and associates. In Z. Dörnyei (ed.), *Attitudes, Orientations and Motivations in Language Learning.* Oxford: Blackwell, 167–210.

Noels, K.A. (2001) New orientations in language learning motivation: towards a model of intrinsic, extrinsic and integrative orientations and motivation. In Z. Dörnyei and R. Schmidt (eds.), *Motivation and Second Language Acquisition.* Honolulu, HI: University of Hawai'i, 43–68.

Norton, B. (1995) Social identity, investment, and language learning. *TESOL Quarterly*, 29(1), 9–31.

Norton, B. (2000) *Identity and Language Learning: Gender, Ethnicity and Educational Change*. Harlow: Longman.

Norton, B. and Toohey, K. (2001) Changing perspectives on good language learners. *TESOL Quarterly*, 35(2), 307–322.

Nunan, D. (ed.) (1992) *Collaborative Language Learning and Teaching*. Cambridge: Cambridge University Press.

Oxford, R.L. (1990) *Language Learning Strategies: What Every Teacher Should Know*. New York: Newbury House.

Peterson, C., Maier, S. and Seligman, M. (1993) *Learned Helplessness: A Theory for the Age of Personal Control*. New York: Oxford University Press.

Pintrich, P.R. and Schunk, D.H. (2002) *Motivation in Education: Theory, Research, and Applications*. Upper Saddle River, NJ: Merrill Prentice Hall.

Rubin, J. (1975) What the "good language learner" can teach us. *TESOL Quarterly*, 9(1), 41–51.

Rueda, R. and Moll, L. (1994) A sociocultural perspective on motivation. In H.F. O'Neil, Jr. and M. Drillings (eds.), *Motivation: Theory and Research*. Hillsdale, NJ: Lawrence Erlbaum, 117–137.

Ryan, R.M. (1991) The nature of the self in autonomy and relatedness. In J. Strauss and G. R. Goethals (eds.), *The Self: Interdisciplinary Approaches*. New York: Springer-Verlag, 208–238.

Ryan, R.M. and Deci, E.L. (2000) Intrinsic and extrinsic motivations: classic definitions and new directions. *Contemporary Educational Psychology*, 25, 54–67.

Schmidt, R. and Savage, W. (1994) Challenge, skill and motivation. *University of Hawai'i Working Papers in ESL*, 12(2), 1–25.

Skehan, P. (1989) *Individual Differences in Second-Language Learning*. London: Edward Arnold.

Swain, M., Brooks, L. and Tocalli-Beller, A. (2002) Peer-peer dialogue as a means of second language learning. *Annual Review of Applied Linguistics*, 22, 171–185.

Ushioda, E. (1996) *Learner Autonomy 5: The Role of Motivation*. Dublin: Authentik.

Ushioda, E. (2001) Language learning at university: exploring the role of motivational thinking. In Z. Dörnyei and R. Schmidt (eds.), *Motivation and Second Language Acquisition*. Honolulu, HI: University of Hawai'i, 93–125.

Ushioda, E. (2003) Motivation as a socially mediated process. In D. Little, J. Ridley and E. Ushioda (eds.), *Learner Autonomy in the Foreign Language Classroom: Teacher, Learner, Curriculum and Assessment*. Dublin: Authentik, 90–102.

Ushioda, E. (2007) Motivation, autonomy and sociocultural theory. In P. Benson (ed.), *Learner Autonomy 8: Teacher and Learner Perspectives*. Dublin: Authentik, 5–24.

van Lier, L. (1996) *Interaction in the Language Curriculum: Awareness, Autonomy and Authenticity*. Harlow: Longman.

Volet, S. and Järvelä, S. (eds.) (2001) *Motivation in Learning Contexts: Theoretical Advances and Methodological Implications*. Amsterdam: Pergamon-Elsevier.

Vygotsky, L.S. (1978) *Mind in Society. The Development of Higher Order Psychological Processes*. Cambridge, MA: Harvard University Press.

Wallace, M. (1998) *Action Research for Language Teachers*. Cambridge: Cambridge University Press.

Williams, M. (2004) Motivation in foreign language learning. In M. Baynham, A. Deignan and G. White (eds.), *Applied Linguistics at the Interface*. London: British Association for Applied Linguistics, in association with Equinox, 167–180.

Williams, M. and Burden, R.L. (1997) *Psychology for Language Teachers*. Cambridge: Cambridge University Press.

Williams, M., Burden, R.L., and Lanvers, U. (2002) "French is the language of love and stuff": student perceptions of issues related to motivation in learning a foreign language. *British Educational Research Journal*, 28(4), 503–528.

Wolters, C. (2003) Regulation of motivation: evaluating the underemphasized aspect of self-regulated learning. *Educational Psychologist*, 34(4), 189–205.

2 Age and good language learners

Carol Griffiths

The role played by age in the development of language by those who already speak other languages (SOL), and the relationship between age and other learner variables such as motivation and aptitude are hotly debated issues. Opinions are divided, sometimes sharply so, over the extent to which the age of the student affects language development, and research aimed at providing evidence for one point of view or another has frequently yielded conflicting results which, often as not, have merely added to the controversy. Although, according to Hyltenstam and Abrahamsson (2003, p. 539), "both the entirely successful adult learner and the slightly unsuccessful child deviate from the unspoken norm", according to Marinova-Todd, Bradford Marshall and Snow (2000), the younger-is-better notion may be a result of misinterpretation of the facts, misattribution of causality and misemphasis on poorer adult learners while underemphasizing good older learners.

The evidence so far

In one of the earliest studies into age-related differences in language development by speakers of other languages, Oyama (1976) studied 60 Italian-born immigrants to the USA. Tape recordings were made of them reading aloud and telling an unrehearsed story. Later they were judged on a five-point scale from no foreign accent to heavy foreign accent. The results indicated that the younger people were when they started learning English the more native-like was their pronunciation. Other studies have shown that, although younger learners are often more successful in the long run, adults may learn more quickly initially. Snow and Hoefnagel-Hohle (1978), who monitored the progress of beginning students of Dutch of varying ages newly-resident in the Netherlands, found that, a few months after arrival, the adolescent and adult students were well ahead of the children in the development of their new language. Within about a year, however, the younger students had caught up with or even passed the levels of the older students. Investigating the levels of attainment of students in a French bi-lingual program in Canada, Harley (1986) discovered that, although older students demonstrated greater overall control of the verb system than younger students after 1,000 hours of instruction, those students who started younger achieved higher levels in the end.

Other studies have not produced such seemingly clear-cut evidence in favor of younger learners. In a very extensive study over ten years and involving 17,000 students of French in Britain, Burstall, Jamieson, Cohen, and Hargreaves (1974) produced results which seemed to indicate that the benefits of early instruction for language development are short lived. Fathman (1975), who looked not only at language performance but at the order of learning specific language structures, concluded that age did not seem to affect the order of language development by those who already speak other languages. She also found that younger students did better on learning phonology but that older students did better on morphology. Neufeld (1978) produced results which seemed to indicate that adults could acquire native-like pronunciation, and a study of Canadian immersion programs by Swain (1981) concluded that an earlier start had much less effect than might have been expected. However, it is difficult to know how far bilingual children, such as in the study by Swain (1981), may be usefully compared with immigrants learning a new language, such as in the studies by Oyama (1976) or Snow and Hoefnagel-Hohle (1978), or with foreign language students such as in the study by Burstall *et al.* (1974), since confounding factors such as length of study and motivation must also be considered.

Although conclusive evidence in favor of one or other point of view has yet to be produced, "there is some good supportive evidence and there is no actual counter evidence" for the advantages of an early start to language development (Singleton, 1989, p. 137). An example given by Cook (1992) concerns adult students who worry about how their children will cope in an English-speaking system. Before long they complain about how much better their children speak English than they do themselves.

My own experience supports Cook's observations. Yasuko, for instance, was an intelligent and conscientious Japanese woman who came to New Zealand to help her 16-year-old daughter settle in to high school. About six months after their arrival I met the daughter, whose ability to communicate confidently and to pronounce English clearly (without, for instance, the typical Japanese r/l confusion) far exceeded her mother's. Her mother's pride in her daughter's progress was mixed with bewilderment at her own perceived slower progress. Wendy was Taiwanese and came to New Zealand with her two sons. She was a highly successful businesswoman with a quick and intelligent mind and a highly motivated language student. But there was no way she could keep up with the language development of her sons, something which she regarded with both satisfaction with them and frustration with herself. Ryong was a highly successful Korean businessman who immigrated to New Zealand with his family. He had spent a lot of time in both Britain and the USA and, therefore had had considerable exposure to English over the years. Even so, once the children started in New Zealand schools, they streaked ahead in their language development. When I met them, I was left with the impression that before long they would be almost indistinguishable from native-speaking children, something which was unlikely ever to be the case with their father.

Although all of the three cases that I have mentioned (and it would be easy to mention more) provide only anecdotal evidence for the idea that younger learners are more successful, their significance should perhaps not be underestimated. It is easy to think of examples such as Yasuko, Wendy, and Ryong. However, with the exception of one case where the child was intellectually sub-normal, and evidently below average even in his own language, I personally cannot think of one case where the parent has been more successful at language development than the child, although I would not want to rule out that it is possible. Much as the more mature of us would like to believe otherwise, and however we might choose to explain the phenomenon, numerically the anecdotes seem to be heavily in favor of the idea that younger learners are more successful language learners than older learners, a belief supported by some well-known case studies.

Schumann (1976) describes a ten-month study of Alberto, a 33-year-old Costa Rican living in the United States of America. Alberto belonged to an unskilled labor group of relatively low socio-economic status. According to a questionnaire, Alberto appeared to have good motivation and positive attitudes towards Americans and American society. However, he socialized mainly with speakers of Spanish, and chose to work at night, which prevented him from attending English classes. Although test results indicated that Alberto was not lacking in cognitive ability, he "evidenced very little linguistic development during the course of the project" (p. 391).

Like Alberto, Wes, a Japanese artist living in Hawaii, was also 33 years old. According to Schmidt (1983), when Wes first arrived in Hawaii, his ability to communicate in English was minimal, although this was not a major problem, since Japanese is widely spoken in Hawaii. Wes was described as extroverted and socially outgoing with a strong drive to communicate, although, like Alberto, he showed "little or no" (p. 143) interest in studying English formally. During a three-year observation period, Wes's ability to communicate orally in English increased at an "impressive rate" (p. 144), although he remained unable to read or write in English and his grammatical control of English "hardly improved at all" (p. 144), leading at times to misunderstandings in interactions with native speakers.

Burling (1981) recounts his own experiences of trying to learn Swedish during his year as guest professor at a Swedish university. Around 20 years older than Alberto or Wes, Burling was in his mid-50s. He had high status, high motivation, and positive attitudes. Nevertheless, in spite of these apparent advantages, Burling judged his own progress as "distinctly unsatisfactory" (p. 280).

Exceptions to the belief that mature learners cannot learn language successfully have been documented, however. One interesting exception is Julie, whose case is discussed by Ioup, Boustagui, El Tigi, and Moselle (1994). At the age of 21, Julie married an Egyptian and moved from England to Cairo. Nine days after her arrival her husband was called away for military service. She was left with non-English speaking relatives in a situation of total immersion until her husband returned 45 days later. After her husband's return Julie used Arabic outside the home and at family gatherings until she started a job as an English teacher where she conversed with the other teachers in Arabic. She received no formal instruction. To assist her language development, Julie kept a note book in which she recorded vocabulary, idioms, and what she observed regarding the structure of the language. She welcomed error feedback and consulted her husband when she had questions. According to Ioup *et al.* (1994), after six months, Julie was communicating well, and after two and a half years she could pass as a native speaker.

Explaining age-related differences in language development

There are many possible explanations for any age-related differences in language development by speakers of other languages. For instance, it is often suggested that there is a critical period for language development during which language can be acquired or learnt more easily than at other stages of life, and "once this window of opportunity is passed, the ability to learn languages declines" (Birdsong, 1999, p. 1). It has been suggested that the critical period lasts until around puberty, at which time the brain begins to lose plasticity, possibly connected with the process of lateralization (Lenneberg, 1967). Others, however, argue that the development of lateralization occurs much earlier than puberty, and we must therefore look elsewhere for an explanation for observed age-related differences in second language development (Dulay, Burt and Krashen, 1982). One possible explanation, according to Long (1990), is the process of myelination which progressively wraps the nerves of the brain in myelin sheaths as the brain matures. Myelination delineates learning pathways in the brain, but reduces flexibility. None of the biological explanations proffered to account for age-related differences in language development is without its controversy. Although much of the evidence seems to point to the fact that younger students are more successful than older students, the exceptions such as Julie (Ioup *et al.*, 1994) render any dogmatic assertions on the subject unsustainable. However, "biological restrictions such as brain maturation should not be so easily overturned" (Bialystok and Hakuta, 1999, p. 177). Because of this, the term "sensitive" period rather than "critical" period has been proposed in order to indicate that there is no "abrupt or absolute criterion after which L2 acquisition is impossible but rather a gradual process within which the ultimate level of L2 attainment becomes variable" (Ioup *et al.*, 1994, p. 74).

Affective factors have been hypothesized as the main reason for the child's eventual superiority in language development (Krashen and Terrell, 1983). Although this may be an over-simplification (Gregg, 1984), it has been suggested that "affective variables may play a more important role than does biological maturation in problems associated with adult second language acquisition" (Schumann, 1975, p. 209). Language shock (which leaves the learner feeling ashamed, anxious, and inadequate) and culture shock (which leaves the learner feeling rejected, disoriented, and uncertain of identity and status) are included by Schumann among these affective variables.

Social pressures also form a major component of these affective factors. Schumann (1976) proposed the concept of social distance to refer to the similarity or dissimilarity of cultures which come into contact with each other. Social distance usually seems to be more of a problem for adults than for children since children are "less culture bound than adults" (Ellis, 1985, p. 109). Peer pressure could conceivably motivate younger learners to learn a second language more successfully. Adults are often quite happy to maintain a distinctive accent; indeed they may do so deliberately in an effort to retain their identity. Young people, however, are often much more strongly motivated by the need to be accepted by their peer groups. "Generalized social changes" are identified by Burling (1981, p. 290) as the main cause of his difficulties when trying to learn Swedish. A child, Burling points out, talks on a narrower range of topics, with less style shifting and less active vocabulary than was expected of himself who, as an adult, "moved into the language backwards" (p. 282). According to Burling, a child does not realize how much he does not know, but an adult is aware of his own limitations and "is likely to give up and conclude that he has lost the capacity to learn a language" (p. 284).

Cognitive differences between children and adults may be another variable contributing to age-related differences in language development.

Older learners' faster initial progress is explained by Krashen (1985) in terms of their ability to obtain more comprehensible input by means of their greater experience, knowledge, and ability to negotiate communication. Older students are able to learn language by consciously thinking about the rules (Ellis, 1985), and cognitive factors could help to explain the findings by Snow and Hoefnagel-Hohle (1978) that older students are initially faster than younger students since they are capable of rationalizing the new language and of utilizing the patterns of their first language for immediate communicative purposes. Older students might also be expected to have a larger repertoire of language learning strategies, established by experience, which they can choose and apply as appropriate. In addition, older students might be expected to be able to exercise better metacognitive control over their learning, for instance by means of time management, and by monitoring and evaluating their own progress. However, "cognitive considerations [. . .] do not address the fact that, in the long run, children typically outperform adults" in language development (Dulay, Burt and Krashen, 1982, p. 271).

Learning situation, emphasized, for instance, by Norton and Toohey (2001) as an important factor in successful learning, may also affect students differently according to their age. Learning situations can vary considerably from naturalistic (where students learn by being immersed in the target language, much the way children learn their first language – recommended by Krashen and Terrell (1983), as the ideal way to learn) to a formal classroom. In turn, classrooms can vary greatly. They may be during the day (typical of primary and secondary schools) or at night (typical of classes for working adults). The methods used may vary from traditional grammar–translation, through highly structured audiolingual to communicative. Some learning situations do not involve face-to-face contact, but are managed by means of correspondence or electronic technology. These different approaches may suit older or younger students depending on factors such as prior learning experience, learning style, metacognitive ability to control their own learning, motivation, what exactly it is they are trying to learn (for instance writing or speaking), and the personal demands which they have on their time and energy (for instance, from family or job).

In addition to maturational, socio-affective, cognitive, and situational explanations for age-related differences in language learning, there is a potentially almost infinite number of individual variables which might conceivably affect a student's ability to learn language. Commonly listed among these variables are gender, culture, personality, learning style, attitude, beliefs, motivation, aptitude, autonomy, and prior learning experience as well as personal factors such as family, job, and health.

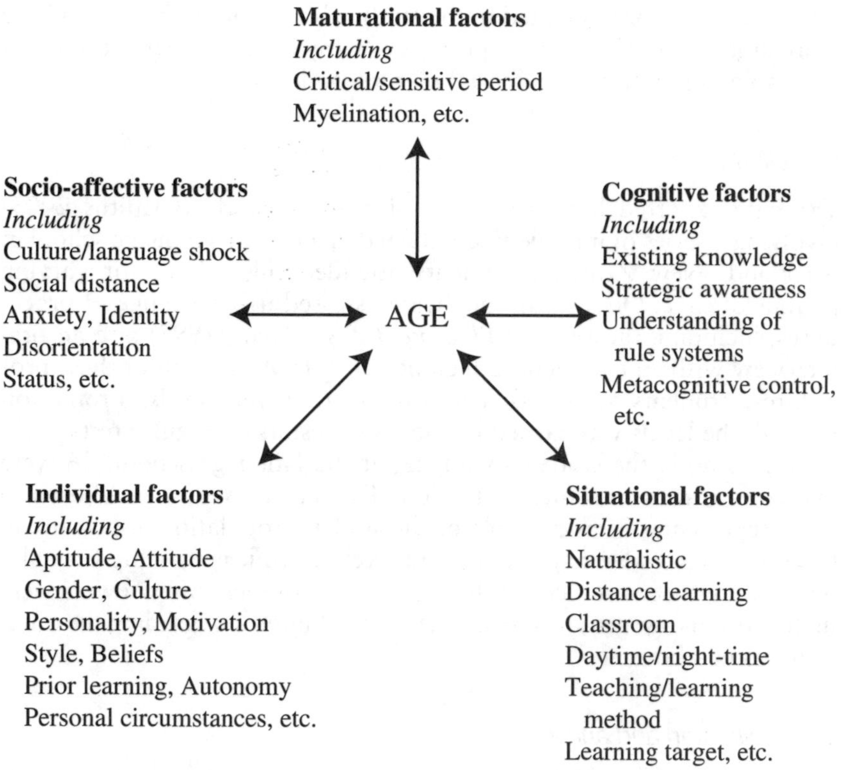

Maturational factors
Including
Critical/sensitive period
Myelination, etc.

Socio-affective factors
Including
Culture/language shock
Social distance
Anxiety, Identity
Disorientation
Status, etc.

Cognitive factors
Including
Existing knowledge
Strategic awareness
Understanding of
  rule systems
Metacognitive control,
  etc.

AGE

Individual factors
Including
Aptitude, Attitude
Gender, Culture
Personality, Motivation
Style, Beliefs
Prior learning, Autonomy
Personal circumstances, etc.

Situational factors
Including
Naturalistic
Distance learning
Classroom
Daytime/night-time
Teaching/learning
  method
Learning target, etc.

Figure 1   Factors which interact with age to influence language learning

When these factors are all combined, they produce an incredibly complicated picture, which Figure 1 models diagrammatically.

The study

Although younger language learners have been researched quite extensively (for instance, Burstall *et al.*, 1974; Swain, 1981), no doubt reflecting the reality that the education of young people is a huge industry, less
research evidence is available regarding mature language learners, for
whom some important questions remain:

• Are older students really less successful at language development than
  younger students?
• If so, what are the factors which contribute to success or otherwise?
• What can a teacher do to help?

Age and good language learners

These questions, investigated in the study which follows, become all the more urgent in the light of the post-war "baby boom" which has created a sizeable population of potential mature students.

Participants

The data reported here were part of a larger study (Griffiths 2003) involving a series of interviews conducted in a private language school in Auckland, New Zealand. Students attended this school for varying periods of time. On arrival, they were assessed using a range of procedures, including the *Oxford Placement Test* (Allan, 1995) and an oral interview with an experienced member of staff. As a result of these procedures, students were assigned to one of seven levels. Promotion through the levels was earned by means of results on regular tests.

From among the students studying at the language school, 26 were invited to a semi-structured interview. The interviewees were chosen to be as representative as possible of the student population, especially in terms of age, gender, nationality, and level of proficiency – the variables which were the main focus of the study. Three of these interviewees were in the 40-plus age group, and are therefore of interest regarding the questions noted above.

Data collection and analysis

Interviewees were asked to complete the 50-item version of the Strategy Inventory for Language Learning (SILL) (Oxford 1990) designed for speakers of other languages learning English in order to provide basic quantitative information about their reported strategy use. Data from the SILL were entered into SPSS and analyzed for frequency of use. An interview guide was also used, consisting of three main questions which dealt with the learners' key strategies, their learning difficulties, and the effects of learner variables on their success. Other interesting comments and insights were also noted by the interviewer, analyzed for common themes, and later written into a report.

Findings

Yuki was 44 years old when she started her English language course at a language school in Auckland, New Zealand. She had already been in New Zealand with her children on a visitor's visa for one year, and she wanted to stay in New Zealand, rather than having to return to Japan leaving her children behind. She therefore applied for a student visa, which meant that she was obliged to attend school. On the Oxford

Placement Test (Allan 1995) she scored 81, which is categorized as a "minimal user" and she was placed in the lowest class (elementary). For some time her attendance was very erratic. She or her children were often sick and she "moved my house" four times. After being warned of the possible consequences of breach of the conditions of her visa, she became more regular. After four months she was moved to a mid-elementary class, and three months later to an upper elementary class. Her ability to communicate remained very low, however, often requiring the services of the Japanese counselor to translate essential information (for instance regarding her immigration status). The results of the monthly tests were also unspectacular. After nearly a year at the language school, and after nearly two years in New Zealand, Yuki was still only in the upper elementary class (the third out of seven levels).

Yuki was not easy to interview because she found it difficult to understand the questions, and, when she understood, found it difficult to express what she wanted to say in English. The English she could manage was frequently extremely ungrammatical: "I can't express myself very well English." According to the results of the SILL she used strategies infrequently. The most difficult aspect of learning English she found to be speaking and writing (production skills). She thought that using the telephone and writing long sentences might be useful strategies to help with these difficulties though she said she did not actually use either of these. As a Japanese, she found English grammar difficult, but was unable to suggest strategies for dealing with the difficulty. The only key strategy she was aware of using was reading easy books in English. Yuki thought English was difficult to learn because "my mind is blank," a condition which she put down to her age.

Although Yuki believed she was too old to learn English, she was far from the oldest student in the school. Hiro was a 64-year-old Japanese man who came to New Zealand to spend a month studying English. His entry test indicated that he was at pre-intermediate level (the fourth out of seven levels), and he studied at this level throughout the month he spent at the school. He said he had spent seven years studying English, but "that was a long time ago" during the war, when he believed he had been handicapped because there were no books, no paper, and he was taught by non-native speakers. According to his SILL results, Hiro used strategies moderately frequently.

As an older Japanese, especially as an older man, interacting with younger students was fraught with cultural difficulties. They could not display superiority without being, in their terms, impolite, and he could not appear to be inferior without losing face in a way that they would all have found socially very difficult. Hiro was, therefore, acutely aware of the need, as an older learner, to develop effective strategies to cope with the social difficulties of interacting with students much younger than himself. One such strategy he used was to busy himself with his note-book when he found classroom communicative activities too threaten-ing. This "opting out" strategy, however, created some problems with classroom dynamics. His teacher was concerned that Hiro spent quite a lot of class time recording new grammar and making long lists of vocab-ulary in his notebook, and even complaining that the class was not given enough "new" grammar and vocabulary. The teacher felt that strategies such as these were not as useful as, for instance, interacting with other students and practicing using the language they already knew, and she also worried that Hiro was perhaps discontented with her teaching. From her point of view, although generally she found Hiro a delightful student, she found it difficult to manage his tendency to be somewhat formal and rigid in his approach to his learning.

When asked his reasons for learning English Hiro said it was just a hobby. He felt that this was a good motivation for learning English, since being relaxed and unworried about the outcome would help him to learn more effectively. As he delightfully put it: "I have worked hard all my life. Now I am going to have some fun!" Hiro was not at the school long enough for any conclusions to be drawn regarding his rate of progress, although, judging by his work over the month, it is quite possible he would have been promoted to the next class after the monthly test had he been there for that. Nevertheless, Hiro's case points to some interest-ing possible implications regarding the needs of older learners and sug-gests some possibly fruitful areas for further research specially designed to investigate age-related differences in language learning.

Like Yuki, Kang was in his forties, and, on arrival, he was initially placed in the lowest class (elementary), but apart from their age and initial starting level, they could hardly have been more different. When the 41-year-old Korean first arrived, his knowledge of English was neg-ligible, although he was evidently fluent in Japanese, so not inexperi-enced as a language learner. Kang had left his wife and young children in Korea and obviously missed them, but he settled single-mindedly to his work. Although according to the SILL he was only a moderate user of strategies, Kang had some interesting strategies of his own. He spent long hours in the self-study room revising lessons, doing homework, and listening to tapes, especially pronunciation tapes, which was the area he found most difficult. An interesting theory that he had was that pronun-ciation is affected by the food we eat, because different kinds of foods require different movements of the mouth and tongue. Accordingly, while in New Zealand, he eschewed his traditional Korean diet and ate Kiwi food instead, a strategy aimed at helping him to get his mouth around the sounds of English.

In addition to this somewhat unusual pronunciation strategy, Kang reported using a list of key language learning strategies, including listening to radio, watching TV, and going to the movies. Kang said he consulted a text book for vocabulary, sentence structure, and grammar, and used a notebook to write down language he picked up from signs, notices, and advertising. He kept a dictionary with him at all times and listened to people talking around him. Unlike some other students who believed that "good" or "bad" teaching was responsible for their success or otherwise, Kang accepted realistically that some teachers are going to be better than others, and that some teachers' styles may affect the way some students learn. Therefore, he believed, students must be flexible in their attitudes and strategies if they are to make the best of their opportunities, and they must accept responsibility for their own learning.

Although age is often considered to be a disadvantage when learning language, Kang was more successful than many of the much younger students with whom he studied. By the end of his seven-month course he was working in the advanced (the top) class, although difficulties remained with typical Korean pronunciation problems such as r/l and f/p discrimination, in spite of seven months of Kiwi tucker! Asked why he thought he had made such good progress, Kang told me: "My heart is one hundred percent want to learn." He wanted to learn English in order to improve his job prospects so that he could provide better opportunities for his family. This strong motivation showed itself in the focus which he brought to his work and in the disciplined and thorough way he went about his study.

Implications for the teaching/learning situation

From a teacher's point of view, the cases described above underline the reality that managing students of different ages in the same classroom is not always without its difficulties. Nevertheless, teachers often respond positively when asked for their reactions to having older students in their classrooms, since mature learners can provide a welcome steadying influence which benefits both the teacher and fellow students. If older and younger students are to be successfully integrated into the same classroom, however, the teacher needs to pay conscious attention to the following aspects of class management:

1 Materials need to be provided which are of interest across a wide age range, or which are targeted to particular age groups within the class.

2 A range of activities needs to be planned, since those which appeal to younger students may be too "childish" for older students, while those which older students enjoy may be too "boring" for younger class members.
3 Tolerance for face-saving mechanisms (such as opting out of threatening activities) should be built into the classroom culture.
4 Students should be allowed to employ idiosyncratic strategies which suit their own learning style or beliefs about how to learn well.

Questions for ongoing research

Is younger better when it comes to language learning? If so, why, and how can teachers and learners manage age-related differences in order to support or achieve successful language learning outcomes? These questions remain open ones. Research to date has tended to be limited to a particular learning situation (in, for instance, England, Canada, or New Zealand) and to employ limited methodology (for instance questionnaires, observation, or interviews). Further research to investigate the question of age in language learning using multiple research methods in a variety of situations is required if meaningful results which might usefully inform teaching practice are to be obtained.

Given an ageing population in many countries of the world, research into how older students learn best is becoming a matter of vital interest to educators concerned with designing and delivering courses for mature students, who often want to complete their education in a way which was not possible for them in their younger years. As a result of improvements in medical care, today's mature learners are often healthy and mentally alert as well as financially secure, and in a position to take advantage of learning opportunities in a way which their own parents often could not. Research into all aspects of the mature learner is urgently required to inform the education industry regarding how best to deal with the demand. What do they want and need? How can a quality product best be delivered? How can older learners learn successfully?

This is not, of course, to suggest that younger learners should be seen as less important – of course not. There are many unanswered questions relating to young learners also: How can achievement be accurately and meaningfully assessed? How can young learners be motivated? The main thrust of educational concern will probably always be young learners who need education at the beginning of their lives and careers. But learning is a lifelong process, and research into how to learn successfully needs to extend across all age groups.

Conclusion

Although consensus is far from universal, most of the evidence regarding age-related differences in language learning would seem to indicate that, overall, younger is better. Possible explanations of this phenomenon include maturational, socio-affective, cognitive, and individual/ psychological factors as well as learning environment and teaching method. When dealing with students of differing ages, teachers need to be flexible in their methods in order that students may be able to learn in the way they feel comfortable and which brings them success.

In spite of the general belief that younger students are more successful at language development than older students, cases such as Julie, Hiro, and Kang demonstrate that it is possible for older students to be good language learners. Rubin (1975) included age as one of the factors requiring further research, and even 30 years later, continued research into age-related learner differences in language development is vitally important in order that learners of all ages might receive optimal support from teachers and educators.

References

Allan, D. (1995) *Oxford Placement Test*. Oxford: Oxford University Press

Bialystok, E. and Hakuta, K. (1999) Confounded age: linguistic and cognitive factors in age differences for second language acquisition. In D. Birdsong (ed.), *Second Language Acquisition and the Critical Period Hypothesis*. Mahwah, NJ: Lawrence Erlbaum, 161–181.

Birdsong, D. (1999) Whys and why nots of the Critical Period Hypothesis for second language acquisition. In D. Birdsong (ed.), *Second Language Acquisition and the Critical Period Hypothesis*. Mahwah, NJ: Lawrence Erlbaum, 1–22.

Burling, R. (1981) Social constraints on adult language learning. In H. Winitz (ed.), *Native Language and Foreign Language Acquisition*. New York: New York Academy of Sciences, 279–290.

Burstall, C., Jamieson, M., Cohen, S., and Hargreaves, M. (1974) *Primary French in the Balance*. Windsor: National Foundation for Educational Research.

Cook, V. (1992) *Second Language Learning and Teaching*. London: Edward Arnold.

Dulay, H., Burt, M., and Krashen, S. (1982) *Language Two*. New York: Oxford University Press.

Ellis, R. (1985) *Understanding Second Language Acquisition*. Oxford: Oxford University Press.

Fathman, A. (1975) The relationship between age and second language productive ability. *Language Learning*, 25(2), 245–253.

Gregg, K. (1984) Krashen's monitor and Occam's razor. *Applied Linguistics*, 5, 78–100.

Griffiths, C. (2003) *Language learning strategy use and proficiency*. (Retrieved from: http//hdl.handle.net/2292/9).

Harley, B. (1986) *Age in Second Language Acquisition*. Clevedon, Avon: Multilingual Matters.

Hyltenstam, K. and Abrahamsson, N. (2003) Maturational constraints in SLA. In C. Doughty and M. Long (eds.), *The Handbook of Second Language Acquisition*. Malden, MA: Blackwell, 539–588.

Ioup, G., Boustagui, E., El Tigi, M., and Moselle, M. (1994) Reexamining the Critical Period Hypothesis: a case study of successful adult SLA in a naturalistic environment. *Studies in Second Language Acquisition*, 16, 73–98.

Krashen, S. (1985) *The Input Hypothesis*. London: Longman.

Krashen, S. and Terrell, T. (1983) *The Natural Approach*. Hayward, California: Hayward Press.

Lenneberg, E. (1967) *Biological Foundations of Language*. New York: Wiley.

Long, M. (1990) Maturational constraints on language development. *Studies in Second Language Acquisition*, 12, 251–285.

Marinova-Todd, S., Bradford Marshall, D., and Snow, C. (2000) Three misconceptions about age and L2 learning. *TESOL Quarterly*, 34(1), 9–34.

Neufeld, G. (1978) On the acquisition of prosodic and articulatory features in adult language learning. *Canadian Modern Language Review*, 32(2), 163–174.

Norton, B. and Toohey, K. (2001) Changing perspectives on good language learners. *TESOL Quarterly*, 35(2), 307–322.

Oxford, R.L. (1990) *Language Learning Strategies: What Every Teacher Should Know*. New York: Newbury House Publishers.

Oyama, S. (1976) A sensitive period in the acquisition of a non-native phonological system. *Journal of Psycholinguistic Research*, 5, 261–285.

Rubin, J. (1975) What the "good language learner" can teach us. *TESOL Quarterly*, 9(1), 41–51.

Schmidt, R. (1983) Interaction, acculturation, and the acquisition of communicative competence: a case study of an adult. In N. Wolfson and E. Judd (eds.), *Sociolinguistics and Second Language Acquisition*. New York: Newbury House, 137–174.

Schumann, J. (1975) Affective factors and the problem of age in second language acquisition. *Language Learning*, 25(2), 209–235.

Schumann, J. (1976) Second language acquisition: The pidginisation hypothesis. *Language Learning*, 26(2), 391–408.

Singleton, D. (1989) *Language Acquisition: The Age Factor*. Clevedon: Multilingual Matters.

Snow, C. and Hoefnagel-Hohle, M. (1978) The critical period for language acquisition: evidence from language learning. *Child Development*, 49, 1119–1128.

Swain, M. (1981) Time and timing in bilingual education. *Language Learning*, 31, 1–16.

3 Learning style and good language learners

Carisma Nel

An enduring question for language researchers is the effect of individual differences on the efficacy of language learning. For example, learners differ from one another in the ways in which they process information from the environment. This proposition of individual differences in information processing is the cornerstone of research on learning styles – which have been defined as learners' "consistent ways of responding to and using stimuli in the context of learning" (Claxton and Ralston, 1978, p. 7) and as their "natural, habitual, and preferred ways of absorbing, processing, and retaining new information and skills which persist regardless of teaching methods or content area" (Kinsella, 1995, p. 171).

The learning style concept

Although it was from psychology that many of the central concepts and theories relating to learning styles originated, in more recent years, research in the area of learning styles has been conducted in domains outside psychology. Several attempts to integrate and synthesize the conceptual field have been made (for instance, Cassidy, 2004; Curry, 1983, 1987, 2000; Jonassen and Grabowski, 1993; Rayner and Riding, 1997; Riding and Cheema, 1991). However, the question of how the style literature should be integrated and organized is still being posed by researchers and teachers alike (for instance, Coffield, Moseley, Hall and Ecclestone, 2004; Desmedt and Valcke, 2004).

According to Curry (1991, p. 249), "there is a bewildering confusion of definitions surrounding learning style conceptualizations and there is a wide variation in the scale and scope of learning, school achievement, and other behavior predicted by the various learning style concepts." As a potentially useful way of looking at learning style, Curry (1983) employs a metaphorical onion with its multiple layers. The first layer of the onion consists of instructional and environmental preferences and constitutes the most observable traits. This layer is open to introspection, is context-dependent, and is not fixed. The second layer of the onion refers to the information processing preferences of the learner.

This relates to the processes by which information is obtained, sorted, stored, and utilized. The next layer is the personality dimension and is described as a "relatively permanent dimension [. . .] apparent only when an individual's behaviour is observed across many different learning situations" (Riding and Cheema, 1991, p. 195). (See Ehrman, this volume, for more information about personality and good language learners).

Five dimensions that mark various preferences have been identified by Dunn and Dunn (1992, 1993). These are environmental preferences regarding sound, light, temperature, and classroom design; emotional preferences addressing motivation, persistence, responsibility, and structure; sociological preferences for private, pair, team, adult, or varied learning relations; physiological preferences related to perceptual strengths, intake, time, and mobility; and processing inclinations based on analytic/global mode, hemisphericity (that is, whether the left or right side of the brain is dominant), and impulsive/reflective preferences.

Individual learners have particular strengths which form the basis of their preferred learning style (Kolb, 1984). These preferences are often expressed in polarized terms, a great number of which have been identified in the literature. Some of the best known of these include divergent vs. convergent (Hudson, 1966), field dependence versus field independence (Witkin, Lewis, Hertzman, Machover, Meisener and Wapner, 1954), global versus analytical (Kirby, 1988), impulsive versus reflective (Kagan, 1965), leveler versus sharpener (Schmeck, 1981), organizer versus nonorganizer (Atman, 1988), right versus left hemisphere (Torrance and Rockenstein, 1988), risk-taking versus caution (Kogan and Wallach, 1964; Kogan, 1971), verbalizer versus visualizer (Richardson, 1977), visual versus haptic (Lewenfeld, 1945), holist versus analytic (Peters, 1977) and holist versus serialist (Pask, 1972). Although style preferences are often presented in terms of dichotomies such as these, many learners, of course, do not exclusively display one style or its bipolar opposite, but operate somewhere on an intervening continuum. For instance, if students have a largely verbal style, this does not necessarily mean that they will not also display elements of visual style.

According to Reid (1987), research has identified four basic perceptual style preferences: visual (for instance reading, charts), auditory (for instance lectures, tapes), kinesthetic (involving physical activity), and tactile (for instance building models or doing laboratory experiments). To these Reid added the dimensions of group versus individual learning preferences to develop the well-known Perceptual Learning Style Preference Questionnaire.

Research into learning style

The concept of learning style relies on the notion that individuals learn in different ways, and there is now a considerable body of research into learning style. A great many factors may influence a student's stylistic preferences, including nationality. A research study conducted by Reid (1987) indicates that Korean students were the most visual in their learning style preferences while Arabic and Chinese language learners expressed a strong preference for auditory learning. Hyland's (1993) Japanese learners favored auditory and tactile styles. In a study conducted by Rossi-Le (1995), Spanish speakers expressed a strong learning style preference for auditory learning, whereas Vietnamese learners preferred visual learning. Reid (1987, p. 101) concludes by suggesting that, although stylistic preferences are relatively stable, students need to be adaptable, since research shows that "the ability of students to employ multiple learning styles results in greater classroom success."

The terms field dependence and field independence are used to describe two extreme dimensions of human perception of stimuli. The more a learner is able to separate relevant material from its context (or field), the more field independent they are said to be (Witkin and Goodenough, 1981). Research into the impact of field dependence/independence on perception suggests that these are stable traits that affect individual responses in a variety of situations. For example, learners who are field dependent are likely to see problems as a whole and have difficulty separating component parts (Witkin and Goodenough, 1981). In contrast, field-independent learners tend to be more analytical and prefer breaking down problems into component parts.

A review of the literature seems to indicate that field independence correlates positively and significantly with success in the language classroom (Brown, 1994; Chapelle, 1995; Chapelle and Roberts, 1986; Chapelle and Abraham, 1990). Abraham (1985) found that language learners with field-independent styles were more successful in deductive lessons (that is, principles are given, consequences and applications are deduced), while those with field-dependent styles performed better in inductive lessons (that is, facts and observations are given, underlying principles are inferred). Naiman, Fröhlich, Stern, and Todesco (1978) found in a study of English-speaking students learning French in Toronto that field independence correlated positively and significantly with imitation and listening comprehension tasks. A study conducted by Dreyer (1992) found a positive and statistically significant relationship between field independence and proficiency as measured by the TOEFL (Test of English as a Foreign Language) test. The results of a study conducted by Dreyer, Wissing, and Wissing (1996) revealed a complex pattern of relationships between cognitive styles and aspects of pronunciation accuracy: in the case of perception of final consonants, field independence, and right hemispheric dominance were related to better performance, while in the case of production (aspiration of initial consonants), field dependence, and left hemispheric dominance were related to better performance.

Learning style instruments

A number of instruments have been specifically developed by language researchers to explore learning styles. These include Reid's (1987) Perceptual Learning Style Preference Questionnaire, Oxford's (1993) Style Analysis Survey, and the Ehrman and Leaver Learning Styles Questionnaire (2003).

The Perceptual Learning Style Preference Questionnaire (Reid, 1987) consists of five randomly arranged statements on each of six learning style preferences (visual, auditory, kinesthetic, tactile, group, and individual). Examples of statements include: "I understand better when I read instructions," and "I learn more when I study with a group." Respondents must rate each statement on a 5-point scale from *strongly agree* to *strongly disagree*, and from this a style profile of the respondent can be constructed.

The Style Analysis Survey (SAS) (Oxford, 1993) is used to determine learners' general approach to learning (that is, it gives an indication of overall learning style preference). The SAS consists of five parts: using physical senses to study or work (visual, auditory, and hands-on), dealing with other people (extroverted versus introverted), handling possibilities (intuitive versus concrete-sequential), approaching tasks (closure-oriented versus open) and dealing with ideas (global versus analytic).

The Ehrman and Leaver (2003) Learning Styles Questionnaire consists of a superordinate construct (synopsis–ectasis) and ten subscales. Ehrman and Leaver (2003, p. 395) explain that, "the synoptic–ectenic distinction addresses the degree of conscious control of learning desired or needed," and they hypothesize that "ectasis controls consciously what synopsis accomplishes through preconscious or unconscious processes." According to them (2003, p. 396), this construct provides detailed and individualized student information while making profiles "comparable across students and, potentially, over time."

With a variety of learning style instruments in use (others include the survey by Cohen, Oxford, and Chi, 2002), it is important to carefully select an instrument according to the unique requirements of the learning context and the purpose of collecting the data (James and

Gardner, 1995). The advantage of such instruments for language teachers is that they enable them to compile a multidimensional profile of students' learning styles using the most commonly identified dimensions so that they can plan and, where necessary, modify their teaching according to their student's needs. For students, such instruments can heighten self-awareness and empower them to maximize their learning opportunities.

Is there a good language learner style?

As noted previously, there are some indications from the research literature that good language learners may be, for instance, more field independent in their learning style. This means that good language learners are better able to manage contextual variables than poorer language learners. Willing (1988), however, following a large-scale study of learning styles in Australia, concluded that stylistic differences were "minimal" (p. 146). It would seem that the dynamic nature of the individual learners and continuously changing contextual factors make the compilation of a generic stylistic profile of the good language learner impossible.

Although learning style appears to be a relatively stable trait, Reid (1987, p. 100) argues that "learning styles are moderately strong habits rather than intractable biological attributes, and thus they can be modified and extended." Chapelle and Roberts (1986) suggest that good language learners are capable of style flexing by adapting their learning style to the needs of a given situation or task. Less successful language learners, on the other hand, are not as adept at flexing when the specific need arises and are more likely to rigidly persist with a particular style even in the face of evidence (such as low grades) that their learning style is not effective.

Implications for the teaching/learning situation

As Cohen and Dörnyei (2002) remind us, students learn in different ways, so that what works well for one learner may not be useful for another. Since learning styles seem to be a relatively stable learner characteristic, teachers may not be able to exert as much influence over this learner variable as, perhaps, over motivation. However, they recommend that teachers should adapt classroom tasks in order to maximize the potential of individual learners with particular learning styles. They also suggest that "It is also possible that learners over time can be encouraged to engage in 'style stretching' so as to incorporate approaches to learning they were resisting in the past" (p. 176).

Learning style and good language learners

According to Bennett (2003, p. 187) "The concept of learning styles offers a value-neutral approach for understanding individual differences [. . .] The assumption is that everyone can learn, provided teachers respond appropriately to individual learning needs." The challenge is to successfully design and deliver language instruction relevant to a multiplicity of learning styles. In order to do this, the teacher needs to consider several areas.

Instructional planning and presentation

It is possible that learning style may vary according to individuals, but also there may be stylistic variation according to gender, age, or nationality. This may mean, for instance, that classes with a majority of male students may have a different dominant style from a mainly female class, and may require different types of activities which cater for their needs. The key for teachers in planning instruction is to be aware of the multiple ways students learn best. In order to identify students' learning styles, teachers might use language style instruments to measure and identify the learners' styles. The learners' style profiles suggested by these instruments can be used as the basis for preparing instruction from that point on.

During the planning and preparation stage, teachers should include a variety of language learning tasks so as to allow learners with different styles to do well and achieve success (cf. Cohen, 2003). Materials should be selected from a variety of scholarly books, refereed journals, the Internet, magazines and newspapers, videos, documents, and so on, since different students will have different interests, and will respond more or less favorably to different stimuli. Teachers should also remember that one of the most important contributions of the learning styles concept to language teaching is the understanding that there is no one "best" method for every student. Although essential language curricula goals may be similar for all students, methods employed must be varied to suit the individual needs of all students and classroom routines should be varied so that all students are able to use their preferred styles at least some of the time (cf. Griffiths on methods, this volume).

Teaching/learning environment construction

It would seem to go without saying that every student learning languages has the right to be successful. In order to actualize that success, teachers need to ask themselves what changes they can make to improve the chances of success for students who are struggling. In addition to recognizing and valuing the uniqueness of learners, teachers need to look at their teaching/learning environments and ask whether their students feel safe, valued, and comfortable; whether the learning environment is supportive; whether language learning is stimulated regardless of style. They also need to consider what they can do to make the teaching/learning environment more attuned to the various needs of their students, given institutional or other constraints.

Assessment

In the interests of accommodating a diversity of learning styles, it is important that there is a variety of assessment components and options built into a language course. The assessment tool can take many forms, including regular assignments, individual or group projects, online or in-class quizzes, student oral presentations, research essays, and term papers. The formats of the tools should be appropriate and may include filling in the blanks, multiple-choice questions, identification of terms, a variety of short and essay questions for the students to select from, and writing papers. In addition, the teacher should provide a variety of appropriate hints and instructions, such as diagrams, tables, or verbal description, to suit a variety of styles.

The interaction of learning style and teaching style

Teachers should also be aware of their own style preferences, which can have a bearing on their students' learning (Harmer, 1998), and they should vary their own teaching styles in planning lessons in order to accommodate multiple learning styles. By understanding students' learning styles, and by being flexible regarding their own teaching styles, teachers can heighten their awareness and be more sensitive in their listening, observation, preparation, presentation, and interaction. Though teachers cannot be all things to all students, they will be more effective if they can provide more variety and choice to accommodate the stylistic differences of their students.

Questions for ongoing research

Regarding learning style, Sternberg (2001, p. 250) has argued "the literature has failed to provide any common conceptual framework and language," while, according to Reid (1998), the concept is still not well understood. The sheer number of dichotomies in the literature conveys something of the current conceptual confusion. Future research should address the issue of theoretical coherence as well as aiming for well-grounded empirical findings, tested through replication.

After more than 30 years of research, no consensus has been reached about the most effective instrument for measuring learning styles and no agreement about the most appropriate pedagogical interventions. The instruments should demonstrate both internal consistency and test–retest reliability, and construct and predictive validity. These are the minimum standards for any instrument which is to be used to redesign pedagogy (Coffield, Moseley, Hall, and Ecclestone, 2004).

Mitchell (1994, p. 18) states that self-report inventories "are not sampling learning behaviour but learners' impressions" of how they learn, impressions which may be inaccurate, self-deluding, or influenced by what the respondent thinks the researcher wants to hear. As Price and Richardson (2003, p. 287) argue "the validity of these learning style inventories is based on the assumption that learners can accurately and consistently reflect a) how they process external stimuli, and b) what their internal cognitive processes are".

There is also widespread disagreement about the advice that should be offered to teachers or tutors. For instance, should the style of teaching be consonant with the style of learning or not? At present, there is no definitive answer to that question, because there is a dearth of rigorously controlled experiments and of longitudinal studies to test the claims of the main advocates. A move towards more controlled experiments, however, would entail a loss of ecological validity and of the opportunity to study complex learning in authentic, everyday educational settings. Curry (1990, p. 52) summarized the situation by commenting that some researchers have carried out studies which have tended to

> validate the hypotheses derived from their own conceptualizations.
> However, in general, these studies have not been designed to
> disconfirm hypotheses, are open to expectation and participation
> effects, and do not involve wide enough samples to constitute valid
> tests in educational settings.

In spite of such biases, Curry (1990) concludes that no one learning style pattern clealy emerges as generally advantageous.

The socio-economic and the cultural context of students' lives and of the institutions where they seek to learn tend to be omitted from the learning styles literature. Learners are not all alike, nor are they all suspended in cyberspace via distance learning, nor do they live out their lives in language laboratories. Instead, they live in particular socio-economic settings where age, gender, race, and class all interact to influence their attitudes to learning. Moreover, their social lives with their partners and friends, their family lives with their parents and siblings, and their economic lives with their employers and fellow workers influence their learning in significant ways. All these factors tend to be played down or simply ignored in most of the learning styles literature and should be addressed in future research.

Conclusion

More than 30 years ago, Rubin (1975) listed learning style among the factors requiring further research in relation to good language learners. Although the learning styles field remains confused (Curry, 1991; Reid, 1998) some tentative generalizations emerge from the research to date. It appears that every learner does have a learning style, consisting of a unique blend of instructional and environmental preferences, of information processing preferences, and of preferences related to personality. Stylistic preferences seem to be relatively stable; however, successful learners do seem to be able to adapt their learning styles to accommodate the requirements of a particular learning task or situation. And no one style which typifies good language learners has been identified.

Since it is difficult to draw together such a diverse and complex area of theory and research, it is important that teachers remember that any theory or model of styles is necessarily a simplification of the complexity of how students learn languages. The failure of research to reach consensus regarding many of the issues surrounding learning styles means that conclusions must be drawn tentatively. However, it would seem sensible to suggest that a primary professional responsibility of language teachers is to maximize the learning opportunities of their students regardless of what their styles might be. A reliable and valid learning styles instrument (for instance Ehrman and Leaver, 2003; Oxford, 1993; Reid, 1987) can be a useful tool in the execution of this responsibility, firstly by helping to diagnose students' preferred learning styles so that teachers can plan and implement effective programs, and secondly to encourage self-awareness among students so that they might enhance their own language learning.

References

Abraham, R. (1985) Field dependence/independence in the teaching of grammar. *TESOL Quarterly*, 19(4), 680–702.

Atman, K.S. (1988) Psychological type elements and goal accomplishment style: Implications for distance education. *The American Journal of Distance Education*, 2(3), 36–44.

Bennett, C. (2003) *Comprehensive Multicultural Education: Theory and Practice* (fifth edition). Boston, MA: Allyn and Bacon.

Brown, H.D. (1994) *Principles of Language Learning and teaching*. Third edition. Englewood Cliffs, NJ: Prentice Hall.

Cassidy, S. (2004) Learning styles: an overview of theories, models and measures. *Educational Psychology*, 24(4), 419–444.

Chapelle, C. (1995) Field dependence/field independence in the L2 classroom. In J. Reid (ed.), *Learning Styles in the ESL/EFL Classroom*. Boston, MA: Heinle & Heinle, 158–168.

Chapelle, C. and Abraham, R.G. (1990) Cloze method: What difference does it make? *Language Testing*, 7, 121–146.

Chapelle, C. and Roberts, C. (1986) Ambiguity tolerance and field independence as predictors of proficiency in English as a second language. *Language Learning*, 36, 27–45.

Claxton, C.S. and Ralston, I. (1978) *Learning Styles: Their Impact on Teaching and Administration*. Washington, DC: National Institute of Education.

Coffield, F., Moseley, D., Hall, E., and Ecclestone, K. (2004) *Should We Be Using Learning Styles? What Research Has to Say to Practice*. London: Learning and Skills Research Centre.

Cohen, A.D. (2003) The learner's side of foreign language learning: where do styles, strategies, and tasks meet? *International Review of Applied Linguistics*, 41, 279–291.

Cohen, A. D. and Dörnyei. Z. (2002) Focus on the language learner: motivation, styles and strategies. In N. Schmitt (ed.), *An Introduction to Applied Linguistics*. London: Edward Arnold, pp. 170–190.

Cohen, A.D., Oxford, R.L., and Chi, J.C. (2002) Learning styles survey, Minneapolis, MN: Center for Advanced Research on Language Acquisition. (Retrieved from: http://www.carla.umn.edu/about/profiles/CohenPapers/LearningStylesSurvey.pdf).

Curry, L. (1983) *Learning Style in Continuing Medical Education*. Ottawa: Canadian Medical Association.

Curry, L. (1987) *Integrating Concepts of Cognitive Learning Style: A Review with Attention to Psychometric Standards*. Ontario: Canadian College of Health Service Executives.

Curry, L. (1990) A critique of the research on learning styles. *Educational Leadership*, 48(2), 50–56.

Curry, L. (1991) Patterns of learning style across selected medical specialities. *Educational Psychology*, 11(3), 247–277.

Curry, L. (2000) Review of learning style, study approach and instructional preference research in medical education. In R.J. Riding and S.G. Rayner (eds.), *International Perspectives on Individual Differences (1): Cognitive Styles*. Stamford, CN: Ablex Publishing, 239–276.

Desmedt, E. and Valcke, M. (2004) Mapping the learning styles "jungle": an overview of the literature based on citation analysis. *Educational Psychology*, 24(4), 445–464.

Dreyer, C. (1992) *Learner variables as predictors of ESL proficiency*. Unpublished Ph.D. thesis. Potchefstroom, South Africa: Potchefstroom University for Christian Higher Education.

Dreyer, C., Wissing, D., and Wissing, M. (1996) The relationship between cognitive styles and pronunciation accuracy in English as a second language. *South African Journal of Linguistics, Supplement* 34, 37–62.

Dunn, R.S. and Dunn, K. (1992) *Teaching Elementary Students Through Their Individual Learning Styles: Practical Approaches for Grades 3–6.* Needham Heights, MA: Allyn and Bacon.

Dunn, R.S., and Dunn, K. (1993) *Teaching Secondary Students Through Their Individual Learning Styles: Practical Approaches for Grades 7–12.* Boston, MA: Allyn and Bacon.

Ehrman, M.E. (this volume) Chapter 4: Personality and good language learners.

Ehrman, M.E. and Leaver, B.L. (2003) Cognitive styles in the service of language learning. *System,* 31, 393–415.

Harmer, J. (1998) *How to Teach English.* London: Longman

Hudson, L. (1966) *Contrary imaginations.* Harmondsworth: Penguin.

Hyland, K. (1993) Culture and learning: a study of the learning style preferences of Japanese students. *RELC Journal,* 24(2), 69–91.

James, W.B. and Gardner, D.L. (1995) Learning Styles: Implications for Distance Learning. *New Directions for Adult and Continuing Education,* 67, 19–32.

Jonassen, D.H., and Grabowski, B.L. (1993) *Handbook of International Differences, Learning and Instruction.* Hillsdale, NJ: Lawrence Erlbaum Associates.

Kagan, J. (1965) Impulsive and reflective children: significance of conceptual tempo. In J.D. Krumboltz (ed.), *Learning and the Educational Process.* Chicago, IL: Rand McNally, pp. 133–161.

Kinsella, K. (1995) Understanding and empowering diverse learners in ESL classrooms. In J.M. Reid (ed.), *Learning Styles in the ESL/EFL Classroom.* Boston, MA: Heinle & Heinle, 170–194.

Kirby, J.R. (1988) Style, strategy, and skills in reading. In R.R. Schmeck (ed.), *Learning Strategies and Learning Styles.* New York: Plenum, pp. 229–274.

Kogan, N. (1971) Educational implications of cognitive styles. In G.S. Lesser (ed.), *Psychology and Educational Practice.* Glenview, IL: Scott, Foresman & Company, pp. 242–292.

Kogan, N. and Wallach, M.A. (1964) *Risk-taking: A Study in Cognition and Personality.* New York: Holt, Rinehart, and Winston.

Kolb, D.A. (1984) *Experiential Learning: Experience as the Source of Learning and Development.* Englewood Cliffs, NJ: Prentice Hall.

Lewenfeld, V. (1945) Tests for visual and haptical aptitudes. *American Journal of Psychology,* 58, 100–112.

Mitchell, D.P. (1994) Learning style: a critical analysis of the concept and its assessment. In R. Hoey (ed.), *Design for Learning: Aspects of Educational Technology.* London: Kogan Page.

Myers, E.I.B. (1962) *The Myers-Briggs Type Indicator.* Palo Alto, CA: Consulting Psychologists Press.

Naiman, N., Fröhlich, M., Stern, H.H., and Todesco, A. (1978) *The Good Language Learner.* Toronto: Ontario Institute for Studies in Education.

Oxford, R.L. (1993) *Style Analysis Survey (SAS)*. Tuscaloosa, AL: University of Alabama.

Pask, G. (1972) A fresh look at cognition and the individual. *International Journal of Man-Machine Studies*, 4, 211–216.

Peters A.M. (1977) Language learning strategies: does the whole equal the sum of the parts? *Language*, 53, 560–573.

Price, L. and Richardson, J.T.E. (2003) Meeting the challenge of diversity: a cautionary tale about learning styles. In C. Rust (ed.), *Improving Student Learning Theory and Practice 10 Years on*. Oxford: Oxford Centre for Staff and Learning Development, Oxford Brookes University, 285–295.

Rayner, S.G. and Riding, R.J. (1997) Towards a categorization of cognitive styles and learning styles. *Educational Psychology*, 17, 5–28.

Reid, J.M. (1987) The learning style preferences of ESL students. *TESOL Quarterly*, 21(1), 87–111.

Reid, J.M. (1998) *Understanding Learning Styles in the Second Language Classroom*. Upper Saddle River, NJ: Prentice-Hall.

Richardson, A. (1977) Verbalizer-visualizer: a cognitive style dimension. *Journal of Mental Imagery*, 1(1), 109–126.

Riding, R. and Cheema, I. (1991) Cognitive styles: an overview and integration. *Educational Psychology*, 11 (3–4), 193–215.

Rossi-Le, L. (1995) Learning styles and strategies in adult immigrant ESL students. In J.M. Reid (ed.), *Learning Styles in the ESL/EFL Classroom*. Boston, MA: Heinle & Heinle, 118–125.

Rubin, J. (1975) What the "good language learner" can teach us. *TESOL Quarterly*, 9(1), 41–51.

Schmeck, R.R. (1981) Improving learning by improving thinking. *Educational Leadership*, 38, 384.

Sternberg, R.J. (2001) Epilogue: another mysterious affair at styles. In R.J. Sternberg and L-F. Zhang (eds.), *Perspectives on Thinking, Learning and Cognitive Styles*. Mahwah, NJ: Lawrence Erlbaum, 249–252.

Torrance, E.P. and Rockenstein, Z.L. (1988) Styles of thinking and creativity. In R.R. Schmeck (ed.), Learning strategies and learning styles New York: Plenum Press, pp. 275–290.

Willing, K. (1988) *Learning Styles in Adult Migrant Education*. Sydney: National Centre for English Language Teaching and Research.

Witkin, H.A. and Goodenough, D.R. (1981) *Cognitive Styles: Essences and Origins*. New York: International Universities Press.

Witkin, H.A., Lewis, H.G., Hertzman, M., Machover, K., Meisener, P.B., and Wapner, S. (1954) *Personality Through Perception*. New York: Harper.

4 Personality and good language learners[*]

Madeline Ehrman

This chapter addresses not just the "good" language learner, but those who may be considered among the best. They are distinguished by performance at "Level Four" (on a five-point scale) on an oral interview test that uses the Interagency Language Roundtable (ILR) level definitions (Federal Interagency Language Roundtable, 1999). Level Four proficiency, also referred to at one time by the American Council on the Teaching of Foreign Languages as "Distinguished" proficiency, implies almost no limitations on the ability of the individual to use the language, including control of multiple registers, fine lexical distinctions, and pragmatic skill close to native. Some refer to this level as "near-native" (Leaver and Shekhtman, 2002).

Those who achieve Level Four are among the true elite of good language learners. Achievement of Level Four in any skill is both very difficult and rare. It is almost never done in a classroom alone, though in the case of gifted learners, it may require only a short exposure to a foreign environment together with very advanced classroom work. For most, however, extended sojourns are the norm. But of course very few, even of those who spend a long time in a country, reach Level Four.

What characterizes Level Four achievers has been an open question for some time. Some of my own research has looked at this question, with intriguing results for motivation, aptitude, cognitive style, native language background, and personality. Personality has been defined as "those aspects of an individual's behaviour, attitudes, beliefs, thought, actions, and feelings which are seen as typical and distinctive of that person and recognized as such by that person and others" (Richards, Platt and Platt, 1998, p. 340). This chapter focuses on personality in particular, using data from the Myers-Briggs Type Indicator (Myers, McCaulley, Quenk and Hammer, 1998), a widely used personality inventory based on the theory of personality originated by Swiss psychologist Carl Jung (1971) which measures personality according to four dichotomous scales (Myers *et al.*, 1998, p. 6):

---

[*]The observations and opinions expressed in this chapter are those of the author and do not represent the official position of the US Department of State.

61

1 Extraversion–Introversion: Extraverts tend to focus on the outer world of things and people, whereas introverts focus more on their inner worlds of internal experiences, including concepts and feelings. They are abbreviated E and I respectively.

2 Sensing–Intuition: Sensing is oriented toward that which can be experienced through the five senses – facts and things, whereas intuition focuses on meanings, possibilities, and the relationships between or among concepts. People who prefer intuition often trust the information they receive without necessarily grounding it on concrete experience. Sensing is abbreviated S, and intuition with N, since I has already been used for introversion.

3 Thinking–Feeling: Thinking refers to making decisions and coming to conclusions primarily on impersonal grounds that takes into account logical consequences. On the other hand, Feeling judgment makes use of personal or social values to make decisions. Note that in this model, Thinking decision-making is not the same as intelligence, nor is Feeling judgment the same as emotion.

4 Judging–Perceiving: These terms refer to whether a person uses Thinking or Feeling judgment to deal with the outside world (Judging) or Sensing or Intuition to deal with the outer world (Perceiving). In practice, Judging types tend to want to come to closure quickly, and Perceiving types want to keep their options open and get all the information they need before taking action.

The four scales combine into 16 possible four-letter types, such as ENFP (extraversion-intuition-feeling-perceiving). We will see that some personality dispositions appear to be advantageous when people learn foreign languages to near-native levels of breadth and depth.

The study

What makes those who achieve Level Four different from those who do not achieve that level? To begin to answer this question, I have been examining data from the Foreign Service Institute (FSI) and conducting interviews with members of the US diplomatic community for some time. The Foreign Service Institute (FSI) is the training arm of the US Department of State. It provides full-time, intensive training in over 60 languages for periods ranging from 24 to 88 weeks, depending on the level of difficulty for native English speakers. The goal is to achieve functional, job-related proficiency for foreign affairs work abroad. For over ten years, the Foreign Service Institute has provided diagnostic and learning advisory services to its language students through the Learning Consultation Service (LCS) which keeps data on individual learner differences based on results of both questionnaires and interviews.

Participants

The current sample was drawn from two databases kept on the learners, one up to 1999 and one from 2000 on. There were nearly 8,000 records and more coming in daily. This study used a sample from those data of 3,145, representing all the records at the time whose last names began with A-Ka (the remainder had not yet been checked and cleared of duplicate records). Of these 3,145, only 2% had achieved Level Four for either speaking/listening or reading or both according to the FSI Oral Proficiency Interview (for details of these measures, see pp. 63–64). The languages in which the Level Fours achieved their high ratings included Chinese, French, German, Hebrew, Indonesian, Italian, Korean, Lao, Portuguese, Russian, Spanish, Swedish, and Turkish. All were learned in adulthood. The average age of those in this sample was 38.4 (standard deviation of 11 years) and there were roughly equal numbers of males and females. Their median education was between the bachelor's and master's degrees. All of these language learners were adults who began the study of the languages in which they have achieved Level Four as adults.

Data collection and analysis

The primary independent measure in this study is the Myers-Briggs Type Indicator (Myers *et al.*, 1998), a questionnaire widely used by educational psychologists, counselors, and organization development specialists. It is a forced-choice, self-report inventory intended to sort individuals into one or the other pole of four main scales. Form M, the version of the MBTI currently used by the LCS, was standardized on a national (US) sample of 3,009 adults over 18, stratified for sex and race. Internal consistency reliability ranges from .90 to .94 on the four scales. Test–retest reliability ranges from .62 to .85. Concurrent validity has been found over a wide range of other personality measures, aptitude tests, and performance. Construct validity has been undertaken through multiple studies examining the degree to which the MBTI ratings differentiate different subpopulations (specifics are in the *Manual*, Myers *et al.*, 1998).

The criterion measure used in this study was the FSI Oral Proficiency Interview. The test yields ratings ranging from 0 to 5 for speaking (the

S-score, which includes interactive listening comprehension) and for reading (the R-score). The full oral interview, including speaking, interactive listening, and an interactive reading test using authentic material, takes over two hours. R-3, for example, indicates reading proficiency level 3 ("professional" proficiency); S-2 represents speaking proficiency level 2 (working proficiency). Other levels are 0 (no proficiency), 1 (survival level), 4 (full professional proficiency, with few if any limitations on the person's ability to function in the language and culture), and 5 (equivalent to an educated native speaker). "Plus" scores (indicating, for instance, proficiency between S-2 and S-3) were coded as 0.5. Thus, for example, a score of S-2+ was coded 2.5. Most students enter FSI with goals of end-training proficiency ratings of S-3 R-3 for full-time training. Up to the present, no one has had an official goal of Level Four, though many overseas missions have indicated that it is highly desirable for some positions.

Analysis was done using SPSS for Windows, version 13. The tests used for the nominal variables that are the subject of this study were frequencies and crosstabs, with significance testing by Fisher's Exact Test.

Findings

The frequency figures show that ISTJ (introversion-sensing-thinking-judging) was the modal (most frequent) personality type in the non-Level Four sample with 266 cases (15.7% of the 16 types) and even with the Level Four group included it was still the modal type in the total sample at 272 (15.4%). The least frequent types were ISFP (introversion-sensing-feeling-perceiving) and ESFP (extraversion-sensing-feeling-perceiving) at 34 (1.9%) and 40 (2.3%) respectively. SP (sensing-perceiving) types were generally infrequent in all groups.

Table 1 displays the findings for the Level Four learners in standard "type table" array.

The only significant result was for INTJ types (introverted-intuitive-thinking-judging) who were significantly over-represented (sig = .027, $p < .05$) among the Level Four students.

In terms of discrete personality characteristics, the most common among those *not* achieving Level Four were E (extraversion), N (intuition), T (thinking), and J (judging). For those achieving Level Four, it was I (introversion), N (intuition), T (thinking), and J (judging). The least well represented, then, were I (introversion), S (sensing), F (feeling), and P (perceiving) for those who had not achieved Level Four, and E (extraversion), S (sensing), F (feeling), and P (perceiving) for those who had achieved Level Four. Intuition was significantly (.002) over-represented among those who had achieved Level Four.

Table 1 MBTI Type Table for Level Four students

ISTJ	ISFJ	INFJ	INTJ
N = 6	N = 2	N = 5	N = 11
9%	3%	7.5%	16.5%
ISTP	ISFP	INFP	INTP
N = 2	N = 0	N = 2	N = 8
3%	0%	3%	12%
ESTP	ESFP	ENFP	ENTP
N = 1	N = 0	N = 5	N = 7
1.5%	0%	7.5%	10.5%
ESTJ	ESFJ	ENFJ	ENTJ
N = 3	N = 4	N = 5	N = 6
4.5%	6%	7.5%	9%

Notes:

N = number of Level Four students in each type.

% = number of Level Four students in the type as a percentage of the total number of Level Fours, rounded to the nearest 0.5.

Within the paired characteristics, intuitive-thinking types (NT) showed the highest frequency overall, whereas sensing-feeling (SF) types were lowest. Of those who had not achieved Level Four, EN (extraversion-intuition), IN (introversion-intuition), and IS (introversion-sensing) types were roughly the same in percentage, and ES (extraversion-sensing) types were considerably less. Of those who had achieved Level Four, EN (extraversion-intuition) and IN (introversion-intuition) types were clearly greater in number than ES (extraversion-sensing) and IS (introversion-sensing) types. Sensing-judging (SJ) types dominated among the non-Level Fours at 33.5%, with intuition-thinking (NT) types close at 32.4%. However, among those who achieved Level Four, intuitive-thinking (NT) types and introverted-intuitive (IN) types were significantly (.007 and .012 respectively) over-represented. Sensing-perceiving (SP) types trailed in both groups with 11.7% and 4.5% respectively.

Among the three-letter combinations, IST (introversion-sensing-thinking) was most frequent among those without Level Four (19.2%), whereas for those with Level Four, it was INT (introversion-intuition-thinking, 28.4%). The least represented combination in the non-Level Four group were those with ESF (extraversion-sensing-feeling) preferences (5.6%) and in the Level Four group those from the EST (extraversion-sensing-thinking), ESF (extraversion-sensing-thinking), and ISF (introversion-sensing-feeling) categories at 6%.

All the sensing types except ESFJ (extraversion-sensing-feeling-judging) are under-represented among those achieving Level Four. On the other hand, all those with NT (intuition-thinking) combinations are over-represented, although only INTJ (introversion-intuition-thinking-judging) is significant (.027).

Intuition

The most striking finding in these data is the importance of intuition among high achieving learners. Intuitives, whether the function is introverted or extraverted, concentrate on meaning, possibilities, and usually accept constant change. Intuitives tend to be oriented toward the future – what might be or what probably will be. They seek hidden patterns and are prone to make associations almost as second nature. They are known to have a strong interest and well-developed ability in reading.

In my own research, I have found that intuition (along with feeling and perceiving) correlates with thin ego boundaries – a kind of openness to experience. This is corroborated by correlations between intuition and "Openness" in the Big Five personality model (McCrae and Costa, 1989). Thin-boundary learners tend to be more receptive to peripheral learning and tolerant of ambiguity than their thicker-boundaried counterparts (Ehrman, 1999; Hartmann, 1991). Thus, we can guess that when it is necessary to adapt to unfamiliar ways of speaking, or to pick up native-like ways of self-expression, and read not only between but behind the lines as is needed at Level Four, a tendency to perceive the world in intuitive ways is likely to be helpful. Pattern matching and recognition is second nature to intuitives, which promotes another area of skill useful in dealing with such linguistic subsystems as register. Because the MBTI was intended to sort people into binary classes, since intuition appears to be an important characteristic of high achievers, the opposite end of the S–N pole (sensing) shows up as relatively less equipped for Level Four learning. There is more discussion of this issue below.

Intuition and thinking

Although intuition was found to be important, not all intuitives were found to be equally over-represented in the group of high achievers. One of these differences is between learners who prefer intuition with thinking (NT), and those who prefer intuition with feeling (NF). The combination of intuition and thinking shows up most often as an interest in intellectual mastery of the world, a liking for analysis as a way of dealing with information, and systems thinking. The specialty of this group

66

is strategic thinking. NT types may be perceived as arrogant by people of other personality types because of their dislike of what they see as incompetence and their very high levels of self-confidence in their domains of interest. At the same time, they are merciless with themselves, never satisfied with current achievement and always attempting to reach higher and higher. If a learner has taken language proficiency as a domain of competence and mastery, it is not surprising that the effort to learn more, deeper, wider, better continues on and on. An NT type on the track of mastery can be relentless. Furthermore, NT types are likely to gravitate naturally to metacognitive strategies such as goal-setting, self-assessment, and self-monitoring – they are also strategic thinkers, and high-level language learning can be something of a campaign.

Another reason that NT types may have an apparent edge is their penchant for analysis and making relatively fine distinctions. One of the hallmarks of Level Four language is precision, especially lexical, including idioms and sayings, but also pragmatic and even grammatical. To achieve these, it is necessary to notice differences and to be able to pick out from the mass of language input what is important. It is not enough to say that two words mean "green," for instance, when one may refer to a clear bluish green, whereas the other is "dusty olive." If there are different words for these two types of green, the Level Four achiever for whom they are relevant, is likely to notice when and how they are used and to come to be able to use them without hesitation. This kind of "sharpening" and "field independence" (Ehrman and Leaver, 2003) is much more characteristic of NTs than of NFs.

Introversion and intuition

Not only are intuitives not all equal as Level Four learners on the thinking–feeling scale, they are quite different on the extraversion–introversion dimension as well. Much of the literature to date has indicated that extraverts are better language learners (Dewaele, 2005; Dewaele and Furnham, 2000; Hokanson, 2000; Naiman, Fröhlich and Stern, 1975; Naiman, Fröhlich, Stern and Todesco, 1978), although there are exceptions (Ehrman, 1994a, 1994b, 1996a). In the case of this study, introversion in combination with intuition is quite significantly over-represented. It appears that the combination of introversion, intuition, and thinking provides something of value. Perhaps introversion brings a sensitivity to archetypal, universal patterns. This is one of the theoretical characteristics of introverted functions: rather than being influenced primarily by outer-world data, they are shaped more by more general and internally accessed archetypes (Jung, 1971).

The way this might work for language learning is that very good language learners react to every language as if it were essentially a manifestation of one language, as suggested by Saunders (1997). This supposes that language universals are roughly the same across languages. These universals correspond to archetypes and are thus especially available to introversion and to intuition. It would not be surprising then, that those with both introversion and intuition would be in tune with the universal substratum of language.

Introversion, intuition, and thinking

One might ask, if introverted intuition makes such a difference, why don't INFJ types, who also have introverted intuition, do equally well? This is where thinking comes in. Thinking promotes sharpening, or remembering differences and learning by means of those differences. This comes more naturally to thinking types than to feeling types, who have a tendency to level or merge different things in their perception. In summary, then, introverted intuition and sharpening (which comes more readily with thinking than with feeling) seem to be important factors in learning language to the Distinguished level.

Judging

In this study, judging is over-represented among those who achieve Level Four. Although judging (versus perceiving) usually represents a preference for an orderly, predictable life, the scale originated as a complex way to determine if the most preferred function is introverted or extraverted. For INTJ types, judging indicates that intuition is used in the introverted mode (sensitivity to archetypes) rather than the extraverted one (focus on the future and its possibilities).

Sensing

Another striking feature of the results of this study is that with the exception of ESFJ (extraversion-sensing-feeling-judging), all the sensing types are clearly (though non-significantly) under-represented among those achieving Level Four. Sensing is thus apparently as disadvantageous to high-level language learning as intuition is helpful to it. Why might this be?

Sensing types are attuned to the world as it is. Extraverted sensing types are highly aware of the present and the physical and factual aspects of the world. They are grounded in "what is." Introverted sensing types are focused on memories of experience as internal facts, but they do not necessarily seek patterns and symbolic meaning, unlike intuitive types. Although this does not mean that sensing types cannot achieve Level Four, sensing is less likely to be attuned to underlying language structure and meaning systems.

Implications for the teaching/learning situation

For the FSI sample at least, intuition, especially introverted intuition, is over-represented among those who achieve very high levels of language proficiency. It is probably related to pattern recognition and analysis, receptivity to direct and indirect input, inferences, tolerance of ambiguity, orientation toward meaning, and sensitivity to universal aspects of language. Thinking appears to be another critical element, but only in combination with intuition: it seems to contribute sharpening tendencies that make possible the kinds of differentiation that promote precision of language. Sensing is under-represented in this sample, and it is possible that this may be at least in part a result of a literal, factual approach that is less oriented to meaning than is intuition.

In spite of the finding that INTJ (introversion-intuition-thinking-judging) personalities are significantly over-represented among the top language learners, teachers should remember that statistics do not predict individual achievement: they only suggest probabilities and directions for assisting those who may not have natural predilections that promote high level language learning. These results suggest that teachers might, for instance, help their learners by not insisting on participation in extraverted activities such as group work against students' natural inclinations, and by providing variety and alternatives in classroom activities to suit students' different personalities. Teachers might help their students to develop intuition by encouraging guessing and extracting meaning from context, to develop thinking by means of analyzing linguistic information, and to develop judging by bringing order into study activities (scheduling, for example).

Questions for ongoing research

The study reported in this chapter must be considered exploratory work. The sample is small and limited to FSI students, who themselves are not typical of language learners by virtue of age, experience, motivation, education, and the context in which they are studying. The participants were not randomly selected: they were those in the LCS database who were in that part of the alphabet that was selected as the source of data.

The MBTI is not the only personality instrument used in the LCS. The Hartmann Boundary Questionnaire also represents personality dimensions, particularly defensive style (Ehrman, 1999; Hartmann, 1991). More could also be learned by an analysis of the total score and the 12 subscales that constitute this measure. More could also be learned by examining the learning strategies used by the several MBTI types who do and do not achieve Level Four. This could be done through a measure for which data exist that examines learning strategies (for instance, the Motivation and Strategies Questionnaire, Ehrman, 1996b) and through interviews, some of which are already being conducted.

It appears to be nearly impossible for those who have begun language study as adults to reach Distinguished Proficiency (particularly in speaking) without at least some time spent where the language is spoken natively. However, the routes taken by various learners to reach their language proficiency vary greatly from one to the other. At one extreme are the few who have a great deal of classroom exposure to the language in their home country and have spent only a few weeks in a native-speaking environment (attested by Bernhardt, 2003). At the other extreme are those who have spent years immersed in the language and culture, with relatively little classroom work. Interviews and examination of learner files in the LCS would tell us much more about different paths to Level Four, including various mixes of classroom work and actual language immersion and use. An open question is the relative importance of formal instruction – perhaps some types need it more than others.

Finally, with a bigger sample of very high achievers, we would want to investigate whether there are differences among those who achieve this level in Western languages as opposed to those who succeed in non-Western languages that are very difficult for most native speakers of English. We would want to know if personality type interacts with language difficulty or language type.

Conclusion

According to the findings of this study, the best language learners tend to have introverted personalities, a finding which runs contrary to much of the literature, and, even, to pedagogical intuition. The best language learners are intuitive and they are logical and precise thinkers who are able to exercise judgment. However, it is clear from the fact that there are high-level language learners in a wide variety of personality categories that motivated individuals can become good language learners whatever their personalities.

References

Bernhardt, J. (2003) Personal communication.

Dewaele, J.-M. (2005) Investigating the psychological and emotional dimensions in instructed language learning: obstacles and possibilities. *Modern Language Journal*, 89(3), 367–280.

Dewaele, J.-M. and Furnham, A. (2000) Personality and speech production: a pilot study of second language learners. *Personality and Individual Differences*, 28, 355–365.

Dörnyei, Z. (2001) *Motivational Strategies in the Language Classroom*. Cambridge: Cambridge University Press

Ehrman, M.E. (1994a) The *Type Differentiation Indicator* and language learning success. *Journal of Psychological Type*, 30, 10–29.

Ehrman, M.E. (1994b) Weakest and strongest learners in intensive language training: A study of extremes. In C. Klee (ed.) *Faces in a Crowd: Individual Learners in Multisection Programs*. Boston, MA: Heinle & Heinle, 81–118.

Ehrman, M.E. (1996a) Psychological type and extremes of training outcomes in foreign language reading proficiency. In A. Horning and R. Sudol (eds.), *Understanding Literacy: Personality Preferences in Rhetorical and Psycholinguistic Contexts*. Cresskill, NJ: Hampton Press, 231–273.

Ehrman, M.E. (1996b) *Understanding Second Language Learning Difficulties: Looking Beneath the Surface*. Thousand Oaks, CA: Sage Publications.

Ehrman, M.E. (1999) Ego boundaries and tolerance of ambiguity in second language learning. In J. Arnold (ed.), *Affect in Language Learning*. New York, Cambridge, Cambridge University Press, 68–86.

Ehrman, M.E. and Leaver, B.L. (2003) Cognitive styles in the service of language learning. *System* 31, 393–415.

Ehrman, M.E. and Oxford, R.L. (1995) Cognition plus: correlates of language learning success. *Modern Language Journal*, 79(1), 67–89.

Federal Interagency Language Roundtable (1999) Language Skill Level Descriptions. (Retrieved from: http://www.govtilr.org/ILRscale1.htm).

Hartmann, E. (1991) *Boundaries in the Mind: A New Psychology of Personality*. New York: Basic.

Hokanson, S. (2000) Foreign language immersion homestays: maximizing the accommodation of cognitive styles. *Applied Language Learning*, 11(2), 239–264.

Jung, C.G. (1921 [1971]) *Psychological Types*. Sir H. Read, M. Fordham, G. Adler, and W. McGuire (eds. Translated by H.G. Baynes and revised by R.F. Hull.), *Collected Works of C.G. Jung Vol. 6*, Bollingen Series 20. Princeton, NJ: Princeton University.

Leaver, B.L. and Shekhtman, B. (eds.) (2002) *Developing Professional-Level Language Proficiency*. Cambridge: Cambridge University Press.

McCrae, R.R. and Costa, P.T. (1989) Reinterpreting the *Myers-Briggs Type Indicator* from the perspective of the Five-Factor Model of Personality. *Journal of Personality*, 57, p. 30.

Myers, I.B., McCaulley, M.H., Quenk, N.L., and Hammer, A.L. (1998) *MBTI Manual: A Guide to the Development and Use of the Myers-Briggs Type Indicator*®, third edition. Palo Alto, CA: Consulting Psychologists Press.

Naiman, N., Fröhlich, M., and Stern, H.H. (1975) *The Good Language Learner: A Report*. Toronto: Ontario Institute for Studies in Education.

Naiman, N., Fröhlich, M., Stern, H.H., and Todesco, A. (1978) The good language learner. *Research in Education Series* 7. Toronto: Ontario Institute for Studies in Education.

Richards, J., Platt, J., and Platt, H. (1998) *Longman Dictionary of Language Teaching and Applied Linguistics*. Addison Longman: China.

Rubin, J. (1975) What the "good language learner" can teach us. *TESOL Quarterly*, 9(1), 41–51.

Saunders, D. (1997) Personal communication.

Ushioda, E. (this volume) Chapter 1: Motivation and good language learners.

5   Gender and good language learners

Martha Nyikos

Gender and its impact upon the ways that the sexes think, reason, and solve problems is once more becoming a hot topic in the popular press, and like any hot topic, it is at once fascinating and controversial. With the help of technology, the last five years of research on the male and female brain have given new insight into differences in their development and modes of information processing (Tyre, 2005). In this chapter we are interested not so much in gender differences *per se*, but in the processes that may contribute to bringing about a language performance differential between boys and girls, women and men. For language educators interested in enhancing the achievement of learners, it is certainly interesting to note that quantitative studies show boys and girls behaving in "strikingly different ways" (Dörnyei, 2005, p. 59).

It is those "different ways" which are the focus of research which seeks to tease out the contribution of gender in the complex array of factors that impact all learning and language learning and pedagogy in particular. Some factors are related to our human state and traits, and others are environmental or situational, dependent on the context or setting.

As educators, our departure point has to include the realization that our own socialized views of gender differences will impact our teaching and judgments. In fact, those views are so subtle and pervasive that they will influence the way we interpret the results being reported in this chapter. Our socialization as gendered beings has influenced our own learning and teaching styles, which in turn affect our students. Regardless of the care we take to give our students many opportunities to discover their optimal learning style, we have to be vigilant of our own subconscious biases and expectations which may manifest themselves in the ways we engage our students in learning.

How is gender defined?

Gender as a broad term is often used to denote not only the biologically based, dichotomous variable of *sex* (that is, male or female) but also the socially constructed roles (i.e., *gender*) which are created by the different ways in which the sexes are raised from birth and socialized within a certain culture (see also Ellis 1994). In this chapter the term *sex* is used in a more restricted sense to denote merely the physical dichotomy of male versus female, while the term gender connotes largely culturally and environmentally formed roles into which males and females are socialized (see also Ushioda, this volume).

Gender is often neglected as a variable in language learning by writers and researchers: "The effects of gender roles, relations and identities are everywhere. Ironically, because of this, in much writing and thinking on English language teaching, gender appears nowhere" (Sunderland, 1994, p. 211). However, Sunderland (2000) points out, a wide range of language phenomena, such as literacy practices, language tests, test performance, self-esteem, styles, and strategies, have been shown to be gendered, since male and female students tend to be represented or to behave or feel differently. The potential for gender to affect language learning can therefore not be ignored.

In this paper the term gender will denote the confluence of biology and socialization, of nature and nurture which in each culture creates the totality of what is conveniently classified as male or female. Despite great variation within each sex, clear and systematic differences in this tightly interwoven complex of characteristics is observable between the sexes. It is on these differences that we focus our research to discover if there are significant variations based on gender in how students learn language.

Biological research reported in recent articles in the popular press are increasingly shedding light on neurological and hormonal differences in the brains of males and females. For example, women have more nerve cells in the left half of the brain where language is centered (Legato, 2005a), and have a richer connection between the two sides of the brain (Tyre, 2005). Women seem to use more of their brains to listen and to speak which "may make activities essential to communication easier for them" (Legato, 2005b, p. 183). Brain scan imagery performed by neuroscientists shows that women utilize the same area of the brain as men to process language but, depending on the linguistic task, women often use both sides of the brain, and, given identical assignments, women activate more areas in their brain than men do (Legato, 2005a). Perhaps most importantly for educators, research has reconfirmed that girls have "language centers" that mature earlier than that of boys (Tyre, 2005, p. 59). These reports in the popular press are important because they are a good indicator of current interest and are most likely to reach parents and help form beliefs and expectations regarding gender differences.

But these findings should not be interpreted as only biological. From infancy on, there are other powerful influences at work. Psychological studies stress gender-specific socialization and expectations which mold gender roles, attributes, and behavior of children from an early age (Beal, 1994; Legato, 2005). It should be noted that individual factors such as spatial, language, and reasoning skills are linked to gender, but not directly attributed to it. As Beal (1994, p. 223) cogently argues, "Children first learn to talk in a social context that varies by gender". Parents talk more to baby girls than boys, responding more to girls' early attempts to use language. Parents have longer and more complex conversations with daughters and encourage more responses from them than sons (Reese and Fivush, cited in Beal, 1994, p. 224). Much of the perceived female superiority in language capability may be due to the added effort which adults tend to lavish on baby girls compared with baby boys. In the crucial early years of life, female brains may be better stimulated due to the subconscious expectations of adults.

Gender socialization may be a key factor in any relative success that women and men of any age have in language learning. The psychological literature is rightfully cautious in designating sources of difference in learning and processing as due to gender. Sociocultural influences shaping young people as gendered beings include many cultural expectations of male and female roles and attribution of certain qualities each should possess, both in society and in the classroom. Today, constructivist views push learning into the social space where students must work collaboratively to achieve the desired goal (Slavin, 1996) as students co-construct their understanding and responses to specific tasks. When we push language acquisition into the social space, we deal with group dynamics and the interplay of social status, personality, learning preferences and individual differences of many kinds. The very nature of cooperative tasks in the classroom is that they bring together many kinds of learning preferences, strategies, and styles which require individuals to work together to negotiate solutions to problems.

Sociocultural theory (Vygotsky, 1978; Donato and McCormick, 1994; Swain and Lapkin, 1998) holds that cognitive development or construction of knowledge occurs as a result of social interaction. Most studies in this area examine the language produced during communicative tasks where negotiation of meaning and cooperation with peers is necessary for completing the linguistic tasks. Gender is a significant, defining dimension of our humanity and as such has at least some influence on the way we learn.

Research into gender in language learning

Rubin's (1975) landmark article marks a significant change in focus from teacher-centered methods to learner-centered approaches. Although a host of factors interact in determining the ease and degree of success in language learning, we will concentrate here only on how gender impacts upon the process. Although we should keep in mind that much of the data are self-reported and thus filtered through a gendered lens of self-perception, some interesting findings have emerged from the research initiatives.

In their review article, Oxford, Nyikos, and Ehrman (1988) argued that women have an early and persistent advantage over men with respect to skills and social integration. These general tendencies are then strengthened and channeled by cultural and societal norms, factors, and institutions. Women encourage conversational partners to talk, remember more details, are more polite, and more likely to try to reach consensus. Women's greater tendency to accept cultural norms and their desire for social approval motivate them to strive for higher grades than men (Nyikos, 1990; Oxford and Nyikos, 1989). Their greater desire for social connection and greater valuation of communicative competence lead them to utilize more social interaction strategies. Women almost invariably use more language learning strategies than men, and make greater use of general study strategies and formal rule-related practice strategies than men. Because women have more complex and tightly knit social connections, they tend to have social interactive learning styles and practice strategies in groups. This sharing may partially explain why research has consistently found that women report at least equivalent but often greater use of learning strategies than men, especially strategies for authentic language use, for communicating meaning, and for self-management as well as for general, social, and affective strategy purposes.

One study modeled language learning strategies and examined the degree to which males and females found one or another particular strategy more effective for learning German (Nyikos, 1990). Various language learning strategies were modeled for different groups of students in beginner's German courses, using the Modern Language Aptitude Test (Carroll and Sapon, 1959) to control for aptitude. As measured by five subsequent quizzes, the study found that women were significantly more successful ($p < .05$) in terms of quiz scores when utilizing color association than men, possibly due to women's socialized sensitivity to color. Similarly, the men were more successful ($p < .05$) when utilizing visual images linking and color association together, possibly due to men's socialized sensitivity to visual data (Nyikos, 1990). Test scores showed that men and women who used "learning strategies that are in tune with their socialized learning style" (Nyikos, 1990, p. 285) had equal chances for success. This provides hope that as individuals mature, they may acquire learning strategies through socialization that are particularly effective for themselves, regardless of what relative role nature and nurture play in language learning strategy choice and use.

Although certain strategies appear to be at least marginally more successfully and efficiently employed by one sex or the other, variation in language learning strategy use between the sexes, although sometimes significant, does not tend to be great in magnitude, as Griffiths (2003) discovered. Using the Strategy Inventory for Language Learning or SILL (Oxford, 1990), Griffiths analyzed the reported frequency of language learning strategy use of 348 students studying English at a private language school in Auckland, New Zealand according to a range of learner variables, including gender. Although female students reported using language learning strategies more frequently on average than males, the difference was neither large nor significant.

It is possible that some of the variation between male and female choices (and implementation) in learning strategies may be due to variation of personality types between the sexes. Ehrman and Oxford (1989, 1990, 1995) measured personality type along four axes: extraversion–introversion, sensing–intuition, thinking–feeling, and judging–perceiving, using the Myers-Briggs Type Indicator (MBTI, Myers 1962). Women tend to prefer the feeling pole of the thinking–feeling measure more often than men, and both sexes on the thinking–feeling personality continuum tend to prefer similar learning strategies. This indicates that perhaps personality type may be an even more significant variable than gender, at least for the preference for certain types of language learning strategies.

Different cultures provide varying opportunities and rewards for the use of specific strategies by the two sexes. For example, in Puerto Rico, Green and Oxford (1995) found that men used television and movies to learn English far more than women because English language programming appealed more to men than women. More specifically, television programs in Puerto Rico are more likely to be broadcast in English if they are sports or action movies whose primary audience is male. Assumptions regarding males' less frequent use of social strategies as compared to females does not hold true for all cultures. For example, in Jordan, where there are single-sex classes, boys used social strategies just as often as did girls (Kaylani, 1996). Most pervasively and powerfully, even within a specific culture, males and females have separate study cultures in which males generally have lower levels of motivation which affect effort and performance: even when student characteristics such as ability, socio-economic status, and parental involvement are statistically controlled, it appears that girls' culture is more study-oriented and supportive of academic achievement (Van Houtte, 2004). Furthermore, according to Gurian and Steven's research (Tyre, 2005), American schools are "girl-friendly", at least partially because the teaching styles of the predominantly female teaching population do not fit the way boys learn. In other words, in considering how gender relates to "good" learning, even the cultures of schools themselves need to be taken into account, emphasizing the importance of situational factors stressed by, for instance, Norton and Toohey (2001)

Studies have consistently found that females place a greater relative importance on and invest more time in language learning than males, because they see greater potential benefit from languages in their future careers and personal lives (Gu, 2002). Women prefer social strategies which stress communication such as forming study groups and practicing with native speakers (Green and Oxford 1995, Jimenez Catalan, 2003). Women also tend to use emotionally supportive affective strategies such as self-encouragement, setting up rewards for their progress and reassuring themselves that they have insufficient background knowledge when encountering difficulties (Young and Oxford, 1997). In general, women are more willing to test the usefulness of a wider array of strategies and consistently use more of them than men (Oxford, Lavine, Felkins, Holloway, and Saleh, 1996). In general, men are more career-oriented, placing lower importance on studying language than on their primary major, they are more goal-oriented and more instrumentally motivated for studying what will be on the next test, and they tend to monitor their progress, such as timing their reading pace and tend to prefer visual strategies such as forming a mental image of a word and labeling objects (Nyikos, 1990). Men also tend to work alone more, summarizing the readings and defining unfamiliar words to themselves (Young and Oxford, 1997). Some studies have shown that women are more flexible in their use of language learning strategies and favor communicative strategies, both of which are qualities of the good language learner (Nyikos, 1987). Men tend to use rote memorization, repetition, and translation more often, all of these tend to be used more heavily by less successful language learners (Nyikos, 1987).

It would seem a natural conclusion that since women tend to desire higher grades more than men and use learning strategies more frequently than men (Oxford, Nyikos, and Ehrman, 1988), that the combination of greater motivation and strategy use should lead to greater success for women in language learning. Most studies show a slight but significant advantage for women (Gu, 2002; Sunderland, 2000). The most notable exception to this is Ehrman and Oxford (1995); they found no correlation between the types of strategies women preferred and those preferred by better language learners in general, nor was there a difference in performance between men and women "by any measure" (Ehrman and Oxford, 1995, p. 81). It is therefore crucial to emphasize once more that differences in language learning preferences between males and females, although in some cases statistically significant, tend to be slight, with far greater variation between individuals than between the sexes.

Implications for the teaching/learning situation

It seems clear that differential language learning success is caused by a combination of nature and nurture. To the degree that these choices are reflective of a deeper match between gender and innate cognitive abilities, gaining understanding of the relative cognitive strengths of each sex will enrich our ability to help students discover, design, and use appropriate strategies that will enable teachers and students to share responsibility for optimal learning in the classroom. Sensitivity to the learning preferences of boys will go a long way to creating a supportive learning environment for male language learners. Our new appreciation of boys' greater need for kinetic, hands-on experience and their intense need for clear-cut, concrete, goal-oriented assignments will help teachers meet their needs more expediently.

Males appear to need to have explicit, essential information, and concrete, visual examples. Due to generally lower motivation, male students also need continuous and concrete reminders regarding the advantages of foreign language study for their future careers. Due to the lower relative importance they place on language studies, males are immediately disadvantaged in their opportunity for social study, whereas females are more likely to form study groups and use social strategies to practice and share information. They are better positioned to co-construct their knowledge through cooperative social interaction. Teachers wishing to foster male participation in study groups should consider helping form these groups. It is essential to help formulate concrete goals and activities which will help students discover and enhance their language learning strategies and find the style that best suits their individual characteristics.

Questions for ongoing research

Although once simplistically regarded in terms of male or female, gender is now understood to be a much more complicated phenomenon which is at least partially socially constructed. The role of gender in language learning, however, is still not well understood. We need considerably more research in order to clarify how gender is interpreted and how it takes its place in a complex web of characteristics that define us as human beings and as learners.

In an age where gender equality has become a basic human right, the idea that there might be gender differences in language learning is not always considered politically correct, and fear of giving offence has, perhaps, nipped potential research initiatives in the bud. In recent years, however, there has been growing concern over the educational performance of boys (for instance Tyre, 2005; Van Houtte, 2004), especially in relation to learning language. Perhaps it is time to put the political niceties in their place and look honestly at the role of gender in language learning, at how gender differences relate to language development, and at the pedagogical implications of gender differences.

Conclusion

The greatest impact of Rubin's (1975) article was that it effectively shifted the focus of language learning from teachers and researchers to the learner by emphasizing that good learners have control over their language learning and could be guided to take even more control. It prompted interest in individual learner differences that led to the synthesis of numerous strands of research into language learning, including strategies, motivation, learning styles, culture, age, personality, aptitude, and gender.

Although females are often believed to be better language learners than males, research evidence for this belief has proven elusive. This may be partly because "gender, as one of the many important facets of social identity, interacts with race, ethnicity, class, sexuality (dis)ability, age, and social status in framing students' language learning experiences, trajectories, and outcomes" (Norton and Pavlenko, 2004, p. 504). Based on the research evidence we have, however, it would seem safe to generalize that both males and females can be good language learners. The ongoing challenge, for researchers, is to discover how students may learn most effectively regardless of gender, and, for teachers, to discover how both their male and female students may be supported to achieve maximum success as language learners.

References

Beal, C. (1994) Boys and girls: the development of gender roles. New York: McGraw-Hill, 213–234.

Carroll, J.B. and Sapon, S.M. (1959) *Modern Language Aptitude Test (MLAT) Manual*. New York: Psychological Testing.

Donato, R. and McCormick, D. (1994) A sociocultural perspective on language learning strategies: the role of mediation. *Modern Language Journal*, 78(4), 453–464.

80

Dörnyei, Z. (2005) Motivational dynamics, language attitudes and language globalization, (unpublished manuscript).

Ehrman, M.E. and Oxford, R.L. (1989) Effects of sex differences, career choice, and psychological type on adult language learning strategies. *Modern Language Journal* 73(1), 1–13.

Ehrman, M.E. and Oxford, R.L. (1990) Adult language learning styles and strategies in an intensive training setting. *Modern Language Journal* 74(3), 311–327.

Ehrman, M.E. and Oxford, R.L. (1995) Cognition plus: correlates of language learning success. *Modern Language Journal* 79(1), 67–89.

Ellis, R. (1994) The Study of Second Language Acquisition. Oxford: Oxford University Press.

Green, J.M. and Oxford, R.L. (1995) A closer look at learning strategies, L2 proficiency, and gender. *TESOL Quarterly* 29(2), 261–297.

Griffiths, C. (2003) *Language Learning Strategy Use and Proficiency*. (http://www.umi.com/umi/dissertations/).

Gu, Y. (2002) Gender, academic major, and vocabulary learning strategies of Chinese EFL learners. *RELC Journal* 33(1), 35–54.

Jimenez Catalan, R.M. (2003) Sex differences in L2 vocabulary learning strategies. *International Journal of Applied Linguistics* 13(1), 54–77.

Kaylani, C. (1996) The influence of gender and motivation on EFL learning strategy use in Jordan. In R.L. Oxford (ed.), *Language Learning Strategies Around the World: Cross-cultural Perspectives*. Honolulu: Second Language Teaching and Curriculum Center, pp. 75–88.

Legato, M.J. (2005a) *Why Men Never Remember and Women Never Forget*. New York: Rodale.

Legato, M.J. (2005b) What you say, what he hears: how to bridge the gap. *Prevention* 57(10), 180–212.

Myers, E.I.B. (1962) *The Myers-Briggs Type Indicator*. Palo Alto, CA: Consulting Psychologists Press.

Norton, B. and Pavlenko, A. (2004) Addressing gender in the ESL/EFL classroom. *TESOL Quarterly*, 38(3), 504–514

Norton, B. and Toohey, K. (2001) Changing perspectives on good language learners. *TESOL Quarterly*, 35(2), 307–322.

Nyikos, M. (1987) *The effects of color and imagery as mnemonic strategies on learning and retention of lexical items in German*. Unpublished doctoral dissertation. Purdue University, West Lafayette, IN.

Nyikos, M. (1990) Sex-related differences in adult language learning: socialization and memory factors. *Modern Language Journal*, 74(3), 273–287.

Oxford, R.L. (1990) *Language Learning Strategies: What Every Teacher Should Know*. New York: Newbury House.

Oxford, R.L. and Nyikos, M. (1989) Variables affecting choice of language learning strategies by university students. *Modern Language Journal*, 73(3), 291–300.

Oxford, R.L., Nyikos, M., and Ehrman, M.E. (1988) Vive la différence? Reflections on sex differences in use of language learning strategies. *Foreign Language Annals* 21, 321–329.

Oxford, R.L., Lavine, R.Z., Felkins, G., Hollaway, M.E., and Saleh, A. (1996) Telling their stories: Language students use diaries and recollective studies. In R.L. Oxford (ed.), Language Learning Strategies Around the World: Cross-cultural perspectives. Manoa: University of Hawai'i Press, 19–34.

Rubin, J. (1975) What the "good language learner" can teach us. TESOL Quarterly 9(1) 41–51.

Slavin, R. (1996) Research on cooperative learning and achievement: what we know, what we need to know. *Contemporary Educational Psychology*, 21, 43–46.

Sunderland, J. (ed.) (1994) *Exploring Gender: Questions and Implications for English Language Education*. Hemel Hempstead: Prentice Hall.

Sunderland, J. (2000) Issues of language and gender in second and foreign language education. *Language Teaching*, 33, 203–223.

Swain, M. and Lapkin, S. (1998) Interaction and second language learning: two adolescent French immersion students working together. *Modern Language Journal*, 82(3), 320–337.

Tyre, P. (2005) Boy brains, girl brains. *Newsweek*, CXLVI(12), 58.

Ushioda, E. (this volume). Chapter 1: Motivation and good language learners.

Van Houtte, M. (2004) Why boys achieve less at school than girls: the difference between boys' and girls' academic culture. *Educational Studies* 30(2), 159–173.

Vygotsky, L. (1978) *Mind in Society: The Development of Higher Psychological Processes*. Cambridge, MA: Harvard University Press.

Young, D.J. and Oxford, R.L. (1997) A gender-related analysis of strategies used to process written input in the native language and a foreign language. *Applied Language Learning* 8(1), 26–43.

6 Strategies and good language learners

Carol Griffiths

In the 30 years since Rubin's (1975) article in *TESOL Quarterly* brought "language learning strategies" to a wide audience, the concept of language learning strategy has been notoriously difficult to define. It has been described as "elusive" (Wenden, 1991, p. 7), "fuzzy" (Ellis, 1994, p. 529) and "fluid" (Gu, 2005, p. 2). Rubin (1975, p. 43) defined language learning strategies as "the techniques or devices which a learner may use to acquire knowledge," and she constructed a list of strategies typical of good language learners. Stern (1975) also published an article on the strategies used by good language learners, among which he included "a personal learning style" (p. 316). The confusion evident even at this early stage in language learning strategy research between basic concepts such as style and strategy has contributed to the difficulties with definition which remain to the present day.

Defining and classifying strategies

A number of studies continued to add to the growing body of knowledge (and controversy) regarding language learning strategies through the remainder of the 1970s and into the 1980s. Think aloud techniques were used by Hosenfeld (1976) to find out more about students' strategies, and another good language learner study was contributed by Naiman, Fröhlich, Stern, and Todesco (1978). The role of conscious language learning strategy choices was examined within a theoretical model of second language learning (Bialystok, 1978, 1981); language learning strategy use in relation to individual student differences was investigated by Wong Fillmore (1979); and the use of mnemonic strategies for the retention of vocabulary was looked at by Cohen and Aphek (1980).

To further complicate the issue of definition, not only does the term "strategy" appear to have different meanings for different writers (such as Rubin, 1975; Stern, 1975; Naiman *et al.*, 1978), but different terminology is employed to cover phenomena which seem to fit within the definition of strategy as it was emerging between the mid-1970s and the mid-1980s. If the terms "learning behaviors" and "tactics" are accepted as being more or less equivalent to "learning strategies"

83

(Larsen-Freeman and Long, 1991), the studies by Wesche (1977) (which discovered that successful language learners employ active learning behaviours in order to learn), by Politzer and McGroarty (1985) (who conducted an exploratory study of how learning behaviours are used in order to gain linguistic and communicative competence), and by Seliger (1984) (who discussed the use of tactics in language development) can be added to the expanding language learning strategy corpus. Larsen-Freeman and Long (1991, p. 199) opt for the term *strategy* "since it was used in perhaps the earliest study in this area and it enjoys the widest currency today." Likewise, according to Ehrman, Leaver, and Oxford (2003), *strategy* remains the term of choice for both researchers and practitioners.

By the mid-1980s, there was "no consensus" and "considerable confusion" (O'Malley, Chamot, Stewner-Manzanares, Kupper, and Russo, 1985, p. 22) regarding the definition of language learning strategies. This confusion and lack of consensus was seen as impeding progress in carrying out and applying research in an area which had the potential to be "an extremely powerful learning tool" (O'Malley *et al.* p. 43). Based on an earlier definition (Rigney, 1978), O'Malley and his colleagues provided a broad definition of language learning strategies as "any set of operations or steps used by a learner that will facilitate the acquisition, storage, retrieval or use of information" (p. 23). Whereas Rubin had divided her strategies into two groups (Direct and Indirect), O'Malley *et al.* identified 26 strategies which they divided into three groups: metacognitive, cognitive, and social. Although some elements of the two taxonomies are similar, by separating Social strategies out into a group of their own, O'Malley *et al.* highlighted the role of interactive strategies in language learning, an important insight, especially at a time when the communicative approach to language teaching and learning was gaining wide acceptance (Littlewood, 1981; Widdowson, 1978).

Language learning strategies were defined by Oxford (1990) as "specific actions taken by the learner to make learning easier, faster, more enjoyable, more self-directed, more effective, and more transferable to new situations" (p. 8). From an extensive review of the literature, Oxford gathered a large number of language learning strategies and created a self-report questionnaire known as the Strategy Inventory for Language Learning (SILL) used by Oxford and others for a great deal of research in the language learning strategy field (for instance Ehrman and Oxford 1989, 1990, 1995; Green and Oxford, 1995; Griffiths 2003a, 2003b; Griffiths and Parr 2000, 2001; Nyikos and Oxford 1993). The strategy items of the SILL are divided into six groups: memory, cognitive, compensation, metacognitive, affective, and social (see Oxford, 1990, for explanations of these categories).

Although several important works on language learning strategies appeared in the late 1980s (for instance Wenden and Rubin, 1987; Skehan, 1989) and 1990s (for instance O'Malley and Chamot, 1990; Wenden, 1991; Cohen, 1998), issues with definition remained unresolved. As the controversy continued into the new millennium, difficulties with theoretical inconsistencies and conceptual ambiguities have, according to Dörnyei and Skehan (2003, p. 610), led educational psychologists to virtually abandon the term *strategy* in favor of *self-regulation*, which refers to the degree to which individuals are active participants in their own learning and includes factors such as cognition, metacognition, motivation, and behavioral and environmental variables used by learners to promote their own learning (Dörnyei, 2005). The need for ongoing theoretical refinement of the language learning strategy concept is acknowledged. However, if the term *self-regulation* is to be useful in any practical sense, the next question must surely be: "What do learners *do* in order to regulate their own learning?" In other words: "What are their strategies?" Strategy selection is included among the characteristics of the self-regulating learner by Winne (1995), which brings the argument almost full circle. Self-regulation is an interesting concept which integrates a number of interrelated factors, including strategy use (Dörnyei, 2005). The self-regulation concept, therefore, does not remove the need for a strategy concept, neither does it do anything to resolve the battles over definition. As Gu (2005) points out, in order to carry out meaningful research, it is necessary to be able to construct an operational definition of what is being researched. With this need in mind, and with 30 years of controversy to draw on, I would like to attempt to pull the areas of consensus together and again attempt a viable definition of language learning strategy. Six essential features emerge:

1 Language learning strategies are what students *do* (Rubin, 1975), suggesting an active approach. The term "actions," however (Oxford, 1990, p. 8), does not take account of the reality that many strategies are mental processes (Macaro, 2006). Although strategies such as thinking, visualizing, or noticing are what students do, they are not exactly actions in the same way as strategies such as reading, writing, or asking questions. The term *activities*, however, can be used to include both physical and mental behavior. The activity focus distinguishes learning strategies from learning style, a related concept with which they are often confused (see Nel, this volume). Learning style is a learner characteristic which relates to learner preferences, the strategies are what they do.

2 Consciousness is argued by many to be a basic characteristic of language learning strategies (for instance, Bialystok, 1978; Oxford,

1990, 2001; Cohen, 1998; Macaro, 2006). Although strategies may be deployed automatically (Wenden, 1991), this is not precisely the same thing as saying that strategies are not deployed *consciously*. Similarly, much of our driving behavior, although automatic (in that, due to practice, we do not need to deliberately decide each action), is, hopefully, neither sub-conscious nor unconscious, but operates somewhere on a continuum between fully deliberate and fully automatic. Indeed, Cohen (1998, p. 4) suggests that "the element of consciousness is what distinguishes strategies from those processes that are not strategic," and he argues that learners who use learning strategies must be at least partially conscious of them even if they are not attending to them fully.

3 Language learning strategies have been described as "optional means for exploiting available information to improve competence in a second language" (Bialystok, 1978, p. 71). It would seem self-evident that strategies are *chosen* by learners, since learners who unthinkingly accept activities imposed by others can hardly be considered strategic given the emphasis on active involvement in the learning process by writers such as Oxford (1990). Strategy choice will depend on contextual factors (such as teaching/learning method, learning situation, or task requirements), individual factors (such as motivation, style, age, gender, nationality/ethnicity/culture, personality, beliefs), and the nature of the learning goal.

4 Strategic behaviour implies goal-oriented, purposeful activity on the part of the learner (Chamot, 2001; Cohen, 2003; Ehrman *et al.*, 2003; Oxford, 2001; Weinstein and Mayer, 1986), and the specification of a goal or intention is listed by Macaro (2006) among his identifying features of strategies. In the case of language learning strategies, the *purpose* is to learn language.

5 Learners use language learning strategies to *regulate* or control their learning (Wenden, 1991). Self-regulation refers to the degree to which individuals are active participants in their own learning (Dörnyei and Skehan, 2003), and Winne (1995) also includes strategies as one of the means used by learners to regulate their own learning.

6 The goal of language learning strategies is the facilitation of learning, a target which distinguishes learning strategies from skills, a concept with which they are often confused. Skills relate to the manner in which language is used (Richards, Platt and Platt, 1992); in other words, learning strategies are used to learn, while skills are employed to use what has been learnt. Skills can, however, be used as a learning strategy, for instance if students decide to read for pleasure in order to expand their vocabulary. The learning goal also distinguishes language learning strategies from other types of learner strategies,

especially communication strategies, whose basic purpose is to maintain communication. Although the distinction between learning strategies and other types of learner strategies is not always so clear in practice (Tarone, 1981), on a theoretical level, communication strategies are intended to maintain communication, whereas language learning strategies are for *learning*.

These six elements, gleaned from 30 years of vigorous debate, when combined, suggest a definition of language learning strategies as:

> *Activities consciously chosen by learners for the purpose of regulating their own language learning.*

The activities can be mental (for instance visualising relationships) or physical (for instance writing notes). Although they are consciously chosen, the choice can operate anywhere on a continuum from deliberate to automatic, and language learning strategies are aimed at learning. I would like to suggest that this definition is broad enough to allow the freedom to research areas within it (a study on the deployment of automatic versus deliberate strategies, for instance, could yield interesting insights), but precise enough to exclude learner characteristics or activities which are not language learning strategies (such as learning style, skills, or communication strategies).

How do good language learners use language learning strategies?

So how does the definition suggested above relate to good language learners? The remainder of this chapter will describe a study into language learning strategy use conducted in a real classroom situation and discuss its implications for teachers and learners before suggesting some practical applications in the teaching/learning situation and questions for further research.

The study

The study was conducted in a private English language school for international students in Auckland, New Zealand. On arrival at the school, students were given the Oxford Placement Test (Allan, 1995), a well-known, commercially available test frequently used by language schools to assess knowledge of grammar and listening skills. In addition, students were interviewed by a member of staff to assess their oral fluency.

87

On the basis of these assessments, students were assigned to one of seven class levels (elementary, mid-elementary, upper elementary, pre-intermediate, mid-intermediate, upper intermediate, or advanced).

Participants

As part of the orientation process, about half-way through their first week, new students attended what was called the Study Skills class. This class was routinely offered only in a student's first week, usually for two hours on a Wednesday afternoon, when regular option classes operated in the school. Option classes were designed to provide variety within the curriculum or to meet particular needs, and students could choose these classes according to their needs or interests. During the Study Skills class, in addition to selecting their ongoing option class for future weeks, new students were introduced to the school's facilities (such as the self-study room) and were encouraged to discuss and reflect upon their strategy use.

Data collection and analysis

During the Study Skills class, 131 students at the beginning of their English language classes completed a questionnaire known as the English Language Learning Strategy Inventory or ELLSI (for further details see Griffiths, 2003b). There were both male (N = 55) and female (N = 76) students from a number of different backgrounds (Argentina, Austria, Brazil, mainland China, Germany, Hong Kong, Indonesia, Italy, Japan, Korea, Lithuania, Switzerland, Taiwan, and Thailand). Ages ranged from 14 to 64.

The ELLSI consists of 32 strategy items (see Table 1 for strategy statements) which students are asked to rate from 1 (low frequency) to 5 (high frequency) according to how often they use them. These data were entered onto SPSS and analyzed for mean frequencies and statistical differences (using the Mann-Whitney U test).

Findings

The students who participated in this study reported an average frequency of strategy use over all ELLSI items of 3.1. When the students were divided into lower level (upper elementary and below, N = 73) and upper level (pre-intermediate and above, N = 58), it was discovered that lower level students reported a lower average frequency of strategy use (average = 2.9) than did higher level students (average = 3.3), a difference which proved to be significant (Mann-Whitney, $p < .05$)

When strategies reportedly used at a high rate of frequency (average = 3.5 or above, Oxford, 1990) were counted, it was found that seven strategy items were reportedly used highly frequently across all students. Lower level students were found to have reported using only five strategy items highly frequently while higher level students reported using fifteen strategy items at this rate. The average reported frequencies of use for each strategy item according to level as well as across all students are set out in Table 1. The overall average reported frequency of strategy use and the number of strategy items reportedly used at a high rate of frequency are summarized at the bottom of the table.

According to these results, it can be seen that higher level students do, indeed, report significantly more frequent use of language learning strategies than do lower level students. Furthermore, the higher level students report using many more (three times as many, in fact) language learning strategies highly frequently than students working at lower levels. In other words, the higher level students report using a much larger repertoire of strategies significantly more frequently than the lower level students. It is, of course, necessary to be cautious about labeling the higher level students as "good" and those at a lower level, by implication, "bad." There are many reasons why students might be in a lower level class, including length of time studying English or the influence of the mother tongue. It is possible that some of the lower level students might make extremely rapid progress and even overtake some of the students who were ahead of them at a previous point in time. In a cross-sectional study such as this one, it is possible only to assess the situation as it exists at a given moment and to consider level as an indicator of success at that point in time.

This is not, of course, to say that every higher level student reports using more strategies more frequently than every lower level student: in any situation involving real and infinitely complex human beings the reality is never that simple. Some studies have discovered that poor language learners use a great many strategies in their unsuccessful efforts to learn (for instance, Porte, 1988; Vann and Abraham, 1990). There may also be difficulties with interpreting Likert scale type instruments (such as the ELLSI) for a number of reasons: frames of reference may not be the same for all respondents, a higher rating may indicate higher awareness rather than more frequent use and so on (Gu, Wen and Wu, 1995). All of these factors combine to paint an extremely complicated picture from which conclusions must be drawn with care and careful consideration given to alternative possibilities. Nevertheless, although it is not possible to generalize the findings of this study to each individual student, viewed overall, the statistics indicate that higher level students report more frequent use of a larger number of language learning strategies than do lower level students,

Table 1 Average reported frequency of language learning strategy use (ELLSI) for lower level, higher level and all students with number of strategies reportedly used highly frequently

ELLSI Statement number	low level	high level	all	Strategy Statement
		Students		
1	3.7	3.9	3.8	Doing homework
2	3.8	4.3	4.0	Learning from the teacher
3	3.3	3.5	3.4	Learning in a native-speaking environment
4	2.4	3.0	2.7	Reading books in English
5	2.5	2.8	2.6	Using a computer
6	2.8	3.5	3.1	Watching TV in English
7	3.0	3.2	3.1	Revising regularly
8	3.2	3.7	3.4	Listening to songs in English
9	1.9	2.4	2.1	Using language learning games
10	1.9	2.7	2.2	Writing letters in English
11	2.3	2.2	2.2	Listening to music while studying
12	3.4	3.7	3.5	Talking to other students in English
13	4.2	4.1	4.2	Using a dictionary
14	2.0	2.7	2.4	Reading newspapers in English
15	3.3	3.6	3.4	Studying English grammar
16	2.9	3.7	3.3	Consciously learning new vocabulary
17	3.5	3.5	3.5	Keeping a language learning notebook
18	3.2	3.6	3.4	Talking to native speakers of English
19	2.7	2.9	2.8	Noting language used in the environment
20	2.7	2.7	2.7	Controlling schedules so that English study is done
21	2.6	2.9	2.7	Pre-planning language learning encounters
22	3.2	3.1	3.2	Not worrying about mistakes
23	2.4	2.2	2.3	Using a self-study centre
24	3.0	3.4	3.2	Trying to think in English
25	3.5	4.1	3.8	Listening to native speakers of English
26	3.4	3.9	3.6	Learning from mistakes
27	3.2	3.5	3.3	Spending a lot of time studying English
28	2.5	3.2	2.8	Making friends with native speakers
29	2.9	3.6	3.2	Watching movies in English
30	2.6	3.2	2.8	Learning about the culture of English speakers
31	2.5	3.1	2.8	Listening to the radio in English
32	1.9	1.9	1.9	Writing a diary in English
	2.9	3.3	3.1	Overall average reported frequency
	5	15	7	Number of strategies reportedly used highly frequently

suggesting a generally positive relationship between the higher level language learner and language learning strategy use.

If we look more closely at the 15 strategy items in Table 1 that higher level students report using highly frequently, we can see that five of them (items 1, 3, 17, 26, 27) relate in one way or another to attempts by the students to manage their own learning. These learners organize themselves to do homework and choose to study in an environment where the target language is spoken. They keep a language learning notebook, learn from their mistakes, and, generally, invest a lot of time in their study. Although some of these strategies are also used highly frequently by lower level students, they are used less frequently by lower level students than by higher level students with the exception of the notebook strategy, where reported frequency is the same. The willingness of these higher level students to employ strategies to regulate their own study accords with the finding by O'Malley et al. (1985) that more proficient students employ more metacognitive strategies than less proficient students (see Anderson, this volume, for further discussion on metacognition).

Four of the strategies reportedly used highly frequently by higher level students relate in some way to the use of resources, including human resources (items 2, 6, 13, 29). These learners use their teacher as a resource and also use a dictionary as a reference. They watch TV and go to movies, resources readily available to them in their environment. Of these strategies, only using a dictionary is reportedly used more frequently by lower level students than by higher level students. This is, perhaps, predictable, since lower level students might be expected to need to refer to a dictionary more frequently than higher level students.

Two of the frequently used strategies are social, involving speaking with others (items 12, 18). Higher level students report talking to other students in English and also to native speakers highly frequently. Higher level students also make frequent use of listening (items 8, 25) as a strategy: they listen to songs and to native speakers talking. Although at one time the explicit teaching of vocabulary was frowned upon (Nation, 1990), it has more recently been recognized that there is a "tremendous communicative advantage in developing an extensive vocabulary" (Thornbury, 2002, p. 13), an advantage of which higher level learners seem to be aware (item 16). Higher level students also report frequently studying grammar. Like vocabulary, the teaching of grammar was out of favor for a number of years, and took some time to emerge from the shadow of the Monitor Hypothesis (Krashen, 1977). More recently, the importance of grammar has been rediscovered by teachers and educators (Thornbury, 1999), and is reportedly frequently used as part of the strategy repertoire of higher level learners (item 15).

In a longitudinal extension to this study, Griffiths (2003b, 2006) discovered that, in addition to the strategy types noted above, students who were successful in terms of their progress through the levels of the school increased the frequency with which they employed reading and writing skills. According, then, to these combined results, the students who make the most rapid progress (good language learners) tend to be characterized by particular behaviors, summarized in the box below:

Higher level learners frequently use a large number of language learning strategies, or activities consciously chosen for the purpose of regulating their own language learning, in particular:

- strategies to manage their own learning (metacognitive)
- strategies to expand their vocabulary
- strategies to improve their knowledge of grammar
- strategies involving the use of resources (such as TV or movies)
- strategies involving all language skills (reading, writing, listening, speaking).

Perhaps almost as interesting as the frequently used strategies are the ones which students report using infrequently (average = 2.4 or below, Oxford, 1990). According to Table 1, higher level students use games (item 9) infrequently as a strategy for language learning, even though games are popularly used in the modern language classroom. They also report infrequently using a self-study centre (item 23), writing a diary (item 32) and listening to music while studying (item 11). Perhaps the infrequent use of the music strategy relates to level of concentration, and indicates that those students who are willing or able to focus single-mindedly on their studies are more likely to be successful? Lower level students report infrequent use of strategies such as reading books and newspapers, and writing letters. Perhaps such strategies need to be introduced with care until a certain threshold of language competence is reached, although it is possible that they may be of benefit to all learners no matter what their level if managed in such a way that confidence and motivation are not lost.

Implications for the teaching/learning situation

Since higher level learners report infrequent use of games (item 9), perhaps teachers might care to consider carefully their use of games in their teaching and to question whether language games really do facilitate effective learning. Perhaps surprisingly, higher level students also report less frequent use of a self-study center (item 23) than lower level students, a phenomenon recorded also by Cotterall and Reinders (2000). Given the huge amounts of money spent on such centers in recent years, the implications of this finding would certainly seem to be worth further research. Another surprisingly low rating was given to the old faithful homework task of diary writing (item 32). Of course, the fact that students report using it infrequently does not necessarily prove that it is not potentially a useful strategy. However, since a low rating was given to this item by both higher and lower level students alike, teachers might like to consider the implications of this finding for their own practice and could very usefully engage in some action research to investigate whether students who write diaries progress more quickly than those who do not.

The question of the use of a dictionary in the classroom can be a contentious one, with some teachers limiting their use or even banning them altogether. While students should probably be encouraged to use other ways to establish meaning before reaching for a dictionary, teachers might care to reflect on the implications of the high reported frequency of this strategy even by higher level learners and on the consequences of students being deprived of this strategy to make sense of what they hear or read or to support what they want to say or write. Considering that use of a dictionary (whether bilingual or English–English, paper or electronic) is a common issue in the language classroom, this might be another useful area for researchers to investigate further.

So, if, on average, higher level learners frequently use a wide variety of language learning strategies, can we conclude that, by helping students to expand their strategy repertoires and encouraging them to use strategies more often, we will help promote good language learning? This was a basic tenet of Rubin's (1975) article. Unfortunately, 30 years of experience has shown that the reality is not quite so straightforward. For instance, it is possible to observe from Table 1 that higher level students report reading newspapers considerably more frequently than lower level students. In the light of this finding, teachers might decide that all students should be given newspaper articles to read, and, indeed, this can be a useful teaching/learning strategy. However, newspaper language is often difficult for those learning a new language, and may well erode confidence and reduce motivation for students who find it discouragingly difficult. Teachers will need to consider carefully the kind of support their students will require if they are to use such a strategy successfully.

Questions for ongoing research

By a process of extraction (one hesitates to compare it to drawing teeth!) from a 30-year literature and amalgamating key elements, a definition has been constructed which suggests what language learning strategies basically are: *activities consciously chosen by learners for the purpose of regulating their own language learning.* However, even after 30 years, some very important questions remain:

1 What are the factors which make particular strategies (defined as above) appropriate and effective given individual learner and learning variables?
2 How can strategies be clustered and sequenced (orchestrated) to be maximally effective for particular individuals, situations, and targets?
3 Where do strategies fit within the super-ordinate construct of self-regulation, and how do they relate to other dimensions of self-regulation such as motivation (see Ushioda, this volume), metacognition (see Anderson, this volume), autonomy (see Cotterall, this volume), and volition (see Oxford, this volume)?
4 On a practical level, how can students be taught to use strategies effectively (see Chamot, this volume)?
5 What are the pedagogical implications of the findings that language games, self-study centers, and diary writing are used infrequently by higher level students?
6 Is dictionary use a useful learning strategy, and how should their use be managed?

All of this presents a picture of daunting complexity. Perhaps we have won some of the battles, but, as the list of questions above clearly trumpets, the war is by no means over.

Conclusion

Individuals are infinitely variable, and any attempt at a one-rule-for-all type conclusion is unlikely to be universally applicable. In addition to strategies, many other learner variables (such as aptitude, learning style, motivation, age, beliefs, culture, gender, personality, metacognition, or autonomy), and learning variables (for instance vocabulary, grammar, pronunciation, function, skills, teaching/learning method, strategy instruction, error correction, or task) have the potential to affect the outcome of language learning efforts, and are considered elsewhere in this volume. All of these variables interact in patterns of great complexity, unique to each individual learner, making any attempts at cause and effect generalizations difficult to justify.

The optimism of 30 years ago, which predicted that if we could only find out what good language learners did we could help all learners to learn successfully has given way to the realization that the task is larger and more complicated than was thought at that point in time (Rubin, this volume). Nevertheless, considerable gains have been made. I believe that the contemporary language learning environment is considerably more learner aware than was the case 30 years ago, though perhaps not universally so. Perhaps this is time for taking stock, for defining what has been achieved to date, but certainly no time for resting on our laurels. We still have a lot to learn about what it is that makes for a good language learner.

References

Allan, D. (1995) *Oxford Placement Test*. Oxford: Oxford University Press.

Anderson, N. (this volume) Chapter 7: Metacognition and good language learners.

Bialystok, E. (1978) A theoretical model of second language learning. *Language Learning*, 28(1), 69–83.

Bialystok, E. (1981) The role of conscious strategies in second language proficiency. *Modern Language Journal*, 65, 24–35

Chamot, A.U. (2001) The role of learning strategies in second language acquisition. In M. Breen (ed.), *Learner Contributions to Language Learning*. Harlow: Longman, 25–43.

Chamot, A.U. (this volume) Chapter 21: Strategy instruction and good language learners.

Cohen, A.D. (1998) *Strategies in Learning and Using a Second Language*. London and New York: Longman

Cohen, A.D. (2003) The learner's side of foreign language learning: where do styles, strategies and tasks meet? *IRAL*, 41, 279–291.

Cohen, A.D. and Aphek, E. (1980) Retention of second language vocabulary over time: investigating the role of mnemonic associations. *System*, 8, 221–235.

Cotterall, S. (this volume) Chapter 8: Autonomy and good language learners.

Cotterall, S. and Reinders, H. (2000) Learner's perceptions and practice in self access language learning. *The TESOLANZ Journal*, 8, 23–47

Dörnyei, Z. (2005) *The Psychology of Language Teaching*. Mulwah, NJ: Erlbaum.

Dörnyei, Z. and Skehan, P. (2003) Individual differences in second language learning. In C. Doughty and M. Long (eds.), *Handbook of Second Language Acquisition* Oxford: Blackwell, 589–630.

Ehrman, M.E., Leaver, B. and Oxford, R.L. (2003) A brief overview of individual differences in second language learning. *System*, 31(3), 313–330.

Ehrman, M.E. and Oxford, R.L. (1989) Effects of sex differences, career choice, and psychological type on adult language learning strategies. *Modern Language Journal*, 73(1), 1–13.

Ehrman, M.E. and Oxford, R.L. (1990) Adult language learning styles and strategies in an intensive training setting. *Modern Language Journal*, 74(3), 311–327.

Ehrman, M.E. and Oxford, R.L. (1995) Cognition plus: correlates of language learning success. *Modern Language Journal*, 79(1), 67–89.

Ellis, R. (1994) *The Study of Second Language Acquisition*. Oxford: Oxford University Press.

Green, J. and Oxford, R.L. (1995) A closer look at learning strategies, L2 proficiency and sex. *TESOL Quarterly*, 29(2), 261–297.

Griffiths, C. (2003a) Patterns of language learning strategy use. *System*, 31, 367–383.

Griffiths, C. (2003b) *Language Learning Strategy Use and Proficiency*. (Retrieved from: http://hdl.handle.net/2292/9).

Griffiths, C. (2006) Strategy development and progress in language learning. *Prospect*, 21(3), 58–76.

Griffiths, C. and Parr, J. (2000) Language learning strategies, nationality, independence and proficiency. *Independence*, 28, 7–10

Griffiths, C. and Parr, J (2001) Strategies for success: how language learning strategies relate to proficiency in language learning. *Many Voices*, 17, 27–31.

Gu, P. (2005) Learning strategies: prototypical core and dimensions of variation. Working paper (Retrieved from: No.10. www.crie.org.nz).

Gu, Y., Wen, Q., and Wu, D. (1995) How often is *Often*? Reference ambiguities of the Likert scale in language learning strategy research. *Occasional Papers in English Language Teaching Vol 5*. ELT Unit, Chinese University of Hong Kong, 19–35

Hosenfeld, C. (1976) Learning about learning: discovering our students' strategies. *Foreign Language Annals*, 9, 117–129.

Krashen, S. (1977) Some issues relating to the Monitor Model. In H. Brown, C. Yorio and R. Crymes (eds.), *On TESOL '77*. Washington DC: TESOL, 144–158.

Larsen-Freeman, D. and Long, M. (1991) *An Introduction to Second Language Acquisition Research*. London and New York: Longman.

Littlewood, W. (1981) *Communicative Language Teaching*. Cambridge: Cambridge University Press.

Macaro, E. (2006) Strategies for language learning and for language use: revising the theoretical framework. *Modern Language Journal* 90(3), 320–337.

Naiman, N., Fröhlich, M., Stern, H., and Todesco, A. (1978) *The Good Language Learner*. Research in Education Series No.7. Toronto: The Ontario Institute for Studies in Education.

Nation, I.S.P. (1990) *Teaching and Learning Vocabulary*. Boston, MA: Heinle & Heinle.

Nel, C. (this volume) Chapter 3: Style and good language learners.

Nyikos, M. and Oxford, R.L. (1993) A factor analytic study of language learning strategy use: interpretations from information-processing theory and social psychology. *The Modern Language Journal*, 77, 11–22.

O'Malley, J.M. and Chamot, A.U. (1990) *Learning Strategies in Second Language Acquisition*. Cambridge: Cambridge University Press.

O'Malley, J.M., Chamot, A.U., Stewner-Manzanares, G., Kupper, L., and Russo, R. (1985) Learning strategies used by beginning and intermediate ESL students. *Language Learning*, 35(1), 21–46.

Oxford, R.L. (1990) *Language Learning Strategies: What Every Teacher Should Know*. New York: Newbury House.

Oxford, R.L. (2001) The bleached bones of a story: learners' constructions of language teachers. In M. Breen (ed.), *Learner Contributions to Language Learning*. Harlow: Longman, 86–111.

Oxford, R.L. and Lee, K.R. (this volume). The learner's landscape and journey: a summary.

Politzer, R. and McGroarty, M. (1985) An exploratory study of learning behaviours and their relationship to gains in linguistic and communicative competence. *TESOL Quarterly* 19, 103–123.

Porte, G. (1988) Poor language learners and their strategies for dealing with new vocabulary. *ELT Journal*, 42(3), 167–171.

Richards, J., Platt, J. and Platt, H. (1992) *Longman Dictionary of Language Teaching and Applied Linguistics*. Harlow: Longman.

Rigney, J. (1978) Learning strategies: a theoretical perspective. In H. O'Neil (Jr) (ed.), *Learning Strategies*. New York: Academic Press, 165–205.

Rubin, J. (1975) What the "good language learner" can teach us. *TESOL Quarterly*, 9(1), 41–51.

Rubin, J. (this volume). Reflections.

Seliger, H. (1984) Processing universals in second language acquisition. In F. Eckman, L. Bell. and D. Nelson (eds.), *Universals of Second Language Acquisition*. Rowley, MA: Newbury House, 36–47.

Skehan, P. (1989) *Individual Differences in Second Language Learning*. London: Edward Arnold.

Stern, H.H. (1975) What can we learn from the good language learner? *Canadian Modern Language Review*, 34, 304–318.

Tarone, E. (1981) Some thoughts on the notion of communication strategy. *TESOL Quarterly*, 15(3), 285–295.

Thornbury, S. (1999) *How to Teach Grammar*. Harlow: Longman.

Thornbury, S. (2002) *How to Teach Vocabulary*. Harlow: Longman.

Ushioda, E. (this volume) Chapter 1: Motivation and good language learners.

Vann, R. and Abraham, R. (1990) Strategies of unsuccessful language learners. *TESOL Quarterly*, 24(2), 177–198.

Weinstein, C. and Mayer, R. (1986) The teaching of learning strategies. In M. Wittrock, *Handbook of Research on Teaching*, third edition. New York: McMillan, 315–327.

Wenden, A.L. (1991) *Learner strategies for learner autonomy*. Englewood Cliffs, NJ; London: Prentice Hall.

Wenden, A.L. and Rubin, J. (eds.) (1987) *Learner Strategies in Language Learning*. London: Prentice Hall.

Wesche, M. (1977) Learning behaviours of successful adult students on intensive language training. In C. Henning (ed.), *Proceedings of the Los Angeles Second Language Research Forum*. English Department, University of California at Los Angeles, 355–370.

Widdowson, H. (1978) *Teaching Language as Communication*. Oxford: Oxford University Press.

Winne, P. (1995) Inherent details in self-regulated learning. *Educational Psychologist*, 30, 173–187.

Wong Fillmore, L. (1979) Individual differences in second language acquisition. In C. Fillmore, D. Kempler and W. Wang, *Individual Differences in Language Ability and Language Behaviour*. New York: Academic Press, 203–228.

7 Metacognition and good language learners

Neil J. Anderson

Metacognition can be defined simply as thinking about thinking (Anderson, 2002, 2005). It is the ability to reflect on what is known, and does not simply involve thinking back on an event, describing what happened, and the feelings associated with it. Metacognition results in critical but healthy reflection and evaluation of thinking that may result in making specific changes in how learning is managed, and in the strategies chosen for this purpose (for a discussion of strategies, see Griffiths, this volume).

Strong metacognitive skills empower language learners: when learners reflect upon their learning, they become better prepared to make conscious decisions about what they can do to improve their learning. O'Malley and Chamot (1990, p. 8) emphasize the importance of metacognition when they state: "students without metacognitive approaches are essentially learners without direction or opportunity to plan their learning, monitor their progress, or review their accomplishments and future learning directions." Metacognition, in language learning, as illustrated in Figure 1 (see p. 100), can be divided into five primary and intersecting components:

1 preparing and planning for learning
2 selecting and using strategies
3 monitoring learning
4 orchestrating strategies
5 evaluating learning.

Views of metacognition

In his great work *Les Miserables*, Victor Hugo wrote, "Where the telescope ends, the microscope begins. Which of the two has the grander view?" (Hugo, 1992, p. 767). The metaphorical telescope and microscope are useful for looking at the concept of metacognition. The addition of a kaleidoscope to the mix provides a deeper understanding of how metacognition is central to an understanding of good language learner behavior.

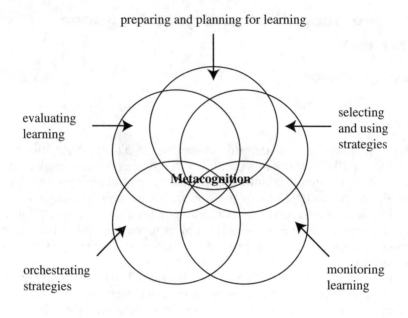

preparing and planning for learning

evaluating
learning

selecting
and using
strategies

Metacognition

orchestrating
strategies

monitoring
learning

Figure 1   A model of metacognition

A telescopic view of metacognition

With a telescopic view of metacognition, we can get an overall view of
the five primary components (see Figure 1).

Preparing and planning for learning

Taking time to prepare for learning and plan what needs to be accomplished makes a major difference in learning. The activation of prior
knowledge is one way of preparing and planning for effective learning.
For example, research by Carrell (1983, 1984) and Carrell and
Eisterhold (1983) has clearly demonstrated that reading comprehension
and reading skills are enhanced when prior, or background, knowledge
is activated. Background knowledge includes all experience that a reader
can bring to a text: life experiences, educational experiences, cultural
experiences, knowledge of how the first language works as well as how
the second language works, and knowledge of how a text can be organized rhetorically. If learners do not have prior knowledge, it will be necessary to build background knowledge prior to asking the students to
engage in the learning task.

100

Selecting and using strategies

The selection of appropriate strategies and knowing when to use them to achieve a particular learning goal is an important aspect of metacognitive behaviour. Many poor language learners are not able to choose useful strategies and do not recognize when to incorporate these strategies into their learning endeavors (Vann and Abraham, 1990). The metacognitive ability of deciding when to use particular strategies indicates that the learner is thinking and making conscious decisions about the learning process. In order to select and use strategies, learners must be familiar with the full range of options available to them. This emphasizes the importance of explicitly teaching strategies in the classroom, for instance by the use of surveys or questionnaires (see implications for the teaching/learning situation).

Monitoring learning

As learners develop the skill of selecting and using appropriate strategies, the next aspect of metacognitive behaviour they develop is the ability to monitor, listed by Rubin (1975) among the behaviors of good language learners. Good language learners are able to recognize when they do not understand and stop to do something about it. Teachers may need to help their students develop monitoring skills, perhaps by means of journals or think aloud protocols (as suggested under implications for the teaching/learning situation).

Orchestrating strategies

Effective strategy use does not occur in isolation. Often we discuss the use of a strategy as if it happens all by itself. Understanding the interdependency of strategy use while engaged in a language learning task is an important learning experience. Being metacognitively aware of strategy use allows good language learners to integrate the use of various strategies in a positive way. Again, surveys or questionnaires (see implications for the teaching/learning situation) followed by discussion may help students orchestrate their strategy use effectively.

Evaluating learning

Thomas Jefferson once said, "He who knows best, best knows how little he knows" (Brainy Quote, n.d.). Good language learners must be able to evaluate the efficacy of what they are doing. Poor learners often do not evaluate the success or failure of their learning. They may not recognize that they lack the ability to self-evaluate. Teachers may facilitate the development of this metacognitive skill by means of evaluation forms, videos, or self-assessment (see implications for the teaching/learning situation).

A microscopic view of metacognition

A microscopic view of each of these five central components of metacognition takes us into five classrooms in different parts of the world.

Preparing and planning for learning

In a recent advanced level, integrated skills class taught by Emma Torres at the Centro Cultural Costarricense Norteamericano (CCCN) in San José, Costa Rica, Ms Torres engaged the learners in a discussion to get them thinking about the topic for the next writing assignment: *Differences Between Men and Women*. Before doing any writing on the topic, Ms Torres allowed the learners to individually identify any gender differences. The class then discussed the differences with a partner. After one minute of discussion with a partner, Ms Torres signalled to the class to change partners. A second conversation about the differences between men and women began. This pattern continued until students had interacted with four or five different class members. As the students move from the oral activities to writing their compositions, they are preparing themselves with the knowledge they need for their compositions. The value of the metacognitive component comes when Ms Torres explicitly points out to the class that this activity will facilitate their writing.

Selecting and using strategies

Joy Janzen, formerly of Moorehead State University, in Minnesota, in the United States, regularly engages her advanced ESL writing students in the selection and use of metacognitive strategies. Professor Janzen engages the class in explicit discussions about what strategic writers do when they write. In particular, she focuses the writers' attention on how to select and use particular strategies for focusing on the audience. The class is learning to select and use particular strategies by thinking recursively and using questions during the writing process.

Monitoring learning

In yet another classroom, this time at the English Language Center at Brigham Young University, in Provo, Utah, in the United States, Mark Wolfersberger teaches an advanced-level business English course.

Mr Wolfersberger allows students to practice monitoring strategies for beginning the writing process through four different writing topics. He has asked the students to prepare to write on the following topic: "Do you agree or disagree with the following statement? People should read only those books that are about real people and established facts. Use specific reasons and details to support your answer." Chen Su Chun from Taiwan shared with her classmates how she monitored her strategies. She immediately thought that she agreed with the statement and proceeded to write without clearly thinking through her reasons for agreeing. As she wrote, she had problems putting together a coherent essay. She stopped writing and realized that the strategy of beginning the writing task without thinking through her reasons was not working for her, and she had to choose another strategy. Chen Su decided to make a list of reasons why she agreed and disagreed with the topic. With this strategy, she realized that she could identify more reasons for disagreeing than for agreeing and that she now had some specific content to write about. Mr Wolfersberger summarized the value of the metacognitive act of monitoring progress, and encouraged the students to stop when they had a problem and redirect their efforts.

Orchestrating strategies

For a view of orchestrating various strategies, we go to the University of Ottawa, in Canada. Professor Laurens Vandergrift is actively engaged in research and teaching of metacognitive strategies as they are linked with the skill of listening comprehension. Professor Vandergrift's pedagogical setting is working with learners of French as a target language. He is currently working with Andy, a native speaker of Kurdish, who spent six years of his life in a refugee camp before emigrating to Canada. Andy has just listened to an audiotape in French and is now listening to the information a second time. As he listens, he verbalizes the various strategies that he orchestrates while listening to a radio announcement in French. Andy uses his background knowledge of radio call-in contests, he identifies vocabulary that he does not know, he guesses at that unknown vocabulary, he expresses doubts about his comprehension. In short, Andy can identify what he knows as well as what he does not know by orchestrating various strategies.

Evaluating learning

Professor Tim Murphey at Yuan Ze University in Chungli, Taiwan, has developed a pedagogical technique that he calls Learner Self-Evaluated Video. Learners are regularly videotaped during class and asked to watch and self-evaluate their speaking performance in English. Professor Murphey has asked the students to share with a partner what they believe their final grade should be for the speaking skills enhancement course for future English teachers. Students are videotaped and then self-evaluate their justification of their final grade. Katie and Dina, two students in Professor Murphey's class, share with each other what they have learned from the course and what they each believe their final grade should be. They engage in healthy, yet critical self-evaluation. They are not superficial in their self-evaluation. They do not automatically say that they deserve an "A" in the course. Nor are they hypercritical of the imperfections they may still be experiencing.

A kaleidoscopic view of metacognition

A kaleidoscope allows us to view a changing pattern. That is the way it is with teaching and learning – no two class sessions are the same. Metacognition is not any one of the five elements discussed here in isolation. It is the blending of all five into a kaleidoscopic view. Each of the five metacognitive skills interacts with the other.

Metacognition is not a linear process moving from preparing and planning to evaluating. More than one metacognitive process may be taking place at a given moment during a learning task. The kaleidoscopic view of metacognition allows us to understand how language acquisition can be accelerated when learners and teachers use metacognition to improve the teaching and learning of language.

Implications for the teaching/learning situation

If we want to develop metacognitively aware language learners, we must have metacognitively aware teachers. Understanding and controlling cognitive processes is an essential skill that classroom teachers can develop in themselves and in the learners with whom they work. Rather than focusing learner attention only on language issues, educators can structure a learning atmosphere where thinking about what happens in the learning process will lead to stronger language skills.

Although researchers such as Skehan (1989), Vann and Abraham (1990) and Wenden (1998) have suggested that explicit teaching of language learning strategies does not ensure a successful learning experience, Dhieb-Henia (2003) concludes that metacognitive training can be an effective tool for teachers to use in helping learners improve their language skills. The promotion of metacognitive behaviour can therefore be a valuable use of instructional time.

There are various pedagogical tools which are available to classroom teachers to help develop metacognition. I will discuss six such tools. Each tool can serve as a stimulus for each of the five components of metacognition and when used regularly in the classroom, along with other tools, can help learners develop the critical but healthy awareness of their development as good language learners.

Language learning surveys or questionnaires

A language learning survey or questionnaire can be a very effective way of providing an initial introduction to learners regarding the importance of developing good language learning skills. These surveys also provide an excellent way of integrating into a classroom discussion all five of the components of metacognition. Various surveys are available, for instance the Strategy Inventory for Language Learning or SILL (Oxford, 1990), the Survey of Reading Strategies or SORS (Mokhtari and Sheorey, 2002; Sheorey and Mokhtari, 2001), and the Perceptual Learning Style Preference Questionnaire (Reid, 1995).

Language learning journals

Riley and Harsch (1999) advocate the use of journals which can serve as a tool for reflection. Teachers can gain insights into learners' metacognition as appropriate prompts are prepared for students to respond to. Sample prompts include:

My learning and practicing plans for next week are:
This week I spoke English with these people:
This week I made these mistakes:
I would like help with:
My self assessment of my performance on today's task is:

Journal prompts that encourage learners to engage in all of the components of metacognition can be prepared.

Learner self-evaluated video

Murphey (2001) and Murphey and Kerry (1996) outline a very effective tool to engage learners in metacognition and practice habits of the good language learner. Learner self-evaluated video allows learners to use a video of a speaking opportunity as a tool to evaluate progress and growth in language development. Each student comes to class with a videotape. The teacher has two video cameras and four video recorders set up so that four students can be videotaped at the same time. The

105

teacher writes a speaking prompt on the board and invites the students to choose a partner and begin the conversation. After two minutes students change partners and have another conversation for two minutes. During each practice opportunity the teacher invites four students to come to the videoing area. The conversations of these learners are recorded. The learners leave the class with a videotape of one conversation and an assignment sheet to do something specific with the videotape. This classroom tool can be extremely useful in engaging learners in specific conversational tasks and engaging learners in reflecting on how they can improve. The learner self-evaluated video method requires sharp metacognitive skills and thus helps learners develop the skills through repeated practice.

The groupwork evaluation form

Most language learning programs engage learners in some type of groupwork in order to provide more speaking opportunities to learners. However, it is rare for teachers to have learners evaluate the use of groupwork. Certainly, if learners work together for an extended period of time with the same group members, students should be asked if the groupwork is meeting the intended purposes. (See Angelo and Cross, 1993, for an example of a groupwork evaluation form.)

Think-aloud protocols

Think-aloud protocols have traditionally been used as a research tool for identifying the mental processes that learners engage in while undertaking a learning task. Think-aloud protocols can also be a very effective pedagogical tool to strengthen metacognitive awareness (Anderson and Vandergrift, 1996; Anderson, 2004). Perhaps the greatest value of think-aloud protocols as a pedagogical tool is that learners are able to articulate their thinking and help each other in the task of language learning. The teacher does not have to be the one to suggest all of the possibilities available to learners. Learners are often more willing to try something that their classmates suggest because they know that their classmates are engaged in the same task of becoming good language learners. The purpose of the think-aloud protocols is to allow learners an opportunity to verbalize the thought processes they engage in while completing a specific task in the language classroom. Through the verbalization, learners become more aware of their strategies and what changes they need to make in order to be better language learners.

Self-assessment on classroom tasks and tests

I use a four-part self-assessment tool when classroom quizzes and tests are administered. Learners respond to parts A, B, and C immediately following the test. Part A asks the learner to review each item on the test and indicate whether they believe they got the answer correct, incorrect, or whether they are not sure. Part B asks them to estimate what they believe their total score will be on the test. It is interesting that learners who are not very metacognitively aware of their performance often do not make a connection between parts A and B and sometimes produce very different responses to these two parts. Part C of the self-assessment is used if an oral interview has been conducted. In order for the oral interview self-assessment to be effective, learners need to know how they will be scored on the interview. Part D of the self-assessment is perhaps when metacognitive skills are used the most. When the tests are corrected and returned to the learners the self-assessment form is also returned. Learners are asked to assess whether they correctly estimated their performance and how they plan to prepare for the next test.

All six of these tools serve as ways for students to become more metacognitively aware of how to become better language learners. By integrating these and other tools into the repertoire of activities used in the classroom, learners get consistent exposure to the components of metacognition.

Questions for ongoing research

Telescopes, microscopes, and kaleidoscopes provide us with special perspectives on metacognition. Which provides the best view? Just like most theories and concepts in the profession of language teaching, we cannot rely on one by itself. We need the perspective of all three to fully understand metacognitive behavior. Ongoing research is required which integrates the three views in a range of situations and with a range of learners of varying characteristics (for instance of different ages, genders, and cultures).

Research has shown that good language learners make frequent use of a wide range of metacognitive strategies (O'Malley and Chamot, 1990; Griffiths 2003). Therefore, the teaching of metacognitive skills may be a valuable use of instructional time to help learners engage metacognitively with the learning task and thereby learn more effectively. How can these metacognitive skills best be taught? A great deal more research is required, considering individual and situational variables, before we can answer this question with any authority.

Conclusion

Many language learners struggle to know how to study effectively and make progress in developing their language skills. Some of these learners rely on teachers and others, or on a structured language program to tell them what to do and how to study in their target language. But good language learners develop metacognitive skills which enable them to manage their own learning, thereby rendering themselves less dependent on others or on the vicissitudes of the learning situation.

While learning from a good teacher in a well-structured language program is very important, it is perhaps even more important for these learners to have meaningful learning experiences on their own. Good teachers and well-structured language learning programs cannot possibly teach learners everything they need to know. Getting good results from studying depends on learners going beyond what teachers and programs provide and developing the kind of metacognitive behaviour which will enable them to regulate their own learning.

References

Anderson, N.J. (2002) *The role of Metacognition in second/foreign language teaching and learning.* ERIC Digest. Washington, DC: ERIC Clearinghouse on Languages and Linguistics. (Retrieved August 16, 2007 from: www.cal.org/resources/digest/0110anderson.html).

Anderson, N.J. (2004) Developing metacognitive awareness. In J. Bamford, and R.R. Day, (eds.), *Extensive Reading Activities for Teaching Language.* Cambridge: Cambridge University Press, pp. 175–180.

Anderson, N.J. (2005) L2 learning strategies. In E. Hinkel (ed.), *Handbook of Research in Second Language Teaching and Learning.* Mahwah, NJ: Lawrence Erlbaum Associates, pp. 757–772.

Anderson, N.J. and Vandergrift, L. (1996) Increasing metacognitive awareness in the L2 classroom by using think-aloud protocols and other verbal report formats. In R.L. Oxford (ed.), *Language Learning Strategies Around the World: Cross-cultural Perspectives.* Manoa: University of Hawai'i Press, pp. 3–18.

Angelo, T.A. and Cross, K.P. (1993) *Classroom Assessment Techniques: A Handbook for College Teachers.* San Francisco: Jossey-Bass.

Brainy Quote (n.d.) *Thomas Jefferson quotes.* (Retrieved August 16, 2007 from: http://www.brainyquote.com/quotes/authors/L/thomas_jefferson.html).

Carrell, P.L. (1983) Background knowledge in second language comprehension. *Language Learning and Communication*, 2, 25–34.

Carrell, P.L. (1984) The effects of rhetorical organization on ESL readers. *TESOL Quarterly*, 18, 441–469.

Carrell, P.L. and Eisterhold, J.C. (1983) Schema theory and ESL reading pedagogy. *TESOL Quarterly*, 17, 553–573.

Dhieb-Henia, N. (2003) Evaluating the effectiveness of metacognitive strategy training for reading research articles in an ESL context. *English for Specific Purposes*, 22, 387–417.

Griffiths, C. (2003) *Language Learning Strategy Use and Proficiency*. (Retrieved from: http://www.umi.com/umi/dissertations/).

Griffiths, C. (this volume) Chapter 6: Strategies and good language learners.

Hugo, V. (1992 [1862]) *Les Misérables*. Translated by C.E. Wilbour. New York: Random House.

Mokhtari, K. and Sheorey, R. (2002) Measuring ESL students' awareness of reading strategies. *Journal of Developmental Education*, 25(3), 2–10.

Murphey, T. (2001) Videoing conversations for self-evaluation in Japan. In J. Murphy and P. Byrd (eds.), *Understanding the Courses We Teach: Local Perspectives on English Language Teaching*. Ann Arbor MI: University of Michigan Press, pp. 179–196.

Murphey, T. and Kerry, T. (1996) LSEV: Learner Self-Evaluated Video. [NFLRC Video 10.] Honolulu, HW: University of Hawai'i, National Foreign Language Resource Center.

O'Malley, J.M. and Chamot, A.U. (1990) *Learning Strategies in Second Language Acquisition*. New York: Cambridge University Press.

Oxford, R.L. (1990) *Language Learning Strategies: What Every Teacher Should Know*. Boston, MA: Heinle & Heinle.

Reid, J. (1995) *Learning Styles in the ESL/EFL Classroom*. Boston, MA: Heinle.

Riley, L.D. and Harsch, K. (1999) Enhancing the learning experience with strategy journals: supporting the diverse learning styles of ESL/EFL students. Proceedings of the HERDSA Annual International Conference, Melbourne, Australia. (Retrieved from: http://herdsa.org.au/vic/cornerstones/pdf/Riley.PDF).

Rubin, J. (1975) What the "good language learner" can teach us? *TESOL Quarterly*, 9(1), 41–51.

Sheorey, R. and Mokhtari, K. (2001) Differences in the metacognitive awareness of reading strategies among native and non-native readers. *System*, 29, 431–449.

Skehan, P. (1989) *Individual Differences in Second Language Learning*. London: Arnold.

Vann, R.J. and Abraham, R.G. (1990) Strategies of unsuccessful language learners. *TESOL Quarterly*, 24, 177–198.

Wenden, A.L. (1998) Metacognitive knowledge and language learning. *Applied Linguistics*, 19, 515–537.

8   Autonomy and good language learners

Sara Cotterall

Defining learner autonomy has been a major preoccupation in much of the research literature on autonomy. Research in learner autonomy explores learners' ability to "take charge of" their learning in both methodological and psychological terms. The focus of research into learner autonomy is on the learners' ability to assume responsibility for their learning (Dickinson, 1987; Holec, 1981; Little, 1991). The central concern is decision-making in the learning process, which both implies a change in role for learner and teacher and raises questions about the willingness and ability of learner and teacher to assume their new roles. The research therefore focuses on both the methodological and psychological aspects of learners' language learning.

Definitions proposed by Henri Holec from the University of Nancy in France, and David Little from Trinity College Dublin dominate much of the discussion. Holec's (1981) report to the Council of Europe describes autonomy as "the ability to take charge of one's own learning" (p. 3) which he sees as involving responsibility for determining learning objectives, defining the contents and progressions of learning, selecting methods and techniques to be used, monitoring the procedure of acquisition, and evaluating what has been acquired. Holec concludes his discussion of what constitutes "taking charge" of one's learning by saying: "The autonomous learner is himself capable of making all these decisions concerning the learning with which he is or wishes to be involved" (Holec, 1981, p. 3).

Two points are worth noting here. Firstly, Holec's wording indicates that he sees autonomy as a *potential* capacity which needs to be developed in learners. Secondly, Holec's definition of autonomy focuses on the technical aspects of learning. The five types of decision he itemizes reflect the focus of many "learning to learn" programs in self access centers; these programs seek to introduce the methodological skills that learners need in order to manage their learning in such settings.

To Holec's definition of the autonomous learner's behaviour, can be added Little's formulation of autonomy, which focuses on the psychological dimension of autonomy. Little (1991, p. 3) argues that: "Essentially, autonomy is a *capacity* – for detachment, critical reflection, decision-making, and independent action. It presupposes, but also entails, that the learner will develop a particular kind of psychological relation to the process and content of his learning." According to Little (1991), the ability to learn autonomously is demonstrated both in learning approach and in the way learning is transferred to other situations.

Elsewhere Little emphasizes that this capacity is universal, rejecting the idea that autonomy is a "western cultural construct and, as such, an inappropriate pedagogical goal in non-Western societies" (Little, 1999, p. 12). Little's final sentence reflects his conviction that an autonomous approach to learning extends beyond the original subject domain and influences the learner's attitudes and behaviors in other settings too.

Benson (2001) introduces a third dimension. In addition to the methodological and psychological aspects of autonomous learning already discussed, Benson claims (2001, p. 49) "that the content of learning should be freely determined by learners." In other words, he argues that autonomous language learners not only decide how and when they learn, and how they think about and manage their learning – but, crucially, they also decide what and where they learn. This introduces a political and a social element to the definition.

I would like to illustrate this third dimension by referring to a class of learners I worked with in an English for Academic Purposes (EAP) program a number of years ago. The learners were highly proficient postgraduates from a range of discipline areas who were attending the course prior to enrolling for master's or doctoral programs. Many of the learners displayed the type of technical learning competence that Holec describes. They could also be considered to have assumed psychological control of their learning, as evidenced by their frequent comments and queries on the relationship between the course activities and the target learning situations for which they were preparing. The dimension of autonomy highlighted by Benson emerged about five weeks into the course when a small group of these learners approached me with a proposal that they no longer attend all class sessions, but instead select the parts of the program they personally judged to be best suited to their purposes. To complement their class participation, they proposed developing individual study programs based on an assessment of their personal needs and priorities. This example of learners asserting their right to determine both the content of their learning and the situation in which that learning takes place illustrates, in my view, what Benson means by the "learning content" level of autonomy. It is an interesting reflection on the challenge that truly autonomous learners can pose to institutions that the learners' sponsor would not agree to their proposal. My own view was that the modifications to the program that the learners suggested would have significantly increased the benefit they obtained from their 12-week course.

Each of the three levels of autonomy (methodological, psychological, and content) highlighted by Holec, Little, and Benson interacts with the other. Benson (2001, p. 50) argues that the three levels are necessarily interdependent since, "Effective learning management depends on control of the cognitive processes involved in learning [. . . which] necessarily has consequences for the self-management of learning [. . .] and control over cognitive processes should involve decisions concerning the content of learning."

Examination of the research in learner autonomy reveals that different researchers and teachers emphasize different aspects of this three-dimensional capacity.

Research into aspects of learner autonomy

Current research on learner autonomy can be grouped under three headings:

Firstly, there are studies which explore the essential nature of learner autonomy. Riley's (1996) evocatively titled paper – "The blind man and the bubble" is a good example. In this paper he discusses the inadequacy of the research tools currently available for researching autonomy, just as the blind man's disability makes him ill equipped to comprehend what a bubble is.

The second group of learner autonomy research studies investigates different means of fostering autonomous behavior among learners. Recent work includes studies on the discourse of learner advising (for instance, Crabbe, Hoffman and Cotterall, 2001), research into the link between learner strategies and learner autonomy (for instance, Hyland, 2000; Nunan, Lai, and Keobke, 1999) and work on the nature of teacher autonomy (for instance, Sinclair, McGrath, and Lamb, 2000).

The third focus of learner autonomy research centers on attempts to measure the effectiveness of efforts to foster autonomous behavior (for instance, Dam and Legenhausen, 1999; Lai, 2001; Sinclair, 1999).

A very recent addition to these three strands of research concerns documentation and analysis of individual learners' language learning "histories." One such account is the focus of the next section of this chapter.

The study

There has been a recent flurry of publications focusing on case studies of individual learners (see, for example, Benson, 2007; Benson and Nunan,

2002, 2005a). The goal of such collections is to "demonstrate the contribution that [. . .] the analysis of learners' stories [. . .] can make" (Benson and Nunan, 2005b, p. 3) to understanding the richness and diversity of second language learners' experiences. In this section of the chapter, excerpts from one such study will be presented which documented the experience of two learners of Spanish – Simon and Harry (not their real names) – enrolled in a first-year course at a university in New Zealand. The aim of the study was to explore the goals, beliefs, and strategies of the learners as part of their ongoing experience of learning Spanish during the course. Excerpts are presented here in an attempt to locate the discussion of learners' use of strategies within a broader consideration of their autonomy as learners.

Participants

Harry was a 29-year-old first-year Bachelor of Arts student; Simon was a 21-year-old first-year Law degree student. Both were native speakers of English. Harry's previous language learning experience included a year of French at secondary school, and a brief period spent living in Spain with his brother, a fluent speaker of Spanish. Simon had recently returned to New Zealand from a year in Denmark on an exchange program, where he reported having been very successful at acquiring the language. While in Denmark, he had also attended introductory Spanish lessons.

The Spanish course in which Harry and Simon were enrolled was a 12-week (one trimester) introductory course. It involved five hours of class contact per week consisting of three one-hour language classes (lecture format), one audio-visual class, and one oral tutorial. The course outline identified the course aims as being to introduce students to the basics of the language through practice in speaking, listening, reading, and writing.

Data collection and analysis

Harry and Simon were interviewed once every two weeks throughout the 12-week trimester. The interviews were highly interactive with the subjects leading much of the discussion following prompts by the interviewer at the beginning of each session. Each audiotaped session lasted approximately one hour, and at the end of each interview, an appointment for the next session was made. Harry and Simon participated in six interview sessions in total. Once the interviews were complete and the data analyzed, the author sent a copy of the draft account to the participants for comment. Both agreed that the account accurately reflected their experience of the Spanish course. Harry also volunteered a number of comments about his experience of participating in the research project and his subsequent attitude to learning Spanish. For a fuller discussion of Harry's experience, see Cotterall (2005).

According to Wenden (1991), autonomous student behavior inevitably involves the use of strategies, which she defines as "operations that learners use to learn a new language and to regulate their efforts to do so" (p. 18). In order to examine the strategy use of these two students, the interview recordings were transcribed and examined for strategy use.

Findings

Several of Rubin's (1975) seven strategies can be identified in the interview transcripts of the two subjects involved in this study. This discussion, however, will focus on just two strategies from Rubin's list:

- The good language learner is prepared to attend to form.
- The good language learner practices.

The good language learner is prepared to attend to form

Simon made a number of comments during the interviews which indicated that he had a keen awareness of the form of target language items. For example, during the second interview, he commented that he had observed similarities in the written form of some vocabulary items in Spanish and Danish:

> I was just writing down some words on my hand like as I was going through the thing like it struck me quite [. . .] like some words are the same [. . .] as Danish and mean completely different things [. . .] yeah um [. . .] the Spanish word for "grey" is *gris* and the Danish for "pig" is also *gris* [. . .] and it's exactly the same word spelt the same I think [. . .] and it means completely different things and I just find that fascinating. [. . .]
>
> (Session Two, 19 mins)

While Simon's comment is not an example of his having identified a pattern within the target language, the fact that he noticed this formal similarity between the two foreign languages indicated that he was sensitive to aspects of the language he was learning. In the third interview, Simon again demonstrated his sensitivity to the formal aspects of the language. When asked if the course had proved difficult for him so far, Simon replied:

> No [. . .] I'm really glad we covered the verb endings again cos now I actually know them so [. . .] I've just written them down [. . .] after a while I found I knew them just cos [. . .] every time they get mentioned [. . .] I'm thinking about them even just off the top of my head sort of I just repeat them like yeah like "o" "s"

> what's "s" or and most of the time I do it with the verb "to go" cos that's one of the easiest to remember but and it's also irregular so that way I learn the verb "to go" as well.
>
> (Session Three, 10 mins)

These comments show not only that Simon understood the need to conjugate the verb in Spanish, and the fact that some verbs do not follow the regular verb paradigm, but also that he acknowledged the need to pay attention to these aspects of linguistic form.

Analysis of the transcripts of Harry's contributions in the interviews also revealed instances of his awareness of the forms of the language. In the second interview he reported on the content of a course test saying:

> There was conjugating verbs you know [. . .] in a sentence and there was a missing gap next to it so you'd have to conjugate the verb [. . .] it was basically verb structure and sentence structure where everything goes and the order of things.
>
> (Session Two, 2 mins)

This comment indicates that he paid attention to the form of the verbs, and by inference, that he understood the way in which changes to the form affected the meaning conveyed by the items. Another instance of Harry paying attention to form involved his attempts at remembering the gender of nouns in Spanish. He explained:

> I try and conjugate a verb and use the right article I mean at the moment for me it's the thing remembering which is masculine which is feminine [. . .] there are a lot more clues in Spanish as there are in French I mean I guess the difference is the rules in Spanish are easier to understand or work out for yourself.
>
> (Session Two, 7 mins)

Here Harry makes use of his concurrent experience of studying French to conclude that there are more obvious patterns in the form of Spanish nouns – presumably the masculine and feminine endings – than in those of French nouns to indicate the noun's gender. Another example of his paying attention to form arose when he commented on the way in which the verb paradigms had been presented to the class:

> We learn the verbs in a strange way like with French you learn all all you know me, you, he, she, it, them, us or we [. . .] do you know what I mean [. . .] whereas in Spanish we learnt me, you and him and her and that was it and then [. . .] it wasn't until about two weeks later that we learnt the plurals and I kind of thought that was a bit strange.
>
> (Session Two, 17 mins)

Autonomy and good language learners

Here Harry's comment reflects the frustration of his preferred learning style in relation to the way in which this grammatical information was presented in class. On another occasion, Harry indicated his awareness of the existence of the polite form of the pronouns and verbs in Spanish, mentioning that when he spoke Spanish to his teacher outside of class, he needed to ask her:

> should I address you formally when we're speaking [. . .] or casually [. . .] and [. . .] you know and that changes almost half the sentence.
>
> (Session Three, 8 mins).

The good language learner practices

The second good language learner characteristic exemplified in the talk of both case study subjects was willingness to practice. During the interviews, as well as reporting on his ongoing learning of Spanish, Simon made frequent reference to his experience learning Danish in Denmark the previous year. Indeed the juxtaposition of these two very different language learning experiences made his commentary much richer. In response to a question about his progress at learning Danish the previous year compared to that of the other exchange students, Simon commented:

> I was the quickest [. . .] I did a bit more work outside the actual course than they did like [. . .] I memorized a whole lot of verbs and the way they sounded and [. . .] their past tense.
>
> (Session One, 16 mins)

In the next session, when asked how he was approaching the learning of verb forms in his Spanish course at university (in New Zealand), Simon reported:

> this year [. . .] I write them down every time he mentions them and . . . I couldn't remember them last year but this time I definitely can I don't know why [. . .] I don't know why. [. . .] maybe [. . .] it's cos I've left them alone and come back or something [. . .] but now I'm finding them really quite easy.
>
> (Session Two, 2 mins)

In both these instances, Simon's comments reflect a willingness to practice, as well as actual instances of his having devoted time and attention to mastering formal aspects of the target language (verb forms in both cases).

A vocabulary practice strategy reported by Harry involved his repeating in Spanish the names of common objects as he moved around his flat. He explained:

116

> I've got little stickers at home all over the house door window open close toaster lightbulb toilet seat you know it's all [. . .] I say them all the time and now it's clothing.

(Session Two, 5 mins)

Harry's strategy of labeling everyday items in his home with the Spanish equivalent for each is a common one. Since it involves the preparation of materials in advance (implying the existence of a preconceived plan for vocabulary learning) and involves repetition, it reflects a commitment to practice.

On the face of it, by attending to form and practicing, both Simon and Harry engaged in good language learner behaviors as part of their study of Spanish at university. However, the outcome of their learning efforts was quite different. While Simon continued throughout the 12-week trimester to achieve good grades on all his in-course tests and completed the course with a grade of "A," Harry's motivation to participate declined significantly in the final weeks of the course, though he did achieve a bare passing grade of "C." It is possible that this outcome was due to the fact that Harry's personal learning agenda and the course agenda were in conflict. Whereas Harry enrolled for the Spanish course in order to broaden his mind and engage with the ideas and values of another culture and civilization, the course agenda appeared to focus almost exclusively on mastery of the grammatical forms of the language. Harry explained it like this:

> Spanish is exciting too [. . .] starting off as [. . .] wow I'm going to do Spanish you know I'm going to learn you know I've been to Spain and I've hung out in that sort of area and thought it was really cool and you know the women are passionate the men are like this and you you know everybody's so fiery and stuff [. . .] and there's the music and [. . .] all that stuff [. . .] is conjured up straight away [. . .] but now it's it's the routine exercises exercises exercises homework homework homework.

(Session Four, 25 mins)

Unfortunately, this (Week 8) comment of Harry's was the first of many subsequent indicators that his personal goals in enrolling for the course were at odds with the course goals, and that his motivation for studying Spanish in that context would not last. In terms of Benson's (2001) notion of learner control over learning content, there was a mismatch between Harry's personal interests and the demands of the learning situation. In order to exercise his autonomy and achieve a good learning outcome, Harry had three choices: he could make some psychological adjustment by coming to terms with the requirements of the course and working within them; he could persuade the learning institution to change its approach; or he could change his learning situation.

Implications for the teaching/learning situation

The brief discussion of the data obtained from the case study reported in this chapter demonstrates that Rubin's (1975) descriptions of the behaviors typical of the good language learner can equally well be applied to the two learners included in this study. However, only one of them succeeded at language learning in terms of the institution's grading system. While both Simon and Harry reportedly paid attention to form and practiced their developing target language skills, only Simon was rewarded with a good course grade. What are we to understand from this?

First and foremost, the data show that learners can adopt the strategies of the "good language learner" without achieving either their own or the course's goals. Clearly, learners involved in institutional language learning may find their autonomy constrained by the goals and practices of the courses in which they enroll. Secondly, a list of generalized abilities or characteristics such as the "good language learner" behaviors needs to be operationalized if it is to be of use to language learners and teachers. For example, language practice needs to be linked to meaningful instances of personal language use if learners are to persist with it.

But more importantly for those interested in promoting learner autonomy, what is also needed – in addition to a set of good learning behaviors is – as Holec suggests (1981, p. 7), "a learning structure in which control over the learning can be exercised by the learner." Such a "structure" allows individual learners to shape and define their learning, and to display their personal autonomy. This may include an individual definition of what constitutes success: many students, for instance, are quite happy with a "C" grade pass.

Questions for ongoing research

According to Cohen (1998), good learners know where their strengths lie and are able to tackle learning problems flexibly. A defining characteristic of autonomous learners is their ability to make decisions about their learning which take account of the context in which they are learning. This suggests that teachers' attention should be focused on understanding their learners, and on helping them develop autonomous control over their learning.

The challenge for ongoing research is how to provide appropriate and effective support for a range of different learner behaviors, and for the ways in which individual learners choose to conduct their language learning in a variety of cultural and educational contexts. To date, a number of means of providing support have been trialled; these include encouraging learners to engage in regular dialogue about their learning (language advising), suggesting that they keep a record of their language learning experiences in the form of a log or journal, and incorporating collaborative project work as part of their learning experience. Each of these interventions needs to be systematically investigated in order to expand our understanding of the kind of support most likely to assist learners in successfully managing their language learning experience.

Conclusion

The implications for teachers of findings from research into learner autonomy are twofold. Firstly, teachers need to accept the heterogeneity of their learners. Learners reflect a range of motivations, cultures, beliefs, learning strategies, styles, and goals. They also differ in age, aptitude, gender and personality. Therefore, they respond differently to different methods and tasks. Secondly, teachers need to acknowledge the powerful influence of context on learning. Gu (2003, p. 18), for instance, claims: "Strategies that work in one educational, cultural and linguistic context might not work in another."

If we accept that our learners will inevitably be diverse and that the contexts in which they learn and use the language will exert a powerful influence, then we must also accept that it is futile to try and develop a teaching approach which will suit all learners, or indeed to promote a unique profile of *the* good language learner. The obvious conclusion is that, as teachers and researchers, we need to pay more attention to individual learners, and their unique motivations, experiences, and stories. An autonomy-fostering approach to language learning is therefore likely to focus first on individual learners' psychological relation to the language learning process, and only then on the strategies they adopt.

References

Benson, P. (ed.) (2007) *Learner Autonomy 8: Teacher and Learner Perspectives.* Dublin: Authentik.

Benson, P. (2001) *Teaching and Researching Autonomy in Language Learning.* Harlow: Pearson

Benson, P. and Nunan, D. (eds.) (2002) *The Experience of Language Learning. Special Issue of the Hong Kong Journal of Applied Linguistics,* 7(2). Hong Kong.

Benson, P. and Nunan, D. (eds.) (2005a) *Learners' Stories: Difference and Diversity in Language Learning.* Cambridge: Cambridge University Press.

Benson, P. and Nunan, D. (2005b) Introduction. In P. Benson and D. Nunan (eds.) *Learners' Stories: Difference and Diversity in Language Learning.* Cambridge: Cambridge University Press, 1–3.

Cohen, A.D. (1998) *Strategies in Learning and Using a Second Language.* London and New York: Longman.

Cotterall, S. (2005) "It's just rules. That's all it is at this stage." In P. Benson and D. Nunan (eds.), *Learners' Stories*. Cambridge: Cambridge University Press, 101–118.

Crabbe, D., Hoffmann, A., and Cotterall, S. (2001) Examining the discourse of learner advisory sessions. *AILA Review*, 15, 2–15.

Dam, L. and Legenhausen, L. (1999) Language acquisition in an autonomous learning environment: learners' self-evaluations and external assessments compared. In S. Cotterall and D. Crabbe (eds.), *Learner Autonomy in Language Learning: Defining the Field and Effecting Change*. Frankfurt: Peter Lang, 89–98.

Dickinson, L. (1987) *Self-instruction in Language Learning*. Cambridge: Cambridge University Press.

Gu, P. (2003) Vocabulary learning in a second language: person, task, context and strategies. *TESL-EJ*, 7/2: 1–4.

Holec, H. (1981) *Autonomy and Foreign Language Learning*. Oxford: Pergamon.

Hyland, F. (2000) ESL writers and feedback: giving more autonomy to students. *Language Teaching Research*, 4(1), 33–54.

Lai, J. (2001) Toward an analytic approach to assessing learner autonomy. *AILA Review*, 15, 34–44.

Little, D. (1991) *Learner Autonomy 1: Definitions, Issues and Problems*. Dublin: Authentik.

Little, D. (1999) "Learner autonomy is more than a Western cultural construct". In S. Cotterall and D. Crabbe (eds.), *Learner Autonomy in Language Learning: Defining the Field and Effecting Change*. Frankfurt: Peter Lang, 11–18.

Nunan, D., Lai, J., and Keobke, K. (1999) Towards autonomous language learning: Strategies, reflection and navigation. In S. Cotterall and D. Crabbe (eds.), *Learner Autonomy in Language Learning: Defining the Field and Effecting Change*. Frankfurt: Peter Lang, 69–77.

Riley, P. (1996) The blind man and the bubble: researching self-access. In R. Pemberton, E. Li, W. Or, and H.D. Pierson (eds.), *Taking Control: Autonomy in Language Learning*. Hong Kong: Hong Kong University Press, 251–264.

Rubin, J. (1975) What the "good language learner" can teach us. *TESOL Quarterly*, 9(1), 41–51.

Sinclair, B. (1999) Wrestling with a jelly: the evaluation of learner autonomy. In B. Morrison (ed.), *Experiments and Evaluation In Self-Access Language Learning*. Hong Kong: HASALD, 95–109.

Sinclair, B., McGrath, I., and Lamb, T. (eds.) (2000) *Learner Autonomy, Teacher Autonomy: Future Directions*. Harlow, Essex: Pearson Education.

Wenden, A.L. (1991) *Learner Strategies for Learner Autonomy*. London: Prentice Hall.

9   Beliefs and good language learners

Cynthia White

Beliefs may not be the first thing that come to mind when reflecting on the good language learner – the role they play may not be as immediately obvious or evident as that of learning strategies or motivation for example. Nonetheless the nature and effects of learner beliefs on language learning have been increasingly recognized since Joan Rubin's 1975 depiction of the good language learner (GLL): beliefs are important because learners hold their beliefs to be true and these beliefs then guide how they interpret their experiences and how they behave. Beliefs can be defined as "mental constructions of experience" (Sigel, 1985, p. 351), which are not only cognitive constructs but also social constructs arising from experience. Benson and Lor (1999) observe that beliefs are always contextualised in relation to some learning task or situation and that beliefs articulated by students are not necessarily held under all circumstances. They conclude that beliefs "can be understood as cognitive resources on which students draw to make sense of and cope with specific content and contexts of learning" (p. 462). In terms of language learning, the domains of beliefs which are acknowledged as relevant are the beliefs learners hold about themselves, about language and language learning and about the contexts in which they participate as language learners and language users.

The idea of the good language learner sprang from questions about how more successful learners approached language learning tasks and the facilitating strategies they brought to the process of learning a language. At around the same time as Rubin's 1975 depiction of the good language learner was published, researchers including Stern (1975), Cohen (1977) and Naiman, Fröhlich, Stern and Todesco (1978) also pursued the question of what can be called "best practices" (Norton and Toohey, 2001) in language learning. These studies in turn gave rise to a well-developed body of research based around the idea that successful learners have particular individual characteristics, affective orientations and learning strategies all of which affect their language learning. Much of the impetus for these studies came from a view that, if we could identify the activities and practices of these good language learners, it would be possible to help less successful students in our teaching and in our advice about how best to learn a language.

Beliefs were not mentioned explicitly in Rubin's (1975) article, but a belief that strategies are efficacious is implicit in the discussion. The beliefs of students are also alluded to, for example, in the observation that "we need also to examine how the good language learner defines opportunity as exposure to many social situations" (p. 44), which is an early recognition that learners have beliefs about such things as what exactly constitutes a language learning opportunity and what more optimal opportunities may be. The 1975 article also foreshadows our understanding that beliefs are highly varied, as in Rubin's discussion of what constitutes a good language learner, focusing on the fact there are many kinds of good language learners who each draw on their preferred means of learning in order to utilize particular learning opportunities. Research over the next three decades was to be concerned with what is going on inside learners' minds and with understanding how opportunities within the environment for language learning act as a modifier of the internal activity occurring in individual learners (Davis, 1995). More recently, notions of environment and opportunity have been revised within a more situated approach to understanding beliefs and good language learners.

Research into the role of beliefs in language learning

In the decade following the appearance of Rubin's 1975 article, the focus of interest widened to include more explicitly what learners thought and believed about language learning. Part of the appeal of research into learner beliefs was the notion that learners' beliefs were likely to affect what they do as language learners – and what they are prepared to do (Abraham and Vann, 1987; Horwitz, 1987, 1988; Wenden, 1986a, 1986b, 1987). At the same time studies devoted to the investigation of learning strategies and self-regulation began to reveal that successful learners develop insights into beliefs about the language learning process, their own abilities and the use of effective learning strategies (Ehrman and Oxford, 1989, 1990; Oxford, 1990; Zimmerman and Martinez-Pons, 1986).

Wenden (1986a, 1986b), for example, carried out interviews with learners and found that alongside describing their strategy use they articulated beliefs, both implicit and explicit, about how best to learn a second language. Further to this, Wenden (1986a) identified learners' explicit beliefs about how best to learn a language as providing the rationale for their particular use of strategies. At around the same time similar observations were made on the basis of investigations carried out by Abraham and Vann (1987) and Horwitz (1988). Abraham and Vann

(1987) proposed a model in which learners' beliefs affect how they approach learning, which in turn directly influences the degree of success achieved in language learning. Horwitz (1987, 1988) included learning and communication strategies as a key belief category in the research instrument she developed, the Beliefs About Language Learning Inventory (BALLI), and such beliefs were seen to underpin the actions learners took.

A decade later, Yang (1999) used the BALLI to examine more closely the relationship between language learners' beliefs and their strategy use, and suggested cyclical relationships between the two: in particular students' self-efficacy beliefs – that is beliefs about their ability to learn a second language – were strongly related to their use of learning strategies, especially functional practice strategies. While Yang's study was based on a quantitative approach to researching beliefs and strategy use, Victori (1999) used an in-depth case study approach with four Spanish students of English, two of whom were more effective and two less effective as writers. In each case a relationship was revealed between the beliefs of writers and the strategies they deployed.

Riley (1996) also argues that beliefs will directly shape learners' strategy use as well as their attitude and motivation. An example he gives is that learners who believe that the ongoing presence of a teacher is necessary to mediate their learning will tend to have problems with any kind of self-directed work. Riley highlights the impact of learner beliefs on language learning by pointing out that beliefs influence motivation, attitudes and learning procedures. And, as Riley points out, "if there is a misfit between what learners believe and the beliefs embedded in the instructional structure in which they are enrolled, there is bound to be some degree of friction or dysfunction" (pp. 152–153).

While the issue of resistance and conflict in relation to learners' beliefs and classroom practices has been widely endorsed, a number of critiques have been put forward challenging the positioning of learners in many studies of beliefs. Barcelos (2003, p. 14), for example, argues that many studies which fall within what she terms a "normative" approach to beliefs could be seen as based on a deficit model "where learners' beliefs are usually described as *erroneous* or *counterproductive*. Learners are viewed, compared and judged according to an ideal view of a good or autonomous language learner". Barcelos then goes on to refer to Benson's (1995) observation that such a portrayal is demeaning, because it suggests an ideal view of the learner that "real" students do not correspond to. An important concern in such critiques relates to methodology: beliefs measured out of context through questionnaires inevitably fail to take account of the experience-based nature of beliefs. Barcelos argues for a more contextual approach which looks at beliefs and actions within particular contexts and traces how they interact and change over time.

Emerging perspectives on the role of beliefs in language learning

In 2001 Norton and Toohey published a commentary in *TESOL Quarterly* tracing the development of research into good language learners and arguing that current research needs to include a focus on how learners' actions are received in particular contexts. Drawing on sociocultural approaches to understanding language learning, they point to the need to shift the focus from individual learners and how they function to the kinds of activities, settings and learning practices available to them within their communities. While, as Kalaja (1995, p. 192) observes, beliefs have been seen mainly as "cognitive entities to be found inside the minds of language learners", they are now seen as socially constructed in specific social, cultural educational and political contexts. Beliefs are recognized as part of students' experiences and interrelated with their environment, and attention is given to beliefs in conjunction with actions and possibilities within particular social contexts. Barcelos (2003) terms this a contextual approach to studying beliefs as opposed to the normative approach referred to earlier.

A longitudinal study within such a contextual approach was developed to explore the expectations and emergent beliefs of learners who entered what was for them a new language learning environment, namely self-instructed language learning (White, 1999, 2003). While the study did not focus specifically at the outset on good language learners, as the research progressed it was evident that students were aware of the need to establish how best to learn a language in that particular context. The initial study (White, 1999) and the extended study (White, 2003) showed clearly the influence of expectations and beliefs on the actions learners were prepared to take and the way they interpreted their experiences within a new learning environment. It also showed the dynamic nature of learners' beliefs as they underwent a period of rapid change and re-evaluated their understanding of the context, what was available to them, and what was required of them. According to this study, the good language learners were those who were successful in this context because they succeeded in adapting their expectations and beliefs to the opportunities available to them and forging a match between those opportunities and their own needs, preferences and abilities. The study, though, also pointed to the fact that for some individuals the affordances of that self-instructed learning context were not able to be accessed in a productive way, and that for those learners the attempts they made to develop a productive interface with that learning context were much less satisfying (White, 2005). While conflicts between their beliefs and what was available to them in the particular configurations of a self-instructed learning environment were evident, some students resolved this by leaving the course, and others succeeded in achieving a more viable way of making progress within the constraints and opportunities as they saw them. From this study we have a picture of good language learners not as those who have particular sets of beliefs but as those who succeed in sensing out the affordances of a particular learning context, and developing a productive interface between their beliefs and attributes and different possibilities and experiences within that context.

Implications for the teaching/learning situation

As mentioned earlier a key factor in the impact of Rubin's (1975) good language learner article is that it spoke to researchers, teachers and learners of the search for ways to improve the processes of language learning. While researchers such as Mori (1999) have raised questions about the malleability of beliefs, particularly through instruction, a number of pedagogical approaches have been developed that are aimed at modifying and reshaping beliefs, including group discussions to raise metacognitive awareness (Wenden, 1991) and using diaries, logs and journals as a means of reflecting on learning. Wenden (1999), for example, argues that teachers should try to understand learner beliefs about language learning and also help them to adopt a more reflective approach to their learning through a four-stage approach:

1 elicitation of learners' beliefs
2 articulation of what has come to awareness
3 confrontation with alternative views
4 reflection on the appropriateness of revising and expanding one's knowledge.

She goes on to suggest that students should be encouraged to acquire new concepts about language learning, and to use their new ideas to seek insights into how they learn and possible reasons for unsuccessful learning outcomes. The difficulty, as Woods (2003) acknowledges, is that we have not, as yet, devoted much attention to studying the efficacy of different ways of restructuring beliefs. Two recent approaches, however, have been developed in classrooms, both based around learners seeing, and changing, themselves.

The first approach is based around the idea of a collaborative forum. In the study described by Ewald (2004) the collaborative forum included 21 students and their teachers with a specific focus on perceptions of small group work. Students were able to express and examine their beliefs through journals, skit presentations which dramatised their behaviour, and questionnaires combined with small and whole group discussions. Such a multifaceted approach was integral to the positive response to the process: students developed an awareness of how they thought and acted in classroom-based small group interactions, and contributed to what Ewald terms an "improved sense of community" (p. 163) as the basis for modifying their own behaviour. A key point here, underlined by Ewald, is that while the different parts of this process may not be appropriate in all contexts the value lay in the fact that teachers were willing to discuss language learning and classroom issues with their students. More importantly, rather than trying to "change" students Ewald suggests it may be more effective for the teacher to focus on helping students to see themselves, and then to collaboratively develop an awareness of the kinds of behaviours that influence their learning.

A second approach carried out by Murphey (1995) and Murphey and Arao (2001) is based around the idea of Near Peer Role Modelling (NPRM) – in this case role models who are somewhat "near" to students in age, gender, interests, ethnicity and so on. Murphey bases his approach on the work of Bandura (1997) who argues that "seeing or visualizing people similar to oneself perform successfully typically raises efficacy beliefs in observers that they themselves possess the capabilities to master comparable activities" (p. 87). Murphey and Arao (2001) traced the impact of a video of four exemplary students who talked about their learning of English and voiced beliefs and attitudes thought to facilitate language development. Results indicated that many of the students' beliefs and behaviors shifted in a positive direction and their rise in motivation persisted. Murphey and Arao argue that this approach is more effective than using lists of strategies or beliefs in the literature since the beliefs emerge from the students themselves. In addition they argue that the similarity in terms of age, ethnicity, interests and gender enhances the intensity of identification. Such an approach is congruent with the notion of identity construction as discussed by Lave and Wenger (1996) whereby learning involves the whole person and involves the construction of identities. One further aspect of the study was that the process of examining students' beliefs and the use of the role models also changed the teacher's beliefs to the point where she made her own classes more interactive. Clearly the value of this approach does not reside in the use of videos, but in finding a way of introducing near peer role models to students in a way that is compelling in a particular socio-cultural setting, and engages the identity of learners.

Questions for ongoing research

To date, narrative enquiry, case studies, discourse analysis, and metaphor analysis (a qualitative method used to assess the structure and content of implicit theories and beliefs, thereby revealing patterns of thought and action) have been found to provide rich sources of data on learner beliefs. The challenge is to develop a more fine-grained approach to studying experiences and practices in particular sociocultural contexts, and looking at how precisely they relate to learner beliefs. What we now know about beliefs and good language learners reveals a number of important avenues for research. Three of the most promising, in my view, arise from the studies discussed in this chapter:

1 The claim that situated awareness might precede change in beliefs (Ewald, 2004) is worthy of further investigation in relation to classroom practices. In particular, attention should be given to finding ways of helping learners to see and understand themselves and to collaboratively develop an awareness of the kinds of actions and behaviours which influence their learning.
2 We need to explore how learners' beliefs assist or constrain them in exercising their agency in particular contexts for language learning and use (Norton and Toohey, 2001).
3 We need more longitudinal studies to see how beliefs develop in relation to learner perspectives on the affordances and constraints of a learning context and to investigate the interplay among those beliefs, learners' actions and their interpretation of experiences (White, 1999, 2003).

Conclusion

Our view of beliefs and good language learners has moved from earlier approaches concerned with identifying and quantifying beliefs to an increasing recognition of the complexity of beliefs and the way they may work in particular circumstances. While earlier approaches focused on the beliefs of individual learners and viewed them as relatively static and unchanging, emerging perspectives draw on sociocultural theory to consider how beliefs are constructed in everyday contexts, and how they may be modified or transformed or come into play in different social contexts. As Benson and Lor (1999) conclude in their study of conceptions of language and language learning, the value of research on learner beliefs may lie not so much in an understanding of the enabling or disabling attributes of particular beliefs as in an understanding of the ways in which learners put their beliefs to use. Equally importantly, our under-standings of good language learners need to encompass a view of beliefs as constructed in everyday practices, shifting and taking shape accord-ing to the social contexts available for learning and using a language.

Looking ahead to the next 30 years of research and practice in rela-tion to learner beliefs and good language learners, I feel confident there is much to look forward to. Ongoing research initiatives are likely to reveal more to us about how we can come to know ourselves as learners and teachers in the intriguing process of language learning.

References

Abraham, R. and Vann, R. (1987) Strategies of two language learners: a case study. In A.L. Wenden and J. Rubin (eds.), *Learner Strategies in Language Learning*. London: Prentice Hall, 85–102.

Bandura, A. (1997) *Self-efficacy: The Exercise of Control*. New York: W.H. Freeman and Company.

Barcelos, A. (2003) Researching beliefs about SLA: a critical review. In P. Kalaja and A. Barcelos (eds.), *Beliefs About SLA: New Research Approaches*. Netherlands: Kluwer, 7–33.

Benson, P. (1995) A critical review of learner training. *Language Learning*, 2(2), 2–6.

Benson, P. and Lor, W. (1999) Conceptions of language and language learning. *System*, 27, 459–472.

Cohen, A.D. (1977) Successful second language speakers: a review of research literature. *Balshanut-Shimushit: Journal of the Israel Association of Applied Linguistics*, 1, 3–21.

Davis, K. (1995) Qualitative theory and methods in applied linguistic research. *TESOL Quarterly*, 29, 427–454.

Ehrman, M.E. and Oxford, R.L. (1989) Effects of sex differences, career choice, and psychological type on adult language learning startegies. *Modern Language Journal*, 73(1), 1–15.

Ehrman, M.E. and Oxford, R.L. (1990) Owls and doves: cognition, personality, and language success. In J.E. Alatis (ed.), *Linguistics, Language Teaching, and the Interdependence of Theory, Practice and Research*. Washington DC: Georgetown University Press, 413–437.

Ewald, J. (2004) A classroom forum on small group work: L2 learners see, and change, themselves. *Language Awareness*, 13(3), 163–179.

Horwitz, E. (1987) Surveying student beliefs about language learning and teach-ing in the foreign language methods course. *Foreign Language Annals*, 18(4), 333–340.

Horwitz, E. (1988) The beliefs about language learning of beginning university foreign language students. *Modern Language Journal*, 72, 283–294.

Kalaja, P. (1995) Student beliefs (or metacognitive knowledge) about SLA recon-sidered. *International Journal of Applied Linguistics*, 5(2), 191–204.

Lave, E. and Wenger, J. (1996) Practice, person, social world. In H. Daniels (ed.), *An Introduction to Vygotsky.* London: Routledge, 143–150.

Mori, Y. (1999) Epistemological beliefs and language learning beliefs: what do language learners believe about their learning? *Language Learning*, 49(3), 377–415.

Murphey, T. (1995) Identity and beliefs in language learning. *The Language Teacher.* 19(4), 34–36.

Murphey, T. and Arao, H. (2001) Reported belief changes through Near Peer Role Modeling. *TESL-EJ*, 5(3), 1–18.

Naiman, N., Fröhlich, M., Stern, H.H. and Todesco, A. (1978) *The Good Language Learner* Research in Education Series No. 7. Toronto: Ontario Institute for Studies in Education.

Norton, B. and Toohey, K. (2001) Changing perspectives on good language learners. *TESOL Quarterly*, 35(2), 307–322.

Oxford, R.L. (1990) Language learning strategies and beyond: a look at strategies in the context of styles. In S.S. Magnan (ed.), *Shifting the Instructional Focus to the Learner.* Middlebury, VT: Northeast Conference on the Teaching of Foreign Languages, 35–55.

Riley, P. (1996) "BATs and BALLs": Beliefs about talk and beliefs about language learning. Paper presented at the International Conference: Autonomy 2000: The development of learning independence in language learning, Bangkok.

Rubin, J. (1975) What the "good language learner" can teach us. *TESOL Quarterly*, 9(1), 41–51.

Sigel, I.E. (1985) A conceptual analysis of beliefs. In: Sigel, I.E.(ed.), *Parental Belief Systems: The Psychological Consequences for Children.* Hillsdale, NJ: Erlbaum, pp. 498–504.

Stern, H.H. (1975) What can we learn from the good language learner? *The Canadian Modern Language Review*, 31, 304–318.

Victori, M. (1999) An analysis of writing knowledge in EFL composing: a case study of two effective and two less effective writers. *System*, 27, 537–555.

Wenden, A.L. (1986a) Helping language learners think about learning. *English Language Journal*, 40(1), 3–12.

Wenden, A.L. (1986b) What do second language learners know about their learning? A second look at retrospective accounts. *Applied Linguistics*, 7, 186–205.

Wenden, A.L. (1987) How to be a successful second language learner: insights and prescriptions from L2 learners. In A.L. Wenden and J. Rubin (eds.), *Learner Strategies in Language Learning.* London: Prentice Hall, 103–117.

Wenden, A.L. (1991) *Learner Strategies for Learner Autonomy.* London: Prentice Hall.

Wenden, A.L. (1999) An introduction to metacognitive knowledge and beliefs in language learning: beyond the basics. *System*, 27, 435–441.

White, C. (1999) Expectations and emergent beliefs of self-instructed language learners. *System*, 27, 443–457.

White, C. (2003) *Language Learning in Distance Education.* Cambridge: Cambridge University Press.

White, C. (2005) Towards a learner-based theory of distance language learning: The concept of the learner-context interface. In B. Holmberg, M. Shelley, and C. White (eds.), *Languages in Distance Education: Evolution and Change*. Clevedon, UK: Multilingual Matters, pp. 55–71.

Woods, D. (2003) The social construction of beliefs in the language classroom. In P. Kalaja and A. Barcelos (eds.), *Beliefs about SLA: New Research Approaches*. Dordrecht; Boston, MA; Kluwer Academic, 201–229.

Yang, N.-D. (1999) The relationship between EFL learners' beliefs and learning strategy use. *System*, 27, 515–535.

Zimmerman, B.J. and Martinez-Pons, M. (1986) Development of a structured interview for assessing students' use of self-regulated learning strategies. *American Educational Research Journal*, 73, 614–628.

10   Culture and good language learners

Claudia Finkbeiner

This chapter will discuss the role of culture and language learning in the classroom. Variations in cultural, ethnic, and national characteristics within and among individual students affect classroom dynamics and therefore influence the decisions which teachers need to make in order to provide an optimal learning environment for all learners. Culture is not an easy concept to define, and is especially difficult to disentangle from concepts such as ethnicity and nationality. Individuals define and interpret these terms differently depending on the sociocultural context they are situated in (Lantolf, 2000). There may be differences of the perceptions of self and others within a given sociocultural context (Finkbeiner, 2006; Kramsch, 1993, 1998), while surface phenomena (such as skin color) are often mistakenly related to categories such as ethnic, national, or cultural belonging. Very frequently these categories are outdated and neither reflect "current racial/ethnic realities" (Kramsch, 1998, p. 44) nor linguistic and cultural truths. In our globalizing world we cannot just glance at the surface and assume we understand others. We need to dive deep not only to understand others but also ourselves (Schmidt and Finkbeiner, 2006a, 2006b).

Many different metaphors have been used to describe culture: for example, culture has been referred to as an iceberg, where only about one-seventh is visible, while the rest is under water and non-observable (Weaver, 1993). Brown (1994, p. 163) describes culture as " 'glue' that binds a group of people together," whereas Hofstede (1997, p. 4) has coined the definition of culture as the "software of the mind." Individuals cannot be defined within one cultural category and as members of one group only; often they belong to many different sub-groups. It is not uncommon for individuals to have dual or even multiple cultural, ethnic, and/or linguistic belongings as well as nationalities. This can change throughout a lifetime. It might therefore be useful to use the concept of *hybrid* cultures and personalities (Bhabha 1994, 1996). According to Bhabha (1994, p. 7):

> the very concepts of homogeneous national cultures, the
> consensual or contiguous transmission of historical traditions, or
> 'organic' ethnic communities – as the ground of cultural
> comparativism – are in a profound process of redefinition

131

and "there is overwhelming evidence for a more transnational or trans-lational sense of the hybridity of imagined communities."

Studies on the role of culture in language learning

When looking at studies on the role of culture in schooling it is impor-tant to remember that research into learning and teaching is inevitably culturally biased by the minds of those who develop the instruments and tests (Hofstede, 1997). This bias can be predicted, for example, when respondents from a non-Western background need to answer question-naires designed by academics with a mainly Western sociocultural back-ground and vice versa (Hofstede, 1997; Elder, 1996). The bias is created by different underlying values, attitudes, and beliefs about what is con-sidered "good" behavior and action. For example, filial piety is consid-ered to be a typical Chinese value. It is strongly connected with honor for ancestors and with full respect for, complete obedience to and finan-cial support of parents. The bias is not just simply the Western versus non-Western dichotomy. It also needs to be considered on a more subtle, sub-cultural level, taking into account the diversity of ethnicity, culture, language, religion, political viewpoint, philosophical belief, sexual ori-entation, age, and gender (Finkbeiner, 2006). Readers' subjective views determine how they interpret items in an instrument or test and how they construct meaning and thus, the "right" or "wrong" answer (Finkbeiner, 2005, pp. 131–170). In some cultures, the answer to an item, such as "I want to achieve higher than my parents did," for example, might con-flict with the value attributed to respect for elders.

In a review of research of the cultural context of language learning, Young (1987) looked at Chinese classrooms. Teaching and learning strategies were found to be very different depending on the language community the language learner belonged to. Chinese learners seem to be used to a much more teacher-centered learning environment than Western learners. Young concludes that Western language teaching methods cannot be simply implemented within the Chinese context: teaching methods must be adapted to the specific learning style of dif-ferent ethnic groups.

Differences according to whether learners originate from an oral or a written culture have been explored by Stavans and Oded (1993), who examined the reading comprehension gap that existed between an Israeli and an Ethiopian group learning English at the same level. It was hypoth-esized that, due to their oral communication tradition, the Ethiopian group would have more difficulties understanding written texts than the learners with a cultural background in written communication. Reading and comprehension strategies were examined. The result showed that there was no direct correlation between cultural differences and reading comprehension difficulties. Hansen-Strain (1989), on the other hand, found group differences in the language development of university students who were from traditionally oral and traditionally written backgrounds. The students from traditionally oral cultures tended to focus more on interpersonal involvement in their speaking and writing than students from traditionally written cultures.

Banya and Cheng (1997) conducted a study with 23 Chinese and English teachers of English and 224 university students of English in south Taiwan. Their research interest was to investigate the interplay of students' beliefs about foreign language learning and of teachers' and students' beliefs across cultures. A special interest was to uncover similarities and differences between teachers' and students' beliefs through comparative analyses. There were interesting group differences, particularly when looking at gender as well as at the success of learning. The following aspects were found to be fundamental assets of good language learners irrespective of culture: low degree of anxiety, willingness to make effort, perceived ease at learning foreign languages and frequent use of language learning strategies. Chinese students and teachers were found to share the same beliefs as to prior experience in language learning, difficulties in language learning, children's superiority, language aptitude, and the important role of practice. When the comparative analyses were carried out, the results indicated that Chinese and American teachers differ in their beliefs.

A study with Japanese (n = 27) and American (n = 34) graduate students as well as their university teachers at Georgetown University (Lutz, 1990, p. 144), showed how the role of expectations in instructional settings can lead to "classroom shock." "The survey revealed that, as expected, Japanese and Americans differed sharply in their expressed appraisal of acceptable and desirable behaviour" (Lutz, 1990, p. 150). The differences could be observed with respect to organization and participation within the classroom setting in general, and "perceptions of what constitutes good student and good teacher behaviour" (Lutz, 1990, p. 148).

Investigating culture and reader response, Finkbeiner (2005) conducted two explorative intercultural studies with 77 high school students aged 16 in grades 9 and 10. As baseline data, American high school students in the USA were included in the survey. The studies were conducted between 1996 and 1997. They were situated within a complex study on the role of reading interest and reading strategies in understanding English texts (Finkbeiner, 1998, 2005). Text reading and follow-up interviews with immediate retrospection were conducted and polarity profiles were distributed to students of English in Taiwan and Germany. With the help of a polarity profile instrument (which allows assessment of readers' text preferences), reader response was measured for three texts. Two extremes within one dimension are used. Several dimensions or indicators make up one main category. This study focused on the following main categories: (a) perception of text difficulty (b) reading interest and emotional text engagement (c) prior knowledge. There were indicators for each category, for example, the following dimensions were used as indicators for emotional text engagement: positive–negative, amusing–serious, engaging–indifferent. A seven-point response scale was employed to indicate the level of agreement at the two ends of the dimensions. The three texts were continuous texts: two were factual and covered the topics "steam" and "zero gravity" and one was literary and covered a "school experience of a migrant child in New York City during the Cold War". Among all groups, the Taiwanese group had the highest emotional values with respect to the factual texts. The highest emotional values with respect to the literary text could be measured for the American students, probably because of prior knowledge and identification with the topic. These results show that reader response cannot be predicted as it depends on how the individual accesses the text, which is highly influenced by individual variables including culture.

Griffiths (2003) stated that the European students in her study appeared to be more effective learners of English than Asian students. This might not be surprising due to the similarity between English and certain European languages. Nevertheless, she also interviewed some highly successful Asian learners, and concluded that nationality was not, in itself, a barrier to language learning success. She suggested that the way students went about their learning, in particular the use of language learning strategies, might be a stronger influence on learning outcomes than culture.

What is the relationship between culture and language learning?

As Rubin pointed out, there might be considerable cultural differences in cognitive learning style. As she notes:

> in some societies, listening until the entire code is absorbed and one can speak perfectly is a reported form of learning; in others successive approximation to native speech is used as a learning strategy; while in still others rote learning is the most common learning strategy.
>
> (Rubin, 1975 p. 49)

With these examples, Rubin looks at institutional background knowledge as an important part of classroom culture, and, as she comments, good language learners may be able to make insightful contributions to the reasons for their learning difficulties and to their preferences for particular methods.

Here the focus is on a target language being taught and learned within a cultural background that might be different from the native culture. According to this, good language learners know about the rules of the specific learning environment and behave accordingly.

It is important to consider different cultural values and beliefs attributed to learning in general and to plurilingualism and language learning in particular as they play a crucial role in how language learning is pursued. No matter where classrooms are situated in the world there is usually a tacit contract between teachers and learners. This contract presupposes how classroom discourse and communication function and how students behave and act within the given framework (Finkbeiner, 2003, 2005). Once learners migrate from X to Y and move from one educational setting into another, not only do they encounter different outer classroom settings but additionally, they have to quickly find out about the underlying rules, values, and beliefs.

Affective factors are another critical area of culturally influenced learner variability (for instance, Schumann, 1975). According to Stern (1983), good language learners manage the emotional and motivational challenges of language learning effectively. As Stern (1983, p. 411–412) explains: "classroom learning as well as immersion in the target language environment each entail specific affective problems which have been characterized as language shock and stress, and as culture shock and stress." Good language learners nevertheless approach the task positively, with energy and persistence. They have positive attitudes towards themselves as language learners, towards language and language learning in general, and towards the language they are trying to learn, its speakers and its culture.

According to Stern (1983), language learning is a process that can be traumatic and lead to language shock and culture shock. According to Hofstede (1997, p. 207) culture shock can be caused by the fact that appropriate behavior, language, underlying beliefs, values, and attitudes are questioned and need to be re-negotiated in a new cultural context: "In a way, the visitor in a foreign culture has to return to the mental stage of an infant, in which he or she has to learn the simplest things over again." Kramsch (1993, p. 205) points out the important fact that "a sphere of interculturality" has to be established in order to be able to relate one's own culture and language ("C1") with the new culture and language ("C2") (Kramsch, 1993, pp. 207–208). We might even go beyond the comparison of similarities and differences and think of the construction of something new, of a *third culture* or *third space* (Bhabha,

1994). It is possible to argue that parallel to Selinker's (1972) interlanguage an interculture or "third space" (Finkbeiner, 2006, p. 28) is developed. The third space is not a physical place. It is a highly active, cognitive, and affective state, it is a "dynamic, fluid, fuzzy, and non-conforming as well as non-normative" construct which "questions existing beliefs, values and feelings about one's own self and about who we are" (p. 28). It happens within or between individuals or groups and can be constructed on an intrapersonal or interpersonal level. The third space might help learners to situate themselves in a safe and non-threatening way in a new world which is created beyond their old and new linguistic and cultural worlds. Yet, we need not romanticize the third space; it might also be a hurtful and harmful experience. This depends on issues of freedom, of individual choice and deliberate action.

Acculturation is an ongoing process which is highly dynamic. It starts pre-natally and ends with death (Finkbeiner, 2006, pp. 28–32). Ideally, third space construction and the development of cultural competence happen throughout the acculturation process (pp. 28–32). This model of acculturation can help in analyzing the cultural processes to which language learning is connected. It regards language learners as cultural beings, and takes account of Piaget's (1954, 1969) and Vygotsky's (1962, 1978) work as a valuable theoretical basis since acculturation is both a highly individual and social process. It puts a strong emphasis on the self. This helps us understand the intercultural processes language learners have to cope with during their individual acculturation process. The acculturation process is influenced by the cultural and sub-cultural groups language learners belong to, but it must be understood as an idealized process. Critical incidents (such as loss of close relatives, social deprivation, war situations, divorce, and so on) might lead to a non-linear acculturation growth. Finally, there are different phases in the acculturation process, which can be of different lengths. Some phases might be skipped and then re-appear at a later stage in life. Re-appearance of "earlier" acculturation processes that were important at the first stage does not imply regression. It only mirrors the dynamics of the acculturation process.

Good language learners are often believed not to have to face culture shock (Stern, 1983, pp. 411–412). Does this imply that the good language learner is culturally more competent than learners who have to face this? The answer to this question is not as easy as we might think. We need to consider that the cultural competence construct is highly complex and multi-faceted. It is dynamic, constantly changing and includes the affective and cognitive dimensions (Bhabha, 1994; Byram, 1997; Finkbeiner, 2006; Hofstede, 1997; Schmidt, 1998; Weaver, 1993). It is connected to cultural sensitivity, cultural awareness, and empathy, as well as the ability to change perspectives and put oneself into the other person's shoes. These qualities allow the good language learner to "navigate smoothly between different cultural and linguistic worlds" (Finkbeiner, 2006, p. 28).

Implications for the teaching/learning situation

In order to successfully teach language to children and adults of different cultures, ethnicities, and/or nationalities, teachers need to become familiar with various methods for teaching diverse populations and develop a strong knowledge of and empathy for the learners. This knowledge includes the learners' cultures and languages, their personality structures, their learning styles, their identities, and their inner selves (Finkbeiner, 2006; Finkbeiner and Koplin, 2002; Schmidt and Finkbeiner, 2006a, 2006b; Wilden, 2006). Only then can adequate and appropriate learning and teaching decisions be made (International Reading Association, 1999). This implies that *good* methods and *good* textbooks cannot be simply imported and *good* language teachers cannot be simply transferred from one cultural context into the next and be expected to be just as successful in the new environment (Son, 2005). Quality of teaching and learning cannot be standardized across cultures, as it is relative (Byram, 1997; Hofstede, 1997).

It is clear that learning is very influenced by culture. In settings where the teacher–student relationship is characterized by a high index in power distance (Hofstede, 1980), classroom communication, for example, might look very different compared to settings where the power distance index is low. This will influence the special characteristics of what *good* communication looks like. We must also be aware that this index may change over time. There are many factors that need to be considered in relation to good language learning. These factors belong to the "software of the mind" (Hofstede, 1997) or the "silent language" (Hall, 1959) and include learning attitudes, learning motivation, and values attributed to learning as well as values associated with learning and education in society. Furthermore, they entail attitudes toward a learning culture based on creative and autonomous learning on the one hand, versus teacher-directed rote learning on the other.

Today we know that culture as well as other learner variables determine whether a language learner has a strong drive to communicate and to learn from communication or not. Culture influences whether learners are inhibited or not, whether and how much they practice and so on. The cultural factor also shapes attitudes towards the role of giftedness and aptitude in society, for instance, whether aptitude is seen merely as an individual factor with personal rights as opposed to a social factor connected to duties for the society. All of these factors may affect the way individual students behave in a learning situation and may require different approaches on the part of the teacher.

Questions for further research

From the research to date, it seems reasonable to generalize that learners from all cultural-ethnic-national backgrounds can be good language learners. It is important for teachers to remember that culture influences learner characteristics and behavior such as prior knowledge and prior experience, learning style, beliefs, motivation, strategies, autonomy, and attitudes towards a particular learning situation. Ongoing research is still required into the relationships among these multiple factors and how they can best be managed in a teaching/learning situation so that learners may derive maximum benefit.

Recent research shows that we have to rethink what we first thought was typical of good language learners. It is not enough to ask "What can the good language learner teach us?" First, we must ask "What is a good language learner?" In this globalizing age the answer to this question is not as straightforward as we might once have thought. The characteristics of "good" and "successful" language learning have to be reconsidered in the light of cultural values.

Conclusion

An "all-inclusive" (Crystal, 1997, p. 75) package is not an option in language teaching and learning once we take personal and cultural diversity into account. There is neither one single method nor one theory that can predict students' learning success in a comprehensive way and still do justice to the miscellany of learners in our classrooms or other learning situations. Individual and cultural diversity influence language learning decisions and choices. They also affect the construct of learning success which needs to be defined according to the learners' sociocultural backgrounds, their values, their attitudes to learning, the specific goals set and the methods applied. Much work remains to be done. The insights from studies may never have been gained if it had not been for the highly valuable discussion around the good language learner initiated by Rubin more than 30 years ago.

References

Banya, K. and Cheng, M.H. (1997) Beliefs About Foreign Language Learning: A Study of Beliefs of Teachers' and Students' Cross Cultural Settings. Paper presented at the Annual Meeting of the Teachers of English to Speakers of Other languages, 11–15 March, 1997. Orlando, FL: ERIC ED411691.

Bhabha, H.K. (1994) *The Location of Culture.* London: Routledge.

Bhabha, H.K. (1996) Culture's in-between. In: S. Hall, and P.D. Gay (eds.). *Questions of Cultural Identity.* London: Sage, 53–60.

Brown, A. (1994) The advancement of learning. *Educational Researcher,* 23(8), 4–12.

Byram, M. (1997) *Teaching and Assessing Intercultural Communicative Competence.* Clevedon: Multilingual Matters.

Crystal, D. (1997) *The Cambridge Encyclopedia of Language,* second edition. Cambridge: University Press.

Elder, C. (1996) The effect of language background on "Foreign" language test performance: the case of Chinese, Italian, and Modern Greek. *Language Learning* 46(2), 233–282.

Finkbeiner, C. (1998) The promotion of explicit and implicit learning strategies: a necessary aim? *Erfurt Electronic Studies in English.* (Retrieved November 9, 2004 from: http://webdoc.sub.gwdg.de/edoc/ia/eese/artic98/finkb/10_98.html).

Finkbeiner, C. (2003) What teachers think about how students read. In: B.D. Biase (ed.) *Developing a Second Language. Acquisition, Processing and Pedagogy Issues in Arabic, Chinese, English, Italian, Japanese and Swedish. Australian Studies in Language Acquisition (ASLA), 10.* Melbourne: Language Australia, 73–94.

Finkbeiner, C. (2005) *Interessen und Strategien beim fremdsprachlichen Lesen. Wie Schülerinnen und Schüler englische Texte lesen und verstehen. [Interests and Strategies in Foreign Language Reading. How Students Read and Comprehend English Texts.]* Tübingen: Narr.

Finkbeiner, C. (2006) Constructing third space together: the principles of reciprocity and cooperation. In P. Ruggiano Schmidt and C. Finkbeiner (eds.), *The ABC's of Cultural Understanding and Communication: National and International Adaptations.* Greenwich, CT: Information Age Publishing, 19–42.

Finkbeiner, C. and Koplin, C. (2002) A cooperative approach for facilitating intercultural education. *Reading Online,* 6(3), (Retrieved July 25, 2005 from: http://www.readingonline.org/newliteracies/lit_index.asp?HREF5finkbeiner/index.html).

Griffiths, C. (2003) *Language Learning Strategy Use and Proficiency.* (Retrieved from: http://www.umi.com/umi/dissertations/).

Hall, E.T. (1959) *The Silent Language.* Garden City, NY: Doubleday/Anchor Books.

Hansen-Strain, L. (1989) Orality/literacy and group differences in second-language acquisition. *Language Learning* 39(4), 469–496.

Hofstede, G. (1980) *Culture's Consequences: International Differences in Work Related Values*. Beverly Hills, CA: Sage Publications.

Hofstede, G. (1997) *Cultures and Organizations: Software of the mind. Intercultural Cooperation and its Importance for Survival*. New York: McGraw-Hill.

International Reading Association. (1999) *Using Multiple Methods of Beginning Reading Instruction. A Position Statement of the International Reading Association*. (Retrieved November 20, 2004 from: http://www.reading.org/downloads/positions/ps1033_multiple_methods.pdf).

Kramsch, C. (1993) *Context and Culture in Language Teaching*. Oxford: Oxford University Press.

Kramsch, C. (1998) Between self and other. In V. Berry and A. McNeill (eds.), *Policy and Practice in Language Education*. Hong Kong: University of Hong Kong, Department of Curriculum Studies, 43–62.

Lantolf, J.P. (ed.) (2000) *Sociocultural Theory and Second Language Learning*. Oxford: OUP.

Lutz, R. (1990) Classroom shock: the role of expectations in an instructional setting. In S.E. Alatis (ed.), *Georgetown University Round Table on Languages and Linguistics*. Washington, DC: Georgetown University Press, 144–156.

Piaget, J. (1954) *Construction of Reality in the Child*. London: Routledge and Kegan Paul.

Piaget, J. (1969) *The Mechanisms of Perception*. London: Routledge and Kegan Paul.

Rubin, J. (1975) What the "good language learner" can teach us. *TESOL Quarterly*, 9(1), 41–51.

Schmidt, P.R. (1998) The ABCs of cultural understanding and communication. *Equity and Excellence in Learning*, 31(2), 28–38.

Schmidt, P.R. and Finkbeiner, C. (eds.) (2006a) *The ABCs of Cultural Understanding and Communication: National and International Adaptations*. Greenwich, CT: Information Age Publishing.

Schmidt, P.R. and Finkbeiner, C. (2006b) Introduction: What is the ABC of Cultural Understanding and Communication? In P.R. Schmidt, and C. Finkbeiner (eds.), *The ABCs of Cultural Understanding and Communication: National and International Adaptations*. Greenwich, CT: Information Age Publishing, 1–18.

Schumann, J. (1975) Affective factors and the problem of age in second language acquisition. *Language Learning*, 25(2), 209–235.

Selinker, L. (1972) Interlanguage. *IRAL*, 10(2), 209–231.

Son, Seung-Nam. (2005) Koreanische Schulkultur – dargestellt aus international vergleichender Perspektive. *Zeitschrift für Erziehungswissenschaft*, 1(8), 53–73.

Stavans, A. and Oded, B. (1993) Assessing EFL reading comprehension: the case of Ethiopian learners. *System* 21(4), 481–494.

Stern, H.H. (1983) *Fundamental Concepts of Language Learning*. Oxford: Oxford University Press.

Vygotsky, L.S. (1962) *Thought and Language*. Cambridge, MA: MIT Press.

Vygotsky, L.S. (1978) *Mind in Society*. Cambridge, MA: Harvard University Press.

Weaver, G.R. (1993) Understanding and coping with cross-cultural adjustment stress. In M. Paige (ed.), *Education for the Intercultural Experience*, Second edition. Yarmouth, ME: Intercultural Press, 137–167.

Wilden, E. (2006) The ABCs Online: using voice chats in a transnational foreign language teacher exchange. In P.R. Schmidt and C. Finkbeiner (eds.) (2006). *The ABCs of Cultural Understanding and Communication: National and International Adaptations*. Greenwich, CT: Information Age Publishing, 189–211.

Young, R. (1987) The cultural context of TESOL – a review of research into Chinese classrooms. *RELC Journal*, 19(2), 15–30.

11 Aptitude and good language learners

Leila Ranta

In her paper on the good language learner, Rubin (1975) identified aptitude, motivation, and opportunity as three factors that account for differential success in language learning. With respect to aptitude, she argued that aptitude tests predict success but do not provide sufficient information to guide pedagogical decision making. Instead, she advocated focusing on the strategies used by good language learners. The celebration of the thirtieth anniversary of Rubin's paper provides an excellent vantage point to view the latest developments in language aptitude research and to revisit the issue of how the concept of aptitude can inform pedagogy.

What is aptitude?

The concept of aptitude current at the time Rubin wrote her paper was that of John Carroll (1962, 1981) who saw foreign language aptitude as a stable cognitive characteristic of those individuals who have a knack or talent for learning other languages. It is defined in terms of speed in language learning. The most widely used measure of aptitude today is still the Modern Language Aptitude Test – MLAT (Carroll and Sapon, 1958) which was designed in the post World War II period to select learners who would be best able to profit from short intensive language courses. It has proved to be a consistent predictor of learning outcomes in a wide variety of contexts (for instance, Carroll, 1981; Gardner and Lambert, 1972). However, despite its predictive utility, the MLAT later came to be devalued by teaching practitioners because of its association with the audiolingual method. The emergence of communicative language teaching (CLT) in the 1980s led to a general neglect of aptitude as a factor worth considering. Krashen (1981) expressed a widely held belief that CLT would be able to level the playing field and cancel out the effect of aptitude on learning success. (See Spolsky, 1995; Dörnyei, 2005; Sawyer and Ranta, 2001 for historical overviews of aptitude research).

Carroll's model of aptitude consisted of four components: phonetic coding ability, rote memory, and two components dealing with the ability to carry out grammatical analysis (grammatical sensitivity and inductive language learning ability). More recent scholarship has attempted to reconceptualize the aptitude construct so as to bring it into alignment with current cognitive theory. McLaughlin (1995) was one of the first to suggest that working memory capacity might be what underlies the predictive power of aptitude tests. Working memory represents the memory processes involved in the simultaneous storage and processing of information in real time (Baddeley and Hitch, 1974; Baddeley, 1986, 1990; Harrington and Sawyer, 1992). The test commonly used by cognitive psychologists to measure working memory capacity is the Reading Span Test (Daneman and Carpenter, 1980) in which a subject is asked to read successive sentences in a set while simultaneously remembering the final word of each sentence. Miyake and Friedman (1998) found that Japanese learners' working memory predicted how native-like their performance was on a measure of syntactic processing in English. Yoshimura (2001) found correlations between aptitude test scores and working memory span. Although these suggest some exciting possibilities, further studies are needed to determine whether working memory is indeed the central component of aptitude as claimed by Miyake and Friedman (1998).

A different approach to reconceptualizing aptitude is found in the work of Grigorenko, Sternberg, and Ehrman (2000) who have developed a new aptitude test, the CANAL-F (Cognitive Ability for Novelty in Acquisition of Language – Foreign) based on the view that a central ability underlying successful language learning is the ability to cope with novelty and ambiguity. The CANAL-F test simulates language learning using an artificial language called Ursulu, testing learners' ability to acquire vocabulary, comprehend extended text, extract grammatical rules and make semantic inferences. The results of the initial validation study look promising: university students' scores on the CANAL-F test correlated with those on the MLAT and with instructor ratings of the students' communication and writing skills, knowledge of vocabulary, overall knowledge and ability to master the target language.

Other reconceptualizations build upon Carroll's model of aptitude in the light of current views of the cognitive processes involved in second language acquisition. Skehan (1998, 2002) has argued that the components of aptitude relate to specific stages in the acquisition process. Thus, phonemic coding ability plays an important role in the early stage where noticing takes place while grammatical sensitivity is most relevant at later stages when patterning takes place; memory becomes very important in the final lexicalizing stage when fluency is achieved. Given ongoing developments in our understanding of the cognitive processes involved in language learning, new components will need to be added to the aptitude model (Skehan, 2002; Dörnyei and Skehan, 2003).

Robinson (2001, 2002) has reconceptualized the components of aptitude into a hierarchical arrangement of *aptitude complexes*, which are combinations of aptitude variables that jointly influence learning in particular situations. Instead of talking about a learner's overall aptitude, Robinson proposes elements of aptitude, such as "aptitude for focus on form via recasts", which is made up of the ability to "notice the gap" and "memory for contingent speech", which consists of a learner's own utterances along with an interlocutor's recasts. In turn, the ability to notice the gap is made up of the metacomponents of perceptual speed and pattern recognition, while memory for contingent speech is made up of working memory capacity and speed of working memory. This more differentiated view of aptitude promises to offer a better framework for investigating how aptitude influences learners' uptake of specific instructional activities.

Aptitude research

Following Carroll, there were few new developments in aptitude research in the 1970s and 1980s with the notable exception of the work of Skehan (1986a, 1986b, 1989). His 1989 book brought attention to the study of individual differences in language acquisition in general and to aptitude in particular. One of the most significant of his contributions during this period was the Bristol Follow-up Study which revealed a connection between first language development and aptitude for other languages. The Bristol study (Wells, 1985) involved 128 children who were studied in the first few years of life. Skehan was able to test these children a decade later when they had begun learning another language in school. What he found was that many of the first language developmental measures such as vocabulary size at 39 months or mean length of utterance at 42 months correlated significantly with scores on various aptitude subtests. The aptitude test scores also correlated with home environment measures associated with the development of decontextualized language. These findings confirm the notion of language aptitude as a stable trait of the individual, as Carroll had posited, but also indicate that it is influenced by experience. In other words, both nature and nurture determine language learning aptitude. A second important contribution by Skehan (1989) was the notion of aptitude-based learner profiles. Hypothetically, a learner can be strong, weak, or average on any of the components of aptitude. These profiles are then likely to have an impact on how the learner responds to different types of instruction. So far, the memory-oriented and the analysis-oriented profiles have been identified in different learner populations (Skehan, 1986a; Wesche,

144

1981; Harley and Hart, 1997) but further research is needed to examine how different aptitude profiles interact with instruction.

Although many still view aptitude test scores as only being relevant in audiolingual or grammar oriented language classrooms, Sawyer and Ranta (2001) show that aptitude measures have predicted learning outcomes in a wide range of contexts, including French immersion classes (Harley and Hart, 1997, 2002), communicative language classrooms (Ehrman and Oxford, 1995), and laboratory experiments of implicit learning (de Graaff, 1997; Robinson, 1997). Of these, the study by Ehrman and Oxford (1995) is worthy of note since it was conducted in the Foreign Service Institute (FSI) context where the MLAT was first trialed. The study examined relationships between a wide variety of learner variables (aptitude, learning strategies, learning styles, personality traits, motivation, and anxiety) and proficiency ratings in speaking and reading a foreign language. The learners were US government employees (N = 282) who had participated in intensive language instruction that was largely communicative but also included some features of audiolingual teaching such as drills and dialogues. Ehrman and Oxford found that the MLAT and an aptitude rating by the instructor were the variables that were most strongly correlated with the FSI ratings of speaking and reading. These proficiency measures correlated with the MLAT as a whole at .50, which is in keeping with the ranges found by Carroll during the audiolingual era.

A review of recent scholarship on aptitude would be incomplete without reference to the large body of research on the phonological problems of at-risk students carried out by Sparks, Ganschow, and their colleagues (see reviews in Sparks and Ganschow, 2001). They have documented the connection between first and other language difficulties. For example, Sparks, Ganschow, Javorsky, Pohlman, and Patton (1992) studied three groups of American high school students: those who were identified as being low risk for failing their first semester in a foreign language, those who were identified as being at high risk for failure, and those identified as learning disabled. Despite average or above average cognitive ability, high-risk learners had problems performing tasks such as correcting spelling and punctuation errors, and identifying isolated words in English. There were, however, no significant differences on tasks involving semantic processing such as reading comprehension. The authors conclude that the difficulties of at-risk students reflect problems with phonological and syntactic processing across languages. Recent work by the Sparks and Ganschow team has demonstrated the benefits of a multisensory structured learning approach for at-risk and learning-disabled students.

Implications for the teaching/learning situation

A useful starting point for discussion of the pedagogical relevance of aptitude is Cook (2001, pp. 125–126). He outlines four possible ways in which teachers can use information about learners' aptitude to:

1 select students who are likely to succeed at language learning;
2 stream students into different classes;
3 provide different teaching for different types of aptitude;
4 excuse students with low aptitude from language instruction.

Options 1 and 4 involve the selection of who does or does not get to participate in language instructional programs. Although Cook argues that the first option is not ethical in countries where education is open to all, it is the case that the Canadian and American government language training programs use the MLAT, along with other instruments, to select suitable candidates for language instruction, since selecting individuals who are likely to be fast and successful language learners ensures that government programs are accountable for their spending (Ehrman, 1998; Wesche, 1981). Option 4 has been addressed extensively in the foreign language teaching literature by Sparks and colleagues (2005). In second language contexts, as opposed to foreign language settings, learners need to acquire proficiency in order to function in daily life and therefore exemption from learning is not the solution. This is where options 2 and 3 are clearly important considerations.

Options 2 and 3 refer to two different types of accommodation to learner aptitude differences by either streaming fast and slow learners on the basis of an overall aptitude score, or by providing instruction attuned to the particular aptitude profile of each learner. Cook himself presents a rather pessimistic view of the viability of option 3, commenting that it would be a luxury to be able to offer varied exercises or parallel classes for students with different needs. An example of how parallel classes can work is provided by Wesche (1981). At that time, the public service commission of Canada offered three types of language instruction to federal civil servants undergoing language training: learners were placed in a class taught using either an analytic, functional, or audio-visual approach depending on their aptitude profile. To be feasible, streaming of this type requires a sufficiently large student population and considerable human and financial resources. Clearly, in most contexts, the more practical solution is to assign teachers the responsibility of adjusting instruction to accommodate learner aptitude profiles. It is not unreasonable to expect teachers to do this since it is a role that is consistent with the principle of learner-centeredness that is central to communicative language teaching (Nunan, 1999). Furthermore, activity types

146

associated with communicative language teaching such as task-based learning and the use of group work structures enable individualization of instruction to learners with varying aptitude profiles within the same classroom.

Individualized instruction can be designed according to either a matching or a compensatory principle. An example of instruction that matched the strengths (or weaknesses) of learners is the Canadian language training program where analytic learners received instruction that emphasized grammatical explanations whereas individuals with auditory and memory abilities were placed in the functional class where instruction emphasized oral activities involving interpersonal situations (Wesche, 1981). In contrast, in compensatory individualized instruction, students are assigned special activities to help them develop in areas of weakness (Rivers and Melvin, 1981). Skehan (1998, 2002) has argued, it is preferable to use compensatory rather than matching individualized instruction for aptitudinal weaknesses because the components of aptitude relate to specific stages in the acquisition process. The following examples illustrate how instructional activities can address the specific needs of two different aptitude profiles.

Helping the less analytic learner figure out the rules

Skehan (1998, p. 204) defines language analytic ability as "the capacity to infer rules of language and make linguistic generalizations or extrapolations". He argues that analytic ability is likely to be particularly important in naturalistic settings where the learner has to impose structure on the input unaided. In such a communication-oriented setting the relationship between learners' analytic abilities and their performance on a range of language proficiency measures was examined (Ranta, 1998, 2002). The learners were all francophone children in grade 6 studying in an English program in Quebec that provided 5 months of intensive language instruction in a single academic year (Lightbown and Spada, 1994). The communicative program provided opportunities for learners to develop their oral fluency in English through oral activities such as games, puzzles, surveys, interviews, presentations, and discussions which were organized around themes relevant to the interests of students. Focus on grammatical form was rare in these classes. Consistent with Skehan's claim, the "good language learners" demonstrated the ability to handle a variety of analytic and decontextualized tasks despite the fact that the instructional content did not promote the development of such skills. A follow-up analysis of the oral production from a subset of those learners (Ranta, 2005) revealed an interesting pattern. Those learners identified as being analytic had progressed more quickly to the higher stages of interlanguage development than learners labelled as being "less analytic". The two groups were not, however, very different on the fluency measures of their speech.

The aim of remediation for less analytic learners is to help them to extract information about linguistic structure from the communicative input and thus "see the trees in the forest". An example of the type of instructional material that can do this comes from a study by White and Ranta (2002) which focused on the third person possessive determiners *his/her* in English. Students were first explicitly taught a rule for deciding when to use the possessive determiners *his* and *her*. The basis upon which a speaker chooses which form to use is very different in French and English and appears to develop in a stage-like manner among francophone learners of English. Typically learners begin using the forms interchangeably or overgeneralize one form before they sort out when each form is to be used. Students were first explicitly taught a "rule of thumb" for deciding when to use *his* and *her*. Presentation of the rule of thumb was followed by a type of consciousness-raising task (Fotos and Ellis, 1991) in which learners, working in cooperative groups, completed a cloze passage where the determiners had been deleted. Each member of the group had to say which form should go into the blank and provide a reason with reference to the rule, and then the group had to come to an agreement about the correct answers. The class did these activities for 30 minutes once a week for five weeks. After this period, oral testing indicated that all of the students had progressed to higher stages in interlanguage development as compared to learners in the Comparison class.

The benefit of instruction is exemplified by the case of Student 17 from the Comparison class. At the end of five months of instruction in the intensive ESL class, this learner had 0% accuracy on his use of the possessive determiners and clearly had not figured out what the forms meant. In the example below, Student 17 and the researcher are discussing a sentence in a written text in which the possessive determiner *her* is incorrect.

> Sentence: *His mother is showing **her** the candles on David's birthday cake.*
>
> S: I change, uh, her for, uh, his because I think it's, uh, his because is, uh, more than one candle, I think.
> R: Mm hm.
> S: I think, uh, I don't know, but, uh, I was thinking, his is for the plural
> R: Mm hm
> S: and, uh, the her, um, uh, is for the, the only, just one.
> R: Mm hm.
> S: Uh, I think is not that.

In contrast, Student 4 in the Rule group moved from stage 1 to stage 7 over the five week period of the experiment. He used *his/her* in his oral production with 80% accuracy and was able to use the rule of thumb to explain why a particular form was correct or not. The effectiveness of this intervention suggests that it provided information about how English grammar works that was accessible to all of the learners. And since it was a relatively brief communicative task making use of engaging texts, even the good language learners who could figure out the rule on their own appeared to be happy doing them.

Helping learners with weak phonological skills to encode sounds and words in an unknown language

A number of researchers have pointed to the importance of auditory abilities as a predictor of success in language learning in the classroom (for instance, Pimsleur, Sundland, and Comfrey, 1964). In the original model of aptitude, phonetic coding ability is defined as the "ability to identify distinct sounds, to form associations between those sounds and symbols representing them, and to retain these associations" (Carroll, 1981, p. 105). This ability includes a special type of memory for phonetic material. This ability is implicated in segmenting speech into words, syllables, and phonemes, and in associating such segments with graphemic counterparts. Skehan (1998) describes this ability as being important for processing auditory input in real time so that it can be passed on to subsequent stages of processing. Furthermore, it is especially important at the earliest stages of language learning in informal learning settings where the main task facing the learner is vocabulary acquisition. The difficulties faced by learners with poor phonemic coding ability are described by Wesche (1981, p. 131):

> Classroom manifestations of difficulties [. . .] include the jumping of syllables or words, and slowness in putting sentences together when speaking the target language; momentary forgetting of the meanings of familiar French words, and production of "one-by one" word strings without "integrating" them into phrases.

For learners weak in phonological skills, a multisensory structured learning approach where learners see, hear and write the language simultaneously can be useful. It is an approach that emphasizes the direct and explicit teaching of spelling–sound relationships and of morphology and syntax (Sparks and Miller, 2000). Sounds and grammar concepts are introduced one at a time. Lessons are sequenced from simple to more complex and include continual review of previously learned letters and sounds. The most important feature of this approach is that new

149

Table 1 A Multisensory structured language lesson

Activity	Time (in minutes)	Description
Sound drills	10–15	Teacher models a new sound while writing it on the board and students repeat while looking at the letter; then they write the sound while saying it aloud. Simple words with the target sound are introduced using the same procedure. Flash cards are then used to review sound–letter correspondances.
Introduction and review of grammatical concepts	10	Teacher explains the new grammar concept in students' own language. Then the rule is explained and modeled in the target language. Students "act out" the language, for example, by having students represent the words in a sentence that are transformed by an operation such as negation.
Introduction and review of vocabulary	10	Students hear, see, and read, and say words repeatedly until they are learned.
Communicative activities	10	Students use the target language vocabulary and grammar they have learned by reading and listening to texts, and engaging in interactive pairwork (e.g., role play, question and answer).

material is always presented such that students use their visual, auditory, and tactile-kinesthetic skills. This means that they pronounce the sounds and write at the same time. Table 1 provides an illustration of what a multisensory structured lesson looks like (based on Sparks, Ganschow, Kenneweg, and Miller, 1991; Sparks and Miller, 2000). This approach was found to be effective with students who were at risk of failing their Spanish course (Sparks, Artzer, Patton, Ganschow, Miller, Hordubay, and Walsh, 1998). Not only did they outperform at-risk students who received traditional instruction, they were not significantly different from the not-at-risk students.

Questions for ongoing research

What are language teachers actually doing to adapt instruction for learners with different aptitude profiles? This is a question which has not been adequately addressed in the language teaching research literature. Bell (2005) surveyed over 400 American university teachers of German, French, and Spanish about their teaching practices and found considerable uncertainty about how to deal with individual differences. For example, in response to the item "Foreign language learners should be put into groups of fast and slow learners", 20% agreed, 57% disagreed and 22% were uncertain. More research is required to determine the most effective ways of dealing with students of varying levels of aptitude.

Horwitz (2000) notes that although there is a long history of calls for individualizing instruction (for instance, Handschin, 1919), there are few reports of relevant empirical research concerning the practices of teachers. We know that experienced teachers think about how to address learners' needs during teaching (Gatbonton, 1999) and that novice teachers struggle with how to do this (Numrich, 1996). Ehrman (1996) notes that the complexity of the task of diagnosing and addressing learners' difficulties cannot be dealt with by means of magic formulas. Her book provides one of the few guides to help teachers understand and diagnose learner difficulties. But in order to develop adequate guidance for novice teachers, we need to have a better picture of what constrains teachers' abilities to provide remedial instruction based on aptitude strengths and the nature of decision-making when teachers do individualize instructional activities. Clearly both qualitative and quantitative situated research on accommodating learner differences is called for.

Conclusion

The discussion in this chapter has focused on the aspects of the aptitude literature that are particularly pertinent to teaching and to the relationship between aptitude and good language learners. In this chapter, I have sought to challenge the still quite prevalent view that aptitude is undemocratic and irrelevant to language learners and teachers. There has been a tendency over the years for scholars and practitioners alike to equate aptitude with a score on the MLAT rather than as an ability that could be measured in different ways. Rather than being merely a score on a test associated with audiolingual teaching, a learner's aptitude reflects strengths and weaknesses in a range of cognitive abilities that underlie the language development process and which interact with other factors such as motivation and opportunity.

Teachers committed to the principle of learner-centeredness should therefore address not only the real-life goals and learning preferences of students but also their cognitive processing needs. It is admittedly a daunting prospect. Nevertheless, accommodating the aptitude profiles of their learners is one way that teachers can provide instruction that will help their students become the best language learners they can be.

References

Baddeley, A.D. (1986) *Working Memory*. Oxford: Clarendon Press.

Baddeley, A.D. (1990) *Human Memory: Theory and Practice*. Hove: Erlbaum.

Baddeley, A.D. and Hitch, G. J. (1974) Working memory. In G. Bower (ed.), *The Psychology of Learning and Motivation*, Vol. 8. New York: Academic Press, 47–90.

Bell, J. (1988) *Teaching Multilevel Classes in ESL*. Markham, Ontario, Canada: Pippin.

Bell, T. (2005). Behaviors and attitudes of effective foreign language teachers: results of a questionnaire study. *Foreign Language Annals*, 38, 259–270.

Carroll, J.B. (1962) The prediction of success in intensive foreign language training. In R. Glaser (ed.), *Training Research and Education*. Pittsburgh, PA: University of Pittsburgh Press, 87–136.

Carroll, J.B. (1981) Twenty-five years of research on foreign language aptitude. In K.C. Diller (ed.), *Individual Differences and Universals in Language Learning Aptitude*. Rowley, MA: Newbury House, 83–118.

Carroll, J.B. and Sapon, S. (1958) *The Modern Language Aptitude Test – Form A*. New York: The Psychological Corporation.

Cook, V.J. (2001). *Second Language Learning and Language Teaching*, third edition. London: Edward Arnold.

Daneman, M. and Carpenter, P. (1980) Individual differences in working memory and reading. *Journal of Verbal Learning and Verbal Behavior*, 19, 450–466.

de Graaff, R. (1997) The eXperanto experiment: effects of explicit instruction on second language acquisition. *Studies in Second Language Acquisition*, 19, 249–275.

Dörnyei, Z. (2005) *The Psychology of the Language Learner*. Mahwah, NJ: Erlbaum.

Dörnyei, Z. and Skehan, P. (2003) Individual differences in second language learning. In C. Doughty and M. Long (eds.), *Handbook of Second Language Acquisition*. Malden, MA: Blackwell, 589–630.

Ehrman, M.E. (1996) *Understanding Second Language Learning Difficulties*. Thousand Oaks, CA: Sage.

Ehrman, M.E. (1998). The Modern Language Aptitude Test for predicting learning success and advising students. *Applied Language Learning*, 9, 31–70.

Ehrman, M.E. and Oxford, R.L. (1995) Cognition plus: correlates of language learning success. *Modern Language Journal*, 79, 67–89.

Ellis, R. (2005) Principles of instructed language learning. *System*, 33, 209–224.

Fotos, S. and Ellis, R. (1991) Communicating about grammar: a task-based approach. *TESOL Quarterly*, 25, 605–28.

Gardner, R. and Lambert, W. (1972) *Attitudes and Motivation in Second Language Learning*. Rowley, MA: Newbury House.

Gatbonton, E. (1999) Investigating experienced ESL teachers' pedagogical knowledge. *Modern Language Journal*, 83, 35–50.

• Grigorenko, E., Sternberg, R., and Ehrman, M.E. (2000) A theory-based approach to the measurement of foreign language learning ability: the Canal-F theory and test. *Modern Language Journal*, 84, 390–405.

Handschin, C.H. (1919) Individual differences and supervised study. *Modern Language Journal*, 3, 158–173.

Harley, B. and Hart, D. (1997) Language aptitude and second language proficiency in classroom learners of different starting ages. *Studies in Second Language Acquisition*, 19, 3, 379–400.

Harley, B. and Hart, D. (2002) Age, aptitude, and second language learning on a bilingual exchange. In P. Robinson (ed.), *Individual Differences and Instructed Language Learning*. Amsterdam/Philadelphia: John Benjamins, 301–330.

Harrington, M. and Sawyer, M. (1992) L2 working memory capacity and L2 reading skill. *Studies in Second Language Acquisition*, 14, 25–38.

Horwitz, E. (2000) Teachers and students, students and teachers: an ever-evolving partnership. *Modern Language Journal*, 84, 523–535.

Krashen, S.D. (1981) Aptitude and attitude in relation to second language acquisition and learning. In K.C. Diller (ed.), *Individual Differences and Universals in Language Learning Aptitude*. Rowley, MA: Newbury House, 155–175.

Lightbown, P.M. and Spada, N. (1994) An innovative program for primary ESL in Quebec. *TESOL Quarterly*, 28, 563–579.

McLaughlin, B. (1995) Aptitude from an information-processing perspective. *Language Testing*, 12, 370–387.

Miyake, A. and Friedman, N.F. (1998) Individual differences in second language proficiency: working memory as "language aptitude". In A.F. Healy and L.E. Bourne (eds.), *Foreign Language Learning: Psycholinguistic Studies on Training and Retention*. Mahwah, NJ: Erlbaum.

Nunan, D. (1999) *Second Language Teaching and Learning*. Boston, MA: Heinle & Heinle.

Numrich, C. (1996) On becoming a language teacher. *TESOL Quarterly*, 30, 131–153.

Pimsleur, P., Sundland, D., and Comfrey, R. (1964) Underachievement in foreign language learning. *IRAL*, 2, 113–150.

Ranta, L. (1998) *Focus on form from the inside: the significance of grammatical sensitivity for L2 learning in communicative ESL classrooms*. Unpublished PhD. Dissertation, Concordia University, Montreal.

Ranta, L. (2002) The role of learners' language analytic ability in the communicative classroom. In P. Robinson (ed.), *Individual Differences and Instructed Language Learning*. Amsterdam/Philadelphia: John Benjamins, 159–180.

Ranta, L. (2005) Language analytic ability and oral production in a second language: is there a connection? In A. Housen and M. Pierrard (eds.),

Investigations in Instructed Second Language Acquisition. Berlin/New York: Mouton de Gruyter, 99–130.

Rivers, W. and Melvin, B. (1981) Language learners as individuals: discovering their needs, wants, and learning styles. In J. Alatis, H. Altman, and P. Alatis (eds.), *The Second Language Classroom*. New York: Oxford University Press, 81–93.

Robinson, P. (1997) Individual differences and the fundamental similarity of implicit and explicit adult second language learning. *Language Learning*, 47, 45–99.

Robinson, P. (2001) Individual differences, cognitive abilities, aptitude complexes and learning conditions in second language acquisition. *Second Language Research*, 17, 368–392.

Robinson, P. (2002) Learning conditions, aptitude complexes and SLA: a framework for research and pedagogy. In P. Robinson (ed.), *Individual Differences and Instructed Language Learning*. Amsterdam/Philadelphia: John Benjamins, 113–133.

Rubin, J. (1975) What the "good language learner" can teach us. *TESOL Quarterly*, 9(1), 41–51.

Sawyer, M. and Ranta, L. (2001) Aptitude, individual differences and L2 instruction. In P. Robinson (ed.), *Cognition and Second Language Instruction*. Cambridge: Cambridge University Press, 319–353.

Skehan, P. (1986a) Cluster analysis and the identification of learner types. In V.J. Cook (ed.), *Experimental Approaches to Second Language Acquisition*. Oxford: Pergamon, 81–94.

Skehan, P. (1986b) The role of foreign language aptitude in a model of school learning. *Language Testing*, 3, 188–221.

Skehan, P. (1989) *Individual Differences in Second Language Learning*. London: Edward Arnold.

Skehan, P. (1998) *A Cognitive Approach to Language Learning*. Oxford: Oxford University Press.

Skehan, P. (2002) Theorising and updating aptitude. In P. Robinson (ed.), *Individual Differences and Instructed Language Learning*. Amsterdam/Philadelphia: John Benjamins, 69–93.

Sparks, R. and Ganschow, L. (2001) Aptitude for learning a foreign language. *Annual Review of Applied Linguistics*, 21, 90–111.

Sparks, R. and Miller, K. (2000) Teaching a foreign language using multisensory structured language techniques to at-risk learners: a review. *Dyslexia*, 6, 124–132.

Sparks, R., Javorsky, J., and Ganschow, L. (2005) Should the Modern Language Aptitude Test be used to determine course substitutions for and waivers of the foreign language requirement? *Foreign Language Annals*, 38(2), 201–210.

Sparks, R., Ganschow, L., Kenneweg, S., and Miller, K. (1991) Use of an Orton-Gillingham approach to teach a foreign language to dyslexic/learning-disabled students: explicit teaching of phonology in a second language. *Annals of Dyslexia*, 41, 96–118.

Sparks, R., Ganschow, L., Javorsky, J., Pohlman, J., and Patton, J. (1992) Test comparisons among students identified as high-risk, low-risk, and learning-disabled in high school foreign language courses. *Modern Language Journal*, 76, 142–159.

Sparks, R., Artzer, M., Patton, J., Ganschow, L., Miller, K., Hordubay, D., and Walsh, G. (1998) Benefits of a multisensory structured language instruction for at-risk foreign language learners: a comparison study of high school Spanish students. *Annals of Dyslexia*, 48, 239–270.

Spolsky, B. (1995) Prognostication and language aptitude testing, 1925–62. *Language Testing*, 12, 321–340.

Wells, C.G. (1985) *Language Development in the Pre-school Years*. Cambridge: Cambridge University Press.

Wesche, M.B. (1981) Language aptitude measures in streaming, matching students with methods, and diagnosis of learning problems. In K.C. Diller (ed.), *Individual Differences and Universals in Language Learning Aptitude*. Rowley, MA: Newbury House, 119–154.

White, J. and Ranta, L. (2002) Examining the interface between metalinguistic task performance and oral production in a second language. *Language Awareness*, 11, 259–290.

Yoshimura, Y. (2001) The role of working memory in language aptitude. In X. Bonch-Bruevich, W.J. Crawford, J. Hellermann, C. Higgins, and H. Nguyen (eds.), *The Past, Present, and Future of Second Language Research*. Somerville, MA: Cascadilla Press, 144–163.

Part II: Learning variables

12 Vocabulary and good language learners[*]

Jo Moir and Paul Nation

At one time the teaching of vocabulary was unfashionable, and it was widely assumed that lexical acquisition could be left to look after itself (Nation, 1990). More recent years, however, have seen renewed recognition of the importance of vocabulary when learning a new language (Griffiths, 2003, 2006). Dating back to around the time that Rubin's article on the good language learner was published in 1975, there has been a more learner-focused view of education. In line with this perspective, there has been increasing interest not only in what is being learnt, but also in language learners themselves, and how they approach the task of learning.

In order to take control of their vocabulary learning, learners need to know what vocabulary to learn, how to go about learning it, and how to assess and monitor their progress. This vocabulary requires a range of learning strategies, such as learning the vocabulary of the subject area (Chung, 2003; Chung and Nation, 2003; Coxhead, 2000) or guessing from context (Nagy, Herman and Anderson, 1985). There are also deliberate learning strategies such as word part analysis, learning using word cards and dictionary use (Nation, 2001) that are important shortcuts to vocabulary growth. Corson (1997), furthermore, argues that new vocabulary needs to be learned both receptively and productively because it is by productive use of such vocabulary that learners signal that they have become part of their particular communities.

The participants in the study reported in this chapter were interviewed in the hope of shedding some light on their personal approach to learning tasks, on their beliefs about learning, and on how effective they were at learning vocabulary. Aspects of word knowledge were investigated, as well as strategies for selecting, revising, self-evaluating, monitoring, learning and memorizing.

[*]Text adapted from *Prospect 17*, 1, 2002, 15–35 with permission from The National Centre for English Teaching and Research. Copyright © Macquarie University, Australia.

The study

This study hoped to determine the extent to which learners were willing (or able) to personalize their own approach to tasks within a curriculum by adapting tasks to meet their own learning needs and preferred learning style, and the extent to which they were successful in their vocabulary learning endeavours.

Participants

The participants in this study were adult students enrolled in an intensive English course for speakers of other languages (ESOL) at a New Zealand university. The task investigated was part of a vocabulary development programme that ran for the duration of the course, and was chosen because it was believed that its continuous nature would allow the participants time to reflect on the task and their own part in the learning process. The vocabulary programme was designed to increase learner awareness of what is involved in vocabulary learning, and to improve productive vocabulary. Learners were required to study between 30 and 40 words of their own choosing each week, using a vocabulary notebook issued to all learners at the beginning of the course. The vocabulary notebook had columns to complete for each word, requiring information relating to pronunciation, meaning, grammatical use, collocations, a sentence containing the target word, and other items from the same word family. Progress in vocabulary learning was monitored through a weekly test, in which learners were required to demonstrate their knowledge of the words they chose to study.

At the beginning of the programme, students were given instruction in a number of vocabulary learning strategies, such as the key-word technique and the use of word cards. Learners were also provided with information giving advice on how to choose vocabulary to study. It was believed that allowing learners to select their own vocabulary would be beneficial in two ways: firstly, self-selecting vocabulary would allow individual learners to focus on vocabulary suited to their own needs and, secondly, selecting their own words would result in increased motivation to learn. A brief profile of each student (whose names have been changed for privacy reasons) is provided in Table 1.

Data collection and analysis

Most of the participants for this study had a receptive vocabulary of between 3,000 and 5,000 words, as tested by Nation's *Vocabulary Levels*

Table 1 The learners involved in the study

Informant	Country of origin	Age/gender	Total years studying English	Years in English-speaking country
Mohamed	Bangladesh	32/M	14.0	0.7
Masa	Japan	23/M	5.0	1.7
Natalie	Hong Kong	24/F	11.0	0.3
Haruko	Japan	32/F	6.0	2.0
Kate	China	27/F	7.0	0.3
Sandy	Korea	27/F	7.0	0.3
Abdi	Somalia	23/M	4.0	0.4
Jack	Korea	20/M	6.0	0.8
Debbie	Sri Lanka	24/F	2.0	0.3
Sun ae	Korea	22/F	6.0	0.4

Test (1990) at the beginning of the programme. They were interviewed in order to elicit information relating to current vocabulary learning behaviour and beliefs about vocabulary learning. The interview was divided into three parts.

Part 1 – Vocabulary learning within the programme

The first part of the interview was intended to elicit information from each of the participants relating to their personal approach to learning vocabulary within the context of the programme. Although all participants were restricted to a certain extent by the confines of the vocabulary learning programme, consisting of a learning notebook and weekly test, it was believed that learners would have a personalized approach to the learning task, adjusted to some extent according to their own needs. Questions in this section of the interview related to aspects of learning, as outlined in Holec's (1981) guidelines for autonomy: personal goal-setting, selection and grading of content, methods and techniques, monitoring and evaluation. It was hoped that responses to these questions would reveal the learners' willingness to make decisions relating to each of these aspects of learning vocabulary in a way that promoted their personal learning.

Part 2 – Other vocabulary learning

The next part of the interview related to participants' vocabulary learning outside the course. It was believed that most participants would have some sort of system for learning vocabulary for personal use. Participants were asked to consider any direct attempts to learn new vocabulary and to describe any strategies or techniques employed. This section of the interview also encouraged participants to consider the relationship between their personal approach to learning and the systematic approach to vocabulary learning used in the course. In the second part of this section, participants were asked about their experience of learning vocabulary in past language courses, in their home country, in New Zealand and in other countries. It was hoped that knowledge of participants' past vocabulary learning experience might provide some insight into current beliefs and behaviour.

Part 3 – Beliefs about vocabulary learning

The third section of the interview related to the participants' personal beliefs about learning vocabulary in a second language. To some extent, most participants had already expressed their beliefs about vocabulary learning in comments made in previous parts of the interview, but this section gave participants the opportunity to expand on ideas and to reflect on their beliefs.

It must be acknowledged that any research method requiring students to describe their own learning behaviour is open to criticism concerning the reliability of the data. It is necessary to consider the possibility that participants are either not sufficiently aware of their own behaviour to offer an accurate description, or have a tendency to direct their responses towards a perceived researcher expectation. One or two of the participants in this study certainly demonstrated a tendency to describe their teachers' instructions rather than their own learning behaviour. However, wherever possible, the researcher deflected such responses and encouraged participants to think more carefully about their actual behaviour and personal beliefs, as is shown in the example below taken from Haruko's interview:

> H: At the beginning of the course J taught us about how to do that. She said we should . . .
> R: OK, that's what J said you should do, can you tell me what you actually do?
> H: (laughs) . . . actually usually I don't do that . . .

In order to increase the reliability of the self-report data, student responses describing behaviour were also supported by examples from notebook work and from vocabulary tests (for more information about the tests, see Moir and Nation, 2002). After the interviews, the data were transcribed and analysed for word selection procedures, aspects of vocabulary knowledge, how vocabulary was learned and memorized, revision practices, and how learning was monitored and self-evaluated.

Findings

While most of the interviews revealed a certain pattern in learner behaviour, one participant, Abdi, differed notably in his approach to the task and in his test results. For this reason, Abdi's behaviour is discussed separately. The behaviour of the other nine learners will be described first.

Nine learners' approaches to vocabulary learning

Analysis of the interview transcripts revealed a surprisingly low level of personalization in the approach that most of the participants were taking to vocabulary learning within the programme. In almost all cases, interviews with the participants revealed limited interaction with the task, and a lack of ownership. Scores from the majority of interview tests conducted with these participants also revealed limited long-term retention of meaning and ability to use items learned for the vocabulary component of the programme.

It is important to stress that the learners spent a considerable amount of time completing the task. Although the time varied from week to week, most participants believed they spent between five and six hours studying vocabulary for the programme. Two participants, Haruko and Sandy, reported spending up to eight or nine hours per week on this task. Interestingly, Abdi, the learner who was approaching the task most effectively, said he spent slightly less time on the task than the other learners: approximately four hours per week. It is clear that these learners were investing a substantial amount of time in this vocabulary development programme, and it is therefore important to investigate how the learners were approaching the task, and how effective the learning really was, in order to determine whether this was time well spent.

Selection of words

Selection of words to be learned each week was the aspect of vocabulary learning in which the participants appeared to demonstrate the least ability to personalize the task, often selecting words that were of limited use or little personal interest. Although some words were selected from a wider range of sources, such as newspapers, personal reading, television or radio, most of the participants elected to select vocabulary from texts presented in class, focusing on academic or "difficult" words. For many, the process of selecting words to study was quite random:

> I don't know this word – I don't know meaning – so I don't know useful or not. I just choose some words I don't know before. This is very popular way for us.
>
> (Haruko)

Although in rare cases participants selected words because of particular personal interest, most of the words chosen in this study were selected purely because they were unknown. Most participants also appeared to place little value on the selection of words to learn, completing this aspect of the task quickly in order to allow time for finding out information about the words and memorizing them for the weekly test:

> I don't have no time to finding the words. Just I open my book and then I just pick up the words.
>
> (Sandy)

Aspects of word knowledge

To a certain extent, information about items to be learned was largely predetermined by the vocabulary workbook with which each student in this programme was expected to work. The need to find such information for each target item was further reinforced by the format of the weekly test. Almost all participants showed a preoccupation with meaning, often at the expense of other crucial aspects of word knowledge. Many of the participants believed that a first language translation of items to be learned was sufficient to enable effective use. Several expressed their lack of interest in depth of word knowledge, stating that aspects of word knowledge such as collocations and other words in the same word family were only learned to fulfil course requirements:

> I need meaning, and then I must fill it [vocabulary learning notebook] with everything. I find everything – collocations and noun, adjective or something, and then family word. Actually, I don't need that, but I have to do because of the test. If I find a word by myself, just meaning is OK for me.
>
> (Sandy)

This apparent lack of value of word knowledge other than meaning was clearly articulated in many of the interviews, demonstrating a general lack of awareness as to how depth of vocabulary knowledge might contribute to ability to use the items both productively and receptively. The participants also often failed to make a connection between depth of word knowledge and their inability to use items communicatively, as is shown in this comment made by Jack in his interview:

> I don't think those things [grammatical information, collocation etc.] is important for me now. Mostly I just find Korea meaning.

The participants were also asked to provide a sentence using each target word for the weekly test. Here again, the majority of the participants demonstrated an unwillingness to personalize the task by creating their own sentences. This approach to learning the target words seemed to have a negative effect on some participants' ability to use the items communicatively. For example, in the case of one of her tested words, Sandy was unable to provide an example of an item in use, because she could not remember the sample sentence she had memorized for the test.

Learning and memorizing words

Rote learning or "memorizing" was the most common strategy used by nine of the ten participants interviewed for this study. All participants spent a considerable amount of time reading over the information recorded in vocabulary learning notebooks, or copying it out several times into larger notebooks. Three of the nine participants also self-tested vocabulary, by covering second-language translations or definitions while reading through the list. Although all students had been instructed on the use of various strategies for learning vocabulary at the beginning of the programme, most of those interviewed had veered away from using these new strategies, preferring to rely on the tried and tested strategy of rote learning. In some cases, the participants had valid arguments for avoiding the use of new vocabulary learning strategies:

> Someone said, you know, find a similar word in my own language, same sound, to help remember, and I tried do that. After that, consequently my English pronunciation become very strange. I don't know, maybe it depend on the people, the student, but [. . .] in my case it make harmful effect for me. I won't do that any more.
>
> (Masa)

A recurrent theme when discussing learning the items chosen was the idea that the words were only learned short term. Many references were made to time constraints in relation to the weekly test and in one case it was explicitly stated that it was only necessary to remember the words for a short time:

> I just memorize that list, reading and writing. It's easy – we have to remember that for just one day.
>
> (Sandy)

While this example is perhaps a little extreme and not representative of the whole group, learning behaviour such as "cramming" on the morning of the weekly test indicates that many of these participants were concerned mostly about remembering the words for the test, rather than as a long-term goal. This is further demonstrated by the general failure to revise items learned after the test.

Revision

Of the nine participants, not one regularly revised words learned in previous weeks, although some recognized the importance of revision and believed lack of it to be contributing to their inability to commit new words to long-term memory. The most common reason cited for failure to revise was lack of time. Participants were busy with other aspects of the programme and revision became less of a priority:

> After the test I am trying to remember and use these words, as because if I don't use this word I can't remember and the word become rusty. But after finishing the test [. . .] each week there is homework for learning next 30 words. I don't get time.
>
> (Mohamed)

Some of the participants believed that teachers should allocate class time to revision of vocabulary, and to follow up vocabulary development by requiring learners to use the new words in writing or speaking.

Self-evaluation and monitoring

Many of the learners believed that they were not learning vocabulary effectively in this part of the programme. It was believed that many of the words had been forgotten, and that they had limited ability to use those words communicatively. Many of the participants attributed their low retention of vocabulary they had studied to the actual words that were selected. Several commented that the words were not useful or relevant to their own lives. Others complained that the words could not be used, making retention of meaning difficult:

> I think it is not very useful because we are memorize for test. Sometimes we forget it – we choose words that are not very common and we forget.
>
> (Debbie)

Interestingly, although selection of words to learn was the aspect of the learning process over which participants had most control, none of these nine participants had made any attempt to alter their selection methods in light of their dissatisfaction with the effects of their current behaviour. This failure to alter personal learning behaviour, even when it is clearly recognized that the system is not working for them personally is perhaps the clearest indication that these learners were not taking responsibility for their own learning, or personalizing the task to meet their own needs.

Case study of an effective vocabulary learner

Abdi, a 23-year-old man from Somalia, was the participant who demonstrated the highest level of responsibility for his own learning. Interestingly, his test results were also considerably higher than any of the other participants (for details, see Moir and Nation, 2002). Abdi's approach to his vocabulary learning, and his beliefs about vocabulary learning demonstrated an awareness both of his own needs and of what is involved in learning vocabulary.

Selection of words

Abdi's process for selecting items to learn was significantly different from the other participants, in that he almost always selected words that were at least partially known:

> Mostly I just choose the words that I already know but I have to improve them or make them clear to me. Or I choose the one that are difficult to me – about how to use them in different situations.

Abdi also chose words to study from a wider range of sources than any of the other participants, selecting words that he found particularly interesting or useful:

> I learn words from talking to people, from TV and from radio. If that word is interesting I write on a small book. I always have a pen and notebook. Later I can put them in this list [vocabulary notebook].

Aspects of word knowledge

Abdi was the only participant to express concerns about levels of knowledge of particular items, demonstrating his awareness of the complexity of knowing a word. Abdi was familiar with the process of looking at different aspects of word knowledge, and placed value on being able to use words appropriately. He was the only participant interviewed who regularly attempted to find out more about the items to learn than was required by the weekly test:

> I try to find out some more sometimes – whether they are spoken, whether they are written, whether informal. Maybe they are old or maybe they are fashion word. I want to know this, so sometimes I find in dictionary, and sometimes I can ask somebody.

Abdi was aware of items having a variety of meanings, usually being able to explain two or more meanings for each of the items tested. He was also aware of the impact that different meanings could have on his own language use:

> If I only know one meaning, or one situation, maybe it's not enough. Maybe I don't understand, or I make a mistake.

Learning and memorizing

Abdi also used a greater range of strategies to learn the words selected each week than any other participant. In addition to a certain amount of re-reading and memorizing, Abdi made flash cards for each word on his list, and carried these cards with him to revise his vocabulary at every available opportunity: while walking, riding on the bus, or having lunch. Abdi made use of small amounts of time to revise his weekly vocabulary. Abdi's other vocabulary learning strategy was to make a direct effort to use those words at every opportunity, in a variety of contexts. He believed that saying the words aloud in a sentence helped him to remember them:

> I try to speak to the native person as much as I can every day [. . .] and try to use new vocabulary [. . .] if I use in different situations I can remember that word. I just talk every day. Sometimes even I talk to myself.

Revision

Like the other participants, Abdi did not make a habit of regularly reviewing all the vocabulary in his notebook, although he did revise any vocabulary that was marked incorrect in the weekly test. However, Abdi did make a consistent effort to use the vocabulary he learned each week in his writing and speaking, constantly reinforcing his understanding of the words and his ability to use them.

Self-evaluation and monitoring

Abdi was the only participant who was confident that he knew all the vocabulary he had learned in the programme, and was able to use each of the words productively, often using more than one meaning of single items. Abdi believed the vocabulary learning programme to be working effectively for him, and was totally happy with his progress. The interview test results confirm Abdi's beliefs relating to the effectiveness of his vocabulary learning.

Explanations

The participants interviewed all wanted to learn vocabulary, and were therefore investing a considerable amount of their study time in developing vocabulary using the programme described. The apparently ineffective approach taken to vocabulary learning by these learners was not due to low motivation or laziness.

Analysis of the interview transcripts revealed a number of possible explanations for the learning behaviour demonstrated by the participants and their failure to personalize the task in order to meet their individual learning needs. These include lack of awareness of what is involved in learning a language and more specifically in learning vocabulary, and the effect of teacher and course expectations (including the weekly tests) on learning.

Language awareness

The learners often showed a limited awareness of their own vocabulary knowledge and of what is involved in knowing a word. Learners often had an inflated idea of their vocabulary size (possibly a result of the test they sat at the beginning of the course) and instead of working a little more on the higher frequency words, learners tended to focus on those that were completely unknown:

> I know first two thousand and three thousand level. I think I have perfect score for that level. I am lucky, I know two thousand and three thousand level already. I have to find some difficult words.
>
> (Mohamed)

Many learners also did not appreciate that knowing a word involves much more than being able to recognise its form and connect it to a meaning. Most of the participants used a very limited range of strategies for vocabulary learning, and many of these reflected their previous learning experience:

> I think course is 85% learning by myself. Teacher not always teach about English in here. This is different from Hong Kong. I suggest teacher can use three hours concentrated teach vocabulary – just use simple English to explain some word meanings.
>
> (Natalie)

The most common strategies were rote learning and copying. Part of the reason for this may relate to the amount of strategy training that the learners received. During the course the learners were introduced to strategies like guessing from context, using word cards, using mnemonic techniques like the keyword technique and word parts, and using dictionaries. But this is not sufficient for effective strategy use. Learners need to not only know about strategies and understand what they involve, but they need to become very comfortable with their use. Until they reach a satisfactory level of comfort with a strategy it is unlikely that they will truly experience its effectiveness and find it as easy to use as their default strategies. Reaching this level of comfort with a strategy involves a considerable investment of time and effort.

Interestingly, Abdi, the most effective of the participants, was the only learner who had been required to choose his own vocabulary to learn in his own country. He was also familiar with the process of learning collocations and grammatical information, emphasising the importance of depth of knowledge. A few participants reported attempts to use new vocabulary creatively and communicatively in their personal learning or also attempted to make connections between new words and prior knowledge when learning vocabulary for personal use:

> Some words it's easy to remember. I try, I can fix that with something I know. But sometimes I can't fix in my mind, so that one just fall out from my head.
>
> (Haruko)

These strategies, however, were not often carried over from learning for personal use to learning within the classroom context.

Teacher/course expectations

In most traditional classroom contexts, the teacher is seen as an authority figure, and learners are generally required to comply with teacher expectations in their learning behaviour. One of the recurring themes in the interview data was the belief that the words that were being studied were not of personal interest to the learners. Although, by selecting their own words to study, learners were theoretically being given the opportunity to personalize the vocabulary development programme to meet their own needs and interests, in fact, learners' choice of words was constrained by implicitly or explicitly stated teacher and course expectations.

> Sometimes I hear a word and I think it is useful. You can use for conversation in every day. But you have to write down in your

vocabulary for test, and I think for teacher this word is too easy, so I just choose some it is difficult and put in my test book.
(Kate)

Implications for the teaching/learning situation

Although the learners in this study were clearly willing workers who spent a lot of time on their learning and were conscientious in completing tasks and preparing for tests, they did not always show the same willingness in personalizing their own learning. There is a big difference between working hard on tasks the teacher has set and shaping the tasks to individual ends. More time may need to be spent on helping learners to decide why they are learning vocabulary and what kind of vocabulary they need to learn. This decision making could involve the teacher working with individuals in personal consultations or small groups, discussing a range of possible goals and working out the appropriate vocabulary to reach these goals. It could involve the teacher modelling a discussion with one learner and then getting the learners to discuss their goals in small groups. Individual learners could then report to the rest of the class on their decisions.

Learners need to reflect on and question their own learning behaviour. This can be done by getting learners to describe to others the way they approach their learning. Initially, a short list of points to cover can help this description. Talking to others and listening to others talk about their approaches to learning can provide an awareness of more options that can be a beginning point for change. Direct teaching about different types of vocabulary and their usefulness, what is involved in knowing a word, strategies for vocabulary learning, and the need to consider revision can help increase awareness. Learners can also keep a written record of their own learning including their reflections on what worked well and what did not. Teachers also need to consider the effect of the tests they use and the suggestions they give to learners. There may seem to be flexibility in a course but the learners may feel that there is a hidden agenda. Discussion between teachers and learners is one way of revealing this.

Learners need to become fluent and comfortable using a few important vocabulary learning strategies. These strategies should include guessing from context, using word cards, using word parts, using mnemonic techniques, especially the keyword technique, and using dictionaries (Nation, 2001). These techniques require a considerable amount of practice and they need to be learned to a point where it is easier to use them than not to use them. Teachers need to develop small syllabuses to develop each of the strategies, moving from teacher control and modelling, to the learners taking over the strategies themselves. This will require several hours of time spread over several weeks for each strategy, but this time can be justified by the returns that control of the strategies brings. The teacher should monitor the development of the strategies and give learners helpful feedback and encouragement. In this way, teachers might contribute to Rubin's (1975, p. 50) aim of "helping the student to learn how to learn a language".

Questions for ongoing research

Although the study described in this chapter has raised some interesting possibilities for helping our students learn vocabulary more effectively, many questions remain. Three in particular stand out:

1 It is clear that students need to personalize the task if they are to learn successfully. However, how exactly can they be motivated to take control of their own vocabulary development, to choose vocabulary appropriate to their own needs and to think beyond the immediate goal of the test?
2 Rote memorization and copying are common strategies for many students who feel comfortable with this kind of learning. Although contemporary teaching methods tend to favour communicative strategies and emphasize understanding rather than mere memorizing, it is not always easy to get students to change their familiar strategy patterns. Should we try to change them? If so, how can this be done?
3 There needs to be more investigation of good language learners like Abdi. How do they develop their skills? How transferable are their skills to less successful students?

Conclusion

Clearly, all the learners in this study believed vocabulary to be important, and they invested a lot of time and effort in learning vocabulary. However, only one of the ten could be considered an effective learner.

Abdi took control of his own learning by selecting words which were interesting and useful and he used a wide range of strategies. He was concerned about appropriate usage and thought beyond just getting a good mark in the weekly test. He was able to reflect on his learning in order to self-evaluate and monitor his progress.

A review of Abdi's data suggests that in order to learn vocabulary effectively, good language learners must have the ability or skills to do the learning, they must have the attitude or willingness to take control of their own learning, and they must develop a reflective awareness of their own approaches to learning. In other words, in addition to ability (which, probably, all ten students in the study had), good learners need autonomy and metacognition (see Cotterall and Anderson, this volume, for more on these topics) if they are to be successful.

References

Anderson, N. (this volume) Chapter 7: Metacognition and good language learners.

Chung, T.M. (2003) A corpus comparison approach for terminology extraction. *Terminology*, 9(2), 221–245.

Chung, T.M. and Nation, P. (2003) Technical vocabulary in specialised texts. *Reading in a Foreign Language*, 15(2), 103–116.

Corson, D.J. (1997) The learning and use of academic English words. *Language Learning*, 47(4), 671–718.

Cotterall, S. (this volume) Chapter 8: Autonomy and good language learners.

Coxhead, A. (2000) A new academic word list. *TESOL Quarterly*, 34(2), 213–238.

Griffiths, C. (2003a) Patterns of language learning strategy use. *System*, 31, 367–383

Griffiths, C. (2003b) *Language Learning Strategy Use and Proficiency*. (Retrieved from: http://wwwlib.umi.com/dissertations/fullcit/3094436).

Holec, H. (1981). *Autonomy in Foreign Language Learning*. Oxford: Pergamon.

Little, D. (1991) *Learner Autonomy: Definitions, Issues and Problems*. Authentik, Dublin.

Moir, J. and Nation, P. (2002) Learners' use of strategies for effective vocabulary learning. *Prospect*, 17(1), 15–35

Nagy, W.E., Herman, P. and Anderson, R.C. (1985) Learning words from context. *Reading Research Quarterly*, 20, 233–253.

Nation, I.S.P. 1990 *Teaching and Learning Vocabulary*. Heinle & Heinle, Boston, MA.

Nation, I.S.P. 2001 *Learning Vocabulary in Another Language*. Cambridge: Cambridge University Press.

Rubin, J. 1975 What the "good language learner" can teach us. *TESOL Quarterly*, 9(1), 41–51.

Wesche, M. and Paribakht, T.S. (1996) Assessing second language vocabulary knowledge: depth versus breadth. *Canadian Modern Language Review*, 53(1), 13–40.

13 Grammar and good language learners

Margaret Bade

According to Rubin (1975), good language learners attend to form (often called "grammar"). Bachman's (1990) model of language competence defines grammar as including vocabulary, morphology, syntax, phonology and graphology, while Purpura (2004) also suggests that we need to view grammar in its broadest sense as including everything speakers know about their language – the sound system (phonology), the system of meanings (semantics), the rules of word formation (morphology), the rules of sentence formation (syntax) as well as an appreciation of vocabulary. Halliday (1994) stresses the functional use of grammar to talk about experiences, to interact with others and to fit in with a wider context. Although these definitions serve to provide a comprehensive view which is in line with current broad views of grammar, aspects of language competence such as vocabulary and phonology are dealt with separately in this volume. For this reason, this chapter will deal with grammar in the narrower sense of "the structure of a language" (Richards, Platt and Platt, 1992, p. 161) and as a set of rules that define how words or parts of words are combined or change to form acceptable units which can be used to convey meaning within a language (Ur, 2003). In language teaching, the view that grammar plays a central role in the language curriculum is often firmly held (Purpura, 2004).

Changing views of grammar

Grammatical analysis dates back to the ancient Greeks, who in the fifth century BC were making observations in their own language on Greek grammar. It was the Alexandrian scholar Dionysios Thrax (*c*.100 BC) who made the first explicit description of the grammar of Greek. Although little attention was paid to syntax (that is how words are strung together to produce sentences), he distinguished eight classes of words (nouns, participles, verbs, conjunctions, prepositions, articles, pronouns, adverbs) with which we are familiar for the description of modern languages. The Romans adopted the grammatical analysis of the Greeks for the description of Latin, as is seen in the Latin grammars of Donatus (AD 400) and Priscian (AD 600). These Latin grammars formed the basis for the teaching of Latin, which was the international medium of communication until the Middle Ages. In the eighteenth century, however, grammars of other languages were examined more closely. Studying particular properties of individual languages can be relevant to the discovery of language universals. European languages and Sanskrit, the ancient language of the Indian Vedic scriptures, were seen to have commonalities. Languages outside the Indo-European family, however, were not easily analysed using the Greco-Latin pattern. In a language like Eskimo, for example, nouns are regularly incorporated into verbs and one single word may correspond to a whole sentence in English or German. Even the traditional analysis of the Indo-European languages led to challenges. For example, whereas in English and Greek the article is a separate word before the noun, in Swedish the article is an ending on the noun, and Latin and Russian do not have articles at all (Davis, 2000; Fromkin, Blair and Collins, 2002).

For the ancients, knowledge seemed to be the ability to state a series of rules. But current thinking suggests that this kind of explicit knowledge about the language does not necessarily guarantee the ability to use the language with grammatical accuracy. Many traditional grammar book rules are prescriptive rather than descriptive, that is they prescribe what is "correct" rather than describing what language users actually do. Some suggest that the explicit knowledge of traditional grammatical rules of a language actually interferes with the acquisition or development of ability to use the language with native-like competence (Tarone and Yule, 1991). Yalden (1991, p. 15) states unequivocally that communication is the prime motivation for learning a language and "it is well known that communication involves more than structure".

Grammatical paradigms such as provided by the grammar–translation method, the situational language teaching method or audiolingual methods have shaped both our current thinking about the definition of grammar in educational contexts and our view of how language is used. The grammar–translation approaches provided the student with almost equal quantities of grammar and vocabulary. The audiolinguists, on the other hand, placed a strong emphasis on the acquisition of the basic grammatical patterns of the language and emphasized everyday language and the direct teaching of the target language. Pronunciation and grammar came at the expense of vocabulary. The audiolingual approach was a strong advocate of the inductive teaching of grammar and there was a focus on the spoken language.

Purpura (2004) views linguistic phenomena from two perspectives: syntactocentric and communication centred. The syntactocentric view of language looks specifically at the way words or linguistic items are arranged in a sentence, and views this arrangement in an operationalized and systematic way. The analysis focuses explicitly on a structural description of how the elements in a language are described operationally when "predicting an 'ideal' speaker's or hearer's knowledge of the language" (p. 6). For example, the following passive voice sentence "Robert was taken to the dentist this afternoon" might be explained by comparing it with an active voice sentence, e.g., "Anne took Robert to the dentist this afternoon." The learners' attention might be drawn to the rules for changing the simple past to the past passive, to rules for pronunciation and spelling and even be compared to ungrammatical passive sentences. This kind of approach to the teaching of grammar might be described as *focussing on forms*, as Ellis (2001, 2006) explains.

A communication-centred perspective of language, by contrast, might not only draw attention to the structural features of the passive voice but also consider aspects of context that might have required the speaker or writer to use the passive rather than the active voice. In other words, the grammar teacher who adopts a more communicative perspective might look at the communicative need for the passive and suggest some alternative ways of looking at why the words might be arranged in a certain way. For example, the teacher might suggest that maybe the speaker wants to emphasize that there was only one person who was going to be taken to the dentist and so Robert becomes the subject; or perhaps the writer or speaker wanted to avoid specifying who took Robert to the dentist. Littlewood (1992) suggests that one of the most characteristic features of communicative language teaching is that it pays systematic attention to communicative as well as structural aspects of language. Good language learners will develop strategies for using language to communicate meanings effectively and they will use the new grammar system to communicate in new situations. This kind of *focus on form* approach involves focussing primarily on the meaning with consideration of the underlying grammar arising out of the communicative activity (Ellis, 2001, 2006).

If we look at some of the ways grammar has been defined in the literature it is perhaps with "accuracy" that we associate grammar most strongly (Nesfield, 1916). Accuracy in the use of words and in the forming of sentences is the end and aim for which grammars have been compiled and systematized in any language, whether ancient or modern. If students have no grammatical rules or principles to refer to for guidance, they have nothing to show them where their mistakes lie or how they are to correct them and so avoid making such mistakes in future. Quirk (1971, p. 77) reinforces the indispensability of knowing grammar when he points out "a language cannot work with words alone". For example, if we put articles, prepositions, tense, number and the conventions of word order into a group of words such as *play, boy, soccer, team* we can arrange them so that they tell us something: *The boys play soccer for the team*. The reader knows who plays soccer and what is played as well as for whom the game is played. Without grammar, however, learners are unable to communicate in all but the most basic situations, an inadequacy of which the learners are themselves often acutely aware, as the small-scale study reported below discovered.

The study

The study aimed to investigate student attitudes towards grammar in order to integrate this into the 20-week course entitled "English for Living and Working in New Zealand". The aims of the course were to enable the students to actively and appropriately participate in New Zealand community and workplace settings. Grammar would clearly be expected to play a role.

Participants

There were 14 students enrolled for the course. Their ages ranged from 20 to 68. They were from China (4), Russia (1), Indonesia (2), Korea (3), Taiwan (1), Thailand (1), India (1) and the Middle East (1). They were a highly motivated group of mostly mature and educated students who were new immigrants, having spent less than two years in New Zealand. Their previous employment included engineering, business, music teaching, medicine, architecture, banking, primary school teaching, university lecturing, nursing, management and information technology. Some had children attending local primary and secondary schools and university. One had sat the language test IELTS and achieved a band 8 (just under native speaker level); another was planning to take this test on completion of the course to gain further qualifications at university level.

Data collection and analysis

A questionnaire was given to the students in the first week of the course and was an especially useful source of data. It consisted of 20 questions, 15 of which were focussed, open-ended questions which allowed the students to analyse what they were doing with their knowledge and why they were doing it. This provided some qualitative data. Five consisted of Yes/No questions which gave quantitative data. The purpose of the questionnaire was to help to find out how best to approach the teaching of grammar with this group of students. The questions related grammar to aspects of the course such as course content, kinds of resources students used to assist in language learning, preferred methodology, feedback and error correction.

The students were given 40 minutes to complete the questionnaire. Once the questionnaires were gathered, they were analysed holistically and according to a scoring rubric. Answers were recorded graphically, showing responses under the four headings: response to content, methodology, attitude to errors and attitude to feedback. Data from the questionnaire were considered alongside information from the pre-course interview and pre-course placement test.

Findings

The results showed a variation in responses according to the students' immediate needs (what the course was going to do for them), prior learning experience (as revealed in their attitudes to feedback and error correction) and approaches to being taught grammar. Predictably, those who had been teacher-trained or who were looking ahead to further their study in New Zealand chose grammar and accuracy as being of paramount importance. Those from the IT and business sector sought to improve their oral skills so that they sounded "like a native speaker". The class was clearly composed of different types of learners with different ways of responding to errors and feedback.

Most noticeable in the answers was the high percentage who gave "study hard", "grammar" and "teacher" as their answers to the question "How do you think you will improve learning English?" and "grammar" as their response to the question "If there was something in the course that you needed the teacher to teach you more of, what would it be?" The students on this course showed an overwhelming desire to be taught grammar, to concentrate on accuracy, and to have their errors corrected. Some of the responses to the questions asked in the survey are reproduced below:

- I like to see model sentences so I can try out my own like this. But sometimes I find I still make mistakes.
- I like to know the rules but I also need to see examples with the rules. Lastly I like to see a short and easy text with these rules and examples of sentences because I know I can learn accurately then.
- I hope the teacher will revisit this grammar point again and again so that I know if I understand it accurately.
- I try to use my time outside the class practising. I give myself different purposes to write for – but limit myself to ten minutes for each purpose with a maximum homework time of one hour.

- Feedback will show me if I need to see the teacher to explain again or I can write to be understood but I still make errors. When I see a mistake it makes me want to correct it.
- I have to think about the definite article and the kind of prepositions all the time and the plural endings and non-count nouns.
- I use my electronic Chinese–English dictionary first but I know I should use the English–English one more to check – I am now getting a hunch when I think I have made an error.
- I don't mind correction because it makes me discover why I make errors.
- I don't want the teacher to think I can't write English well. I am a professional adult and yet I still make lots of errors in my writing. I don't want this.
- To improve my English is a current task. I need more grammar help.
- I am just interested in how to write successfully!!!

Implications for the teaching/learning situation

As a result of the study described above a number of microstrategies that would help students learn grammar could be identified:

Cognitive strategies
- Modelling sentences
- Utilizing rules and also examples
- Consulting a dictionary
- Analysing form and meaning
- Revising grammar points
- Coping with variations in sentence structure

Self-monitoring strategies
- Students recognizing own errors
- Critiquing/accepting advice from teachers/peers
- Accepting teachers' feedback
- Learning to be reflective
- Students setting their own grammar goals
- Seeing grammar as an active process

As a result of the study described above, grammar was integrated in all modules of the course using different methods and forms of feedback. It proved mostly effective. Some students found it particularly difficult to maintain consistent accuracy in some grammar points over the course (use of articles, third person "s"), as displayed in their writing assessments, while others saw gradual improvement in their weekly summary

179

writing, particularly in their use of tenses. A student who sat IELTS at the end of the course without additional instruction gained entry to university. Another student was accepted into the MBA, while another was short-listed for a job as a lecturer in social work. There are some success stories from this study which show that outcomes for balancing grammar in all four skills can be effective.

Teachers need to be sensitive to the needs of their students. For those who are concerned with how best to teach grammar to varied groups of learners, it can be valuable to use a learner-centred questionnaire which has questions which encourage students to analyse their use of language and give their own feedback on aspects of the course on which they are about to embark. Teachers should get to know the kinds of learners they have in their class and particularly gain ideas of their attitudes towards learning. This can assist with course planning. It can also assist with the overall success of their students' learning and instruction. For the majority of learners in this study, grammar was obviously something that needed to be visible in the lesson.

The age range of the subjects in the group had no noticeable effect on the results in grammar accuracy. My oldest learner's grammar improved markedly over the course. He was a very motivated learner (he had been a university teacher himself in China) and there were factors outside the classroom also: his daughter, with whom he lived, worked in Auckland and spoke fluent English, and his grandchild, who was also in the house, enjoyed her grandfather teaching her. This was similar to at least half the class who had sons and daughters attending local schools. They reported their learning from this class helped them relate to their children's learning of English.

Thornbury (1999, p. 17) writes: "Many learners come to language classes with fairly fixed expectations as to what they will do there." Grammar instruction is often demanded by students because it fulfils cultural expectations (Scarcella and Oxford, 1992), and teachers of such students will be under considerable pressure to conform to student demands. Furthermore, there has been research which suggests that good language learners develop strategies for learning grammar (Griffiths, 2003, 2006). It would be simplistic to suggest that there are easy answers to these kinds of pressures, but teachers need to consider what it is that they are trying to do, whom it is that they are trying to do it for, and the best way of doing it in the given context.

Students' expectations and previous language learning experience are likely to have a powerful effect on their level of motivation (Tarone and Yule, 1991), and it has been shown in many studies that motivation bears a strong relationship to achievement in language learning (for instance Gardner and Lambert, 1972; Gardner, 1980; Gardner, 1985). More recent work carried out by Dörnyei (1998), Oxford (1996) and Ushioda (this volume) also affirm the importance of motivation. This is not necessarily to suggest that student expectations (for instance regarding the importance of grammar) should always be fulfilled: there may well be times when expectations need to be modified. Nevertheless, teachers need to consider what their students expect from their time in class and, if necessary, consider how to modify the expectations or their own preconceived ideas if motivation is not to suffer.

In many communicative classrooms, grammar is taught, but it is presented to the students with an approach to second language learning that is task-based, interactive and communicative: in other words, through a management of interaction that is jointly constructed by teacher and learner. It is integrated in an informal way and connected with features of what constitutes, for instance, writing a report or writing an essay. The aim is to draw students' attention to the way a report or an essay is organized and to give students opportunities to communicate in the target language, using appropriate form. Teachers should consider whether tasks (for more on task-based learning see Rubin, this volume), which are commonly used as a component of instruction in contemporary classrooms, are appropriate for their own students. Designing a task means that the participants must be engaged as if they were language users in the real world.

Questions for ongoing research

Because research is still continuing in order to provide more valid and reliable data about how instruction contributes to acquisition, conclusions regarding the most effective ways for teaching grammar must remain tentative. According to Ur (2003, p. 83), one of our jobs as teachers is to assist our students in making the "leap" from form-focussed accuracy work to fluent production, by providing a "bridge", characterized as "a variety of practice activities that familiarize them with the structures in context, giving practice both in form and communicative meaning." Does this mean that explicit grammar teaching by means of traditional methods such as teacher explanation of rules followed by exercises is less effective than getting students to use grammar in the course of completing a task? This remains an under-researched question.

It is not usually difficult to convince learners that grammar is important when learning language. But some learners must be convinced that different teaching styles, such as learning grammar inductively or deductively, or presenting students with tasks to complete in pairs (focus on form) can be as effective as traditional methods (focus on forms) in teaching grammar, and although more and more teachers are adopting a communicative approach, learners are often the ones who need to be convinced of the effectiveness of communicative methods. How can students be persuaded of the benefits of a communicative approach? Indeed, how about the even more basic question of whether a communicative approach is, in fact, better than traditional methods? Or, even more basically, what is "better", in what situation, and for whom?

As mentioned earlier, motivation of the learner plays a key role and, as Oxford and Nyikos (1989), have shown, motivation often leads to learners using different kinds of learning strategies which can facilitate greater skill in language learning. However, motivation is affected by age (for more on this see Griffiths, this volume), by variations in stages of development, and by the situation in which the learning is taking place. How do these factors affect the way grammar is taught and students' receptivity to the chosen methods?

Focus on form as an instructional technique is fundamental to the contemporary language classroom but debate has surrounded the question as to whether this approach can accomplish and facilitate successful grammar acquisition in different classroom settings (Sheen and O'Neill, 2005; Poole, 2005). Studies carried out by Poole (2005) and Williams (1999) highlighted benefits to students' vocabulary learning rather than to specific linguistic code features. However, research undertaken by Ellis, Basturkmen and Loewen (2001, 2006) and Basturkmen, Loewen and Ellis (2001), has demonstrated that focus on form instruction can also be effective in promoting grammar acquisition.

Conclusion

A knowledge of grammar is essential for clarity of communication in both the written and the spoken form. Obviously, a language course which consisted entirely of grammar to the detriment of communicative learning would not achieve this goal. But when grammar is given its proper place and taught in such a way that it does not overshadow other elements of language teaching, it is often welcomed by students as a very effective way of moving towards that mastery of the language to which good language learners aspire.

Research has not yet made it definitively clear whether teaching/learning approaches that include a focus on grammar have an advantage over those that don't (Ellis, 1985; Long, 1988). However, what we can probably be reasonably assured of is that the study of grammar has been with us for a long time and may well always be with us.

References

Bachman, L.F. (1990) *Fundamental Considerations in Language Testing*. Oxford: Oxford University Press.

Basturkmen, H., Loewen, S. and Ellis, R. (2004) Teachers' stated beliefs about incidental focus on form and their classroom practices. *Applied Linguistics*, 25(2), 243–272.

Davis, J. (2000) *A Crash Course in English Grammar*. Stuttgart: Ernst Klett Verlag.

Dörnyei, Z. (1998) Motivation in foreign and second language learning. *Language Teaching*, 31, 117–135.

Ellis, R. (1985) *Understanding Second Language Acquisition*. Oxford: Oxford University Press.

Ellis, R. (2001) Investigating form-focused instruction. In R. Ellis (ed.), *Form-focused Instruction and Second Language Learning*. Malden, MA: Blackwell, 1–46.

Ellis, R. (2006) Current issues in the teaching of grammar: an SLA perspective. *TESOL Quarterly*, 40(1), 83–107.

Ellis, R., Basturkmen, H. and Loewen, S. (2001) Learner uptake in communicative ESL lessons. *Language Learning* 51: 281–318.

Ellis, R., Loewen, S. and Basturkmen, H. (2006) Disentangling focus on form. A response to Sheen and O'Neill (2005). Applied Linguistics, 27(1), 135–141.

Fromkin, V., Blair, D. and Collins, P. (2002) *An Introduction to Language*, fourth edition. Victoria, Australia: Nelson Thomson Learning.

Gardner, R. (1980). On the validity of affective variables in second language acquisition: conceptual, contextual and statistical considerations. *Language Learning*, 30, 255–270.

Gardner, R. (1985) *Social Psychology and Second Language Learning*. London: Edward Arnold.

Gardner, R. and Lambert, W. (1972). *Attitudes and Motivation in Second Language Learning*, Rowley, MA: Newbury House.

Griffiths, C. (2003) Patterns of language learning strategy use. *System*, 31, 367–383.

Griffiths, C. (2006) Strategies for successful learning in an English-speaking environment. *Journal of Asia TEFL*, 3(2), 141–163.

Griffiths, C. (this volume) Chapter 2: Age and good language learners.

Griffiths, C. (this volume) Chapter 6: Strategies and good language learners.

Griffiths, C. (this volume) Chapter 20: Teaching/learning method and good language learners.

Halliday, M. (1994) *An Introduction to Functional Grammar*, second edition. London: Edward Arnold.

Littlewood, W. (1992) *Communicative Language Teaching. An Introduction*. Cambridge: Cambridge University Press.

Long, M.H. (1988) Instructed interlanguage development. In L.M. Beebe (ed.), *Issues in Second Language Acquisition: Multiple Perspectives*. New York: Newbury House/ Harper & Row, 115–141.

Nesfield, J.C. (1916) *Manual of English Grammar and Composition*. London: Macmillan & Co. Ltd.

Oxford, R.L. (ed.) (1996) *Language Learning Strategies Around the World: Crosscultural Perspectives*. Honolulu, HI: University of Hawai'i Press.

Oxford, R.L. and Nyikos, M. (1989) Variables affecting choice of language learning strategies by university students. *Modern Language Journal*, 73(3), 291–300.

Poole, A. (2005) The kind of forms learners attend to during focus on form information: a description of an advanced ESL writing class. *Asian EFL Journal*, 7(3), 1–13.

Purpura, J.E. (2004) *Assessing Grammar*. Cambridge: Cambridge University Press.

Quirk, R. (1971) *The Use of English*. London: Longman Group Limited.

Richards, J.C. (1992). *The Language Teaching Matrix*. Cambridge: Cambridge University Press.

Richards, J., Platt, J. and Platt, H. (1992) *Longman Dictionary of Language Teaching and Applied Linguistics*. Harlow: Longman.

Rubin, J. (1975) What the "good language learner" can teach us. *TESOL Quarterly*, 9(1), 41–51.

Rubin, J. (this volume) Chapter 23: Tasks and good language learners.

Scarcella, R.C. and Oxford, R.L. (1992) *The Tapestry of Language Learning*. Boston, MA: Heinle & Heinle Publishers.

Sheen, R. and O'Neill, R. (2005) Tangled up in form: critical comments on "Teachers' stated beliefs about incidental focus on form and their classroom practices" by Basturkmen, Loewen and Ellis. *Applied Linguistics*, 26(2), 268–274.

Tarone, E. and Yule, G. (1991) *Focus on the Language Learner*. Oxford: Oxford University Press.

Thornbury, S. (1999) *How to Teach Grammar*. Harlow: Longman.

Ur, P. (2003) *A Course in Language Teaching. Practice and Theory*. Cambridge: Cambridge University Press.

Ushioda, E. (this volume) Chapter 1: Motivation and good language learners.

Williams, J. (1999) Learner-generated attention to form. *Language Learning*, 49(4), 583–625.

Yalden, J. (1991) *Principles of Course Design for Language Teaching*. Cambridge: Cambridge University Press.

14 Functions and good language learners

Zia Tajeddin

Following disenchantment with grammar-based and situation-based methods, a functional approach to the teaching and learning of language was embraced in order to highlight the importance of learner-centered goals, a learner-centered view of language learning, and the analysis of learner needs for using language to communicate and interact with others. As the functional approach flourished, the concept of "function" gained multiple interpretations, such as the purpose of an utterance, the use to which a particular grammatical form is put, and the communicative purpose of a piece of language (Berns, 1984; Finocchiaro and Brumfit, 1983; Guntermann and Phillips, 1982; van Lier, 2001; Woodward, 2001). Our main questions from the point of view of the current volume are: how do good language learners develop functional competence (or the ability to use the language they are learning in real communication) and how can teachers facilitate the process?

Theoretical background

Over the years there have been a number of approaches to the teaching of language functions among which the Prague and the British traditions are perhaps the best known. Following Saussure (1916), the Prague school of linguistics viewed language as a system of units (for instance, sentence, word, morpheme, or phoneme), each serving some purpose or function and functionally related to other units (Berns, 1990; Crystal, 1991). The functional perspective on language set up by the Prague school is shown in its view of language as consisting of devices fulfilling certain functions and being understood only when the functional relation of each device to others is analyzed (Menšíková, 1972). In addition to its theoretical concern with language, the Prague school had an interest in the practical application of its theory to the teaching and learning of functions, centered on the need to understand the relationship of form to meaning and function in the course of learning a new language.

The British tradition, also referred to as Firthian linguistics (Davis, 1968; Palmer, 1973) and the London school (Sampson, 1980), is another school of linguistics whose functional view was central to its conception of language. Firth (1957), the founder of the school, drew heavily on Malinowski's (1935) context of situation to frame his view of language as a system functioning in some environment or context. Following Malinowski, Firth argued for the centrality of the notion of context, with an emphasis on meaning. Insisting on language as a means primarily used by people to function in society, Firth construed meaning as function in context. Each function, in his view, can be split into a series of component functions, defined as the use of a language form in relation to a context. In other words, as function in context, meaning was not studied only in word-based semantics or in a separate area of linguistics. Rather, the statement of the functions of linguistic elements in their context was looked on as the principle underlying all linguistic description (Berns, 1990).

Many of Firth's proposals about language function have been developed by neo-Firthian scholars, whose main theoretician is Halliday. In Halliday's theory, language function has a dual status. The first refers to the uses or functions that reflect the developmental needs of an infant, inter alia instrumental and regulatory. The second concerns the transition to adult language. While this language, according to Halliday (1978), maintains its originally functional character, the concept of "function" in it undergoes a substantial change in that it is no longer synonymous with "use" but gains a more abstract nature, turning into a kind of metafunction. Through metafunction, the various adult uses of language receive a symbolic expression in a systematic and finite form. For Halliday, uses in the adult language are simply "the selection of options within the linguistic system in the context of actual situation types" (Halliday, 1978, p. 46); as such, it is not possible to enumerate language uses in a very systematic way. In Halliday's view, adult language is made up of a small number of functional components. The influence of the British tradition is evident both in the implications of its functional view of language for the promotion of function acquisition and use by learners, and in the practical involvement of linguists drawing on this tradition to respond to the burgeoning demand for language learning.

Research into the functional use of language

In the literature on the development of language learners' ability to comprehend and perform language functions, the term *speech acts* is often used to refer to language functions in order to place the relevant research under the rubric of pragmatic competence and interlanguage development. One example of this terminological preference is Flowerdew's (1990) reference to Wilkins's (1976) classification of language functions as a taxonomy of speech acts. Over the last two decades, there has been a growing literature on pragmatic development from general pragmatic, sociopragmatic, and pragmalinguistic perspectives, and along with it, the comprehension and production of speech acts/language functions by learners. Research in this area has focused on issues such as individual differences in pragmatic development, pragmatic transfer, and cross-cultural comparison.

Individual differences in pragmatic development

Individual differences in functional learning and use include a range of characteristics like language proficiency, age of arrival, gender, motivation, social and psychological distance, and social identity (Kasper and Rose, 2002), and the impact of these factors on learners' production and recognition of speech acts, such as apologies, compliments, greetings, requests, and refusals (for instance, Hassall, 1997; Hill, 1997; Houck and Gass, 1996; Maeshiba, Yoshinaga, Kasper, and Ross, 1996; Matsumura, 2003; Omar, 1991; Robinson, 1992; Rose, 2000; Safont Jordà, 2005; Sameshima, 1998; Takahashi and Beebe, 1987; Takahashi and DuFon, 1989; Trosborg, 1987, 1995). Most studies carried out on the role of proficiency point to its positive effects on functional competence. That is, although even beginning learners can learn to comprehend and produce speech acts, learners at more advanced levels can build up a larger repertoire of speech acts and have a higher capacity to benefit from pragmatic instruction. Trosborg (1987) reported on the expansion of learners' repertoire of apology use as their proficiency level increased. The participants in Takahashi and DuFon's (1989) study exhibited more preference for direct requests in line with their proficiency level. Maeshiba *et al.* (1996) found that advanced Japanese learners of English outperformed the intermediate learners in emulating native English speakers' pragmatic behavior. Sameshima (1998) examined performance of request, refusal, and apology by three levels of Chinese speakers of Japanese. The results indicated that learners' linguistic performance of speech acts more closely approximated that of native speakers as their level became more advanced. Safont Jordà's (2005) study on the use of request formulations in the oral and written production tasks by subjects at beginning and intermediate levels showed that the latter outperformed the former in the quantitative and qualitative use of request forms.

However, the research by Takahashi (1996) and Matsumura (2003) failed to account for improvement in speech act use. Takahashi (1996) noted that higher level learners did not seem to improve their performance of request acts. The study by Matsumura (2003) aimed to account for variation in pragmatic development of 137 Japanese learners of

English in terms of their different levels of English and amount of exposure. Using the degree of approximation to native speech act behavior to assess the learners' pragmatic development in various advice-giving situations, Matsumura suggests that the pragmatic development, as evidenced by significant mean differences, cannot be attributed to higher levels of English, and that the amount of exposure has greater potential to account for the development of pragmatic competence in language learning. As these findings indicate, a mismatch sometimes exists between learners' language level and their pragmatic competence, indicating a failure to draw on proficiency gains to use speech acts appropriately in different contexts and situations. Therefore, good language learners need greater awareness of the fact that pragmatic competence does not automatically evolve in the process of language learning and that they need a focus on the pragmatic aspect of language.

Pragmatic transfer

A number of studies have addressed the issue of pragmatic transfer from the first language to the new language. Takahashi and Beebe (1987), for instance, hypothesized that proficiency in the target language is positively correlated with positive pragmatic transfer from the first language, although this hypothesis was rejected by Maeshiba *et al.* (1996), who carried out an apology study with intermediate and advanced Japanese ESL Learners. Cohen's (1997) account of his experience in an intensive course in Japanese as a foreign language supports the positive correlation hypothesis in that his insufficient Japanese resources made him unable to produce utterances in Japanese according to first language pragmatic norms. Higher-proficiency learners are more likely to display pragmatic transfer since they have the necessary linguistic resources to do so; by contrast, lower-proficiency learners do not have such resources and hence they will tend to reveal less pragmatic transfer.

Cross-cultural comparison

Many researchers, according to Safont Jordà (2005), have adopted a cross-cultural perspective to study functional development (for instance, Blum-Kulka, House, and Kasper, 1989; Ebsworth, Bodman, and Carpenter, 1996; Eisenstein and Bodman, 1986, 1993; Holmes, 1989; Olshtain and Cohen, 1983; Murphy and Neu, 1996; Nelson, Al-Batal, and Echols, 1996; Olshtain and Weinbach, 1993). Blum-Kulka *et al.* (1989) addressed cross-cultural variation in the use of requests and apologies by native and non-native speakers. Results from their study shed light on differences between native speakers and language learners in their use of linguistic realizations for various situations and provided insights into the transfer of certain pragmatic norms. Eisenstein and Bodman (1993) analyzed the use of expressions of gratitude by native and non-native speakers of American English from different cultural backgrounds. Their non-native subjects showed certain problems with the adjustment of more complex linguistic forms in certain contexts. Further, non-native speakers' expressions and perceptions of gratitude appeared to be culture bound. In a similar vein, the study by Ebsworth *et al.* (1996) into expressions of gratitude revealed that learners' cultural background played a role in their performance. Olshtain and Weinbach (1993) carried out a study of apologies and complaints produced by native speakers and non-native speakers of Hebrew. According to their findings, non-native speakers produced longer stretches of discourse, were affected by the social distance in their selection of particular formulae, and displayed a higher degree of variability in their responses. Murphy and Neu (1996) also found that culture affected the production of given speech acts. Hence, as Safont Jordà (2005) suggests, the use of speech acts is influenced by the situational and contextual norms underlying language use related to different cultural backgrounds. Good language learners are likely to be sensitive to these varying factors.

Implications for the teaching/learning situation

The functional approach has had far-reaching implications for language teaching and learning. It has been heavily relied on to inform language teaching and learning, particularly in the areas of syllabus design organized around language functions, and of teaching methodology which is effective in presenting and practicing language functions and giving language learners a feeling of success and achievement in the use and interpretation of language functions.

The theoretical germ of the function-based syllabus can be clearly perceived in the functional view of the Prague school. From the vantage point of the school, language is a tool which enables the community using it to perform a number of functions serving the needs and wants of mutual understanding. The development of the function-based syllabus also owes an enormous debt to the contribution of the London school, particularly that of Halliday. His theory of language acquisition as mastery of linguistic functions had a great impact on Wilkins' (1976) functional syllabus. Founded on this theoretical background, largely sociolinguistic by nature, the functional syllabus organizes learning activities pragmatically in terms of communicative functions or speech acts. It focuses on what learners want to do or what they want to accomplish through speech (Finocchiaro and Brumfit, 1983). The key features related to the teaching of functions to language learners are:

1 meaning is paramount
2 dialogs are centered around communicative functions
3 sequencing is determined by the consideration of content, function, or meaning.

Mixed results have been reported regarding the effect of instruction on functional competence in a new language. Cohen and Tarone (1994) found that training had a positive effect on the written speech act behavior of the learners in their study. Olshtain and Cohen (1990), however, failed to find clear-cut evidence of the efficacy of the instruction program on learners' development of apologies, and although Salazar Campillo (2003) found a qualitative increase in the use of requests by 14 English non-native speakers after pragmatic instruction, the effect was not maintained in delayed tasks. Overall, however, research results largely lend support to the instruction of speech acts and the benefits learners gain from a functional focus (Cohen, 2005). Therefore, the instructed learning of speech acts seems to be a necessity (Bardovi-Harlig, 2001) since pragmatic functions and relevant contextual factors are often not noticed by learners despite prolonged exposure (Schmidt, 1993).

If we accept the importance of instruction for learners to develop pragmatic ability, particularly in view of the fact that learners generally have limited functional competence (Fukushima, 1990), the next question has to be: What kind of instruction is best? A distinction is often made between explicit and implicit instruction. The difference between explicit and implicit teaching of the pragmatic routines of attention getting, apology, and thanking to 14 learners of Japanese was the focus of the study by Tateyama, Kasper, Mui, Tay, and Thananart (1997). In the explicit group, the learners discussed the different functions, were exposed to teacher examples and explanation, received a handout illustrating and explaining the difference in the use of the routine formulae according to social context, and finally watched video clips relevant to the formulae. By contrast, the implicit group only watched the video and was prompted to notice formulaic expressions. The results revealed higher ratings for the role-plays in the explicit group. Takahashi (2001) examined the enhancement of pragmatic performance by a group of Japanese learners of English using four input conditions, including explicit teaching. The participants' request performance was found to have been affected most strongly by explicit teaching. Trosborg (2003) found a slight advantage for the explicit teaching of pragmatic routines related to the handling of complaints. Ishihara (2004) looked at the interim and delayed impact of explicit pragmatic instruction on learners' complimenting and responding to compliments. The learners' performance on an interim discourse completion task showed that their production of and response to compliments improved as the instruction progressed, although a delayed post-test showed the maintenance of pragmatic enhancement in only a subset of the learners. In addition to those studies focusing on speech act production, there have been those entailing the enhancement of speech act perception and interpretation. For example, Eslami-Rasekh, Eslami-Rasekh, and Fatahi (2004) provided Iranian advanced learners of English with explicit instruction through teacher-fronted discussions, cooperative grouping, role-plays, and other relevant tasks. The results of the post-test revealed that the learners' perception of the speech acts of requesting, apologizing, and complaining improved significantly. As Eslami-Rasekh (2004) pointed out, even advanced learners may not be well aware of speech acts because a commendable knowledge of language will not necessarily lead to a corresponding level of pragmatic knowledge required for appropriate communication. It follows that learners need explicit metapragmatic attention to enhance their functional competence.

Another common distinction is between inductive and deductive instruction. While deductive instruction is based on the provision of metapragmatic information through the explicit instruction of speech acts before learners are engaged in practice activities, inductive instruction allows learners to engage in the analysis of speech acts in order to arrive at the generalization themselves (Rose and Kasper, 2001). Rose and Ng (2001) employed a control group and two treatment groups to investigate the effect of deductive and inductive instruction on compliments and compliment responses. The results of a discourse completion test showed that the learners in both treatment groups (that is, both the deductive and inductive treatment groups) outperformed those in the control group in their responses. This suggests firstly that instruction in pragmatics can make a difference in a language learning context, and secondly that learners can gain from both deductive and inductive instruction to acquire greater pragmatic competence.

Questions for ongoing research

Research on the production and interpretation of language functions/speech acts by language learners has shed some light on the patterns of pragmatic development, the function-form interaction, the effect of instruction, and the significance of individual differences. However, ongoing research on speech acts, as Kasper and Rose (2002) suggest, needs to be more directly informed by language learning theories, and there are still many under-researched areas.

1 Existing investigations have been conducted with participants from a small number of cultures and linguistic backgrounds. Are results similar in different learning environments?

2 What is the effect on speech act learning of such individual differences as age, motivation, proficiency level, learning strategies, and social distance?

3 What is the effect of function-based activities in the more recent teaching methods and syllabus types, such as the task-based syllabus and the lexical syllabus?

4 What is it that good language learners do to develop functional competence that less successful learners do not, and how can insights into this question be used to promote functional development?

Conclusion

The functional approach arrived on the scene in the 1970s to help language learners acquire communicative competence. It broadened the horizons of learning by contributing to the burgeoning of interest in the concepts of a functional view of language learning, a learner-centered focus, the analysis of learner needs, and learner-centered goals.

Functions are one of the units of organization in the hybrid or multi-dimensional syllabus (Johnson, 2001) and functions feature prominently in any method or textbook aimed to satisfy the communicative needs of language learners. This is the result of recognition that pragmatic competence is one of the vital components of language that good language learners need to acquire (Eslami-Rasekh, 2004). Further, functions are gaining increasing attention with the rise of interlanguage pragmatics and the corresponding research into the learning, use, and instruction of functions/speech acts. However, the question of how good language learners develop functional competence (that is, how they learn to use the language) and how insights into this question might be used to assist less successful learners (Rubin, 1975) remains largely unaddressed and presents a fertile ground for further research.

References

Bardovi-Harlig, K. (2001) Empirical evidence of the need for instruction in pragmatics. In K.R. Rose and G. Kasper (eds.), *Pragmatics in Language Teaching*. New York: Cambridge University Press, 13–32.

Berns, M. (1984) Functional approaches to language and language teaching: another look. In S. Savignon and M. Berns (eds.), *Initiatives in Communicative Language Teaching II*. Reading, MA: Addison-Wesley, 3–21.

Berns, M. (1990) *Contexts of Competence: Social and Cultural Considerations in Communicative Language Teaching*. New York: Plenum Press.

Blum-Kulka, S., House, J., and Kasper, G. (1989) *Cross-Cultural Pragmatics: Requests and Apologies*. Norwood: Ablex Publishing Corporation.

Cohen, A.D. (1997) Developing pragmatic ability: insights from the accelerated study of Japanese. In H.M. Cook, K. Hijirida, and M. Tahara (eds.), *New Trends and Issues in Teaching Japanese Language and Culture*. Honolulu: University of Hawaii, Second Language Teaching and Curriculum Center, 137–163.

Cohen, A.D. (2005). Strategies for learning and performing L2 speech acts. *Intercultural Pragmatics*, 2–3, 275–301.

Cohen, A.D. and Tarone, E. (1994) The effects of training on written speech act behavior: stating and changing an opinion. *MinneTESOL Journal*, 12, 39–62.

Crystal, D. (1991) *A Dictionary of Linguistics and Phonetics*. Oxford: Blackwell.

Davis, P. (1973) *Modern Theories of Language*. Englewood Cliffs, NJ: Prentice Hall.

Ebsworth, M., Bodman, J.W., and Carpenter, M. (1996) Cross-cultural realization of greetings in American English. In S. Gass and J. Neu (eds.), *Speech Acts Across Cultures*. Berlin: Mouton de Gruyter, 89–107.

Eisenstein, M. and Bodman, J.W. (1986) "I very appreciate": expressions of gratitude by native and non-native speakers of American English. *Applied Linguistics*, 7, 167–185.

Eisenstein, M. and Bodman, J.W. (1993) Expressing gratitude in American English. In G. Kasper and S. Blum-Kulka (eds.), *Interlanguage Pragmatics*. Oxford: Oxford University Press.

Eslami-Rasekh, Z. (2004) Enhancing the pragmatic competence of NNEST candidates. Paper presented at the 38th TESOL Convention, Long Beach, California.

Eslami-Rasekh, Z., Eslami-Rasekh, A., and Fatahi, A. (2004) The effect of explicit metapragmatic instruction on the speech act awareness of advanced EFL students. *TESL-EJ*, 8(2). (Retrieved May 5, 2006 from http://www.writing.Berkeley.edu TESL_EJ/ej30/az.html).

Finocchiaro, M. and Brumfit, C. (1983) *The Functional-Notional Approach: From Theory to Practice*. Oxford: Oxford University Press.

Firth, J.R. (1957) *Papers in Linguistics 1934–1951*. London: Oxford University Press.

Flowerdew, J. (1990) Problems of speech act theory from an applied perspective. *Language Learning*, 40(1), 79–105.

Fukushima, S. (1990) Offers and requests: performance by Japanese learners of English. *World Englishes*, 9, 317–325.

Guntermann, G. and Phillips, J.K. (1982) *Functional-Notional Concepts: Adapting the Foreign Language Textbook*. Washington, DC: Center for Applied Linguistics.

Halliday, M.A.K. (1978) *Language as Social Semiotic: The Social Interpretation of Language and Meaning*. Baltimore, MD: Edward Arnold.

Hassall, T.J. (1997) *Requests by Australian learners of Indonesian*. Unpublished doctoral dissertation. Canberra, Australian National University.

Hill, T. (1997) The development of pragmatic competence in an EFL context. Unpublished doctoral dissertation. Tokyo, Temple University Japan.

Holmes, J. (1989) Sex differences and apologies: one aspect of communicative competence. *Applied Linguistics*, 10, 194–213.

Houck, N. and Gass, S. (1996) Non-native refusal: a methodological perspective. In S. Gass and J. Neu (eds.), *Speech Acts Across Cultures*. Berlin: Mouton de Gruyter, 45–63.

Ishihara, N. (2004) Exploring the immediate and delayed effects of formal instruction: teaching giving and responding to compliments. *MinneTESOL/WITESOL Journal*, 21, 37–70.

Johnson, K. (2001) *An Introduction to Foreign Language Learning and Teaching*. Essex: Pearson Education.

Kasper, G. and Rose, K.R. (2002) Pragmatic development in a second language. *Language Learning*, Vol. 52, Supplement.

Maeshiba, N., Yoshinaga, N., Kasper, G., and Ross, S. (1996) Transfer and proficiency in interlanguage apologizing. In S. Gass and J. Neu (eds.), *Speech Acts Across Cultures*. Berlin: Mouton de Gruyter, 155–187.

Malinowski, B. (1935) *Coral Gardens and their Magic*. London: Allen and Unwin.

Matsumura, S. (2003) Modelling the relationships among interlanguage pragmatic development, L2 proficiency, and exposure to L2. *Applied Linguistics*, 24 (4), 465–491.

Menšíková, A. (1972) Sentence patterns in the theory and practice of teaching the grammar of French as a foreign language. In V. Fried (ed.), *The Prague School of Linguistics and Language Teaching*. London: Oxford University Press, 43–61.

Murphy, B. and Neu, J. (1996) My grade's too low: the speech act set of complaining. In S. Gass and J. Neu (eds.), *Speech Acts Across Cultures*. Berlin: Mouton de Gruyter, 191–216.

Nelson, G.L., Al-Batal, M., and Echols, E. (1996) Arabic and English compliment responses: potential for pragmatic failure. *Applied Linguistics*, 17, 411–432.

Olshtain, E. and Cohen, A.D. (1983) Apology: a speech act set. In N. Wolfson and E. Judd (eds.), *Sociolinguistics and Language Acquisition*. Rowley, MA: Newbury House, 18–35.

Olshtain, E. and Cohen, A.D. (1990) The learning of complex speech behavior. *The TESL Canada Journal*, 7, 45–65.

Olshtain, E. and Weinbach, L. (1993) Interlanguage features of the speech act of complaining. In G. Kasper and S. Blum-Kulka (eds.), *Interlanguage Pragmatics*. Oxford: Oxford University Press, 108–122.

Omar, A.S. (1991) How learners greet in Kiswahili. In L.F. Bouton and Y. Kachru (eds.), *Pragmatics and Language Learning (Vol. 2)*. Urbana-Champaign, IL: Division of English as an International Language, University of Illinois, Urbana-Champaign, 59–73.

Palmer, F.R. (1968) *Selected Papers of J.R. Firth, 1952–1959*. Bloomington, IN: Indiana University Press.

Robinson, M.A. (1992) Introspective methodology in interlanguage pragmatics research. In G. Kasper (ed.), *Pragmatics of Japanese as Native and Target Language (Technical Report No. 3)*. Honolulu, HI: University of Hawaii at Manoa, Second Language Teaching and Curriculum Center, 27–82.

Rose, K.R. (2000). An exploratory cross-sectional study of interlanguage pragmatic development. *Studies in Second Language Acquisition*, 22, 27–67.

Rose, K.R. and Kasper, G. (eds.) (2001) *Pragmatics in Language Teaching*. New York; Cambridge: Cambridge University Press.

Rose, K.R. and Ng, C. (2001) Inductive and deductive teaching of compliments and compliment responses. In K.R. Rose and G. Kasper (eds.), *Pragmatics in Language Teaching*. New York: Cambridge University Press 145–170.

Rubin, J. (1975) What the "good language learner" can teach us. In: *TESOL Quarterly*, Vol. 9(1), March 1975, pp. 41–51.

Safont Jordà, M.P. (2005) *Third Language Learners: Pragmatic Production and Awareness*. Clevedon: Multilingual Matters Ltd.

Salazar Campillo, P. (2003) Pragmatic instruction in the EFL context. In A. Martinez Flor, E. Usó Juan and A. Fernández Guerra (eds.), *Pragmatic Competence and Foreign Language Teaching*. Castelló de la Plana, Spain: Publications de la Universitat Jaume I, 233–246.

Sameshima, S. (1998) Communication task ni okeru nihongo gakusyusha no tenkei hyougen/bunmatsu hyougen no syuutokukatei: Chuugokugo washa no "ira" "kotowari" "shazai" no baai (The acquisition of fixed expressions and sentence-ending expression by learners of Japanese). *Nihongo Kyouiku (Journal of Japanese Language Teaching)*, 98, 73–84.

Sampson, G. (1980) *Schools of Linguistics: Competition and Evolution*. London: Hutchinson.

Saussure, F. de (1959) [1916] *Cours de Linguistique Générale*. (*Course in General Linguistics*, translated by W. Baskin.) New York: McGraw-Hill.

Schmidt, R. (1993) Consciousness, learning, and interlanguage pragmatics. In G. Kasper and S. Blum-Kulka (eds.), *Interlanguage Pragmatics*. Oxford: Oxford University Press, 21–42.

Takahashi, S. (1996) Pragmatic transferability. *Studies in Second Language Acquisition*, 18, 189–223.

Takahashi, S. (2001) The role of input enhancement in developing pragmatic competence. In K.R. Rose and G. Kasper (eds.), *Pragmatics in Language Teaching*. New York; Cambridge: Cambridge University Press, 171–199.

Takahashi, T. and Beebe, L.M. (1987) The development of pragmatic competence by Japanese learners of English. *JALT Journal*, 8, 132–155.

Takahashi, S. and DuFon, M.A. (1989) Cross-linguistic influence in indirectness: the case of English directives performed by native Japanese speakers. Unpublished manuscript, Department of English as a Second Language, University of Hawaii at Manoa.

Tateyama, Y., Kasper, G., Mui, L., Tay, H., and Thananart, O. (1997) Explicit and implicit teaching of pragmatic routines. In L.F. Bouton (ed.), *Pragmatics and Language Learning (Vol. 8)*. Urbana-Champaign, IL: Division of

English as an International Language, University of Illinois, Urbana-Champaign, 163–178.

Trosborg, A. (1987) Apology strategies in natives/non-natives. *Journal of Pragmatics*, 11, 147–167.

Trosborg, A. (1995) *Interlanguage Pragmatics: Requests, Complaints and Apologies*. New York: Mouton de Gruyter.

Trosborg, A. (2003) The teaching of business pragmatics. In A. Martinez Flor, E. Usó Juan and A. Fernández Guerra (eds.), *Pragmatic Competence and Foreign Language Teaching*. Castelló de la Plana, Spain: Publications de la Universitat Jaume I, 247–281.

van Lier, L. (2001) Language awareness. In R. Carter and D. Nunan (eds.), *The Cambridge Guide to Teaching English to Speakers of Other Languages*. Cambridge: Cambridge University Press, 160–165.

Wilkins, D.A. (1976) *Notional Syllabuses*. London: Oxford University Press.

Woodward, T. (2001) *Planning Lessons and Courses*. Cambridge: Cambridge University Press.

15 Pronunciation and good language learners

Adam Brown

In her 1975 article, Rubin states that "the good language learner has a strong desire to communicate" (p. 46). Linguists declare that, of the two main mediums for communication in human language (the spoken and written), it is the spoken medium that has primacy (see, for instance, Brown, 2005). All human languages have had a spoken form, while there are many languages that have had no written form. Humans learn to communicate in speech at an earlier age than in writing. Most people spend far longer communicating in speech/listening than they do in writing/reading. Good language learners therefore do not neglect pronunciation. Writers have often compared the process of learning to pronounce another language with that of learning other physical activities, such as swimming. That is, learning to pronounce is a physical activity involving parts of the body (tongue, lips, vocal cords, lungs, etc.) that have to be coordinated well in order to produce the desired effect.

Bloom and Krathwohl's (1956) often-quoted taxonomy of educational objectives (commonly known as *Bloom's taxonomy*) provides a classification of possible objectives of courses, in three categories. The first, *cognitive* domain deals with knowledge of a factual nature that is presented, and learnt, during a course of instruction. This is clearly important when learning to swim, as it is necessary to know what to do with hands and feet, how to hold the body in the water, when to take breaths, etc. It is also of importance when learning the pronunciation of another language as, by definition, all such learners already speak (pronounce) at least one first language. This is not to say that speakers know consciously what they do with their vocal organs when pronouncing their first language(s), but that many of these articulatory habits will need to be changed for the language being learnt. Cognitive aspects are learnt by having them presented in an organized and interesting way, and can be tested by traditional pen-and-paper examinations to check that they have been understood and remembered.

Secondly, the *psychomotor* domain covers the physical skills needed. There is a world of difference between knowing what to do with the body in order to swim, and being able to do it. For this reason, swimming lessons contain a great deal of practice in the water in a swimming pool. Similarly, psychomotor aspects of pronunciation are learnt by practical classes in which learners speak. This may seem an obvious statement. However, there are many countries in the world where English language classes do not contain much in the way of practical exercises giving learners the opportunity to pronounce the language. Psychomotor aspects of pronunciation are tested by requiring learners to speak. Again, this may seem obvious. However, tests are often conducted by, for example, requiring learners to discriminate recordings of phonemes, words and sentences. Tests such as this are clearly listening tests rather than tests of pronunciation. On many courses, pronunciation is not explicitly tested at all.

The final aspect of Bloom's taxonomy is the *affective* domain. This relates to the learners' feelings about what is being learnt and the learning situation. Those learning to swim are more likely to succeed if they appreciate the importance of being able to swim (for instance, in an emergency), and if the classes take place in a warm atmosphere, not only in terms of the camaraderie and encouragement in the class, but also the temperature of the water. In many respects, affective considerations may be the most important for pronunciation teaching, for several reasons. Perhaps most significantly, many teachers pay little attention to the affective side of language teaching. There is great potential for embarrassment, ridicule and loss of face, especially with such a physical activity as pronunciation. Learners also need to appreciate that pronunciation is an important element of learning a language. Research (for instance, Willing, 1988) suggests that learners are aware of its importance. In a questionnaire survey among Singaporeans, Indians and Thais, Shaw (1981) found that each nationality group rated speaking as their worst of the four skills (speaking, listening, writing, reading), but chose speaking as the skill that they wanted to be their best. As Shaw (1981, p. 116) concludes, "if these statistics are a true reflection of reality, there is a great difference between what the students want and what they are getting from their English classes."

Pronunciation targets

Good language learners know what they are aiming for. In terms of pronunciation, the range of possible targets may be shown by the following quotations (from Ellis and Sinclair, 1989, pp. 66–67). Purificacion, a learner from Spain, says, "I'm sure I make a lot of mistakes when I speak – but I no care – the people they understand me – mostly." For her, intelligibility is the main criterion. However, it is only a fairly minimal level of intelligibility. Hers is a utilitarian outlook – she has, for instance, no desire to be mistaken for a native speaker.

In contrast, Herbert, a learner from Germany, asserts, "I want my English to be perfect and I always try very hard to be correct." He wants to perfect the image of a good speaker (pronouncer) of English and would probably be happy if people mistook him for a native speaker.

Maria Elena, a learner from Colombia, admits, "I feel strange when I speak English – like a different person." For her, the way she speaks, whether her native language or a foreign one, is an intimate part of who she is, and she does not feel any desire or need to change her identity in this way.

The three concerns described above – intelligibility, image and identity – are different, but equally valid. We cannot say that Herbert is wrong to want to speak like a native speaker, any more than we can criticize Maria Elena for being proud of, and wanting to preserve, her Colombianness. The fact that the criteria of image and identity pull in different directions (image towards a native pronunciation, identity towards a local one) has important implications for pronunciation teachers. Jenkins (2000) has approached this problem by proposing a Lingua Franca Core. Her basic premise is that, since non-native speakers of English far outnumber native, we should turn our attention to interactions between non-native speakers, the concerns of native speakers being irrelevant. The Lingua Franca Core is a statement, based on empirical research findings, of pronunciation features that must be pronounced accurately to avoid potential breakdowns in communication.

Learner variables

Rubin (1975) pointed out that good language learning depends on several variables including motivation, aptitude and opportunity. These form the subject of the next sections of this paper.

Before we examine each of these considerations, it is worthwhile here to describe an often-quoted piece of research by Purcell and Suter (1980). This is in fact a statistical re-examination of work done by Suter (1976), and thus may be considered reliable from the statistical perspective. The pronunciation accuracy of 61 non-native speakers of English was rated by 14 judges. The speakers were immigrants to the USA, with Arabic, Japanese, Persian and Thai as their native languages. They also responded to 16 questions about personal details and self-ratings according to various other criteria that had been proposed by writers as important variables. The results show that only four of the variables were statistically significant – the other factors did not contribute to any statistical correlation. The four, in order of importance, were first language, aptitude for oral mimicry, length of time in an English-speaking country and/or living with a native speaker, and strength of concern for pronunciation accuracy.

Two worrying conclusions follow from this. Firstly, these four factors are not aspects of the learning situation over which teachers have much control, if any at all. This emphasizes that much of the responsibility for pronunciation learning lies with the learner rather than the teacher. Secondly, of the factors relating to formal classroom training, none were found to be of any statistical significance. However, other writers have cast doubt on this finding, arguing that it is not the amount of training but quality that is important.

Motivation

Motivation (Ushioda, this volume) is often divided into two dichotomies: internal and external motivation, and integrative and instrumental motivation. Internal motivation comes from the individual and the learning situation; that is, the learners find what goes on in class interesting. External motivation is generated by factors such as culture, parents and financial reward. Integrative motivation is driven by the desire of learners to associate themselves with the culture (lifestyle, history, music, art, sport, literature, etc.) of the speakers of that language. Instrumental motivation is utilitarian in nature: learning the language for a specific purpose such as passing an examination, meeting the requirements for entry to an educational institution, applying for a job, and doing international business. Since accent is a strong marker of cultural identity, it is intuitive to think that learners with strong internal and integrative motivation would achieve better pronunciation than others. However, integrative motivation was one of Purcell and Suter's factors, and was found to be of no statistical significance.

One area in which motivation is thought to be of great importance is fossilization. This is the situation where a learner's pronunciation has plateaued, that is, reached a certain level and has failed to improve despite subsequent instruction and favourable exposure to the language. This is often the case with adult migrants to native-speaking countries such as the UK, USA and Australia. It is often claimed that this is because the speakers have passed a critical age (Lenneberg, 1964), after which language learning becomes more difficult and, for some learners, impossible.

Acton's (1984) procedure for dealing with fossilized learners is based on four principles:

1 The responsibility for success in the course is placed on the students.
2 The most important learning and change must go on outside the class.

3 The focus of the course is on overall communicative effectiveness and intelligibility, rather than pronunciation *per se*.
4 Many of the activities are aimed at getting participants to find ways of using in spontaneous speech what they are capable of doing in formal pronunciation exercises.

Since Acton's subjects had been passed over for promotion at work because of their poor pronunciation and communication skills, motivation was not a problem. However, because of the demands of the course, there was a dropout rate of 25%, and a further 25% did not complete enough of the work to demonstrate significant, lasting change. Reports by workmates of the remaining 50% indicated improvement in the learners' speech, and the learners themselves were enthusiastic about the programme, and intended to continue to use the techniques after the course.

Aptitude

It is intuitive to think that some learners "have better ears and mouths" than others, that is, that they have a natural flair for pronunciation (and listening). Indeed, Purcell and Suter (1980) found aptitude for oral mimicry to be the second most important determinant of pronunciation accuracy.

Strevens (1974) stressed the importance of mimicry, by distinguishing two ways in which learners could acquire the pronunciation of another language. The first he called the innocence principle, which suggests that most learners can learn to pronounce a new language simply by means of mimicry, although the ability to do this tends to diminish with age. Mimicry is, after all, how we learn the pronunciation of our native language(s). This was contrasted with the sophistication principle which suggests that: older learners can benefit more than younger learners from formal instruction. Good language learners know whether they have an aptitude for acquiring pronunciation by imitating sounds, or whether detailed descriptions of what the vocal organs are doing is necessary.

Opportunity

The third most important factor in Purcell and Suter's research was found to be length of time in an English-speaking country and/or living with a native speaker. Again, it is intuitive to think that living in an environment where the language is spoken, and therefore being exposed to it every day, would provide ideal opportunities to acquire the language, and its pronunciation. However, the case of fossilized speakers, many of whom migrated to native-speaking countries many years before, shows that other factors are equally important. One of these would be the use that is made of this opportunity.

For instance, many international students come to Auckland, the largest city in New Zealand. This would seem to present ideal conditions for acquiring a high level of English and its pronunciation. Future employers of these students probably expect that, having gained an English-medium degree in an English-speaking country, these graduates would have good language and pronunciation skills, and an understanding of cultural differences, and thus be ideal candidates for posts requiring international communication. However, Auckland also has a sizeable international resident population. Many of these students fail to take full advantage of the opportunity, but instead share accommodation and hang out with other students who speak their own language, eat at ethnic restaurants, read the newspaper in their own language and so on. Good language learners extract maximum benefit from immersion opportunities, by interacting more with the host culture and language, making local friends, watching local television and reading local newspapers and using homestays with local families.

Opportunity is thus only a benefit if advantage is taken of the opportunity. As Acton (1984) emphasized, the most important learning and change must go on outside the class and after the course. This was also stressed in research carried out by Macdonald, Yule and Powers (1994) and Yule and Macdonald (1995). There are three elements to any course. Firstly, teaching refers to the materials that the teacher prepares, and the way that they are delivered in class, which are the teacher's responsibility. Secondly, learning depends partly on the teacher and whether the materials and delivery are good; however, it depends more significantly on factors relating to the learner such as motivation and boredom. Finally, effective teaching and learning cannot be said to have taken place if, once the course has finished, the learners do not use the knowledge, skills and attitude acquired during the course. Yule, Macdonald and Powers therefore used three significant points in the learning process: the start of the course, the end of the course, and a point two days after the end of the course. The real proof of the pudding is whether students put into practice after the course what they have learnt during it. This seems especially relevant for pronunciation.

Implications for the teaching/learning situation

Many learners, and unfortunately many teachers, treat pronunciation as if it were a separate aspect of language learning. If pronunciation is explicitly handled at all, it is often covered in class slots divorced from the rest of the syllabus. However, given that pronunciation is an indispensable aspect of communicating in speech, and given that successful communication is the basic aim of language learning, pronunciation should be seen as relating to various other communicative aspects of language. Wise teachers will exploit these connections, and seek ways to integrate pronunciation work into other language work, and avoid presenting pronunciation tasks in isolation. Good language learners will understand this interrelationship. Three examples of this are enough to make the point: listening, spelling and nonverbal features.

Writers (e.g. MacCarthy, 1976) have argued whether a learner needs to be able to hear a sound distinction in order to be able to pronounce it. However, listening, as the receptive aspect of the spoken medium, clearly has connections with speech, as its productive aspect. They are two sides of the same coin. Most learners, on hearing their own recorded voice, are surprised at how they sound and are often quite capable of saying what their strengths and weaknesses are in terms of pronunciation. Modern computer technology (for instance Microsoft Sound Recorder) makes sound recording very easy. Learners can then easily record and hear themselves, submit recordings to the teacher, and exchange recordings with other people, whether other learners or native speakers. Listening to authentic English voices in realistic situations is an important component in the popular *Streaming Speech* materials (Speech in Action, no date) which aim to capture natural speech and break it down into learnable chunks. Although, as Cauldwell (2005) points out, natural speech can be messy and frustrating for learners, it is important that students are challenged if they are to develop the ability to pronounce a new language in such a way that it is easily understood.

Good learners of English also need to be aware of the problems of English spelling. English spelling is based on the alphabetic principle, that is the symbols (letters) in the spelling represent the individual consonant and vowel sounds (phonemes) in the pronunciation. However, English is probably the worst example of this among languages of the world. This means that learners probably speak a native language that is spelt much more regularly than English, and good language learners learn early on that English is very different in this respect. For instance, many learners of English regularly pronounce what is spelt with the letter 's' as an /s/ sound. However, while the English letter 's' often represents

/s/ (e.g. *chase*), it also often represents /z/ (e.g. *phase*). For the plural suffix, it may represent /s/ (e.g. *cats*), /z/ (e.g. *dogs*) or /ɪz/ (e.g. *horses*). It is often part of the representation of /ʃ, ʒ/ (e.g. *sugar, fusion*). In many words of French origin, it is silent, that is, it does not represent any sound (e.g. *debris*). Furthermore, it is often difficult or impossible to give rules covering the various pronunciations of particular letters. This means that the correspondence between letters and sounds (and vice versa) is far from one-to-one, and is the reason why English dictionary entries use phonemic symbols in transcriptions (see Brown, 2005).

Finally, non-verbal features are a neglected area of language teaching. In our native languages, we all use gestures, facial expressions and so on when conversing. In English, these nonverbal features often coincide with pronunciation features, especially stress of various kinds. For example, the placement of the tonic syllable (the intonationally most prominent syllable in an utterance) can be emphasized by beating gestures of the hands and wide-open eyes. In a contrastive context, the difference between the pronunciation of *I don't like Jane* in the following sentences can be shown clearly in this way.

1   I don't *like* Jane – I love her.
2   You may think I like her, but I *don't* like Jane!

Many language learners have been found to use little or no nonverbal features in class, even those learners who seem to use nonverbal features expressively when speaking in their native language. Good language learners, however, use nonverbal communication to support pronunciation.

Questions for ongoing research

Writers have often reminded us that research has failed to show any clear correlation between pronunciation teaching and improved pronunciation. Does this mean that we should give up the attempt? As teachers, we hope not. However, research should perhaps be directed to three key questions.

Firstly, many teachers, maybe as a result of such research findings, sweep pronunciation teaching under the carpet, and do not deal with it in any systematic way. Research, along the lines of Macdonald (2002), is important as it tries to establish why teachers are often so reluctant to deal with pronunciation. Macdonald found that relevant factors included the lack of a pronunciation requirement in the curriculum, and the lack of a systematic way of assessing students' pronunciation. Further investigation of these factors would be fruitful.

Secondly, Macdonald also found that there was a lack of suitable materials for pronunciation teaching. Clearly, if poor materials are used, it is not surprising that, according to research findings, teaching may not lead to improved pronunciation. Research could therefore be directed towards assessing the effectiveness of particular types of material. There is a saying in ELT circles, that a drill is a device used for boring. Drills have their place in focusing learners' attention on specific points of pronunciation. However, they cannot be called communicative at all. The same is true of phoneme discrimination exercises of the *Ship or sheep?* (Baker, 2006) variety. In fact, very few published pronunciation materials can truly be called communicative. Innovative ways of making pronunciation work communicative should be explored.

Finally, pronunciation writers have increasingly emphasised the importance of learner factors in the process. If learners do not know what they are aiming for, do not see how pronunciation relates to other aspects of language, do not feel that the burden of their learning lies with them, feel embarrassed at opening their mouths and perhaps producing poor pronunciation, do not see why pronunciation is important outside the classroom and so on, then any teaching is unlikely to be successful. Learner factors, shown to be important by the research of Purcell and Suter (1980), should also form the focus of pronunciation research.

Conclusion

Pronunciation is an important aspect of language learning, a fact that good learners are aware of. As in other areas of language learning, they must approach the task in an appropriate way. This involves having motivation to learn, being willing to attempt new, "exotic" sounds even at the risk of embarrassing failure, exploiting opportunities for exposure to the language, and realizing that pronunciation is not a separate skill but relates to all other aspects of language learning. In these ways, they will strive to achieve their differing goals in pronunciation and language learning, and achieve their desired levels of intelligibility. Acceptable pronunciation facilitates the drive to communicate in speech, which Rubin (1975) includes among the characteristics of good language learners.

References

Acton, W. (1984) Changing fossilized pronunciation. *TESOL Quarterly*, 18(1), 71–85. Also in A. Brown (ed.) (1991) *Teaching English pronunciation: a book of readings*. London: Routledge, 120–135.

Baker, A. (2006) *Ship or sheep?* (third edition). Cambridge: Cambridge University Press.

Bloom, B.S. and Krathwohl, D.R. (1956) *Taxonomy of Educational Objectives: The Classification of Educational Goals, by a Committee of College and University Examiners. Handbook I: Cognitive Domain.* New York: Longmans, Green.

Brown, A. (2005) *Sounds, Symbols and Spellings.* Singapore: McGraw-Hill.

Cauldwell, R., (2005) Bricking up and streaming down: two approaches to naturalness in pronunciation materials. Paper presented at University College London, Phonetics Teaching and Learning Conference. (Retrieved 6 April, 2007 from www.phon.ucl.ac.uk/home/johnm/ptlc2005/pdf/ptlcp36.pdf).

Ellis, G. and Sinclair, B. (1989) *Learning to Learn English: A Course in Learner Training.* Cambridge: Cambridge University Press.

Jenkins, J. (2000). *The Phonology of English as an International Language.* Oxford: Oxford University Press.

Lenneberg, E.H. (1964) The capacity of language acquisition. In J.A. Fodor and J.J. Katz (eds.), *The Structure of Language: Readings in the Philosophy of Language.* Englewood Cliffs, NJ: Prentice Hall, 579–603.

MacCarthy, P. (1976) Auditory and articulatory training for the language teacher and learner. *English Language Teaching Journal,* 30, 212–219. Also in A. Brown (ed.) (1991) *Teaching English Pronunciation: Book of Readings.* London: Routledge, 299–307.

Macdonald, D., Yule, G. and Powers, M. (1994) Attempts to improve English L2 pronunciation: the variable effects of different types of instruction. *Language Learning,* 44, 75–100.

Macdonald, S. (2002) Pronunciation views and practices of reluctant teachers. *Prospect,* 17(3), 3–18.

Microsoft (n. d.) Sound Recorder. (Retrieved 25 March 2007 from www.microsoft.com/resources/documentation/windows/xp/all/proddocs/en-us/app_soundrecorder.mspx?mfr=true).

Purcell, E.T. and Suter, R.W. (1980) Predictors of pronunciation accuracy: a reexamination. *Language Learning,* 30(2), 271–287.

Rubin, J. (1975) What the "good language learner" can teach us. *TESOL Quarterly,* 9(1), 41–51.

Shaw, W.D. (1981) Asian student attitudes towards English. In L.E. Smith (ed.) *English for Cross-Cultural Communication.* New York: St Martin's Press, 108–122.

Speech in Action (n. d.) Streaming speech. (Retrieved 25 March 2007 from www.speechinaction.com.).

Strevens, P. (1974) A rationale for teaching pronunciation: the rival virtues of innocence and sophistication. *English Language Teaching Journal,* 28, 182–189. Also in A. Brown (ed.) (1991) *Teaching English pronunciation: A book of readings* London: Routledge, 96–103.

Suter, R.W. (1976) Predictors of pronunciation accuracy in second language learning. *Language Learning,* 26, 233–253.

Ushioda, E. (this volume) Chapter 7: Motivation and good language learners.

Willing, K. (1988) *Learning Styles in Adult Migrant Education.* Adelaide: National Curriculum Resource Centre.

Yule, G. and Macdonald, D. (1995) The different effects of pronunciation teaching. *International Review of Applied Linguistics*, 33(4), 345–350. Also in J. Morley (ed.) (1994) *Pronunciation pedagogy and theory: new views, new directions.* Alexandria, VA: TESOL, 111–118.

16   Listening and good language learners

Goodith White

In a first language, listening is the first skill which learners usually develop: they listen to an utterance, then they repeat it, later they learn to read it, and finally they learn to write it. This natural sequence does not always apply to the learning of languages other than the first, where the graphic skills (reading and writing) often precede the aural/oral skills, perhaps because students are learning in an environment where aural input is not always readily available. This frequently results in listening skills being underdeveloped and undermines students' confidence regarding their target language competence.

Good listeners

The first thing to point out about good listeners is that understanding the language of a spoken text is only one part of what they need to be able to do. Effective listeners need to operate a number of skills simultaneously as they receive a spoken message (Anderson and Lynch, 1988; Lynch, 1998). They need to refer to three different areas of knowledge (schematic, contextual and linguistic) in order to make sense of the message. As far as linguistic knowledge is concerned, listeners need to perceive the incoming sounds and store them in working memory, while beginning some processing of the stored language by separating it into manageable segments. They also scan the incoming message in order to sample bits of language which may hold the key to the meaning of the message, and parse words and phrases by matching them with representations already stored in long-term memory. At the same time listeners refer to contextual information in order to construct hypotheses concerning the meaning of what they have sampled and what may come next (Macaro, 2001). That contextual information includes the physical setting in which the message was produced, the participants, and the co-text (what has already been said). Listeners also make use of schematic knowledge to understand meaning, and this includes knowledge of how discourse is organized, as well as how language is used in a particular society, and factual knowledge of the topic which is being talked about. It is obvious from this brief description that knowledge

208

of the language system (phonology, stress, intonation, lexis, syntax) is not sufficient in itself to interpret the meaning of a spoken message, and that listening involves combining bottom-up processing of sounds with top-down expectations for messages which draw on much wider schematic and contextual knowledge of language in use.

In real life it is often closely linked with speaking, with listeners becoming speakers and vice-versa in the blink of an eye. Reciprocal or interactive listening, in which the listener interacts with the speaker to achieve the purpose of the interaction, and in which the listener can ask for clarification and provide verbal and non-verbal feedback (nodding, saying "mmm" and so on) has been rather neglected in language class-rooms (Vandergrift, 1997a; Richards, 1990). English for Academic Purposes (EAP) classes, for example, often focus almost exclusively on non-reciprocal listening in terms of helping students to listen to lec-tures, and fail to take adequate account of the fact that they also need to interact with fellow students socially, and with tutors and students in tutorials, as well as with those beyond the academic environment. This focus on non-reciprocal listening extends to general English classrooms. In a typical listening lesson, students hear pre-recorded material on audio or video tapes, DVD or the Internet. This material is usually controlled by the teacher so that students themselves are unable to interact with the tape by stopping it and replaying it if they fail to understand something. Moreover, students are typically asked to understand and remember transactional information from an oral text (facts, figures, names, etc.) rather than interactional information such as attitude and opinion. In other words, students are encouraged to focus on *what* has been said rather than *why* and *how* it has been said. Obviously, if we are to prepare students adequately for the kinds of listening they will do outside the classroom, we need to encourage and provide opportunities for both interactive and non-reciprocal listening, and to ask students to focus on both transactional and interactional information in what they hear, whichever is appropriate for the kind of text they are listening to and their purpose in doing so. If students are to practise interactive as well as non-reciprocal listening, this has implications for strategy use. Class-room activities need to help students not only to use language learning strategies, but also the kinds of receptive communication strategies, com-monly involved in interactive listening (Vandergrift, 1997a) such as sig-nalling for the speaker to continue.

Language learners often think that all their difficulties in listening are due to their inadequate knowledge of the target language. However, as we have seen, they also need to be able to make use of various kinds of non-linguistic information in order to make sense of spoken messages, and to be able to communicate their current level of comprehension to

209

speakers. There are also other skills which effective listeners need which apply whether listening in the native language or to a target language, such as motivation, concentration and empathy towards the speaker. They are seldom discussed in language classrooms and yet they are important, and a natural part of the metacognitive and social strategies described by O'Malley and Chamot (1990). It is interesting to discover that native speakers are by no means perfect themselves in these skills, and there is a considerable literature devoted to training first language listeners in these skills, particularly in the fields of business and therapy. Brownell (1986, p. 2), for instance, who is mainly interested in increasing effective listening in business, points out that "without a doubt, most of us [first language speakers] have inadequate listening skills", and she goes on to propose training in six important aspects of listening: hearing, understanding, remembering, interpreting, evaluating and responding. Fromm (1998, pp. 192–193) calls listening "an art" and suggests that, among other characteristics, listeners should aim for "complete concentration" and "a capacity of empathy with another person [. . .] strong enough to feel the experience of the other as if it were his own." I would suggest that, in particular, empathy (understanding why a speaker wants to communicate a particular message) is vital for understanding, and often left out of the picture when teaching or learning how to be an effective listener in a target language.

We also need to think about the role which listening can play in language development in general. Good language learners realize that listening plays a vital role in language development (as we will see in the next section), but they also need to recognize that for language development to truly take place, it is important that intake (that is, listening to a spoken message) is also accompanied by opportunities for output (for instance, Swain, 1985) and that listening is part of a wider social interaction and negotiation of meaning (for instance, Gass and Varonis, 1994). In other words, listening is necessary for language learning to take place, but it is not enough in itself to ensure that it does, and that some form of language production will inevitably be involved in the whole process.

Research into how good language learners develop listening skills

Studies such as that by Feyten (1991) show that learners who are most proficient in listening make more progress in language development generally. Good language learners are aware of the importance of opportunities provided by listening for language acquisition. Griffiths' research on strategies (2003, 2006, this volume) shows that successful learners make use of chances to watch TV and movies, listen to native speakers and notice language use in the environment, which presumably includes language they hear.

If we move from listening as a resource for language learning to the question of how good language learners seek to improve their ability to listen in a target language, there are a number of noteworthy findings from research. O'Malley, Chamot and Kupper (1989), for instance, carried out an important study of the mental processes second language listeners used in order to understand spoken messages. They aimed to access these processes by using a think-aloud procedure in which they interrupted students during the course of a listening activity and asked them what they were thinking. The researchers focused on the strategies which were used by effective and ineffective listeners. Although the findings might have been prejudiced by the fact that the students had already been divided into good and bad listeners before the experiment, the results were of great interest. They found that effective target language listeners were able to employ efforts to redirect attention when they felt that their concentration was slipping and listen for intonation and pauses. They were able to listen for larger chunks of language such as phrases and sentences, focusing on individual words only when there was a breakdown in communication, and infer the meaning of new words which were important for comprehension. They were also able to employ a variety of strategies to solve decoding problems and use contextual and schematic knowledge as well as linguistic knowledge to interpret meaning. The researchers concluded that effective target language listeners were able to use a variety of strategies, and that "instructional approaches which rely exclusively upon teacher input [. . .] for their effectiveness are failing to draw upon what the students can contribute to the learning process" (O'Malley et al., 1989, p. 434).

Vandergrift (1997b) found that metacognitive strategies had great potential for enhancing success in target language listening. He argued that the effective use of metacognitive strategies gave learners an overview of how well other listening processes were working. In particular, he singled out comprehension monitoring as a kind of superordinate metacognitive strategy that determined the use of other metacognitive strategies, such as paying attention to important points (see Anderson, this volume, for further discussion of metacognition in language learning).

Bacon (1992, p. 161) emphasised the individual nature of strategy use in target language listening: "individuals will apply different strategies depending on their personality, cognitive style and the task in hand." She asked students to listen to two different radio broadcasts, one of which contained more narrative elements than the other. She found that the more narrative passage produced better comprehension and students were able and willing to report a greater number of strategies for that passage. Men and women appeared to use different strategies depending on the order in which they heard listening passages and the difficulty of the passages. Women reported using more metacognitive strategies, while the men reported feeling more confident about listening in a target language. The women were less flexible in their approach to the listening and tried to listen for gist, and not to translate, while the men were not ashamed to try any strategy that appeared to work. However, the choice of strategies did not appear to produce different levels of comprehension between men and women. As Macaro (2001, p. 102) comments about the study:

> we should therefore remind ourselves that we should not impose strategy use on learners but make learners aware of the range of strategies available and that a different response may be needed according to the type of passage they are listening to.

Recent research on listening strategies, for instance Rost (2002, p. 155), has focused on defining a small set of "teachable" strategies out of the almost infinite list of possibilities which seem to be consistently associated with successful listening. The five strategies that seemed to be linked to success were:

1 Predicting information or ideas prior to listening
2 Inferring from incomplete information
3 Monitoring comprehension
4 Asking for clarification
5 Providing a personal response to what has been heard.

Implications for the teaching/learning situation

An important question is: Is strategy training at all effective? Is it any use for the teacher to overtly instruct language learners in the use of listening strategies? In an important study, Thomson and Rubin (1996) demonstrated that strategy instruction over a period of two years significantly improved the listening ability of a group of students learning Russian. It also showed the usefulness of training students to use particular strategies for particular types of listening, that is, drama, interviews and news reports. Other studies (for instance, Rubin, 1988; O'Malley and Chamot, 1990; Vandergrift, 1997b), confirm the effectiveness of instruction. As Vandergrift (1997b, p. 170) remarks: "the few studies carried out in listening strategy instruction suggest that students can indeed be instructed in strategy use to enhance their performance on listening tasks."

If we think about the strategies which good language learners might employ in order to become better listeners, and to support and build up listening skills, it is useful to refer back to O'Malley and Chamot's three basic categories of metacognitive, cognitive and social/affective strategies (1990). In the lists below, I attempt to synthesize some of the listening strategies which have been mentioned in the literature (for instance, Rost and Ross, 1991; Bacon, 1992; Rost, 1999; Vandergrift, 1997a, 1999) as important for successful listening, while emphasizing that this list is illustrative rather than exhaustive:

1 *Cognitive strategies*: these are activities which learners use to remember and develop language and to facilitate comprehension.
    • predicting what a piece of listening will be about, or what language/ information will come next;
    • drawing inferences when information is not stated or has been missed;
    • guessing meaning of unknown words;
    • using intonation and pausing to segment words and phrases;
    • other micro-strategies to do with processing language – identifying stressed words, listening for markers, listening for structures etc.;
    • using schematic and contextual information (top-down) together with linguistic information (bottom-up) to arrive at meaning;
    • visualizing the situation they are hearing about;
    • piecing together meaning from words that have been heard.

2 *Metacognitive strategies*: these are activities which learners use to organize, monitor and evaluate how well they are understanding.
    • focusing attention, concentrating and clearing the mind before listening;
    • applying an advance organizer before listening (*I think the topic is going to be . . , so . . .*);
    • going in with a plan (*I'm going to listen for . . . words I know/key words/cognates . . .*);
    • getting used to speed and finding ways of coping with it;
    • being aware when they are losing attention and refocusing concentration;
    • deciding what the main purpose of listening is;
    • checking how well they have understood;
    • taking notes;
    • paying attention to the main points;
    • identifying listening problems and planning how to improve them.

3 *Socio-affective strategies*: these are activities in which learners interact with other people in order to help their comprehension and encourage themselves to continue listening.
   - asking for clarification;
   - checking that they have got the right idea;
   - providing themselves with opportunities for listening;
   - motivating themselves to listen;
   - lowering anxiety about listening;
   - providing a personal response to the information or ideas presented in the piece of listening;
   - empathizing with the speaker and trying to understand the reason for a particular message.

If we refer back to Rubin's (1975) characteristics of the good language learner, we notice that they are present in the listening strategies listed above; that is, good language learners are willing and able to guess, to learn from communication with others, to take risks, to attend to form and meaning by synthesizing linguistic and non-linguistic knowledge, to create opportunities for language practice and to self-evaluate performance.

Reinders (2004) gives some sensible advice about strategy instruction in the classroom. He suggests starting out by establishing which strategies students already use. There are a number of ways of finding out what these are: through classroom discussions, teacher observation of students, asking students how they perform language tasks, getting them to keep learner diaries, or using questionnaires. These provide useful points from which class and teacher can progress towards making existing strategies more effective, and discovering and employing new strategies. Reinders outlines a method of teaching strategies which consists of:

- discussing how a certain strategy might help to solve a particular listening problem;
- modelling it;
- getting the students to try it out;
- evaluating how effective it was.

A wide range of listening materials and suggestions for listening activities is available (for instance, Helgesen, Brown and Smith, 1997; White, 1998). Teachers could follow the procedure outlined above with the activities they choose for their classes in order to raise students' awareness of strategy options, to provide them with an example, to encourage experimentation, and to empower students with the ability to self-evaluate. Teachers should especially look for listening activities which are as much as possible devised and controlled more by the students than the teacher, since this increase in student autonomy is, in my opinion, one of the keys to successful learning (for further discussion of autonomy, see Cotterall, this volume).

Questions for ongoing research

There is now a considerable and growing literature on research into skill development and strategy use by different types of target language listener. However, the methodology for teaching listening skills and strategies still seems somewhat undeveloped and old-fashioned (see White, 1998 and 2006).

How can we best teach students to listen effectively? I would suggest it is this area which now needs work, because good language learners deserve good language teaching to assist the development of listening skills, and to develop an all-round competence which is often lacking among students who are frequently led into a target language, using methods which favour the development of graphic skills, leaving important listening skills to suffer from relative neglect. We urgently need research to inform the development of effective listening materials, equipment and teaching methodology.

Conclusion

Listening is usually the first skill which children develop as they begin to acquire the ability to communicate by means of language, and it remains an important skill throughout life. This is no less true for those learning a language other than their first. Good language learners need to activate non-linguistic knowledge about physical context, topic, ways in which discourse is organized and so on, in order to understand a spoken message. They should view listening as an important medium for developing language but also need to be aware that in order to develop language effectively, they need to practise the language they hear, either by responding to the spoken message and/or by producing some of the language they have heard in other situations. They also need to develop a range of receptive communication strategies which will enable them to cope with interactive listening.

Good language learners are able to use a number of strategies which vary according to the individuals' learning styles, the task and the type of listening in which they are engaged. However, there do seem to be some strategies which are more closely associated with successful listening than others, particularly prediction, inferring, monitoring and clarifying. Although it has been demonstrated that instruction in listening strategies can improve listening ability, further research is required to rectify the relative neglect of listening skills in target language development methodology to date.

References

Anderson, A. and Lynch, T. (1988) *Listening*. Oxford : Oxford University Press.
Anderson, N. (this volume) Chapter 7: Metacognition and good language learners.
Bacon, S.M. (1992) The relationship between gender, comprehension, processing strategies, and cognitive and affective responses in foreign language learning. *The Modern Language Journal*, 76(2), 160–175.
Brownell, J. (1986) *Building Active Listening Skills*. New Jersey: Prentice Hall.
Cotterall, S. (this volume) Chapter 8: Autonomy and good language learners.
Feyten, C.M. (1991) The power of listening ability: an overlooked dimension in language acquisition. *Modern Language Journal*, 75, 173–180.
Fromm, E. (1998) *The Art of Listening*. New York: Continuum.
Gass, S. and Varonis, E. (1994) Input, interaction, and second language production. *Studies in Second Language Acquisition*, 16, 283–302.
Griffiths, C. (2003) Patterns of language learning strategy use. *System*, 31, 367–383.
Griffiths, C. (2006) Strategies for successful learning in an English-speaking environment. *Journal of Asia TEFL*, 3(2), 141–163.
Griffiths, C. (this volume) Chapter 6: Strategies and good language learners.
Helgesen, M., Brown, S. and Smith, D. (1997) *Active Listening*. Cambridge: Cambridge University Press.
Lynch, T. (1998) 'Theoretical perspectives on listening'. In W. Grabe (ed.), *Annual Review of Applied Linguistics*, Vol. 18. Cambridge: Cambridge University Press, 3–19.
Macaro, E. (2001) *Learning Strategies in Foreign and Second Language Classrooms*. London and New York: Continuum.
O'Malley, J.M. and Chamot, A.U. (1990) *Listening Strategies in Second Language Acquisition*. Cambridge: Cambridge University Press.
O'Malley, J.M., Chamot, A.U., Kupper, L. (1989) Listening comprehension strategies in second language acquisition. *Applied Linguistics*, 10(4), 418–437.
Reinders, H. (2004) Learner strategies in the language classroom: which strategies, when and how? *Guidelines*, 26(1), 31–35.
Richards, J.C. (1990) *The Language Teaching Matrix*. Cambridge: Cambridge University Press.
Rost, M. (1999) Developing listening tasks for language learning. *Odense Working Papers in Linguistics*, Denmark: University of Odense, 49–60.
Rost, M. (2002) *Teaching and Researching Listening*. London: Longman.
Rost, M. and Ross, S. (1991) Learner use of strategies in interaction: typology and teachability. *Language Learning*, 41, 235–273.

Rubin, J. (1975) What the "good language learner" can teach us. *TESOL Quarterly*, 9(1), 41–52.

Rubin, J. (1988) Improving foreign language listening comprehension. Project No. 017AH70028. Washington, DC: US Department of Education.

Swain, M. (1985) Communicative competence: some roles of comprehensible input and output in its development. In S. Gass and C. Madden (eds.), *Input in Second Language Acquisition*, Rowley, MA: Newbury, 235–253.

Thompson, I. and Rubin, J. (1996) Can strategy instruction improve listening comprehension? *Foreign Language Annals*, 29(3), 331–342.

Vandergrift, L. (1997a) The Cinderella of communication strategies: reception strategies in interactive listening. *The Modern Language Journal*, 81(4), 494–505.

Vandergrift, L. (1997b) The strategies of second language (French) listeners: a descriptive study. *Foreign Language Annals*, 30(3).

Vandergrift, L. (1999) Facilitating second language listening comprehension: acquiring successful strategies. *ELT Journal*, 53(4), 73–78.

White, G. (1998) *Listening*. Oxford: Oxford University Press.

White, G. (2006) Teaching listening: time for a change in methodology. In E. Uso and A. Martinez-Flor (eds.), *Current Trends in Learning and Teaching the Four Skills Within a Communicative Approach*. Amsterdam: Mouton de Gruyter.

17 Speaking and good language learners

Yasushi Kawai

Clear pronunciation (see Brown, this volume) is an important aspect of the ability to speak effectively. However it does not in itself ensure oral competence. It is quite conceivable, for instance, that a speaker might be able to pronounce perfectly an utterance which makes no sense or which is totally inappropriate, as Eliza Doolittle in Shaw's *Pygmalion* demonstrated so memorably. The skill of speaking involves a pragmatic element which has attracted a great deal of attention in recent years (see, for instance, Kasper and Rose, 2002), and the importance of helping students to develop sociopragmatic competence with speech acts in their target language is now well recognized (see, for instance, Cohen, 2005). Oral communication involves an interactive social aspect which sets it apart from other language skills and creates a whole extra dimension with which the learner must come to terms. So, although good pronunciation is necessary for clear speech, it is by no means sufficient for the development of good speaking skills.

Although interest in oral communication is alive and active, it is not a novel focus. In fact, the development of speaking skills in a target language has long been a central issue in the minds of learners, teachers, and researchers. The linguistic studies around the turn of the twentieth century (for instance, Gouin, 1892; Sweet, 1899) were linked to the development of oral skills. This emphasis on speaking rather than writing was also stressed in audiolingualism (Fries, 1945), in input-based instruction (Krashen and Terrel, 1983), and in interaction-based (Long, 1983) or output-based theories (Swain, 1985). In the communicative approach (for instance Brumfit and Johnson, 1979; Littlewood, 1981; Widdowson, 1978), the development of oral skills is no doubt the focal point of language instruction (Lazaraton, 2001). The development of oral skills has always been of paramount importance, since "a large percentage of the world's language learners study English in order to develop proficiency in speaking" (Richards and Renandya, 2002, p. 201).

However, developing oral skills in a second language is not an easy task. When the learner is not in the target language environment, it is likely that learning to speak that language will be especially difficult, since learners have minimum exposure to the target language and culture, which is crucial to understanding sociolinguistic traits (such as genre and speech styles), paralinguistic traits (such as pitch, stress, and intonation), nonlinguistic traits (such as gestures and body language) and cultural assumptions in verbal interaction (Shumin, 2002).

How do good language learners develop speaking skills?

Studies conducted in China, Japan, and the USA indicate that good language learners use a variety of strategies to develop speaking ability. Those who develop good oral skills appear to be frequent strategy users regardless of culture and learning context.

Huang and van Naerssen (1987) investigated tertiary level students of English in China. Subjects were given an oral test and a learning strategy questionnaire that included formal practice (such as listening to and doing pattern drills, listening in order to improve pronunciation, memorizing and reciting texts, imitation, re-telling stories, reading aloud, and reading in order to learn vocabulary items or grammatical structures which can be used when speaking); functional practice (such as using language for communication, thinking or talking to oneself, and using listening or reading to provide models for speaking); and monitoring (such as paying attention to the use of linguistic forms and modifying language responses). The results indicated that the high performers on the oral test used more functional practice than the middle and low performers.

A series of investigations of "expert" second language speakers in Japan was conducted by Takeuchi (2003). He asked 18 expert English speakers including simultaneous interpreters, professors, and diplomats about their learning experiences in the course of language development. Common responses were: practicing phonological aspects in the beginning stage; memorizing formulaic expressions and illustrative sentences with pattern practice in the beginning and early intermediate stages; listening practice using dictation, reading aloud repeatedly, utilizing context and multimedia in building oral vocabulary in the beginning and intermediate stages; engaging in intensive, periodical, and continuous self-study in the late beginning to intermediate stages; trying to find opportunities to speak English including naturalistic communication with native speakers, self-talk and simulated conversation practice with peers in the intermediate stage.

Varela (1999) investigated the effect of grouping, selective attention, cooperation, note-taking, self-assessment, and self-talk on the development of oral presentation skills in sixth, seventh and eighth grade classes of English for speakers of other languages in the USA. Forty-one students were divided into the experimental group with strategy-instruction and the control group without it. Videotaped pre-test and post-test oral presentations were rated on organization, clarity, vocabulary choice, eye contact, volume, and pace. Strategy use was investigated by means of interviews. The results indicated that the experimental group improved their oral presentations significantly more than the control group. The experimental group also reported an increase in strategy use and there was correlation between strategy use and presentation performance.

These three studies indicate that good language learners frequently use a variety of strategies to develop speaking ability. However, despite the wide interest in strategy use and the development of oral skills, there are very few lists of strategies for developing speaking skills in the literature, although two lists labeled *strategies for speaking* do exist. The first list by Rubin and Thompson (1994) addresses nine potential problems that arise during speaking tasks, including pronunciation problems, dealing with recurring mistakes, managing correction, creating practice opportunities, accuracy issues, communication breakdowns, conversation difficulties, comprehensibility, and rules of interaction. The second speaking strategy list was developed by Weaver, Alcaya, Lybeck, and Mougel (1994). This list includes strategies to be used before conversation, during conversation, and after conversation.

Strategy instruction and oral skill development

The teachability of strategies for learning oral communication skills to less successful learners is a contentious issue in language learning research (Dörnyei, 1995). According to Cohen, Weaver, and Li (1995) there have been "relatively few studies investigating the benefits of providing second language learners with formal training in the applications of strategies for speaking" (pp. 3–4). However, there are some.

The effect of strategy instruction on speaking ability was investigated by O'Malley and Chamot (1990). High school students studying English for speakers of other languages were divided into three groups. The first group was taught metacognitive, cognitive, and social/affective strategies. The second group was taught cognitive and social/affective strategies. The third group (the control group) did not receive strategy instruction. Audiotaped pre-test and post-test speaking tasks were rated by two judges on a five-point scale that examined delivery, accuracy, and organization. The results indicated that the group that was taught all three strategies outperformed the other two. The group that was taught two strategies came next and the third group, the control group, which did not receive strategy instruction, was rated the lowest.

Another investigation which studied the effect of strategy instruction on improving speaking ability was conducted by Dadour and Robbins

(1996). A college English speaking course in Egypt conducted explicit strategy instruction. Experimental groups received strategy instruction, and control groups did not. Oral proficiency tests incorporating role-plays were conducted as pre-test and post-test. Students were provided with an Arabic translation of Oxford's (1990) Strategy Inventory for Language Learning (SILL) to assess their strategy use. The results indicated that the experimental groups outperformed the control groups on the oral proficiency test, and that the experimental group also utilized more language learning strategies.

Yet another study to investigate the effect of strategy instruction was conducted in French and Norwegian language courses in a university in the USA by Cohen *et al.* (1995). The courses focused mainly on speaking skills. The experimental group received strategy-based instruction; the control group did not. Participants took pre-tests and post-tests consisting of three speaking tasks: self-description, story retelling, and city description. Their taped performance was evaluated by assessing self-confidence in delivery, grammar, and vocabulary, and story elements and ordering. The results indicated that the experimental group outperformed the control group in one task (city description) though not in the other two tasks.

Thus, based on these studies, there is evidence to suggest that strategy instruction can improve performance in oral skills. However, the number of empirical studies is still limited. In order to accumulate useful information regarding how good language learners develop oral skills, ongoing research studies are essential.

Study 1

In order to augment the limited research done so far regarding the development of oral skills, an action research project was set up to investigate the effects of task-based strategy instruction for oral discussion in a Japanese university. In this university, both faculty professors and students supported the development of speaking ability in English, but students tended to be reserved when oral English communication was required in class.

Participants

The participants in this study were 50 freshman engineering students (48 males and two females) enrolled in a 15-week required English class. In order to get these speakers to use the target language in communicative tasks, an electronic chat programme was used as a bridge toward face-to-face interactions. Although electronic chat and face-to-face conversation cannot be considered identical speech acts (e-chat, for instance, lacks gesture, intonation, and other paralinguistic features such as turn-taking), the justification for using an electronic chat programme was that it might ease the anxiety, timidity, or intimidation in face-to-face interaction, and help reserved learners to participate more actively.

Data collection and analysis

During the first half of the semester, students did not receive strategy instruction. They just participated in discussion using an electronic chat programme, summarized the discussion on an electronic bulletin board, and then discussed the same topic face-to-face. After the first half of the semester, data were collected using a self-report questionnaire that investigated how students participated in electronic and face-to-face interactions. The question was: *How did you participate in discussions?* Positive responses included: *I dominated in discussions* and *I actively participated in discussions.* Less active responses included: *I may not be so active but I was not reluctant to speak* and *I participated, but I was more often listening to others.* The least active response was: *I was not involved with discussions.*

In the second half of the semester, task-based strategy instruction was conducted to enhance the further participation in chat and face-to-face discussions. This instruction included the following:

1 Learners were given an overview regarding how target language oral interaction proceeds and the strategies they could use to facilitate this interaction.
2 Learners were given a list of common, generally useful expressions (such as *May I ask a question . . .? Could you please repeat/clarify/ explain . . .? I would like to know why . . .? Let me give you an example . . ., On the other hand . . .*) which they then practiced in preparation for speaking encounters.
3 In order to help students focus on the face-to-face discussion task, they wrote a model conversation on paper as a group, then individually prepared and rehearsed their own remarks.

After the second half of the semester, questionnaire data were again collected. One student was missing on the day of data collection and 49 students answered questions. The responses were grouped into positive, less active, and the least active regarding chat discussions and face-to-face discussions. The results for the first half of the semester and the second half of the semester were compared for both discussion types.

Findings

According to responses to the questionnaire administered after the first half of the semester, 79.6% of the students actively participated in chat discussions. This number increased to 89.8% in the second half of the semester. On the other hand, less active students drastically decreased from 20.4% to 10.2%. There was none who was not involved in discussions at all in either semester.

Participation in face-to-face oral interactions also increased in the second half of the semester, though the effect was smaller than that in electronic discussion. In the first half of the semester, 34.7% actively participated. In the second half of the semester this number increased to 40.8%. Those who were less active decreased from 65.3% to 55.1%. Unfortunately, 4.1% were not involved in face-to-face discussion in the second semester.

The results of this study suggest that strategy instruction for group discussions in English is effective both for chat discussion and oral face-to-face discussions. The effect was especially obvious in chat discussions, but less obvious in face-to-face discussions. It is possible, however, that only one semester of instruction may not have been enough for a clear effect to be evident. In addition, only a few task-based strategies were introduced specifically regarding face-to-face interaction, and the strategies did not include affective strategies such as self-encouragements to handle intimidation and anxiety.

In order to identify effective but missing strategies, a second study was conducted during which two Japanese speakers of English provided their views on language learning.

Study 2

The study described in this section of the chapter was small scale and relatively informal. A questionnaire was sent via email to two proficient speakers of English as a second language in order to identify their strategies.

Participants

The participants in this study were two Japanese adult English speakers, who will be called Naomi and Erika. Naomi is a simultaneous interpreter. Erika is a high school English teacher. Both have used English professionally for 20 years; thus, their English communication ability is unquestionably higher than the majority of Japanese college graduates.

Both women developed their English ability in Japan although they occasionally visited English speaking countries.

Data collection and analysis

An open-ended questionnaire was emailed to the interviewees who were known to the researcher via a professional association. The questionnaire included the following three questions:

1 If you were a college student, how would you prepare for a discussion class?
2 What difficulties would you foresee during the discussion?
3 What would you do to overcome those difficulties?

They were encouraged to give as many responses as they could. After completing the questionnaire, they emailed their responses back. Additional questions were sent when the researcher found some interesting responses. The responses were compared and similarities and differences were examined. Then, the focus was placed on anxiety control, and pre-task, in-task, and post-task strategies.

Findings

Although Naomi is not a particularly shy Japanese woman, she is also not particularly sociable or extroverted. When asked if she was good at speaking with other people, she replied it was troublesome to talk to strangers; however, it was a part of her job to encourage others to speak. She was also asked if she had felt anxious or scared while learning to speak English. She said that was not the case, because, in the beginning stage, native speakers knew she had limited English proficiency and thus adjusted their level of speaking. Later on, after Naomi became better at communicating in English, she managed to make herself understood using the English ability she had at the time.

   How, then, had Naomi managed to avoid developing English speaking anxiety? One clear answer was her way of preparing for English speaking tasks in advance. Naomi gave detailed explanations regarding how she would have prepared for the face-to-face interactions. She wrote she would have gathered as much information as possible that related to the discussion topic using as much English material as she could find. She also would have collected useful English expressions and then summarized the issues. She would have practiced versatile expressions such as *I agree with the first point you raised, but may I ask you a few questions?* that could be used regardless of the topic. Naomi also would have simulated discussions with an individual or with a group, in which she would have tried to find concepts that were difficult to express in English. Then, she would have tried to determine if her inability to express what she meant was due to lack of understanding or lack of English ability. After all of this preparation, she would have practiced her remarks aloud in several different ways, thereby enabling her to choose the best and the easiest ones to utilize. In order to reduce anxiety about speaking in a foreign language, she also stressed the importance of daily activities such as reading aloud, singing songs in English and making comments in English while watching TV.

Even after this elaborate preparation, she still expected difficulties in pursuing the task. She was asked what problems she would have expected to face and what she would have done to overcome those problems. Naomi wrote she might have been reserved and hesitant because she would be considering the feelings of the other participants. Due to her limited English ability, she might not have been able to express subtleties and perhaps would have gone to extremes with her opinions. She might have had difficulty with the flow of the discussion and she might not have had the courage to state her opinions at the right moment. In order to overcome these difficulties, she would have been determined to ask at least one question, or she would have adopted a strategy of temporary agreement if she could not come up with a viable response.

Unlike Naomi, Erika is a distinctly extroverted and sociable person. She considers it easy to talk to strangers and to make friends with them. In spite of her easygoing personality, she did experience fear and anxiety when speaking English. Erika often felt that the other person spoke too fast, used unfamiliar vocabulary and did not understand what she was trying to say. In order to overcome these problems, Erika repeated questions or asked the other person to repeat their remarks. Another fundamental strategy was to increase her vocabulary and to employ functional practice in order to use learned expressions.

Erika wrote she would have done the same kind of task preparation as Naomi. She would have gathered information regarding the discussion topic through books, the Internet, and interviews. She would have translated the information into English. She also would have sought help from native speakers if they were available. Erika, like Naomi, would have sought out expressions frequently used in discussions and practiced her remarks orally in advance. She would have also anticipated other people's remarks. In addition, she would have reviewed discussion procedures.

Like Naomi, Erika also anticipated difficulties. There would have been times when she would not have understood some remarks due to lack of vocabulary, pronunciation, or some unexpected issues. To solve these problems, Erika would have used confirmation questions, asked questions based on concrete examples, and taken notes while participating in discussion. But she emphasized the importance of precautionary measures and post-task evaluation. She would have tried to imagine as many scenarios as possible and prepare for them. After the class, she would have looked up the expressions that she did not understand in a dictionary so she would be able to use them on other occasions.

The importance of planning strategies is emphasized by these two good language learners. In preparation for face-to-face discussions, they wrote they would practice orally in advance, since pre-task preparation is a confidence builder. It also seems important to practice speaking aloud in a target language on a daily basis in order to overcome the fear of actually using the language. They would also adopt social strategies such as simulating discussions with peers. This enables them to select manageable language items at their own language level, which is also another confidence builder. For in-task strategies, they would prepare emergency measures for possible communication breakdowns. Post-task activities are also important, especially learning from failures which might mitigate the fear of future failures. These strategies were missing in Study 1, where only pre-task strategies were emphasized. These two good language learners suggest in-task and post-task strategies are also important.

Implications for the teaching/learning situation

Oral competence is an important goal for many learners (Richards and Renandya, 2002). Perhaps, therefore, an important role for teachers who are aiming to improve their students' ability to speak effectively may be to find ways to provide support for learners with various kinds of learning styles so that they can learn in the ways which suit them best. Study 1, in this chapter, is an example of the use of an electronic chat program to scaffold a task for reserved learners to help them gain the confidence to face interactive opportunities, without allowing the fear of making mistakes and appearing foolish to cripple their drive to communicate and develop speaking skills.

In order to develop these skills, students need strategies. The good language learners in Study 2 provided a variety of strategies. It may be helpful to organize these strategies into three different levels:

1 Strategies to facilitate development of underlying oral skills (such as "rules" of intonation, turn taking etc.). These are general skills which are not limited to a particular situation, but which all speakers need to learn.

2   Strategies to facilitate better oral communication skills (such as learning useful vocabulary and expressions for typical communicative situations). Learning at this level might include word families (such as for education, employment, or accommodation) and functional grammar (such as expressing opinions, giving information, or making requests).

3   Strategies to facilitate the completion of particular speaking tasks (such as rehearsing particular communicative situations). The language required for these kinds of tasks will be specific, and more focused than for levels 1 and 2.

The learners in Study 2 demonstrated a variety of strategies in all three levels; however, it is important to notice that they intended to integrate these three aspects in preparation for and during the performance of an assigned task. Level 1 and 2 skills are definitely important for any kinds of oral communication. The development of communication skills, however, requires practice in specific contexts. Strategies at level 3 might appear to be micro tactics on the surface, but they are also crucial to develop other aspects of language skills associated with levels 1 and 2. It is suggested, therefore, that more attention be paid to level 3 strategies.

Questions for ongoing research

Many questions related to how good language learners develop speaking skills remain to be answered. The results of Study 1 showed positive results regarding the effectiveness of task-based strategy instruction for electronic chat and face-to-face oral discussions, but studies that employ a wider variety of strategies are required. Also, studies investigating kinds of oral communication other than discussion will be needed. Research on language learning in classroom environments requires active participation of the teacher-researcher since observations and continuous reflections on teaching and learning are essential. Accumulation of action research projects will help advance knowledge in this area.

Study 2 provided possible strategies missing in the instruction in Study 1 and suggested the importance of in-task and post-task strategies. This study was small-scale; more interviews involving a wider range of interviewees in a variety of settings are needed to gather relevant information. By assembling more data, classifying strategies into groups and researching their effects on the development of speaking skills, task-based strategy lists for various types of interaction can be developed for use in the teaching/learning situation.

The first study reported in this chapter was carried out in a Japanese context among young university students, most of whom were male. However, it is possible that students of other nationalities and ages and with a different gender mix might respond differently to the kind of electronic chat scaffolding described in this study. Similarly, both of the participants in the second study were mature Japanese females. It would be useful to investigate whether the findings of this study are generalizable to males and other age groups and nationalities.

Conclusion

A reserved attitude in oral communication does not necessarily indicate the speaker's lack of motivation or inability to communicate in a target language. Study 1 indicates that even those who are not willing to participate in face-to-face interaction can and will participate actively in electronic chat discussions. The effect of task-based strategy instruction was evident in both electronic and oral face-to-face discussions; however, the effect was not as great in oral discussions as in electronic discussions. This indicates that there are strategies specific to face-to-face oral discussions which need to be emphasized and practiced if students are to gain confidence in this kind of interaction.

A review of the available literature seems to indicate that those who develop good speaking skills tend to use a wide variety of strategies. However, it seems to be not so much the number of strategies, but the selection and combination of them which is vital in the development of second language oral proficiency. The successful English learners in this study showed that, although their strategy use was not identical, there were several strategies which they both employed. They both prepared for oral encounters in advance. They asked questions and exposed themselves regularly to spoken English (for instance, songs, TV, movies, native speakers). They also both made a conscious effort to actively engage in real oral communication by interacting in the target language, and they both monitored and evaluated their own learning.

A salient characteristic of good language learners is active participation in and contribution to their own learning (Chamot, Barnhardt, El-Dinary and Robbins, 1999). Since the ability to speak well in a target language is an important goal for many learners, perhaps an important role for teachers may be to find ways to provide support (especially for more reserved students) so that learners have the motivation to practice, and the confidence to face interactive opportunities free of the anxiety which might otherwise inhibit their endeavors.

References

Brown, A. (this volume) Chapter 15: Pronunciation and good language learners.

Brumfit, C.J. and Johnson, K. (1979) *The Communicative Approach to Language Teaching*. Oxford: Oxford University Press.

Chamot, A.U., Barnhardt, S., El-Dinary, P.B. and Robbins, J. (1999). *The Learning Strategies Handbook*. New York: Longman.

Cohen, A.D. (2005) Strategies for learning and performing L2 speech acts. *Intercultural Pragmatics*, 2(3), 275–301.

Cohen, A.D., Weaver, S.J., and Li, T.U. (1995) *The impact of strategies-based instruction on speaking a foreign language*. Minneapolis, MN: National Language Resource Center. (ERIC Document Reproduction Service No. ED394322).

Dadour, E.S., and Robbins, J. (1996) University-level studies using strategy instruction to improve speaking ability in Egypt and Japan. In R.L. Oxford (ed.), *Language Learning Strategies Around the World: Cross-cultural Perspectives*. Honolulu: University of Hawai'i Press, 157–166.

Dörnyei, Z. (1995) On the teachability of communication strategies. *TESOL Quarterly*, 29(1), 55–85.

Fries, C.C. (1945) *Teaching and Learning English as a Foreign Language*. Ann Arbor, MN: University of Michigan Press.

Gouin, F. (1892) *The Art of Teaching and Studying Languages*. London: George Philip.

Huang, X-H. and Van Naerssen, M. (1987) Learning strategies for oral communication. *Applied Linguistics*, 8(3), 287–307.

Kasper, G. and Rose, K. (2002) *Pragmatic Development in a Second Language*. Oxford: Blackwell.

Krashen, S.D. and Terrel, T.D. (1983) *The Natural Approach: Language Acquisition in the Classroom*. San Francisco: Alemany Press.

Lazaraton, A. (2001) Teaching oral skills. In M. Celce-Murcia (ed.), *Teaching English as a Second or Foreign Language*. Boston, MA: Heinle & Heinle, 103–115.

Littlewood, W. (1981) *Communicative Language Teaching*. Cambridge: Cambridge University Press.

Long, M. (1983) Native speaker/non-native speaker conversation in the second-language classroom. In M. Clarke and J. Handscombe (eds.), *On TESOL 82*. Washington, DC: TESOL, 207–225.

O'Malley, J.M. and Chamot, A.U. (1990) *Learning Strategies in Second Language Acquisition*. Cambridge: Cambridge University Press.

Oxford, R.L. (1990) *Language Learning Strategies: What Every Teacher Should Know*. New York: Newbury House.

Richards, J.C. and Renandya, W.A. (2002) *Methodology in Language Teaching*. Cambridge: Cambridge University Press.

Rubin, J. and Thompson, I. (1994) *How to be a More Successful Language Learner*. Boston, MA: Heinle & Heinle.

Speaking and good language learners

Shumin, K. (2002). Factors to consider: Developing adult EFL students' speaking abilities. In J.C. Richards and W.A. Renandya (eds.), *Methodology in Language Teaching*. Cambridge: Cambridge University Press, 204–211.

Swain, M. (1985) Communicative competence: some roles of comprehensible input and comprehensible output in its development. In S.M. Gass and C.G. Madden (eds.), *Input in Second Language Acquisition*. New York: Newbury House, 235–253.

Sweet, H. (1899) *The Practical Study of Languages: A guide for Teachers and Learners*. London: Dent.

Takeuchi, O. (2003) *Yoriyoi gaikokugo gakushuho wo motomete* (In pursuit of better language learning). Tokyo: Shohakusha.

Varela, E. (1999) Using learning strategy instruction to improve English language learners' oral presentation skills in content-based ESL instruction. In R.L. Oxford (ed.), *Strategy Research Compendium: Language Learning Strategies in the Context of Autonomy*. New York: Columbia University, 76–77.

Weaver, S.J., Alcaya, C., Lybeck, K., and Mougel, P. (1994) Speaking strategies: a list compiled by teachers in the experimental sections of the strategies-based instruction experiment. Unpublished document, National Language Resource Center, University of Minnesota, Minneapolis MN. Later published in A.D. Cohen (1998). *Strategies in Learning and Using a Second Language*. London: Longman.

Widdowson, H. (1978). *Teaching Language as Communication*. Oxford: Oxford University Press.

18 Reading and good language learners

Karen Schramm

Although in a first language, linguistic input is usually initially received via listening (see White, this volume), it is often via reading that students are exposed to a language other than their first. This chapter explores the target language reading process of good language learners. Before we look at empirical examples from speakers of other languages learning to read in English that highlight the importance of action-orientation in the target language reading classroom, we will briefly explore the interactive cognitive processes involved in reading. The chapter concludes with implications for the teaching and learning of target language reading.

Target language reading as a cognitive process

When we enjoy our newspaper or a good book, we are usually unaware of how amazingly complex a skill reading is. As language teachers, however, we often observe our students experiencing comprehension problems that make us wonder how the process of reading might work in the mind, and how we can best support our bilingual or multilingual students who are trying to develop reading skills in a new language.

Several disciplines – psychology, linguistics, and education, in particular – are involved in researching reading and have constantly refined their research methodology to inquire into this elusive process, hidden from direct observation. Research methods span a wide continuum from highly controlled psycholinguistic experiments (using, for example, eye movement tracking, reaction times to linguistic stimuli, or neurophysiological measurements such as brain scans), to ethnographic studies that rely on participant observation, documentation, interpretation, and discussion with informants in authentic reading contexts over extended periods of time.

Central to cognitive definitions of reading is the concept of meaning construction that characterizes reading not as a passive way of getting information, but as an active process of constructing understanding. The activation and use of topic-specific pre-knowledge as well as the psycholinguistic processing of text information both play an important role in meaning construction. We will therefore briefly look at each of these two aspects.

In a process called elaboration, readers integrate pre-knowledge elements into their mental models. The availability of such pre-knowledge depends on interests (Bügel and Buunk, 1996; Finkbeiner, 2005) which means that texts based on unfamiliar cultural information pose a higher reading challenge than texts based on one's own culture/s (Brantmeier, 2005; Steffensen and Joag-dev, 1992). These top-down processes are crucial for meaning construction, but it is also important to point out that elaborations are only possible after bottom-up activation of the particular knowledge domains (Hudson, 1988; Roller and Matambo, 1992; also see Nassaji, 2002). On the basis of the constructed mental model at a particular time during the reading process, readers form expectations about the up-coming text information. If these hypotheses are correct, they help the readers process the text information; if readers cannot confirm their hypotheses, however, they usually pay increased attention to text processing or even revise their mental model. On the basis of the constructed meaning, readers also make intended inferences about information that is only implied in the text. For example, *fish* might be understood specifically as *shark* when reading about a fish that attacked a swimmer (Rickheit and Strohner, 1990, pp. 537–539).

Readers also integrate text information into their mental model in a bottom-up process. This clearly presents a particular challenge for target language readers who only have limited linguistic pre-knowledge of that language. Our discussion, of the perceptual and psycholinguistic processes involved in constructing a propositional textbase from the black and white marks on the pages in a text, will proceed from letter and word recognition via syntactic parsing and semantic processing, to the creation of local and global coherence. However, this linear presentation does not imply that these bottom-up processes are sequential. Instead, they interact with each other as well as with the top-down processes involving pre-knowledge that we discussed above.

For the perception of visual information on the page, readers' eyes do not move evenly across the lines, but "jump" in so-called saccades from one fixation point to the next. Under usual circumstances, first language readers do not fixate every word; instead 1.2 words per fixation have been found to be an average for readers of English (Just and Carpenter, 1980). At a speed that usually ranges from 200–250 milliseconds per fixation for first language readers, these saccades bring new information into the foveal area of the retina where visual acuity is best (Inhoff and Rayner, 1996; Noordman and Vonk, 1994). The resulting iconic representations are analyzed into graphemes by pattern recognition mechanisms that are based on the detection of distinctive features of graphemes as well as on orthographic knowledge about the probability of letter combinations. At this processing level, differences in writing systems and directions clearly present challenges for the reader of a new language. However, even when a reader's first and new or target language share the same alphabet (assuming the reader can read in their first language), their weaker associations concerning letter combinations in the target language, their lesser knowledge of the new orthography, as well as interference from first language orthography increase the processing difficulties as compared to reading in their first language (for further research on orthographic features, see Akamatsu, 2003; Berkemeier, 1997; Birch, 2002; Koda, 1999; Nassaji, 2003).

A central research question concerning the next processing level of word recognition has been whether it requires the activation of the phonological code in working memory or whether words can be recognized directly on the basis of the visual code only. By now, the concept of a dual access to the mental lexicon – that is either direct visual access or access via phonological recoding – has largely been agreed on (Grabe and Stoller, 2002; Katz and Feldman, 1996). The mental lexicon provides semantic and syntactic information about a particular lexical item. A challenge for those trying to read in a language other than their first arises from the fact that not all words a student reads are represented in their mental lexicon. In such cases, readers can ignore the unknown word, consult a dictionary (or another source such as a friend or the teacher), infer it from the context, and/or analyze it into morphological components (Fraser, 1999; Fukkink and de Glopper, 1998). But even when readers of a new language process a word that is indeed represented in their mental lexicon, at the beginning levels, their lexical access is not as automatic as it is in reading in their first language (also see Fukkink, Hulstijn, and Simis, 2005; Qian, 2002).

Syntactic parsing relies on grammatical knowledge that first language readers usually possess to a much higher degree than those learning to read in a new language. Empirical studies have singled out entities such as complex nominal phrases or hypothetical conditional clauses as being especially problematic for learners of English (Berman, 1992; Cooper, 1992). Teachers who deal with students from different linguistic backgrounds should realize that the syntactic strategies of target language readers are often based on the morpho-syntactical characteristics of their specific first languages. When readers use these language-specific processing strategies for reading in their target language, they often pay more attention to unimportant morpho-syntactical information than to important clues. For example, a reader with English as the first language will usually transfer the strategy of paying attention to word order even when reading in another language with a rather flexible word order, such as Korean, which native readers process without paying attention to word order (Karcher, 1994; Koda, 1993, 1994, 2005).

Beyond the clause and sentence level, readers need to establish local coherence on the basis of connectors such as conjunctions (for example, *because*, *although*) or pronominal adverbs (for instance, *therefore*, *thereafter*) and on the basis of co-reference established by linguistic devices such as pronouns (for example, *the woman–she–her*) or semantic relations (for instance, *keyboard–mouse–type*) (Chung, 2000; Ozono and Ito, 2003). Global coherence is also of great importance. An essential theoretical distinction in this respect is the one by van Dijk and Kintsch (1983) into macrostructures and superstructures of texts. Macrostructures represent the condensed content of texts and consist of macropropositions. Readers create such macropropositions by recursively applying the macrorules of selection, deletion, generalization, and construction onto propositions of the original textbase. This is often hard for those who are reading in a language other than their first, who consequently have more trouble answering comprehension questions at this deeper processing level than factual questions at the surface level of the text (Oded and Walters, 2001; Perkins and Brutten, 1992). The term superstructure, on the other hand, refers to text forms. Since Kaplan's (1966) provocative article on cultural thought patterns, the field of contrastive rhetoric has further inquired into organizational differences of texts in different cultures, and reading research has established that target language texts based on first language rhetorical conventions lead to better comprehension and recall (for instance, Chu, Swaffar, and Charney, 2002), suggesting that readers in a target language need to build their knowledge about culture-specific text forms in order to be able to make top-down use of it in their target language reading. A systematic progression with respect to text forms is thus an important aspect of a target language reading class.

Although this brief overview has concentrated on major cognitive aspects of reading in a language other than the first, it is important to remember that metacognitive, social, and affective aspects are also crucial to the understanding of what is involved in target language reading. Metacognition on reading involves strategy awareness and perceived strategy use as well as the actual regulation and control of the reading process (Schramm, 2006). Social practices relating to the use of texts vary greatly according to culture, and educational cultures in particular (Bell, 1995; Heath, 1983), while affective factors such as interests (Finkbeiner, 2005) as well as attitudes and beliefs (Kamhi-Stein, 2003) also play major roles in target language reading.

How do good language learners develop reading skills?

To inquire into the question of how good language learners develop reading skills in a language other than their first, Schramm (2001) conducted a qualitative analysis of 16 hours of think-aloud protocols obtained from German undergraduate students reading an American psychology textbook in English. The analysis was based on insights from the growing number of reading strategy studies that have evolved from Rubin's (1975) concept of the good language learner (for a recent overview of studies on target language reading strategies, see Schramm, 2006). Three interrelated action levels involved in reading were identified:

1 The first level is the higher-level activity in which the reading process is embedded. In our examples, the higher-level activity is a psychology class with lectures, discussions, and exams.
2 The second level is characterized by the reader's specific goal for interaction with the author by means of reading, for instance, the reading of a psychology textbook for the purpose of passing the psychology class exam.
3 The third level consists of action to secure comprehension when comprehension problems have been evaluated as threatening the reader's goal.

Goal-orientation on these three levels was found to be charateristic of good language learners. This section therefore presents empirical examples that demonstrate the more successful readers' mental actions.

First, it is important to realize that readers usually have a goal in mind. The exceptions to this authentic reading praxis are the many classrooms in which reading is done for the sake of reading or language learning only. In other contexts, readers read to find information that they are interested in using in some meaningful way. Such use can result in immediate subsequent action (for instance, buying ingredients for a particular dish after having consulted a cookbook or going to the train station at a particular time after having consulted the schedule). More abstract ways of using information can involve decision-making (for instance, about which product to buy or which plan to pursue to tackle a complex problem), emotional stimulation (for instance, about experiences such as love or fear), and display or supply of knowledge (for instance, in exams, business meetings, or own texts) to name only a few examples. Our first empirical example illustrates the impact of a reading goal. This example has been taken out of the retrospection of a German psychology student who explains how her color-coding strategy has been initiated by, and now serves, her oral participation in a psychology class. This example shows how the higher-level goal that reading is to serve influences subsequent action.

Example 1: Colors

Interviewer: And how did you come up with the idea [of using two different colors]?

Student: Because it always was so terribly important in Ms X's class. Because we always had to read these texts, and during the next class, we had to comment on them or something like that, and either she really only wanted the theory or something like that, or she wanted many examples. And I spent the first two sessions on nothing else but searching my text to find out which part is a theory, which part is an example. And that was senseless searching, that was ((1s)) a stupid use of time. And then, later on, I marked it in two colors. And, depending on what she asked during the next session, I could find it more quickly.

(translated from Schramm 2001, p. 254)

Double brackets with a number indicate pauses in seconds.

On a second level, reading involves linguistic interaction with the author in a dilated speech situation (Ehlich, 1984). Since the author and reader are separated by a local and/or a time distance, the written text bridges their two isolated speech situations so that they can cooperate despite their separation. This cooperation is not only based on a shared goal such as, in our examples, passing psychological knowledge from one generation to the next, but also on culture-specific knowledge about how people usually cooperate to achieve this specific purpose – a purpose that has come up many times before in their society and the pursuit of which has therefore evolved into inter-individually shared, routine patterns of action (Ehlich and Rehbein, 1979; Rehbein, 1977).

The bold print in Example 2 shows how another German reader of English reconstructs the teaching goal of the textbook authors. Note that in the example the reader focuses on finding out what the authors want to do. Based on such a reconstructed goal, readers can organize their individual mental action to interplay with the reconstructed action that the author is pursuing.

The think-aloud data allow us to retrace the reader's intense reconstruction of the authors' goal from a text passage on light perception. At first, she is surprised that the textbook authors mention an alien creature, and she asks herself what "he" might want to do. After she has processed the text for another twelve seconds, she verbalizes the recon-

---

Example 2: Alien Creature

((clicks tongue, 1s)) ((sighs, 1s)) "alien creature"? Well· **(What) does he want now?** ((laughs, 1s)) ((11s)) ((inhales audibly, 1s)) (Oh yes,) and **now • he wants us/ they want us to** somehow get at • • how that can be measured, the light, • • and at which point one can see it. ((8s)) **Yes, there it is again,** "to determine the minimum" • • • "magnitude of a stimulus" ((2s)) "that can be" ((2s)) Well, that • • the minimum limit • **is what one, you know, always tries to find out.** At which point one can detect anything at all.

(translated from Schramm 2001, CD, Fig. 6.17)

Single brackets indicate that utterance parts are not clearly audible.

Double brackets indicate non-phonological, acoustic information and pauses (in seconds).

Quotation marks indicate reading aloud from text.

Underlining indicates emphasis.

• indicates a short pause, • • a medium pause, • • • a long pause under 1 second.

---

structed goal (*they want us to*), which she finds confirmed after another eight seconds of reading (*Yes, there it is again*).

So far, we have seen the integration of reading into a higher-level activity and reading as inter-individual action of reader and author for a specific purpose. On a third level, good readers take action to secure comprehension. Characteristically, their decision to take action is based on an evaluation of the comprehension problem with regard to the pursuit of the reading goal, which they established in relation to their sociocultural context. In other words, good readers do not take action to solve comprehension problems that do not endanger their reading goal. Less successful readers, on the other hand, tend to worry about comprehension problems that are not relevant to the pursuit of the reading goal, and/or they tend to ignore, or find easy pseudo-solutions to comprehension problems that put them at risk of not achieving their reading goal (Schramm, 2001).

Example 3 shows a successful reader acting to secure comprehension (in bold). When she asks the question "First or later?" she is unsure whether the bones that she has just read about transmit sound *from* the oval window or *to* the oval window. She goes back to the relevant text elements to find that bones are "the first thing," and then makes notes in the margin that document her findings. This example illustrates the third level of intra-individual action to secure comprehension; it is subordinate to the purposeful cooperation with the author as well as the superordinate activity that determines the reading goal.

Example 3: Mechanical Bridge

Okay. So, first it transmits ((5s)) the vibrations to the • *oval window*. ((2s)) And then ((3s)) um ((1s)) they are transduced ((2s)) into mechanical impulses. ((35s)) "*Sound*"-wave goes through the • "*Eardrum*". ((2s)) Transmitted to the "Oval window". ((3s)) And there, then, . . . ((4s)) • • • **First or later?** ((5s)) So· • • ((clears her throat, 1s)) ((4s)) First • the *eardrum* is still clear. Then, ((9s)) then this chamber reaches the *oval window*. ((24s)) **Yes, so the first thing are the, ((1s)) the um/ these bones.** ((2s)) (*Eardrum*). ((2s)) *Then* ((2s)) um ((4s)) follows ((2s)), *then* ((4s)) oval ((3s)) (*window*).

> *(translated from Schramm 2001, CD, fig. 8.23)*

Single brackets indicate that utterance parts are not clearly audible.

Double brackets indicate non-phonological, acoustic information and pauses (in seconds).

Quotation marks indicate reading aloud from text.

• indicates a short pause, • • a medium pause, • • • a long pause under 1 second.

Italics represent use of English in the German think-aloud.

Implications for the teaching/learning situation

According to Schramm's findings, good readers are able to develop clear goals for their reading, and they are able to reconstruct the author's goal and action steps from the text and to relate information from the text to their own goals. Also, good readers are able to monitor their own comprehension, evaluate problems, and take appropriate action. These findings are in line with several other studies on cognitive and metacognitive strategy use (see the overview in Schramm, 2006). Below, we incorporate our findings into a set of recommendations which teachers might use to advise students:

Level 1: reading for the higher level goal

- Before you start reading, establish your reading goal(s). Think about (or ask your teacher) why you want to (or have to) read this text.
- Activate your pre-knowledge, skim the text, and build necessary pre-knowledge from encyclopedias, the Internet, and other sources.

- After reading, when you actually use the text information, think about which of your thoughts during and after reading were most helpful for accomplishing the task.
- When you use the text information, also think about how, during and after reading, you could have better prepared for actually using the text information.

Level 2: cooperating with the author

- Think about what the author's goal is and how this relates to your own personal goal in reading the text.
- Observe which steps the author makes to pursue the text goal(s).
- Skip or skim any sections that do not help you to reach your reading goal(s).
- Think about whether the text allows you to reach the author's goal(s) and, more importantly, your own goal(s).

Level 3: securing comprehension of the text

- Watch out for inconsistencies between what you read and your own background knowledge. Make a note of such inconsistencies for later action (e.g., class discussion).
- Watch out for inconsistencies between what you read and previous text information. If an inconsistency threatens your reading goal, look again at the preceeding passages in the text and try to resolve the inconsistency.
- Watch out for ideas that seem unrelated to other ideas in the text. If they seem relevant, take the time to inquire into their connections to the text (e.g., by studying the links between sentences such as connectors and co-reference).
- When you get bored, frustrated, or nervous, do something about it (e.g., choose another text to pursue your goal, or get help).

Although the language in these recommendations is reasonably difficult, and may need to be simplified for lower level learners, by presenting these ideas to their students, teachers can raise learners' awareness of how they might go about improving their ability to read effectively in their target language. Practice, evaluation, and transfer of reading strategies are also necessary for sustained learning effects. It is therefore essential to organize reading instruction in meaningful and contextualized ways that actually require – and motivate – action on all three levels.

Questions for further research

Three aspects of particular relevance for classroom instruction on target language reading emerge from this action-level perspective. First, it seems plausible that readers' concepts of the action levels vary from reader to reader. Depending especially on their sociocultural background, target language readers might conceptualize the role that reading plays in various higher-level actions, the established ways in which authors and readers interact for specific purposes, and the options of how to go about comprehension repairs in quite different ways. Research on sociocultural variation in reading as mental action, on sociocultural clashes in the target language reading classroom, or on (rather problematic) unnoticed misunderstandings in the cooperation with the author therefore seem to be promising lines of research for target language reading instruction.

Secondly, many of the strategies suggested on pp. 238–239 are rather broad. It would be useful to further examine these strategies and to identify some of the micro-strategies involved. Strategies such as what to do if a word is unknown, how to segment text into semantic "chunks", and how to cope with unfamiliar grammatical constructions are all critically important for students reading in a language other than their first.

Thirdly, most research on target language reading strategies has so far focused on differences between good and poor readers. However, such studies only provide us with rather indirect clues concerning classroom or self-study interventions that might (or might not) be useful for poor target language readers. It consequently seems desirable that future investigations focus on actual learning outcomes of reading strategy interventions, which aim to empower self-regulated and autonomous target language readers.

Conclusion

From our discussion of the three levels involved in learning how to read in a language other than the first, a picture of good target language learners emerges who are firstly aware of the higher-level activity that determines their specific reading goal and who regulate and control their reading with respect to this activity. Secondly, good language learners are able to reconstruct the author's goal and linguistic action steps from the text, and organize their mental action steps into an interplay with the author's linguistic action steps. Thirdly, good learners monitor their comprehension, evaluate comprehension problems with respect to the pursuit of the specific reading goal, and take comprehension-securing action on the basis of such evaluation. These results concerning the functional action-orientation of good target language readers call for the integration of reading instruction into authentic study, work, or community contexts that, from this particular perspective, seem indispensable for successful target language reading development.

References

Akamatsu, N. (2003) The effects of first language orthographic features on second language reading in text. *Language Learning*, 53(2), 207–231.

Bell, J.S. (1995) The relationship between L1 and L2 literacy: Some complicating factors. *TESOL Quarterly*, 29(4), 687–704.

Berkemeier, A. (1997) *Kognitive Prozesse beim Zweitschrifterwerb. Zweitalphabetisierung griechisch-deutsch bilingualer Kinder im Deutschen* (Cognitive processes in the acquisition of a second script. Second literacy learning of German by Greek-German bilingual children). Frankfurt: Lang.

Berman, R.A. (1992) Syntactic components of the foreign language reading process. In J.C. Alderson, and A.H. Urquhart (eds.), *Reading in a Foreign Language* (fifth edition). London/New York: Longman, 139–156.

Birch, B. (2002) *English L2 Reading: Getting to the Bottom.* Mahwah, NJ: Erlbaum.

Brantmeier, C. (2005) Effects of reader's knowledge, text type, and test type on L1 and L2 reading comprehension in Spanish. *Modern Language Journal*, 89(1), 37–53.

Bügel, K. and Buunk, B.P. (1996) Sex differences in foreign language text comprehension: the role of interests and prior knowledge. *Modern Language Journal*, 80(1), 15–31.

Chu, H.-C.J., Swaffar, J., and Charney, D.H. (2002) Cultural representations of rhetorical conventions: the effects on reading recall. *TESOL Quarterly*, 36(4), 511–541.

Chung, J.S. (2000) Signals and reading comprehension – theory and practice. *System*, 28(2), 247–259.

Cooper, M. (1992) Linguistic competence of practised and unpractised non-native readers of English. In J.C. Alderson and A.H. Urquhart (eds.), *Reading in a Foreign Language* (5th edition). London/New York: Longman, 122–135.

Ehlich, K. (1984) Zum Textbegriff (About the term "text"). In A. Rothkegel, and B. Sandig (eds.), *Papiere zur Textlinguistik Vol. 52. Text – Textsorten – Semantik (Papers in Textlinguistics).* Hamburg, Germany: Buske, 9–25.

Ehlich, K. and Rehbein J. (1979) Sprachliche Handlungsmuster (Linguistic patterns of action). In H.-G. Soeffner (ed.), *Interpretative Verfahren in den Sozial- und Geisteswissenschaften* (Interpretative methods in the social sciences and humanities). Stuttgart, Germany: Metzler, 243–274.

Finkbeiner, C. (2005) *Interessen und Strategien beim fremdsprachlichen Lesen. Wie Schülerinnen und Schüler englische Texte lessen und verstehen* (Interests and strategies in foreign language reading. How students read and understand English texts). Tübingen, Germany: Narr.

Fraser, C.A. (1999) Lexical processing strategy use and vocabulary learning through reading. *Studies in Second Language Acquisition*, 21, 225–241.

Fukkink, R.G. and de Glopper, K. (1998) Effects of instruction in deriving word meaning from context: a meta-analysis. *Review of Educational Research*, 68(4), 450–469.

Fukkink, R.G., Hulstijn, J., and Simis, A. (2005) Does training in second-language word recognition skills affect reading comprehension? An experimental study. *Modern Language Journal*, 89(1), 54–75.

Grabe, W. and Stoller, F.L. (2002) *Teaching and Researching Reading*. Harlow, England: Pearson Education.

Heath, S.B. (1983) *Ways with Words: Language, Life, and Work in Communities and Classrooms*. Cambridge: Cambridge University Press.

Hudson, T. (1988) The effects of induced schemata on the 'short circuit' in L2 reading: non-decoding factors in L2 reading performance. In P.L. Carrell, J. Devine, and D.E. Eskey (eds.), *Interactive Approaches to Second Language Reading*. Cambridge: Cambridge University Press, 183–205.

Inhoff, A.W. and Rayner, K. (1996) Das Blickverhalten beim Lesen (Eye movements during reading). In H. Günther, and O. Ludwig (eds.), *Schrift und Schriftlichkeit – Writing and its use. Ein interdisziplinäres Handbuch internationaler Forschung – An interdisciplinary handbook of international research*, Vol. 2. Berlin/New York: de Gruyter, 942–957.

Just, M.A., and Carpenter, P.A. (1980) A theory of reading: From eye fixations to comprehension. *Psychological Review*, 87(4), 329–354.

Kamhi-Stein, L.D. (2003) Reading in two languages: how attitudes toward home language and beliefs about reading affect the behaviors of "underprepared" L2 college readers. *TESOL Quarterly*, 37(1), 35–71.

Kaplan, R. (1966) Cultural thought patterns in intercultural education. *Language Learning*, 16(1), 1–20.

Karcher, G.L. (1994) *Das Lesen in der Erst- und Fremdsprache. Dimensionen und Aspekte einer Fremdsprachenlegetik* (Reading in a first and foreign language. Dimensions and aspects of foreign reading teaching) (2nd edition). Heidelberg, Germany: Groos.

Katz, L. and Feldman, L.B. (1996) The influence of an alphabetic writing system on the reading process. In H. Günther and O. Ludwig (eds.), *Schrift und Schriftlichkeit – Writing and its use. Ein interdisziplinäres Handbuch internationaler Forschung – An interdisciplinary handbook of international research*, Vol. 2. Berlin/New York: de Gruyter, 1094–1101.

Koda, K. (1993) Transferred L1 strategies and L2 syntactic structure in L2 sentence comprehension. *Modern Language Journal*, 77(4), 490–500.

Koda, K. (1994) Second language reading research: problems and possibilities. *Applied Psycholinguistics*, 15, 1–28.

Koda, K. (1999) Development of L2 intraword orthographic sensitivity and decoding skills. *Modern Language Journal*, 83(1), 51–64.

Koda, K. (2005) *Insights into Second Language Reading: A Cross-linguistic Approach*. Cambridge: Cambridge University Press.

Nassaji, H. (2002) Schema theory and knowledge-based processes in second language reading comprehension: A need for alternative perspectives. *Language Learning*, 52(2), 439–481.

Nassaji, H. (2003) Higher-level and lower-level text processing skills in advanced ESL reading comprehension. *Modern Language Journal*, 87(2), 261–275.

Noordman, L.G.M. and Vonk, W. (1994) Text processing and its relevance for literacy. In L. Verhoeven (ed.), *Functional Literacy: Theoretical Issues and Educational Implications*. Amsterdam/Philadelphia: Benjamins, 75–93.

Oded, B. and Walters, J. (2001) Deeper processing for better EFL reading comprehension. *System*, 29(3), 357–370.

Ozono, S. and Ito, H. (2003) Logical connectives as catalysts for interactive L2 reading. *System*, 31(2), 283–297.

Perkins, K. and Brutten, S.R. (1992) The effect of processing depth on ESL reading comprehension. *Journal of Research in Reading*, 15(2), 67–81.

Qian, D.D. (2002) Investigating the relationship between vocabulary knowledge and academic reading performance: An assessment perspective. *Language Learning*, 52(3), 513–536.

Rehbein, J. (1977) *Komplexes Handeln: Elemente zur Handlungstheorie der Sprache*. (Complex action: Elements of the action theory of language). Stuttgart, Germany: Metzler.

Rickheit, G. and Strohner, H. (1990) Inferenzen: Basis des Sprachverstehens (Inferences: Basis of language comprehension). *Die Neueren Sprachen*, 89(6), 532–545.

Roller, C.M. and Matambo, A.R. (1992) Bilingual readers' use of background knowledge in learning from text. *TESOL Quarterly*, 26(1), 129–141.

Rubin, J. (1975) What the "good language learner" can teach us. *TESOL Quarterly*, 9(1), 41–51.

Schramm, K. (2001) *L2-Leser in Aktion. Der fremdsprachlichen Leseprozeß als mentales Handeln* (L2-readers in action. The foreign language reading process as mental action). Münster, Germany/New York: Waxmann.

Schramm, K. (2006) Cognitive and metacognitive aspects of the L2 reading process: research and teaching perspectives. *Babylonia* 3/2006, 25–30.

Steffensen, M.S. and Joag-dev, C. (1992) Cultural knowledge and reading. In J.C. Alderson and A.H. Urquhart (eds.), *Reading in a Foreign Language* (5th edition). London/New York: Longman, 48–61.

van Dijk, T.A. and Kintsch, W. (1983) *Strategies of Discourse Comprehension*. New York: Academic Press.

White, G. (this volume). Chapter 16: Listening and good language learners.

19   Writing and good language learners

Louise Gordon

Getting learners to engage in writing in the target language with any degree of enthusiasm can be a challenge for teachers. Perhaps this reflects the effort which must be exerted in order to write competently in a first language: doing the same in a new language therefore seems altogether too difficult. And to make it even more difficult for aspiring target language writers, in addition to linguistic knowledge, the socio-cultural nature of writing, involving prior knowledge, knowledge of genre and register, and cultural expectations may in fact hinder attempts to transfer competence in first language writing to another language (Hyland, 2003).

Writing in the language classroom is often seen as an extension of or support for the other skills. It may, for example, be used to consolidate the learning of grammar or vocabulary or be used as preparation for a speaking activity: jotting down intended dialogue will give the students time to think and therefore improve confidence and fluency. The opportunity to write in order to become a better writer does not often predominate in the language classroom (Harmer, 2004).

Given, however, that there are many language learners who go on to do further studies in the target language, competency with writing in the target language is becoming increasingly relevant to the needs of speakers of other languages. Therefore, it is not uncommon that classes are now given over to the specific teaching of this skill. As a result, different theories have emerged over the past 20 years to provide teachers with a framework with which to guide students on the path to proficiency.

Theories of writing

At one end of the theoretical continuum, writing is seen as an extension of grammar and therefore focuses on accuracy. At the other end, the communication of meaning is paramount, accuracy a side issue. Somewhere in between, other approaches such as process, genre, or functional orientations attempt to balance out the form–meaning dichotomy. Perhaps as a consequence of the complexity of writing, the different theories over the course of time have not superseded one another, but are often used together so as to provide language learners with an array of tools necessary to helping them develop proficiency with writing in the target language (Hyland, 2003).

When writing is used as a support skill in the language classroom it is usually approached from a teaching orientation which is product-centered, meaning that the teacher will immediately correct any mistakes in grammar and language form, therefore not giving learners the opportunity to attend to their own weaknesses with either form or in conveying meaning. This approach not only ignores how meaning is developed, but it also fails to recognize that the writer, regardless of purpose or form, must go through a number of stages before producing a final text (Hyland, 2003). It is the process approach which proposes that, since experienced writers go through the cognitive stages of planning, composing and revising in a manner that is recursive, so too should those hoping to improve their ability to write. The process approach encourages students to plan and draft and, as a consequence of revising, of deliberating over the extent to which the draft effectively conveys meaning, or in response to peer or teacher feedback, they may need to re-plan or re-draft what they have written (Flower and Hayes, 1981).

Feedback, with its potential to transform a writer's text, has a really important role in process writing but it is not without its drawbacks. First among these is the tendency for learners to add or delete ideas in their draft only in response to teacher feedback. In other words, unless teachers are discerning in how feedback is given, they can foster student dependency. By perfunctorily adding or deleting, in accordance with teacher feedback, the learner is failing to engage in the writing process and, as a consequence, the overall ability to write will not improve. Peer feedback can fall short of what it is intended to achieve, either because peers lack sufficient knowledge themselves to provide accurate feedback, or because student peers may be apprehensive about offering constructive criticism. Feedback, if it is to be useful, will inspire writers to re-plan, re-draft, or re-edit their texts so as to best convey their intended meaning. The form of their writing, the grammar and vocabulary, are not attended to until the final draft. This delay in responding to grammar is one of the strengths of this approach as students are encouraged to express their ideas without their flow of thought being impeded by their concern for correctness.

However, one of the shortcomings of process writing, as identified by Swales (1990), is that it puts too much emphasis on the cognitive processes of writing with too little regard given to the social forces, which help to shape a text. This weakness provides the ideal entry point for considering the use of the genre approach, in conjunction with process. This approach holds that writing is not simply an outcome of internal processes, but is also determined by purpose and context. So all writing is done with a purpose in mind, whether it is to write a postcard, a love letter, a newspaper article, or a university essay, and these various purposes influence the overall structure and features of a text such as coherence (Harmer 2004). Context, being the social influences operating beyond the page, determines such linguistic features of a text as register. In teaching according to this approach, an expert text will be analyzed before the teacher models how to write such a text along with learner input. Students, once aware of how such a text is constructed, are then free to independently use the model to write their own texts (Hyland 2003).

Once the students begin to write according to the chosen genre, the process orientation can be implemented, with the learners developing their text by following the cognitive stages of planning, composing, and revising. One of the advantages of using the genre approach along with process is that an initial focus on genre, examining how the rhetorical and linguistic features of a text are constructed so as to achieve a particular purpose, helps the teacher to prepare the students to write. Once the thinking processes necessary to composing such a text have been modeled, then the students may engage in the cognitive stages recommended by the process approach in order to construct their own text. Using the two collaboratively helps to resolve one of the weaknesses of process writing which puts too much emphasis on the writer as an independent producer of texts and too much emphasis on "the writer and the writer's internal world" (Swales, 1990, p. 220) without considering the socio-cultural nature of writing. The genre approach gives the learner more initial support, with analysis of and modeling how to construct a text for a particular purpose before learners engage in the process of creating their own. Process and genre together, in recognizing that writing is both personal and social, help to address a major potential difficulty of learning to write in a new language: that the prior knowledge, experience, and cultural expectations that a learner brings to the classroom may be incompatible with those which render a piece of writing in the target language effective.

Another perspective on the teaching of writing is the functional approach. Underlying this approach is the idea "that particular language forms perform certain communicative functions and that students can be taught the functions most relevant to their needs" (Hyland, 2003, p. 6). In this respect, it is a development on the approach which teaches writing as an extension of grammar. With a view to helping students write effective essays, the functional approach will break a paragraph down into its component parts, identify topic and supporting sentences, and discuss the different purposes for which these may be written, whether it be to describe a process, to list ideas or to provide an example. From identifying the overall purpose of a paragraph, students can be taught how coherence and cohesion are developed. Analysis then shifts from paragraph to essay level (with its overall structure of introduction, body, and conclusion) and opportunity will be provided for students to develop competence with this structural form.

One of the weaknesses of the functional approach, as Hyland (2003) points out, is that it fails to attend to meaning and purpose. The students may be getting plenty of practice with language patterns but they are not engaging in any writing which for them has any real meaning or purpose. Consequently, once they have been exposed to a plethora of scaffolding texts intended to help them to develop competence with writing for a particular function, if they are then required to write at a level that challenges their communicative competence, meaning can be compromised or even neglected. Instead they may simply randomly depend on language patterns that are supposed to be effective for the particular function. As a result the student may fail to respond effectively to the assigned task and ideas may merely be randomly pasted together with very little development of cohesion and coherence at sentence, paragraph, or essay level.

So, how do good language learners develop writing skills? In an attempt to throw some light onto this important question, a small-scale exploratory study was conducted at a private tertiary educational institution in Auckland, New Zealand.

The study

To identify the characteristics of good writers, interviews were conducted with two students who had produced impressive work while progressing towards proficiency with their writing. These two students were both aiming to study for a Bachelor's degree at a tertiary institution for international students in Auckland, New Zealand. In order to complete their studies, they were both required to write sometimes quite complicated assignments in English. Since both of them were struggling with the written component of their chosen courses, they were enrolled in courses which focused on the development of writing skills.

Participants

The younger student was only 16 years old. She was Indonesian, and studying in a Foundation course designed to prepare her for further study at degree level. The older student was 23. She was Chinese, and already studying at degree level. Both students were enrolled in courses which involved the development of the ability to write in their target language (English). They both displayed better than average writing ability, and were interviewed in order to explore possible explanations for their success.

Data collection and analysis

The participants were invited to an informal interview and asked a series of questions relating to how they managed the writing process. Questions asked related especially to how much they read in the target language and the extent to which they believed this to be a help when writing. How did they attend to vocabulary and grammar, and how did they cope with uncertainty? How did they make sure their meaning was clear? Were they interested in writing? Were they prepared to spend time perfecting their writing? Did they write for other than classroom/assignment purposes? Notes were taken while the interviewees were talking and later analyzed for common themes.

Findings

The responses to the questions indicated that these two successful students used several broad strategies in the process of developing their writing skills. Although, with only two respondents, conclusions must be considered tentative at this point, the following strategies were found to be characteristic of these two good writers.

1 Good writers read

For anyone interested in writing, even in their first language, reading is invaluable, and this is no different for those trying to learn a new language (Griffiths, 2002, 2003a, 2003b, 2004; Schramm, this volume). Among other benefits it can help them to develop ideas for an assigned writing task as well as to build the rhetorical structures and vocabulary required to express their ideas for a specific purpose. Both respondents were keenly aware of how reading helped them to write more effectively. Whenever they are given a writing task their first destination would be the library or the Internet. For one of the respondents, referring to the Internet was not a matter of putting herself at the mercy of its magnitude; she had specific websites and publications she would consult, and this would be where her preparation to write would begin. Reading would not only help the learners to generate ideas before beginning to write, if they found themselves floundering mid-task they would again go back to reading, not just once but as many times as necessary.

2 Good writers attend to vocabulary

A large and appropriate vocabulary is an essential tool for those wanting to express themselves in a new language (Nation, 1990; Moir and Nation, this volume), and one of the respondents was especially aware of how reading helped her build the foundation necessary to express her ideas in writing. This she would not leave to chance. When reading she would make notes of new vocabulary in a book designated for this purpose. As well as defining the word as appropriate to her needs, she would record how the word had been used. When writing she would experiment with the use of the new vocabulary, using the context in which she had seen it used as a guide. As well as using the vocabulary she had encountered while reading, she would use unfamiliar vocabulary from the thesaurus, even if she was not sure whether she was using it correctly.

3 Good writers develop strategies to manage a degree of uncertainty

For those learning a new language, there are many uncertainties: uncertainty about the requirements of a task, uncertainty about how to express their ideas or uncertainty about their own ability to do either. As Hyland (2003) comments, one of the problems for speakers of other languages is that they are learning to write while learning the language. Both respondents were prepared to negotiate the difficulties intrinsic to operating within this zone of uncertainty, a characteristic identified by Naiman, Fröhlich, Stern, and Todesco (1978) as typical of good language learners. In fact, these respondents would turn it to their advantage by using, for example, unfamiliar vocabulary with the intention of better developing their understanding of how this word is used within the context of a given subject. They would not, however, use this vocabulary merely at random: through reading they would have identified this vocabulary as essential to effectively expressing ideas on a designated topic. The genre approach to the teaching of writing tries to bridge the gap between the familiar and unfamiliar by analyzing features of an effective text and deciding how the writer has met the socio-cultural expectations of writing for a specific purpose. Such a method tries to diminish writer uncertainty, but such a strategy will only to a small degree compensate the writer who is not prepared to read on the topic.

4 Good writers attend to meaning

The respondents would initially ensure that they clearly understood the required task. This meant that once they started researching, their reading would be more focused. Before beginning to write they both planned, and, for one of the respondents, this involved writing out topic sentences. Once she had drafted her ideas, she would revise her writing, checking that the supporting ideas were relevant to the main ideas, and that the meaning was clear throughout.

5 Good writers attend to grammar

Attention to form was identified by Rubin (1975) and by Griffiths (2003a, 2003b) as typical of successful language learners. With one of the respondents, although she would not let form interfere with her initial attempt to compose, once she had finished her writing she checked her grammar on the Word program. The other respondent took less initiative, correcting her grammar in response to teacher feedback. So both respondents, although they would not allow grammar to impede their flow of thinking, took care with their grammar while writing.

6 Good writers work with their writing until it effectively responds to the set task and the ideas expressed are clear and coherent

Both respondents were prepared to independently revise their writing for relevance and clarity before submitting it to their teacher. And, if the task involved them re-composing their writing, they were prepared to exert themselves in order to improve the relevance, appropriacy and clarity. And doing this was no small task, for, as one of the respondents commented, in order to produce 500 words she could be sitting down for five hours. But this was the price she was prepared to pay, for she knew that the very act of persisting would render results she could not have foreseen. It is the process approach to the teaching of writing which encourages the learner to revise until both the meaning and form of the writing are purposeful and clear.

7 Good writers actively generate their own interest to write

Motivation is an essential characteristic of successful language learners (Ushioda, this volume). Attending to all that needs to be done in order to improve the ability to write requires persistence. From the start to the finish, good writers retain their motivation, be it intrinsic or extrinsic. Often this is no small achievement, for frequently the learner will be required to write on a topic that fails to ignite any flame of interest. Good writers, however, navigate their way around this initial disinterest. How? Just as the two respondents read to generate ideas and to generate vocabulary, they read to generate interest.

8 Good writers create opportunities to write outside the classroom

It is the writer who uses the language reflectively outside the classroom who is most likely to benefit. For example, in the keeping of a journal or writing letters there is the opportunity to gain a fresh perspective on what is being learnt and to obtain valuable practice and reinforcement. So just as Rubin (1975) says, it is the good language learner who creates opportunities to learn and develop skills rather than passively waiting for opportunities to arrive.

Implications for the teaching/learning situation

In spite of personal, social, and cultural differences, proficiency with writing in a target language is not unattainable, but the extent to which it is achieved can vary according to individual variables such as aptitude, motivation, and opportunity, as discussed by Rubin (1975). Out of these three variables, as Rubin points out, there is dissension as to the extent to which aptitude can be modified. Some regard it as an unvarying characteristic, others assert that it can be enhanced through training, while still others allude to the intricate relationship between aptitude and motivation (see Ranta, this volume).

Just as a student endowed with aptitude may, through lack of motivation, squander an opportunity to learn, the inverse may often hold true: less able students, may perceive an opportunity to learn as more valuable and therefore apply themselves to the task of learning with greater urgency. The capable student may dissipate the opportunity believing that another will arise later when their motivation is higher. A less able student, however, may not languish under such complacency: a sense of urgency will imbue efforts to learn the language. In fact, as Rubin (1975) comments, it is this sense of urgency and the motivation to communicate as well as a willingness to exert themselves which impel learners towards competence. And certainly, gaining proficiency with target language writing requires consistent exertion over an extended period of time.

Fundamental to maintaining such a level of motivation is the importance of having a goal to work towards. In the case of language learners, the goal could be to go on to complete further studies in the target language or to use the language for work-related purposes once they return home. However, even though learners may be required to engage in writing once their goal is achieved, this motivation alone does not necessarily create the right conditions for learners to gain proficiency or even communicative competence with target language writing (for further discussion of motivation, see Ushioda, this volume).

So herein, it could be said, lies the responsibility of the teacher: to provide the opportunities for learners to develop effective writing skills in the target language. In turn, it is the responsibility of the learner to exploit the opportunity to learn. These variables (aptitude, motivation, and opportunity), cannot be considered in isolation: they must favorably co-exist in the language learner, since only then can the personal, social, and cultural divergences that exist between learning to write in a first and target language be successfully navigated and aspirations aligned with achievements.

Questions for ongoing research

In the complex task of language learning, even high aptitude, strong motivation, and abundant opportunity do not guarantee success. The imperative now is to identify strategies, or activities consciously chosen by learners for the purpose of regulating their own learning (Griffiths, this volume), which will help contribute towards success with learning to write in a second language.

Although the findings from the study reported in this chapter suggest some interesting possibilities regarding how good learners learn to write in a language other than their first, the findings are from a small-scale and informal study and can be regarded only as tentative. In order to produce more robust findings which might usefully inform classroom practice, more participants are required representing a range of learner variables (for instance gender, age, nationality etc.). Studies should be conducted in a variety of learning situations (for instance, high school, university, distance learning, native/non-native etc.). A more rigorous methodology might include a more structured list of questions, more exact recording and transcribing procedures, and more consultation with other professionals over interpretation.

Furthermore, all of the strategies identified in this study are extremely broad. It would be useful in terms of informing classroom practice to conduct further in-depth research to investigate the specific micro-strategies involved in strategies such as attending to grammar or meaning. What exactly do students do when they use macro-strategies such as these? With the adjustments noted above, some interesting findings might emerge from a replication of this study.

Conclusion

Writing in a new language can be a difficult skill to develop, and it is often not regarded as a high priority in modern communicative language classrooms. However, especially for those wishing to pursue further studies in the new language, the development of writing skills may well be essential. Over the years, various methodologies have been favored by educators, such as the process, genre, and functional approaches, and these varying approaches can be more or less successful for different students, for different purposes and in different situations.

With only two respondents, it is not possible to draw firm conclusions from the current small-scale study, and a larger-scale survey of how good language learners develop writing skills in a target language would be a useful direction for further research, as well as looking at the strategy areas in more depth. Nevertheless, indications from the current study suggest that students who learn to write successfully in a new language share several common characteristics. Successful writers read in the new language and attend to vocabulary. They have strategies to manage a degree of uncertainty, and they attend to both meaning and form. Furthermore, they create their own interest and opportunities to write and they persist until their writing is satisfactory. According to the study reported in this chapter, although developing the ability to write in a new language can be difficult, students who display these characteristics may maximize their chances of success.

References

Flower, L., and Hayes, J. (1981) A cognitive process theory of writing. *College Composition and Communication*, 32, 365–87.

Griffiths, C. (2002) Using reading as a strategy for teaching and learning language. *ERIC Database of Educational Documents*. (Retrieved from: http://www.eric facility.org).

Griffiths, C. (2003a) Patterns of language learning strategy use. *System*, 31, 367–383

Griffiths, C. (2003b) *Language Learning Strategy Use and Proficiency.* (Retrieved from: http://hdl.handle.net/2292/9).

Griffiths, C. (2004) Studying in English: language skills development. *Occasional Paper No. 5*. Auckland, New Zealand: Centre for Research in International Education. (Retrieved from: http://www.crie.org.nz).

Griffiths, C. (this volume) Chapter 6: Strategies and good language learners.

Harmer, J. (2004) *How to Teach Writing*. Essex: Pearson Education.

Hyland, K. (2003) *Second Language Writing*. Cambridge: Cambridge University Press.

Moir, J. and Nation, P. (this volume) Chapter 2: Vocabulary and good language learners.

Naiman, N., Fröhlich, M., Stern, H., and Todesco, A. (1978) *The Good Language Learner*. Research in Education Series No.7. Toronto: The Ontario Institute for Studies in Education.

Nation, P. (1990) *Teaching and Learning Vocabulary*. Boston, MA: Heinle & Heinle.

Ranta, L. (this volume) Chapter 11: Aptitude and good language learners.

Rubin, J. (1975) What the "good language learner" can teach us. *TESOL Quarterly*, 9(1), 41–51.

Schramm, K. (this volume) Chapter 18: Reading and good language learners.

Swales, J. (1990) *Genre Analysis: English in Academic and Research Settings*. Cambridge: Cambridge University Press.

Ushioda, E. (this volume) Chapter 1: Motivation and good language learners.

20 Teaching/learning method and good language learners

Carol Griffiths

In recent years, individual learner variables, such as those discussed in Part 1 of this volume, have been increasingly recognized as important factors in students' success or otherwise as language learners. However, in order to understand what it is that makes a good language learner, it is important to look at not only the characteristics of the individual learner, but at "the contexts in which individuals learn" (Norton and Toohey, 2001, p. 318). It is quite possible that various aspects of a given situation may affect different learners in quite different ways, and may relate to the opportunities which a given learning context affords. One such aspect which is often an integral part of a given learning context is teaching/learning method.

Over the years many different methods and approaches to the teaching and learning of language to and by speakers of other languages (SOL) have come and gone in and out of fashion (Griffiths and Parr, 2001). Indeed "the proliferation of approaches and methods is a prominent characteristic of contemporary [. . .] language teaching" (Richards and Rodgers, 1986, p. vii). This has been put down to "the pendulum effect in language teaching" (Nunan, 1991, p. 1), an effect which Celce-Murcia (2001, p. 3) attributes to "the fact that very few language teachers have a sense of history about their profession and are thus unaware of the [. . .] many methodological options they have at their disposal". In order to raise awareness of the options, this chapter aims to review the most commonly employed language teaching methods which have been used in recent times (since the middle of the twentieth century), and will report on a small-scale research project aimed at discovering students' views on the effectiveness of various methods.

Derived from the way Latin and Greek were taught, the grammar–translation method, as its name suggests, relied heavily on the teaching of grammar and practicing translation as its main teaching and learning activities (Richards, Platt, and Platt, 1992). The major focus of this method tended to be reading and writing, with very little attention paid to speaking and listening. Vocabulary was typically taught in lists, and a high priority was given to accuracy and to the ability to construct correct sentences. Instruction involved translating to and from the target language and was typically conducted in the students' native language. Grammar–translation tended to be a very teacher-driven method, with little consistent attention being given to the learners' perspectives (Tarone and Yule, 1989). It tended to be assumed that if learners simply followed the method they would, as a matter of course, learn language.

The audiolingual method grew partly out of a reaction against the limitations of the grammar–translation method, and partly out of the urgent war-time demands for fluent speakers of languages such as German, Italian, and Japanese. The "Army Method" was developed to produce military personnel with conversational proficiency in the target language. After the war, the "Army Method" attracted the attention of linguists already looking for an alternative to grammar–translation and, in order to avoid the militaristic connotations, became known as the audiolingual method. By the 1960s, audiolingualism was widespread (Richards and Rodgers, 1986). In direct contrast to the grammar–translation method, the audiolingual method was based on the belief that speaking and listening are the most basic language skills and should be emphasized before reading and writing (Richards, Platt and Platt, 1992). Audiolingual teaching methods depended heavily on drills and repetition, which were justified according to behaviorist theories that language is a system of habits which can be taught and learnt on the stimulus, response, and reinforcement basis that behaviorists believed controlled all human learning, including language learning. Since audiolingual theory depended on the automatic patterning of behavior by means of rote learning, repetition, imitation, memorization, and pattern practice (Stern, 1992), there was little or no recognition given to any conscious contribution which the individual learner might make in the learning process. Indeed, learners were discouraged from taking initiative in the learning situation because they might make mistakes, which were rigidly corrected (Roberts and Griffiths, this volume, Chapter 22). In the early 1960s, audiolingualism was commonly seen as a major breakthrough which would revolutionize the teaching and learning of languages. However, by the end of the 1960s the limitations of the audiolingual method were beginning to make themselves obvious. Contrary to audiolingual theory, language learners did not act according to behaviorist expectations. They wanted to translate things, demanded grammar rules, found endless repetition boring and not conducive to learning (Hutchinson and Waters, 1990).

It was at this time, in the mid-to late 1960s, that the ideas of the highly influential linguist, Noam Chomsky (for instance Chomsky, 1965, 1968) began to have a major effect on linguistic theory. Chomsky postulated that all normal human beings are born with a Language Acquisition Device (LAD) which enables them to develop language from an innate set of principles which he called the Universal Grammar (UG). Chomsky's theory of Transformational-Generative Grammar attempts to explain how original utterances are generated from a language user's underlying competence. Chomsky believed that behaviorist theory could not explain the complexities of generative grammar and concluded that "the creative aspect of language use, when investigated with care and respect for the facts, shows that current notions of habit and generalisation, as determinants of behavior or knowledge, are quite inadequate" (Chomsky, 1968, p. 84).

Although Chomsky's theories directly related mainly to first language learners, his view of the learner as a generator of rules was taken up by Corder (1967) who argued that language errors made by language learners indicate the development of underlying linguistic competence and reflect the learners' attempts to organize linguistic input. The intermediate system created while the learner is trying to come to terms with the target language was later called "interlanguage" (IL) by Selinker (1972) who viewed learner errors as evidence of positive efforts by the student to learn the new language. This view of language learning allowed for the possibility of learners making deliberate attempts to control their own learning and, along with theories of cognitive processes in language learning promoted by writers such as McLaughlin (1978) and Bialystok (1978), contributed to a research thrust in the mid-to-late 1970s aimed at discovering how learners employ learning strategies to promote the learning of language (for instance Rubin, 1975; Stern, 1975; Naiman, Fröhlich, Stern and Todesco, 1978). The idea that teachers should be concerned not only with "finding the best method or with getting the correct answer" but also with assisting a student in order to "enable him to learn on his own" (Rubin, 1975, p. 45) was, at the time, quite revolutionary.

At much the same time, however, as researchers were working to develop an awareness of language learning as a cognitive activity, Krashen (for instance Krashen, 1976, 1977) took off in almost exactly the opposite direction. Challenging the rule-driven theories of the grammar–translation method, the cognitive view of learners being able to consciously control their own learning, as well as the audiolingual behaviorist theories that language can be taught as a system of habits, Krashen proposed his five hypotheses. Summarized briefly (Krashen and Terrell, 1983), these consist of the Acquisition-Learning Hypothesis (conscious learning is an ineffective way of developing language, which is better acquired through natural communication); the Natural Order Hypothesis (grammatical structures of a language are acquired in a predictable order); the Monitor Hypothesis (conscious learning is of very little value to an adult language learner, and can only be useful under certain conditions as a monitor or editor); the Input Hypothesis (language is acquired by understanding input which is a little beyond the current level of competence); and the Affective Filter Hypothesis (a learner's emotions and attitudes can act as a filter which slows down the acquisition of language. When the affective filter is high it can block language development). Taken to their extreme, Krashen's hypotheses led to the belief that conscious teaching and learning were not useful in the language learning process, and that any attempt to teach or learn language in a formal kind of a way was doomed to failure.

According to Gregg (1984, p. 94), however, "each of Krashen's hypotheses is marked by serious flaws". Contrary to the learning/acquisition hypothesis, McLaughlin (1978), approaching the issue from a cognitive psychologist's point of view, proposed an information-processing approach to language development whereby students can obtain knowledge of a language by thinking through the rules until they become automatic, while Pienemann (for instance Pienemann, 1985, 1989), postulated that language can be taught and learnt when the learner is ready (Teachability Hypothesis). Nevertheless, in spite of the many challenges, Krashen's views have been and remain very influential in the language teaching and learning field. Even a harsh critic such as Gregg, who censures Krashen for being "incoherent" and "dogmatic" admits that "he is often right on the important questions" (Gregg, 1984, pp. 94–95), and in as far as Krashen (for instance Krashen, 1981) believed that language develops through natural communication, he might be considered one of the driving forces behind the communicative language teaching movement which is in vogue to the present day.

An important theoretical principle underlying the communicative language teaching movement was called "communicative competence" by Hymes (1972). Communicative competence is the ability to use language to convey and interpret meaning, and it was later divided by Canale and Swain (1980) into four separate components: grammatical competence (which relates to the learner's knowledge of the vocabulary, phonology and rules of the language); discourse competence (which relates to the learner's ability to connect utterances into a meaningful whole); sociolinguistic competence (which relates to the learner's ability to use language appropriately); and strategic competence (which relates to a learner's ability to employ strategies to compensate for imperfect knowledge).

Another cornerstone of communicative language teaching theory is the belief that how language functions is more important than knowledge of form or structure. The concept of the communicative functions of language promoted by Wilkins (1976) has had a strong influence on contemporary language learning programs and textbooks. Other well-known figures in the field have consolidated and extended the theories of communicative language teaching. For instance, Widdowson (1978) argued that by using a communicative approach language can be developed incidentally, as a by-product of using it, while Littlewood (1981) stresses the need to give learners extensive opportunities to use the target language for real communicative purposes, an emphasis which highlights the importance of language skills (see the respective chapters by Goodith White, Kawai, Schramm, and Gordon, this volume) and suggests the usefulness of a task-based approach (see Rubin and McCoy, this volume).

Other less widely adopted language teaching and learning methods and approaches include, among others: situational language teaching (whereby grammar and vocabulary are practiced through situations); the natural method (which emphasises natural acquisition rather than formal grammar study); the direct method (which uses only the target language); the total physical response method (which stresses the importance of motor activity); the silent way (which encourages the teacher to be silent as much as possible); and suggestopedia (which attempts to harness the influence of suggestion, such as music or art, on human behavior).

It would probably be fair to say that to a greater or lesser extent all of these various methods and approaches have had some influence on the contemporary language learning and teaching field, which has tended in recent years to move away from dogmatic positions of "right" or "wrong" and to become much more eclectic in its attitudes and willing to recognize the potential merits of a wide variety of possible methods and approaches, as noted by writers such as Larsen-Freeman (1987) and Tarone and Yule (1989). The term *postmethod* has even been used to indicate that contemporary language teaching does not adhere to any one rigid methodology (for instance, Brown, 2002; Kumaravadivelu, 2001; Tajeddin, 2005), but synthesizes aspects of various methods (Bell, 2003) in order to accommodate the needs of the teacher, the learners, and the situation. However, although a historical look at language teaching/learning methodology may help to put the changes which have occurred over the years into perspective, it does nothing to establish which of the many methods are used by successful language learners.

The study

In an attempt to investigate the important question of how teaching/learning methods relate to successful language learning, a small scale and relatively informal research project was undertaken in an English language school in Auckland, New Zealand.

259

Participants

The participants were 37 students who came from a variety of backgrounds: most were from mainland China, Korea, Taiwan, and Japan with a few from Russia, Hong Kong, Saudi Arabia, and India. These participants were mature students with ages ranging from early 20s to late 30s. Those included in this research were at intermediate level or above, and so had already demonstrated a reasonable level of language learning ability. Although care needs to be taken not to suggest by implication that lower level learners are necessarily "bad" learners (they may, in fact, make rapid progress from an initial low-level placement), the questionnaire was considered by the teachers of the lower-level classes to be too difficult and time consuming at that point in time. Therefore, those classes chosen to be included in this study consisted of already quite successful or "good" language learners.

Data collection and analysis

The instrument used was a questionnaire designed to explore students' preferences regarding teaching/learning method. It consisted of 13 items (see Table 1 for questionnaire items) which students were asked to rate from 1 (strongly disagree) to 5 (strongly agree) according to how they liked to learn a new language. The questionnaire was filled out by students in class and later collected. The data were entered onto SPSS and average ratings for each item calculated and ranked. Questionnaire items focused on features of particular methods:

- Grammar–translation: items 1, 2, 3
- Audiolingual: items 4, 5
- Communicative language teaching: item 6
- Functional: item 7
- Situational language teaching: item 8
- The natural method: item 9
- The direct method: item 10
- Total physical response: item 11
- The silent way: item 12
- Suggestopedia: item 13

Findings

The questionnaire results are set out in Table 1, sorted in order of highest to lowest average rating. As can be seen from Table 1, the items which received the highest ratings relate to spoken language and interaction, while the desire to expand vocabulary also rates highly, followed by

Table 1 Results of questionnaire regarding preferred learning methods

Item	I like to learn a new language	Rating
4	by hearing language spoken	4.4
6	by interacting with others	4.3
2	by memorizing vocabulary	4.1
5	by repeating the language many times	4.0
7	by learning how language functions (e.g. requesting or complaining)	4.0
8	by learning the language related to particular situations	3.9
11	by being active	3.9
13	in a pleasant environment	3.9
9	in a natural environment rather than in a classroom	3.7
3	by memorizing grammar rules	3.4
10	by using only the target language	3.0
1	by translating to or from my first language	2.9
12	From a teacher who is silent as much as possible	2.2

repetition and a wish to develop functional competence. Six more items (relating to a liking for situational language, activity, a pleasant environment, a natural learning environment, grammar, and use of the target language) rate in the neutral-to-agree range (3 to 4). The only items which fall into the disagree range (less than 3) are translating to or from the first language and having a silent teacher. The last of these might be interesting to consider in relation to contemporary trends to denigrate too much "teacher talk".

A few students added comments to the questionnaire form about other methods they had found effective. Several mentioned liking to watch TV or movies and listen to songs and radio: in other words their preferred learning method involved using the media, or resources available in the environment. Some said they wanted to focus on skills (e.g. writing), others that they found tasks (e.g. looking for a flat) useful, while still others mentioned that they liked to have all their mistakes corrected. One student mentioned finding dictation useful for improving listening skills, a time-honoured method often neglected or even scorned in contemporary communicative classrooms. Another student mentioned the need for teaching/learning methods to bridge the gap between classroom and everyday life, since in class "we study perfect and great vocabs, but outside class we stuck".

Implications for the teaching/learning situation

These results would seem to indicate that higher-level language learners tend to be very eclectic in their preferences regarding learning method.

Rather than reporting a liking only for methods which emphasize, for instance, grammar, repetition, or vocabulary, these students gave relatively high ratings to a wide range of methods, suggesting that there is more than one way to learn language well, and that good language learners can flexibly employ the methods which best suit themselves and/or their situations in order to achieve their learning goal.

From the point of view of informing teaching practice, these findings would seem to support the eclecticism recommended by writers such as Tarone and Yule (1989) who suggest that eclecticism involves "picking and choosing some procedures from one methodology, some techniques from another, and some exercise formats from yet another" (p. 10) rather than trying to decide whether lesson procedures, techniques, or formats fit in with some pre-determined theory. Eclectic approaches have, therefore, sometimes been criticized as atheoretical. As Tarone and Yule (1989, p. 10) continue, eclecticism has been criticized, "particularly by advocates of one methodology or another, as resulting in a hodge-podge of conflicting classroom activities assembled on whim rather than upon any principled basis". In fact, they argue, effective eclecticism requires great effort and knowledge, and places much responsibility on individual teachers to apply appropriate principles to the selection of suitable procedures and materials for their students.

The importance of a principled approach to eclecticism is echoed by Larsen-Freeman (1987), who writes (p. 55): "It is not uncommon for teachers today to practice a principled eclecticism, combining techniques and principles from various methods in a carefully reasoned manner."

Questions for ongoing research

Although the study described in this chapter was on too small a scale for firm conclusions to be drawn, it suggests some interesting questions for further research. Would the same or similar results be obtained if there were more participants involved? This study took place in a situation where students were studying in an environment where the target language was spoken. Would students learning in their own native-language environment give similar ratings, especially to items such as "I like to learn a new language by hearing language spoken"? The students in this study belonged to a fairly narrow age range (20s to 30s). Would younger or older students give similar responses? Do students from different national backgrounds give varying responses? And if a longitudinal study were conducted, which methods would be found to be preferred by those who made the fastest progress?

The comments added by some students to their questionnaire suggest the need for some adaptations to the survey. Extra items might include: I like to learn a new language by concentrating on skills, by means of tasks, by having all my mistakes corrected, by using the media. When considering additions to the questionnaire, the issue of whether the item is truly a method or merely a student's individual strategy would need to be resolved. For instance, is "using the media" a method or a strategy? Is it, perhaps, a method in the media studies class and a strategy for a student who decides to read newspapers to expand his vocabulary? These questions may not always be easy to decide absolutely, but if theoretically justifiable, additional items would contribute to a more comprehensive instrument for assessing learner preferences regarding method.

Conclusion

Over the years, a wide range of methods has been used in order to teach and learn language. These methods range from grammar–translation to audiolingual to communicative, but there are also a number of others, such as the natural method and suggestopedia. Rather than keeping rigidly to one or other method, contemporary approaches tend to be eclectic, so that it is not uncommon to find some grammar, some pattern drilling, some communicative interaction, some tasks and so on all within one lesson.

Since the findings from the study reported in this chapter suggest that good learners use a wide variety of learning methods, rather than keeping rigidly to a single method, the implication would seem to be that teachers need to look for methods which best suit the needs of their particular learners in a given situation. They need to be resourceful, flexible and ready to adapt and try a variety of methods in order to help their students achieve success in language learning.

References

Bell, D. (2003) Method and postmethod: Are they really so incompatible? *TESOL Quarterly*, 37(2), 325–336.

Brown, H.D. (2002) English language teaching in the "post-method" era. In J. Richards and W. Renandya (eds.), *Methodology in Language Teaching: An Anthology of Current Practice*. Cambridge: Cambridge University Press, 9–18.

Bialystok, E. (1978) A theoretical model of second language learning. *Language Learning*, 28(1), 69–83.

Canale, M. and Swain, M. (1980) Theoretical bases of communicative approaches to second language teaching and testing. *Applied Linguistics*, 1, 1–47.

Celce-Murcia, M. (2001) Language teaching approaches: An overview. In M. Celce-Murcia (ed.), *Teaching English as a Second or Foreign language* (third edition) (pp. 3–110). Boston, MA: Heinle & Heinle.

Chomsky, N. (1965) *Aspects of the Theory of Syntax.* Cambridge, MA: The MIT Press.

Chomsky, N. (1968) *Language and Mind.* New York: Harcourt, Brace & World.

Corder, S.P. (1967) The significance of learners' errors. *International Review of Applied Linguistics*, 5, 160–170.

Gregg, K. (1984) Krashen's monitor and Occam's razor. *Applied Linguistics*, 5, 78–100.

Griffiths, C. and Parr, J. (2001) Language-learning strategies: theory and perception. *ELT Journal*, 55(3), 247–254.

Hymes, D. (1972) On communicative competence. In J. Pride and J. Holmes (eds.), *Sociolinguistics* (pp. 269–293). Harmondsworth, UK: Penguin.

Hutchinson, T. and Waters, A. (1990) *English for Specific Purposes: A Learning-centred Approach.* Cambridge: Cambridge University Press.

Kawai, Y. (this volume) Chapter 17: Speaking and good language learners.

Krashen, S. (1976) Formal and informal linguistic environments in language acquisition and language learning. *TESOL Quarterly*, 10, 157–168.

Krashen, S. (1977) Some issues relating to the Monitor Model. In H. Brown, C. Yorio and R. Crymes (eds.), *On TESOL '77* (pp. 144–158). Washington, DC: TESOL.

Krashen, S. (1981) *Second Language Acquisition and Second Language Learning.* Oxford: Pergamon Press.

Krashen, S. (1985) *The Input Hypothesis.* London: Longman.

Krashen, S. and Terrell, T. (1983) *The Natural Approach.* Hayward, CA: Hayward Press.

Kumaravadivelu, B. (2001) Towards a postmethod methodology. *TESOL Quarterly* 35, 537–560.

Larsen-Freeman, D. (1987) From unity to diversity: twenty-five years of language-teaching methodology, *Forum*, 25(4), 2–10.

Littlewood, W. (1981) *Communicative Language Teaching.* Cambridge: Cambridge University Press.

McLaughlin, B. (1978) The Monitor model: some methodological considerations. *Language Learning*, 28, 309–32.

Moir, J. and Nation, P. (this volume) Chapter 12: Vocabulary and good language learners.

Naiman, N., Fröhlich, M., Stern, H., and Todesco, A. (1978) *The Good Language Learner.* Research in Education Series No.7. Toronto: The Ontario Institute for Studies in Education.

Norton, B. and Toohey, K. (2001) Changing perspectives on good language learners. *TESOL Quarterly*, 35(2), 307–322.

Nunan, D. (1991) *Language Teaching Methodology.* New York: Phoenix.

Pienemann, M. (1985) Learnability and syllabus construction. In K. Hyltenstam and M. Pienemann (eds.), *Modelling and Assessing Second Language Acquisition* (pp. 23–75). Clevedon, UK: Multilingual Matters.

Pienemann, M. (1989) Is language teachable? Psycholinguistic experiments and hypotheses. *Applied Linguistic*, 10, 52–79.

Richards, J., Platt, J., and Platt, H. (1992) *Longman Dictionary of Language Teaching and Applied Linguistics*. Harlow: Longman.

Richards, J. and Rodgers, T. (1986) *Approaches and Methods in Language Teaching*. Cambridge: Cambridge University Press.

Roberts, M. and Griffiths, C. (this volume) Chapter 22: Error correction and good language learners.

Rubin, J. (1975) What the "good language learner" can teach us. *TESOL Quarterly*, 9(1), 41–51.

Rubin, J. and McCoy, P. (this volume) Chapter 23: Tasks and good language learners.

Schramm, K. (this volume) Chapter 18: Reading and good language learners.

Selinker, L. (1972) Interlanguage. *International Review of Applied Linguistics*, 10, 209–230.

Stern, H.H. (1975) What can we learn from the good language learner? *Canadian Modern Language Review*, 34, 304–318.

Stern, H.H. (1980) *Fundamental Concepts of Language Teaching*. Oxford: Oxford University Press.

Stern, H.H. (1992) *Issues and Options in Language Teaching* (edited posthumously by P. Allen and B. Harley). Oxford: Oxford University Press.

Tarone, E. and Yule, G. (1989) *Focus on the Language Learner*. Oxford: Oxford University Press.

Tajeddin, Z. (2005) A critique of the inception and premises of the postmethod paradigm. *ILI Language Teaching Journal*, 1(1), 1–14.

White, G. (this volume) Chapter 16: Listening and good language learners

Widdowson, H. (1978) *Teaching Language as Communication*. Oxford: Oxford University Press.

Widdowson, H. (1990) *Aspects of Language Teaching*. Oxford: Oxford University Press.

Wilkins, D. (1976) *Notional Syllabuses*. Oxford: Oxford University Press.

21 Strategy instruction and good language learners

Anna Uhl Chamot

An aspect of teaching/learning methodology which has attracted a great deal of debate over the years is the issue of strategy instruction. A major premise of the research on the strategies of "good" language learners initiated by Rubin (1975) is that the strategies used by successful learners of languages can be taught to students who are struggling to learn a new language, thus making them better language learners. In the 30 years since Rubin's article, the effectiveness of strategy instruction has been questioned (for instance, Vann and Abraham, 1990). Nevertheless, others have developed well-recognised strategy instruction models (such as Chamot, Barnhardt, El-Dinary and Robbins, 1999; Cohen, 1998; and Grenfell and Harris, 1999), and research has shown that, under the right conditions, strategy instruction can be effective (for instance, Nunan, 1997; O'Malley, 1987).

Thirty years ago, it was commonly believed that "good" language learners used learning strategies while "bad" language learners did not. This fallacy was exposed by studies that compared effective and less effective language learners and found that both used learning strategies, often the less effective learners using as many strategies as the more successful language learners (O'Malley and Chamot, 1990). Further research examined the quality of learning strategy use and found that strategic learners have metacognitive knowledge about their own thinking and learning approaches, a good understanding of what a task entails, and the ability to orchestrate the strategies that best meet both the task demands and their own learning strengths (see Anderson, this volume). Thus, simple counts of learning strategy use can be misleading – it is how learning strategies are used that determines how useful they are.

Basic research on language learner strategies concerns the identification and description of learning strategies used by language learners and the correlation of these strategies with other learner variables such as proficiency level, age, gender, motivation, and the like (Chamot and El-Dinary, 1999; El-Dib, 2004; Green and Oxford, 1995; Griffiths, 2003b; Oxford and Burry-Stock, 1995). Current research is also investigating the effect of the task itself and the influence of the target language on the selection and use of learning strategies (Chamot and Keatley, 2004;

266

Oxford, Cho, Leung and Kim, 2004). Applied research on language learning strategies investigates the feasibility of helping students become more effective language learners by teaching them some of the learning strategies that descriptive studies have identified as characteristic of the "good language learner" (Rubin, 1975, 1981; Stern, 1975).

Identification of language learning strategies

Research on learners' strategies has clarified what a learning strategy is – and is not – though the debate is by no means settled (see Gu, 2005; Griffiths, this volume). Learning strategies are for the most part unobservable, though some may be associated with an observable behaviour. For example, a learner could use *selective attention* (unobservable) to focus on the main ideas during a listening comprehension exercise and could then decide to *take notes* (observable) in order to remember the information. In almost all learning contexts, the only way to find out whether students are using learning strategies while engaged in a language task is to ask them. Verbal report data are used to identify language learners' strategies because observation does not capture mental processes (Cohen, 1998; O'Malley and Chamot, 1990; Rubin, 1975; Wenden, 1991). Although self-report may be inaccurate if the learner does not report truthfully, it is still the only way to explore learners' mental processing. Grenfell and Harris (1999, p. 54) have described this dilemma in the following way: "It is not easy to get inside the 'black box' of the human brain and find out what is going on there. We work with what we can get, which, despite the limitations, provides food for thought."

Researchers have asked language learners to describe their learning processes and strategies through retrospective interviews, stimulated recall interviews, questionnaires, written diaries and journals, and think-aloud protocols concurrent with a learning task. Each of these methods has limitations, but each provides important insights into unobservable mental learning strategies. In retrospective interviews, learners are asked to describe what they were thinking or doing during a recently completed learning task (see O'Malley and Chamot, 1990). The limitation is that students may forget some of the details of their thought processes or may describe what they perceive as the "right" answer. A stimulated recall interview is more likely to accurately reveal students' actual learning strategies during a task because students are videotaped while performing the task, and the interviewer then plays back the videotape, pausing as necessary, and asking students to describe their thoughts at specific moments during the task (Robbins, 1996).

The most frequently used and probably the most efficient method for identifying students' learning strategies is through questionnaires. The limitations are that students may not remember the strategies they have used in the past, may claim to use strategies that in fact they do not use, or may not understand the strategy descriptions in the questionnaire items. For these reasons, some studies have developed questionnaires based on tasks that students have just completed. The reasoning behind this approach is that students will be more likely to remember and to report accurately if relatively little time has elapsed (see Chamot and El-Dinary, 1999; Ellis and Sinclair, 1989; Fan, 2003; Kojic-Sabo and Lightbown, 1999; National Capital Language Resource Center, 2000a, 2000b; O'Malley and Chamot, 1990; Oxford *et al.*, 2004; Ozeki, 2000; Rubin and Thompson, 1994; Weaver and Cohen, 1997). The limitations of this approach are that, to date, there has been no standardization of either tasks or follow-up questionnaires, so that it is impossible to make comparisons across studies.

The greatest numbers of descriptive studies have utilized a questionnaire developed by Oxford (1990), the Strategy Inventory for Language Learning (SILL). This instrument has been used extensively to collect data on large numbers of language learners (see Cohen, Weaver and Li, 1998; Griffiths, 2003a; Nyikos and Oxford, 1993; Olivares-Cuhat, 2002; Oxford, 1990; Oxford and Burry-Stock, 1995; Wharton, 2000). The SILL is a standardized measure with versions for students of a variety of languages, and as such can be used to collect and analyze information about large numbers of language learners. It has also been used in studies that correlate strategy use with variables such as learning styles, age, gender, proficiency level, and culture (Bedell and Oxford, 1996; Bruen, 2001; Green and Oxford, 1995; Griffiths, 2003b; Nyikos and Oxford, 1993; Oxford and Burry-Stock, 1995; Wharton, 2000). Oxford and her colleagues are currently working on a task-based questionnaire to complement the SILL (Oxford *et al.*, 2004).

Diaries and journals have also been used to collect information about language learners' strategies. In these, learners write personal observations about their own learning experiences and the ways in which they have solved or attempted to solve language problems (see, for example, Carson and Longhini, 2002). Student learning strategy diaries have also been used to collect data about pronunciation strategies (Peterson, 2000). As with other verbal reports, learners may not necessarily provide accurate descriptions of their learning strategies. Rubin (2003) suggests using diaries for instructional purposes as a way to help students develop metacognitive awareness of their own learning processes and strategies.

Another research tool with applications to instruction is the think-aloud individual interview in which the learners are given a task and asked to describe their thoughts while working on it. The interviewer may prompt with open-ended questions such as, *What are you thinking right now? Why did you stop and start over?* Recordings of think-aloud interviews are analysed for evidence of learning strategies. Verbal protocols have been used extensively in reading research in first language contexts, where they have provided insights not only into reading comprehension processes but also into learners' affective and motivational states (Afflerbach, 2000). The rich insights into language-learning strategies provided through think-aloud protocols tend to reveal on-line processing, rather than metacognitive aspects of planning or evaluating (see Chamot and Keatley, 2003; Chamot, Keatley, Barnhardt, El-Dinary, Nagano and Newman, 1996; Cohen *et al.*, 1998; O'Malley, Chamot and Küpper, 1989).

The tools that researchers have used to identify language learning strategies are especially valuable for discovering students' current learning strategies before beginning to give instruction. For example, teachers can ask students to complete a language task, and then lead a classroom discussion about how students completed the task and point out the learning strategies that students mention. Teachers can also develop a questionnaire appropriate for the age and proficiency level of their students and have students complete it immediately after completing a task. For a more global picture of their students' learning strategies in general, teachers might want to use the SILL. When strategy instruction is underway and students show evidence that they understand and are using some of the strategies independently, teachers could ask them to keep a diary or journal about their use of strategies in the language class and in other contexts, thus encouraging transfer. Most importantly, teachers can make their own thinking public by "thinking aloud" as they work on a task familiar to students, commenting on their own strategies as they go. All of these approaches can help students develop their own metacognition about themselves as strategic learners.

Models for language learning strategy instruction

A number of models for teaching learning strategies in both first and second language contexts have been developed (see, for example, Chamot *et al.*, 1999; Cohen, 1998; Graham and Harris, 2003; Grenfell and Harris, 1999; Harris, 2003; Macaro, 2001; O'Malley and Chamot, 1990; Oxford, 1990; Pressley, El-Dinary, Gaskins, Schuder, Bergman, Almasi, and Brown, 1992).

Table 1 compares three current models for language learning strategy instruction. These instructional models share many features. All agree on

Table 1 Models for language learning strategy instruction

SSBI* Model (Cohen, 1998)	CALLA** Model (Chamot *et al.*, 1999; Chamot, 2005)	Grenfell and Harris (1999)
Teacher as diagnostician: Helps students identify current strategies and learning styles.	**Preparation:** Teacher identifies students' current learning strategies for familiar tasks.	**Awareness raising:** Students complete a task, and then identify the strategies they used.
Teacher as language learner: Shares own learning experiences and thinking processes.	**Presentation:** Teacher models, names, explains new strategy; asks students if and how they have used it.	**Modelling:** Teacher models, discusses value of new strategy, makes checklist of strategies for later use.
Teacher as learner trainer: Trains students how to use learning strategies.	**Practice:** Students practise new strategy; in subsequent strategy practice, teacher fades reminders to encourage independent strategy use.	**General Practice:** Students practise new strategies with different tasks.
Teacher as coordinator: Supervises students' study plans and monitors difficulties.	**Self-Evaluation:** Students evaluate their own strategy use immediately after practice.	**Action Planning:** Students set goals and choose strategies to attain those goals.
Teacher as coach: Provides ongoing guidance on students' progress.	**Expansion:** Students transfer strategies to new tasks, combine strategies into clusters, develop repertoire of preferred strategies.	**Focused Practice:** Students carry out action plan using selected strategies; teacher fades prompts so that students use strategies automatically.
	Assessment: Teacher assesses students' use of strategies and impact on performance.	**Evaluation:** Teacher and students evaluate success of action plan; set new goals; cycle begins again.

*Styles and Strategies-Based Instruction
**Cognitive Academic Language Learning Approach

the importance of developing students' metacognitive understanding of the value of learning strategies and suggest that this is facilitated through teacher demonstration and modelling. All emphasize the importance of providing multiple practice opportunities with the strategies so that students can use them autonomously. All suggest that students should evaluate how well a strategy has worked, choose strategies for a task, and actively transfer strategies to new tasks. All three models begin by identifying students' current learning strategies through activities such as completing questionnaires, engaging in discussions about familiar tasks, and reflecting on strategies used immediately after performing a task. These models all suggest that the teacher should model the new strategy, thus making the instruction explicit.

Although the three models in Table 1 have many features in common, the CALLA model is recursive rather than linear so that teachers and students always have the option of revisiting prior instructional phases as needed (Chamot, 2005). The Grenfell and Harris (1999) model, on the other hand, has students work through a cycle of six steps, then begin a new cycle. The Cohen (1998) model has the teacher take on a variety of roles in order to help students learn to use learning strategies appropriate to their own learning styles. The Grenfell and Harris model provides initial familiarization with the new strategies, then has students make personal action plans to improve their own learning, whereas the CALLA model builds in a self-evaluation phase for students to reflect on their use of strategies before going on to transfer the strategies to new tasks. In summary, current models of language learning strategy instruction are solidly based on developing students' knowledge about their own thinking and strategic processes and encouraging them to adopt strategies that will improve their language learning and build proficiency.

Implications for the teaching/learning situation

The preponderance of research on language learning strategies has been descriptive, as researchers have sought to discover what learning strategies are reported by learners of different languages. The methods and findings of this research have important instructional applications, such as the identification of students' strategies before, during, and after strategy instruction and the impact of students' culture and prior school experiences on their acquisition and use of strategies. While less extensive than descriptive language learning strategy research, strategy intervention research has suggested important issues related to instruction, such as the influence of culture and context, explicit versus implicit and integrated versus discrete strategy instruction, language of instruction, and the transfer of strategies to new tasks.

Influence of culture and context

The learner's goals, the context of the learning situation, and the cultural values of the learner's society have a strong influence on choice and acceptability of language learning strategies. For example, in a culture that promotes individual competition and has organized its educational system around competitive tasks, successful language learners may prefer strategies that allow them to work alone rather than social strategies that call for collaboration with others.

Two SILL studies illustrate some of the learning strategy preferences reported by students in different cultural contexts. A study of ethnic Chinese bilingual Singaporean university students studying French or Japanese found that students reported a preference for social strategies (involving interaction with others) as well as a disinclination to use affective strategies to control feelings or emotions (Wharton, 2000). Another study looked at the language learning strategies of university students in an advanced level Spanish writing class and compared achievement on a writing sample between those students speaking Spanish as a first or heritage language and those learning Spanish as a language other than their first (Olivares-Cuhat, 2002). As could be expected, students with a Spanish language background were graded higher on their writing samples than the other students, but, more interestingly, they also showed a greater preference for affective and memory strategies and these latter were highly correlated with their writing achievement. Preliminary findings of a current study of learning strategies used by university students of less commonly taught languages indicate that, while both heritage speakers of Arabic and students of Arabic as a non-primary language share many of the same challenges and consequent learning strategies for learning Modern Standard Arabic (MSA), they also demonstrate differences (Keatley, Chamot, Spokane and Greenstreet, 2004). For instance, heritage speakers reported using metacognitive strategies to overcome interference from their Arabic dialects when they attempted to speak Modern Standard Arabic, but, unlike the students who spoke other languages, had no difficulty in discriminating Arabic sounds and hence did not report any learning strategies for listening comprehension.

The implications for teaching are that language teachers need to find out what learning strategies students are already using for the different tasks they undertake in the language classroom. An open discussion of reasons why students use the strategies they identify can help teachers understand cultural and contextual factors that may be influencing their students. This can lead to clarification of the task demands where there is a mismatch with students' current learning strategies. By understanding the task more clearly, students are likely to be more motivated to try new strategies to complete it successfully.

Strategy instruction: explicit versus implicit and integrated versus discrete

Research on reading and writing instruction in first language contexts strongly argues for explicit strategy instruction (Graham and Harris, 2000; National Reading Panel, 2000; Pressley, 2000; Pressley and Harris, 2001). Explicit learning strategy instruction essentially involves the development of students' awareness of the strategies they use, teacher modelling of strategic thinking, student practice with new strategies, student self-evaluation of the strategies used, and practice in transferring strategies to new tasks (Chamot *et al.*, 1999; Grenfell and Harris, 1999; Harris, 2003; Oxford, 1990). Although implicit strategy instruction may help to reinforce strategic awareness (Griffiths, 2003b), most researchers agree on the importance of explicitness in strategy instruction (Anderson, in press; Chamot *et al.*, 1999; Cohen, 1998; Nunan, 1997; O'Malley and Chamot, 1990; Oxford and Leaver, 1996; Shen, 2003).

However, there is less agreement on the issue of whether strategy instruction should be integrated into the language curriculum or taught separately. While many argue that integrated instruction provides students with opportunities and motivation to practise learning strategies with authentic language learning tasks (Chamot and O'Malley, 1994; Chamot *et al.*, 1999; Cohen, 1998; Grenfell and Harris, 1999; Nunan, 1997; Oxford and Leaver, 1996), others have voiced concerns. For example, strategies learned within a language class are less likely to transfer to other tasks (Gu, 1996), and, from a practical point of view, it is easier to plan for one discrete strategy course than to prepare all teachers to teach strategies (Vance, 1999; Weinstein, 1994).

Given the current state of knowledge about learning strategy instruction, teachers should certainly opt for explicit instruction, although they should be aware that implicit (embedded) messages can also be powerful. And, practical difficulties notwithstanding, teachers should probably integrate the instruction into their regular course work, rather than providing a separate learning strategies course, where lack of student motivation can be a major obstacle (Griffiths, 2003b; Wenden, 1987). An ideal situation would be one in which all teachers in all subject areas teach learning strategies, as students would then be more likely to transfer strategies learned in one class to another class. This approach is currently being carried out in at least two school districts in the USA through

273

a process of continuing professional development for all teachers. Both school districts report that student achievement overall, as measured by standardized test scores, has improved significantly over the years in which learning strategy instruction has been implemented (Hodge, personal communication, 2004; Schreiber, personal communication, 2004).

Language of instruction

Language of instruction is not an issue in learning strategy research in first language contexts, as the strategies are taught in the students' native language. This is not the case, however, where students are being instructed in their target language. Beginning level language students do not yet have the proficiency to understand explanations in the target language of why and how to use learning strategies. However, if learning strategy instruction is postponed until intermediate or advanced level courses, beginners will be deprived of strategies that can make their language learning more successful and increase their motivation for further study. It is probably impossible not to use the first language during strategy instruction for beginning to low intermediate level students (Macaro, 2001).

Some recent studies of beginning level proficiency second language learners have provided learning strategy instruction in the native language (for instance, Cunningham Florez, 2000; Rybicki, 2002). Other studies have used a combination of the native and target languages (for instance, Chamot and Keatley, Grenfell and Harris, 1999; Ozeki, 2000; 2003). From these few studies, it seems clear that the issue of language of instruction in teaching language learning strategies is far from resolved. If all students in a language class speak the same first language, and the teacher also knows that language, initial learning strategy instruction can be in the native language. The drawback is that use of the native language takes time away from exposure to and practice in the target language. Alternatively, teachers have been urged to give the strategy a target language name, explain how to use it in simple language, and repeatedly model the strategy (Chamot *et al.*, 1999). Grenfell and Harris (1999) recommend staying within the target language as much as possible, but acknowledge that for most beginning level classes, getting students started on reflecting on their own learning may well have to be done through the first language.

Transfer of strategies to new tasks

Early research on learning strategies in first language contexts found that students often were unable to transfer strategies to new tasks, but later studies showed that transfer increased significantly when teachers helped students understand their own learning processes and metacognition (Belmont, Butterfield and Ferretti 1982). Similarly, language learning strategy researchers have argued for the central role of metacognitive knowledge and metacognitive learning strategies in language learning (Anderson, 2002, in press; Chamot, 2001; Chamot *et al.*, 1999; Grenfell and Harris, 1999; Harris, 2004; O'Malley and Chamot, 1990; Rubin, 2001; Thompson and Rubin, 1996; Vandergrift, 2002; Wenden, 2002).

A call for research on "the transfer of learning strategies from the L1 to the L2 – and from the L2 to additional languages and even back to the L1" (Chamot, 2001, p. 42) has not inspired many investigations! However, a study is currently underway that is investigating transfer of strategies taught in the first language to the target language as well as factors that assist or hinder such transfer (Harris, personal communication, 2004). In a preliminary study, semi-structured interviews were conducted with a small group of 12-year-old students in their second year of target language study in schools in London (Harris, 2004). These students had been exposed to learning strategy instruction in their English classes, so they were asked to make judgements on 16 different strategies as to whether each strategy was useful *only* for learning English, *only* for learning the target language, for learning any language, or not useful. Differences were found between high attaining and low attaining students in that the high attainers used more metacognitive strategies and were making some transfers of strategies from their English class to their target language class, whereas low attainers were less likely to use metacognitive strategies or make transfers from English.

Questions for ongoing research

Over the years, strategy intervention research has taken a back seat compared with descriptive strategy research. It is difficult to see why this should have been the case given that pedagogical application has always been stated as the major driving purpose for research in this area. Perhaps it is time that strategy instruction was moved to the front seat and serious efforts were made to address the question: How can we instruct our students in effective strategy use?

A number of important questions remain either unanswered or only partly answered. Among these are: What is the effect of culture on strategy use, and how does this need to be allowed for in the teaching/learning situation? Are different strategies more or less appropriate in various learning contexts, and if so, which ones are appropriate where? Is instruction better delivered explicitly or implicitly? Is integrated or discrete instruction more effective? What is the effect of language of instruction? How can we teach students to transfer strategies to new tasks? Are there differences in the ways good language learners process strategy instruction compared with less successful students? A great deal of work remains to be done before we can claim to have definitive answers to any of these questions.

Conclusion

This chapter has examined a number of issues in language learning strategy research and practice that are important in helping students become more successful language learners. However, while we have learned much about the usefulness of including the kinds of strategies used by good language learners in target language education, much still remains to be investigated.

In 1975 Joan Rubin opened a new chapter in language teaching and learning by proposing that teachers learn from what students can teach us about successful language learning. Thirty years later, we are still exploring the implications of this idea and what it truly means to have a learner-centred, strategic classroom which facilitates effective language learning.

Thirty years ago, teaching/learning methods were focused on the *teacher*. We were still looking for the perfect method that teachers could adopt to make successful language learners of their students. Joan Rubin turned all of these methods on their heads. She asked: "What do students do to learn – especially, what do good language learners do to learn?" Her message was, and is, that student learning processes should guide what teachers do. The strong implication is that no one method can reach every student and that instruction should be learner-centred. Since Joan's landmark work on what the good language learner can teach us (Rubin, 1975), language pedagogy has increasingly explored language learning from the learner's perspective. Thank you, Joan!

References

Afflerbach, P. (2000) Verbal reports and protocol analysis. In M.L. Kamil, P.B. Mosenthal, P.D. Pearson and R. Barr (eds.), *Handbook of Reading Research, Volume III*. Mahwah, NJ: Lawrence Erlbaum, 163–179.
Anderson, N.J. (2002) The role of metacognition in second language teaching and learning. *ERIC Digest*, April 2002. Washington, DC: Center for Applied Linguistics.

Anderson, N.J. (in press). L2 learning strategies, in E. Hinkel (ed.), *Handbook of Research in Second Language Teaching and Learning*. Mahwah, NJ: Lawrence Erlbaum.

Anderson, N.J. (this volume) Chapter 7: Metacognition and good language learners.

Bedell, D.A. and Oxford, R.L. (1996) Cross-cultural comparisons of language learning strategies in the People's Republic of China and other countries. In R.L. Oxford (ed.), *Language Learning Strategies Around the World: Cross-Cultural Perspectives*. Honolulu, HI: University of Hawai'i Press, 47–60.

Belmont, J.M., Butterfield, E.C. and Ferretti, R.P. (1982) To secure transfer of training: instruct self-management skills. In D.C. Detterman and R.J. Sternberg (eds.), *How and How Much Can Intelligence Be Increased?* Norwood, NJ: Ablex, 147–154.

Bruen, J. (2001) Strategies for success: profiling the effective learner of German. *Foreign Language Annals*, 34(3), 216–225.

Carson, J.G. and Longhini, A. (2002) Focusing on learning styles and strategies: a diary study in an immersion setting. *Language Learning* 52(2), 401–438.

Chamot, A.U. (2001) The role of learning strategies in second language acquisition. In M.P. Breen (ed.), *Learner Contributions to Language Learning: New Directions in Research*. Harlow, England: Longman, 25–43.

Chamot, A.U. (2005) The Cognitive Academic Language Learning Approach (CALLA): an update. In P.A. Richard-Amato and M.A. Snow (eds.), *Academic Success for English Language Learners: Strategies for K-12 Mainstream Teachers*. White Plains, NY: Longman, 87–101.

Chamot, A.U. and El-Dinary, P.B. (1999) Children's learning strategies in immersion classrooms. *The Modern Language Journal*, 83(3), 319–341.

Chamot, A.U. and Keatley, C.W. (2003) Learning strategies of adolescent low-literacy Hispanic ESL students. Paper presented at the 2003 Annual Meeting of the American Educational Research Association, Chicago, IL.

Chamot, A.U. and Keatley, C.W. (2004) Learning strategies of students of less commonly taught languages. Paper presented at the 2004 Annual Meeting of the American Educational Research Association, San Diego, CA.

Chamot, A.U. and O'Malley, J.M. (1994) *The CALLA handbook: Implementing the Cognitive Academic Language Learning Approach*. White Plains, NY: Addison Wesley Longman.

Chamot, A.U., Barnhardt, S., El-Dinary, P.B. and Robbins, J. (1999) *The Learning Strategies Handbook*. White Plains, NY: Addison Wesley Longman.

Chamot, A.U., Keatley, C., Barnhardt, S., El-Dinary, P.B., Nagano, K. and Newman, C. (1996) *Learning strategies in elementary language immersion programs*. Final report submitted to Center for International Education, US Department of Education. Available from ERIC Clearinghouse on Languages and Linguistics.

Cohen, A.D. (1998) *Strategies in Learning and Using a Second Language*. London: Longman.

Cohen, A.D., Weaver, S. and Li, T-Y. (1998) The impact of strategies-based instruction on speaking a foreign language. In A.D. Cohen, *Strategies in Learning and Using a Second Language*. London: Longman, 107–156.

Cunningham Florez, M. (2000) The plot thickens: beginning level English language learners as strategists. *Practitioner Research Briefs, 1999–2000 Report Series*. Charlottesville, VA: Virginia Adult Education Research Network. ERIC Document Reproduction Service ED 444 391; FL 801 393.

El-Dib, M.A.B. (2004). Language learning strategies in Kuwait: links to gender, language level, and culture in a hybrid context. *Foreign Language Annals*, 37, 85–95.

Ellis, G. and Sinclair, B. (1989) *Learning to Learn English: A Course in Learner Training. Teacher's Book*. Cambridge: Cambridge University Press.

Fan, M.Y. (2003) Frequency of use, perceived usefulness, and actual usefulness of second language vocabulary strategies: a study of Hong Kong learners. *Modern Language Journal*, 87(ii), 222–241.

Graham, S. and Harris, K.R. (2000) The role of self-regulation and transcription skills in writing and writing development. *Educational Psychologist*, 35, 3–12.

Graham, S. and Harris, K.R. (2003) Students with learning disabilities and the process of writing: a meta-analysis of SRSD studies. In L. Swanson, K.R. Harris and S. Graham (eds.), *Handbook of Research on Learning Disabilities*. New York: Guildford, 323–344.

Green, J.M. and Oxford, R.L. (1995) A closer look at learning strategies, L2 proficiency, and gender. *TESOL Quarterly*, 29(2), 261–297.

Grenfell, M. and Harris, V. (1999) *Modern Languages and Learning Strategies: In Theory and Practice*. London: Routledge.

Griffiths, C. (2003a) Patterns of language learning strategy use. *System*, 31, 367–383.

Griffiths, C. (2003b) *Language learning strategy use and proficiency* (PhD thesis). (Retrieved from: http://www.umi.com/umi/dissertations/).

Griffiths, C. (this volume) Chapter 6: Strategies and good language learners.

Gu, P.Y. (1996) Robin Hood in SLA: what has the learning strategy researcher taught us? *Asian Journal of English Language Teaching*, 6, 1–29.

Gu, P. (2005) Learning strategies: prototypical core and dimensions of variation. Working paper No.10. (Retrieved from: www.crie.org.nz).

Harris, V. (2003) Adapting classroom-based strategy instruction to a distance learning context. *TESL-EJ*, 7(2) (Retrieved from: http://cwp60.berkeley.edu:16080/TESL-EJ/ej26/a1.html).

Harris, V. (2004). Personal communication.

Harris, V. (2004) Cross-linguistic transfer of language learning strategies: preliminary findings. Unpublished manuscript.

Hodge, M. (2004) Personal communication.

Keatley, C., Chamot, A.U., Spokane, A. and Greenstreet, S. (2004) Learning strategies of students of Arabic. *The Language Resource*, 8(4), May 2004. (Retrieved from: http://www.nclrc.org/nectfl04ls.pdf).

Kojic-Sabo, I. and Lightbown, P.M. (1999) Students' approaches to vocabulary learning and their relationship to success. *Modern Language Journal*, 83(2), 176–192.

Macaro, E. (2001) *Learning Strategies in Foreign and Second Language Classrooms*. London: Continuum.

National Capital Language Resource Center (2000a) High school foreign language students' perceptions of language learning strategies use and self-efficacy. Unpublished research report. ERIC Document Reproduction Service ED 445 517; FL 026 388.

National Capital Language Resource Center (2000b) Elementary immersion students' perceptions of language learning strategies use and self-efficacy. Unpublished research report. ERIC Document Reproduction Service ED 445 521; FL 026 392.

National Reading Panel (2000) Report of the National Reading Panel: Teaching children to read. (Retrieved from: http:/www.nichd.nih.gov/publications/ nrp/smallbook.htm).

Nunan, D. (1997) Does learner strategy training make a difference? *Lenguas Modernas*, 24, 123–142.

Nyikos, M. and Oxford, R.L. (1993) A factor analytic study of language learning strategy use: interpretations from information-processing theory and social psychology. *Modern Language Journal*, 7, 11–22.

Olivares-Cuhat, G. (2002) Learning strategies and achievement in the Spanish writing classroom: a case study. *Foreign Language Annals*, 35(5), 561–570.

O'Malley, J.M. (1987) The effects of training in the use of learning strategies on learning English as a second language. In A.L. Wenden and J. Rubin (eds.), *Learner Strategies in Language Learning*. UK: Prentice Hall, 133–143.

O'Malley, J.M. and Chamot, A.U. (1990) *Learning Strategies in Second Language Acquisition*. Cambridge: Cambridge University Press.

O'Malley, J.M., Chamot, A.U. and Küpper, L. (1989) Listening comprehension strategies in second language acquisition. *Applied Linguistics*, 10(4), 418–437.

Oxford, R.L. (1990) *Language learning strategies: what every teacher should know*. New York: Newbury House.

Oxford, R.L. and Burry-Stock, J.A. (1995) Assessing the use of language learning strategies worldwide with the ESL/EFL version of the Strategy Inventory for Language Learning. *System*, 23(2), 153–175.

Oxford, R.L. and Leaver, B.L. (1996) A synthesis of strategy instruction for language learners. In R.L. Oxford (ed.), *Language Learning Strategies Around the World: Cross-Cultural Perspectives*. Honolulu, HI: University of Hawai'i Press, 227–246.

Oxford, R.L., Cho, Y., Leung, S. and Kim, H-J. (2004) Effect of the presence and difficulty of task on strategy use: an exploratory study. *International Review of Applied Linguistics*, 42, 1–47.

Ozeki, N. (2000) Listening strategy instruction for female EFL college students in Japan. Tokyo: Macmillan Language House.

Peterson, S.S. (2000) Pronunciation learning strategies: a first look. Unpublished research report. ERIC Document Reproduction Service ED 450 599; FL 026 618.

Pressley, M. (2000) What should comprehension instruction be the instruction of? In M.L. Kamil, P.B. Mosenthal, P.D. Pearson and R. Barr (eds.), *Handbook of Reading Research, Volume III*. Mahwah, NJ: Lawrence Erlbaum, 545–561.

Pressley, M. and Harris, K. (2001) Cognitive strategies instruction. In A.L. Costa (ed.), *Developing Minds: A Resource Book for Teaching Thinking* (third edition). Alexandria, VA: Association for Supervision and Curriculum Development.

Pressley, M., El-Dinary, P.B., Gaskins, I., Schuder, T., Bergman, J.L., Almasi, J. and Brown, R. (1992) Beyond direct explanation: transactional instruction of reading comprehension strategies. *Elementary School Journal*, 92(5), 513–555.

Robbins, J. (1996) *Between "Hello" and "See You Later": Development of Strategies for Interpersonal Communication in English by Japanese EFL Students*. Published Ph.D. Dissertation, University Microfilms, International. UMI number: 9634593. Ann Arbor, MI: University of Michigan.

Rubin, J. (1975) What the "good language learner" can teach us. *TESOL Quarterly*, 9(1), 41–51.

Rubin, J. (1981) Study of cognitive processes in second language learning. *Applied Linguistics*, 11, 117–131.

Rubin, J. (2001). Language learner self-management. *Journal of Asian Pacific Communication*, 11(1), 25–37.

Rubin, J. (2003) Diary writing as a process: simple, useful, powerful. *Guidelines*, 25, 2.

Rubin, J. and Thompson, I. (1994) *How to Be a More Successful Language Learner*. Second edition. Boston, MA: Heinle & Heinle.

Rybicki, A. (2002) Developing effective study skills while studying a foreign language. Master of Arts Action Research Project, Saint Xavier University and SkyLight Professional Development Field-Based Master's Program. ERIC Document Reproduction Service ED 466 628; FL 027 367.

Schreiber, J. (2004) Personal communication.

Shen, H-J. (2003) The role of explicit instruction in ESL/EFL reading. Foreign Language Annals, 36/3, p. 424–433.

Stern, H.H. (1975) What can we learn from the good language learner? *Canadian Modern Language Review*, 31, 304–318.

Thompson, I. and Rubin, J. (1996) Can strategy instruction improve listening comprehension? *Foreign Language Annals*, 29(3), 331–342.

Vance, S.J. (1999) Language learning strategies: is there a best way to teach them? Unpublished manuscript. ERIC Document Reproduction Service ED 438–716; FL 026–146.

Vandergrift, L. (2002) It was nice to see that our predictions were right: developing metacognition in L2 listening comprehension. *The Canadian Modern Language Review*, 58, 555–575.

Vann, R. and Abraham, R. (1990) Strategies of Unsuccessful Language Learners. *TESOL Quarterly*, 24(2), 177–198.

Weaver, S.J. and Cohen, A.D. (1997) Strategies-based instruction: a teacher-training manual. Minneapolis, MN: Center for Advanced Research on Language Acquisition, University of Minnesota.

Weinstein, C.E. (1994) Students at risk of academic failure: learning to learn classes. In K.W. Pritchard and R.M. Sawyer (eds.), *Handbook of College Teaching: Theory and Applications*. Westport CT: Greenwood.

Wenden, A.L. (1987) Conceptual background and utility. In A.L. Wenden and J. Rubin (eds.), *Learner Strategies in Language Learning.* Englewood cliffs, NJ; London: Prentice-Hall International, 1–14.

Wenden, A.L. (1991) *Learner Strategies for Learner Autonomy.* London: Prentice-Hall International.

Wenden, A.L. (2002) Learner development in language learning. *Applied Linguistics*, 23(1), 32–55.

Wharton, G. (2000) Language learning strategy use of bilingual foreign language learners in Singapore. *Language Learning*, 50(2), 203–244.

22 Errors and good language learners

Michael Roberts and Carol Griffiths

Over the years, various teaching and learning methods have approached errors in language learning from quite different theoretical and practical standpoints. An ongoing problem is a definition of "error." Should an error be related to native-speaker utterances, as suggested by Lennon (1991)? Although defining error in these terms has some appeal, there is wide variation among those who would consider themselves to be native speakers, so whose variety is to be taken as the standard? Or should an error be judged according to whether it is grammatically correct or whether it is acceptable, as discussed by James (1998)? Although grammar may be a relatively objective criterion, able to be decided upon by some higher authority such as a reference grammar book, what is accepted as "correct" is by no means absolutely uniform across language varieties, while acceptability is a highly subjective measure. In spite of many years of debate, a review of the literature reveals that there is no "unproblematic" (Ellis and Barkhuizen, 2005, p. 56) definition of error.

The behaviorist view

The behaviorist approach to language learning expounded by Skinner (1957) saw language learning as a process of habit formation – the acquisition of a series of responses to external stimuli developed through a process referred to as operant conditioning. Under this approach language errors were considered to be counter-productive because they led to the formation of bad habits, which, if left uncorrected resulted in fossilization.

The two-pronged strategy to counter this problem involved (1) the avoidance of error through contrastive analysis, and (2) the treatment of error with rigorous correction practices. The Contrastive Analysis Hypothesis (CAH) put forward by Lado (1957) and others, claimed that the similarities and differences between learners' first language and their target language, respectively, accounted for the relative ease or difficulty of learning various language features. By focusing attention on the differences, teachers could help learners avoid the error trap.

282

The cognitive view

Skinner's view was strongly challenged by Chomsky (1959) in his review of Skinner's work. Chomsky maintained that language learning was a process of rule formation, that it is a cognitive process. He was fascinated by what has been referred to as Plato's problem, or the logical problem of language acquisition, that is how such a perfect product could result from such an impoverished input. In his parlance, the output was under-determined by the input (Chomsky, 1981). Noting that the hypotheses formed by language learners were not completely random, but seemed to be constrained in some way, he postulated a species-specific (human), domain-specific (language), biological endowment: a genetically encoded predisposition to learn languages. Sometimes referred to as the Language Acquisition Device (LAD) or Universal Grammar (UG), this facility consists of a core of principles encoding what is possible in the whole range of human languages, and a set of parameters which encode the paths of variability across languages.

These parameters are initially set at the most restrictive (non-inclusive, least marked) position. As learners encounter language input (however imperfect), they are able to glean enough evidence to "trigger" the correct setting of the parameter for that particular language. Chomsky also talks about positive and negative evidence. Direct negative evidence (overt correction) is usually not available to first language learners and indirect negative evidence (that is, noticing the absence) is not considered strong enough to trigger the setting. Thus, parameter setting requires positive evidence (presence of a feature in the input).

The interlanguage view

Building on this view, Corder (1967), in his seminal article on the significance of learner error made several important observations that shaped the path of research in years to come. He noted a distinction between *input*, or what is made available to the student, and *intake*, or what is taken in. He also noted that the learner agenda often differs from the teacher agenda and that the learner's *built-in syllabus* is probably more efficient than the teacher-imposed one. He makes a distinction between *mistakes*, which are performance slips, and *errors*, which are evidence of the learner's interim, and as yet incomplete, language system, and which he referred to as transitional competence (later called "interlanguage" by Selinker, 1972). Corder ascribed a threefold importance to errors: they provide evidence of progress to the teacher, they provide evidence to researchers of how language is learned, and they are a device

283

by which learners learn, testing and modifying their hypotheses about language.

The notion of a built-in syllabus excited researchers in the 1970s who thought that if they could find what this built-in syllabus was, they could solve all the problems of language teaching and learning. The now famous morpheme studies of Burt and Dulay (1980) showed common acquisition orders across a variety of language types, suggesting that interference from the first language was not the main factor involved. This led them to develop their Creative Construction Hypothesis which asserted that learners recreated the "rules" or mental representations of the target language by a process of inferring them from the input. The common acquisition orders discovered in the morpheme studies led to the inclusion of the Natural Order Hypothesis in Krashen's (1985) Monitor Model.

The communicative view

Krashen built his Monitor Theory around the notion that comprehensible input was the necessary and sufficient condition for language acquisition to occur (the Input Hypothesis), and that there was a distinction between the acquired system and the learned system (the Acquisition-Learning Hypothesis). He incorporates Corder's notion of a built-in syllabus in his Natural Order Hypothesis, and attempts to explain why children do so much better learning a first language, than adults do learning a second language by postulating a set of affective attributes such as poor motivation, anxiety, and inhibition which can block the functioning of the Language Acquisition Device (the Affective Filter Hypothesis). Working with Terrell (1983) he developed the Natural Approach, a teaching method which sees the role of classroom teaching as one of providing comprehensible input in communicative contexts and in a supportive affective environment. Under this approach, error correction, structural grading, and grammar explanations are proscribed.

While Burt and Dulay's studies concentrated on correct performance, or what was successfully acquired, there were those who felt that in so doing they were overlooking a very important aspect of language development, which Wode, Bahns, Bedey, and Frank (1978) referred to as pre-target like regularities. These were errors in the sense of Corder's characterization of errors as systematic, but they seemed to show up regularly in the interlanguage systems of learners regardless of their first language. A series of studies looking at these so-called *developmental sequences* for aspects of language such as negation, interrogatives and plurals, concluded that these sequences were obligatory, unrelated to first language background, and impervious to instruction. This last finding appears to be the basis for at least some skepticism about the effectiveness of error correction, if not justifying the extreme view of proscription.

The information processing view

The need for the Affective Filter Hypothesis in Krashen's Monitor Theory to explain the difference in outcomes between child first language acquisition and language acquisition by adults who already speak other languages suggests that apart from affect, Krashen is ascribing the same process to both. In contrast, Bley-Vroman (1989), argues that the two processes are very different and while processes and outcomes suggest that Universal Grammar might be available to children in the acquisition of their first language, the processes and outcomes of adult language learning exhibit more characteristics in common with general skill learning. In particular he points out that, unlike child first language acquisition, adult language learning is characterized as a conscious, effort-filled process, dependent on intrinsic factors such as intelligence and motivation, and resulting in variable success. He notes that the Universal Grammar facility in children seems to atrophy around the time of their entry into adolescence and the onset of what Inhelder and Piaget (1958) refer to as the stage of formal operations – the ability to conceptualize in the abstract and infer generalizations from data. If we accept Bley-Vroman's Fundamental Difference Hypothesis, and in particular his observation that adult language acquisition is similar to general skill learning, then an explanation which includes the development of automaticity becomes attractive.

Krashen's insistence in the Acquisition-Learning Hypothesis that these two processes run on parallel tracks which never converge has been referred to as the non-interface position, that is, learning can never become acquisition. In contrast, McLaughlin, Rossman, and McLeod (1983) suggest an information processing model which sees language acquisition as a process of skill development, progressing from a conscious, effort-filled endeavor which cannot share mental resources with other tasks at the same time (analogous to linear processing) to an unconscious, effortless operation which can be performed in a multi-task environment (analogous to parallel processing). This constitutes an interface position in which learning becomes acquisition through the development of automaticity. Krashen's proscription of error correction in the Natural Approach is no doubt based on his desire to recreate a teaching and learning environment that is faithful to the one in which children

285

acquire their first language. It embraces the notion that caregivers respond to the content of a child's utterance rather than the form, and his belief that adult language acquisition is basically the same process as a child's acquisition of its first language. If we accept that acquisition of language by adults who already speak other languages is more closely related to general skill development, the theoretical motivation for adopting a proscriptive stance on error correction disappears.

Effectiveness of error correction/corrective feedback

If there is no theoretical basis for proscribing error correction, more pragmatic considerations regarding its effectiveness in facilitating learning become paramount. Illustrative of this position is that taken by Long (1977) who suggests that much of the corrective feedback supplied to language learners is erratic, ambiguous, ill-timed, and ineffective in the short-term, while Truscott (1996) maintained that error correction was ineffective and even harmful.

A model for the effectiveness of corrective feedback in relation to rule fossilization is outlined by Vigil and Oller (1976). They suggest that fossilization occurs when certain linguistic items, rules, and sub-systems become prematurely entrenched before they have achieved target-like status. To prevent this from occurring there is a need for a destabilizing influence on the system until it achieves target-like status. Their model looks at the expectation of feedback in two channels: affective and cognitive. An expectation of negative affective feedback will cause the learner to give up attempts to communicate. An expectation of positive affective and cognitive feedback will predispose towards fossilization. An expectation of positive affective feedback and negative cognitive feedback, will maintain destabilization of learners' interlanguage systems until they have achieved target-like status. The implication for classroom teachers is that they need to create an expectation of positive feedback in the affective domain in order for students to profit from the destabilizing effects of error correction.

Corrective feedback should be modeled on that given by native speakers to non-native speakers outside the classroom, according to Day, Chenowith, Chun, and Luppescu (1983). Their description of such feedback as clear and consistent is in sharp contrast with Long's (1977) findings about classroom error correction noted above. They found that native speaker feedback typically occurred in the turn immediately following the erroneous utterance and was most often direct and focused. The errors which invited feedback were those which inhibited conversation, such as factual errors, discourse errors and vocabulary items. Syntactic errors, which seem to be the focus of most of classroom error correction, were corrected only 7% of the time compared with 89.5% for errors of fact, 35% for discourse errors and 15% for vocabulary errors. They conclude by citing Judd's (1978) assertion that as syntax errors will only disappear with the passage of time, teachers would do better to focus their attention on vocabulary enrichment exercises.

The literature on corrective feedback is extensively reviewed by Chaudron (1988). He suggests that the question of whether or not errors should be corrected should ultimately be determined by how effective correction is. Chaudron notes that the practice of error correction should be restricted to those which are related to the pedagogic focus of the lesson and suggests, with Hendrickson (1978), that it should be used judiciously, focusing on types of error that inhibit communication, that are repeated frequently, and that have a highly stigmatizing effect on the listener. Alternatives to teacher correction of errors are also noted: self correction by students (Wren, 1982) and student peer correction (Long and Porter, 1985).

An interesting study which attempted to measure the value of corrective feedback in informing the learning process was conducted by Tomasello and Herron (1989). They developed an instrument which they referred to as the "Garden Path" technique comprising a group of sentences for which using a strategy of first language (English) transfer would result in target language (French) error. These errors were in turn immediately corrected by the teacher. The control group were just taught the French form and told it differed from the English. They found that the Garden Path group performed significantly better than the control group on post-test.

The role of consciousness in language learning is discussed by Schmidt (1990). Schmidt proposes that intake is that part of the input that the learner notices. Citing the study of his own acquisition of Brazilian Portuguese (Schmidt and Frota, 1986), Schmidt notes that in order to benefit from correction learners must first notice that they are being corrected – in other words, conscious noticing is a pre-condition for input to become intake.

In order to investigate the degree to which corrective feedback helps learners improve the accuracy of their writing over time, Bitchener (2003) surveyed 53 adult migrants who were divided into three groups: one which received direct written corrective feedback and a five-minute teacher-student conference; another which received direct written feedback only; and a third which received no corrective feedback. According to the results, those who received both written feedback and a conference session did significantly better than those who received only written feedback or no feedback. Bitchener (2003, p. 85) concludes that the results suggest "that some treatment conditions may better facilitate the progress that learners make in acquiring greater accuracy over the use of some problematic linguistic features".

While teaching a beginning Japanese language class at a North American University, Roberts (1995) observed that in spite of frequent correction, the same errors persisted. In conducting a peer observation of a colleague, the same phenomenon was observed. In a number of instances the students appeared not even to notice that the teacher was trying to correct their utterances. A growing feeling that excessive error correction was counter-productive motivated a determination to test student awareness and the effectiveness of the error correction.

The participants in Roberts's (1995) study were students in a first year Japanese language class at a North American University, and were all native speakers of North American English. The teacher was a native speaker of Japanese. Her permission was received to video the class, but she was not told that the focus of the study was on error correction, so as not to influence her focus in this area. A 50-minute class was video-taped, transcribed, and analyzed for instances of error correction activity by the teacher. Three student volunteers from the class were invited to view the video and note as many instances of error correction activity by the teacher as they could find in a single viewing of the tape. They were asked to note the meter reading at the point where the correction occurred and comment on the nature of the error. While they only had one viewing of the tape, the subjects were told they could stop the tape and repeat a section if they wished. Interestingly, none of them exercised this option. Instances of error correction activities were tabulated by the researcher and categorized according to a taxonomy of correction types. Similarly, errors were categorized according to a taxonomy of error types. Instances of noticing of error correction activity by the three subjects who viewed the tape, and instances of their correctly understanding the nature of the error from the activity observed on the tape were also tabulated across correction and error categories.

There were 92 instances of corrective feedback activity by the teacher in the 50-minute class. Since the three students who were recruited to view the videos had been asked to focus on error correction, they might have been expected to have had a heightened awareness of error correction compared with other students just sitting in the class. However, in spite of the focus of their search, they noticed less than 50% of the error correction. In even fewer instances were they able to demonstrate understanding of the nature of the errors by means of their comments. Roberts (1995) concludes that, for corrective feedback to be effective, learners must both notice and understand the nature of the correction.

How do good language learners deal with corrective feedback?

In order to explore how good language learners deal with corrective feedback, Griffiths (2006) observed two English language students from East Asia studying at the same language school in Auckland, New Zealand, and living in the same homestay accommodation. Meg, who was 26 years old had studied English for six years at school and needed English to improve her job prospects. Kay, who was 19 years old, had studied English for three years at school and wanted to study at university (subject unspecified).

They started at the language school at the same time and both were placed in the Elementary class. However, it soon became evident that Meg was making much faster progress than Kay. A number of differences in their strategy use was noted, including differences in the ways they dealt with errors. Meg firstly noticed when she was being corrected and then made an effort to use and remember the correct form. If there was something she did not understand she would ask. Griffiths (2006) provides an example of this behavior:

> Meg: I will meet my friend at 30 past 1.
> Homestay mother: At 1:30?
> Meg: Yes, 1:30 (*picking up the correction*). How about half past one? Is that correct?
> Homestay mother: That is also correct. You can say either.

By comparison, Kay paid scant attention to corrective feedback and frequently repeated the same errors time after time, for instance, repeatedly referring to Meg as "he", apparently oblivious to the error and to attempts to correct her.

At the end of the 10-week homestay period, Meg had already moved to the Pre-intermediate class and was ready to be promoted to Intermediate, while Kay was still struggling at Elementary level. According to Roberts' (1995) conclusion, it is possible that Meg's ability to notice and understand error correction may have contributed to her faster progress compared with Kay. As Rubin (1975) observed, good language learners learn from their own mistakes.

Implications for the teaching/learning situation

As Ellis (1994, p. 585) concludes, "probably the main finding of studies of error treatment is that it is an enormously complex process". Although this complexity no doubt contributes to the lack of unanimity regarding the effectiveness of error correction, the study by Griffiths (2006) suggests that for students who are aware of and act on correction, error feedback can be a useful and effective means of helping to develop competence in a target language.

Error correction is often considered "a vital part of the teacher's role" (Harmer, 1998, p. 62) and "one of the things that students expect from their teachers" (Harmer, 2001, p. 59). Faced with these expectations, teachers need to develop techniques to attract students' attention to correction and to provide cognitive input regarding correct language form. The decision of the need for error correction needs to be linked to the focus of the lesson activity in which it occurs. If the focus is on developing fluency/confidence in communicating, then the error should only be corrected if it impedes communication of meaning. If the focus is on grammatical accuracy in the use of a particular language feature, errors of form relating to the feature of focus should not be ignored. Of course, in correcting errors of form there is a variety of strategies ranging from very subtle non-verbal communication, alerting the learner to the need to monitor their utterance, to the less subtle interventionist approach of cuing, repeating, or recasting.

However, in order to avoid demotivation, correction needs to be done in such a way that the student's affective needs are also considered, as Vigil and Oller (1976) point out. Decisions regarding which errors to correct and how to achieve a balance between correction and encouragement are not straightforward (Hedge, 2000). Although error correction may be a recognized part of language instruction, "too much of it can be discouraging and demoralizing" (Ur, 1996, p. 171). Nevertheless, Ur (2000, p. 16) makes it clear that she considers correction important:

> first, because that's what learners want, and, all things being equal, I think we teachers should respect learners' wishes; and second because even if correcting is only of limited effectiveness, commonsense would argue that if there's one thing that is less effective than correcting, it is: not correcting.

Decisions regarding correction may well depend on a teacher, in a split second in front of a class, weighing considerations such as institutional or course demands and individual student needs against each other: a responsibility not to be taken lightly. Nevertheless, "there is increasing evidence that learners progress faster with meaningful language practice in a rich linguistic environment with an informed policy of error correction on the part of the teacher" (Hedge, 2000, p. 15).

Questions for ongoing research

Opinions regarding the effectiveness of error correction in language learning have been sharply divided over the years. At one end of the continuum is the position which holds that all errors must be rigidly corrected to avoid the development of unchangeably bad linguistic habits, while at the other extreme is the argument which maintains that all error correction is ineffective and may even have negative consequences for the learner.

According to Griffiths (2006), the good learner in her study learned from her mistakes, whereas the poorer learner ignored correction. This finding accords with the finding by Roberts (1995) that effective correction is both noticed and understood by learners, and also with Rubin's observation that good learners use their mistakes to improve their own language abilities.

If, however, we assume that error correction can be effective, questions remain as to how it is best carried out. Is it better to correct implicitly, perhaps by means of recasts, as used by the homestay mother in the example reported by Griffiths (2006), or is direct correction which the student cannot fail to notice more effective? Is it better to correct a student immediately, perhaps causing loss of face, or is it better to leave correction until later, when the student may already have forgotten the context of the error? To what extent do situational factors have an impact on error correction decisions: do we need different techniques for one-to-one correction from what might be appropriate in a classroom? And how about learner variables such as age? Do we need to use a different approach to correcting older learners from what we use for younger learners? All of these questions remain to be clarified.

Conclusion

As a result of the expectations mentioned by Harmer (1998, 2001), the appropriateness of correction of learner errors when teaching speakers of other languages (SOL) is a question that exercises the minds of all language teaching practitioners at some stage or other of their careers. As beliefs about the way in which languages are learned have changed, there has been a change in the way in which errors are perceived and in views about how teachers should respond to their students' errors. These views have ranged all the way from rigid correction of all errors to total proscription of all error correction.

Amid the controversies, teachers have often been left to manage the practicalities of the teaching/learning situation with little guidance.

Given however, that issues of error correction have been attracting a lot of interest in recent years (for instance, Ellis and Barkhuizen, 2005), hopefully teachers can look forward to more guidance from researchers regarding the relationship between error correction and the promotion of excellence in language learning among their students.

References

Bitchener, J. (2003) Does corrective feedback help L2 learners improve the accuracy of their writing over time? *New Zealand Studies in Applied Linguistics*, 9/2, 73–87.

Bley-Vroman, R. (1989) What is the logical problem of foreign language learning? In Gass, S., and J. Schachter (eds.) *Linguistic Perspectives on Second Language Acquisition*. Cambridge: Cambridge University Press, 41–68.

Burt, M. and H. Dulay. (1980) On acquisition orders. In Felix, S. (ed.) *Second Language Development: Trends and Issues*. Gunter Narr Verlag, Tubingen, 267–327.

Chaudron, C. (1988) *Second Language Classrooms: Research on Teaching and Learning*. Cambridge: Cambridge University Press.

Chomsky, N. (1959) Review of *Verbal Behavior* by B.F. Skinner. *Language*, 35, 26–58.

Chomsky, N. (1981) Principles and parameters in syntactic theory. In N. Hornstein, and D. Lightfoot (eds.), *Explanations in Linguistics: the Logical Problem of Language Acquisition*. London: Longman, 32–75.

Corder, S. (1967) The significance of learner errors. *International Review of Applied Linguistics*, 5, 161–170.

Day, R., Chenowith, N., Chun, A., and Luppescu, S. (1983) Foreign language learning and the treatment of spoken errors. *International Review of Applied Linguistics*, 5, 161–170.

Ellis, R. (1994) *The Study of Second Language Acquisition*. Oxford: Oxford University Press.

Ellis, R. and Barkhuizen, G. (2005) *Analysing Learner Language*. Oxford: Oxford University Press.

Griffiths, C. (2006) Strategies for successful language learning in an English-speaking environment: insights from a case study. *The Journal of Asia TEFL*, 3(2), 141–164.

Harmer, J. (1998) *How to Teach English*. London: Longman.

Harmer, J. (2001) *The Practice of English Language Teaching* (third edition). London: Longman

Hedge, T. (2000) *Teaching and Learning in the Language Classroom*. Oxford: Oxford University Press.

Hendrickson, J. (1978) Error correction in foreign language teaching: recent theory, research, and practice. *Modern Language Journal*, 62, 387–398.

Inhelder, B. and Piaget, J. (1958) *The Growth of Logical Thinking from Childhood to Adolescence*. New York: Basic Books.

James, C. (1998) *Errors in Language Learning and Use: Exploring Error Analysis*. London: Longman.

Judd, E. (1978) Vocabulary teaching and TESOL: a need for re-evaluation of existing assumptions. *TESOL Quarterly*, 12, 71–76.

Krashen, S. (1985) *The Input Hypothesis*. London: Longman.

Krashen, S. and Terrell, T. (1983) *The Natural Approach*. New York: Pergamon.

Lado, R. (1957) *Linguistics Across Cultures*. Ann Arbor, MI: University of Michigan Press.

Lennon, P. (1991) Error: some problems of definition, identification and distinction. *Applied Linguistics*, 12, 180–196.

Long, M. (1977) Teacher feedback on learner error: mapping cognitions. In H. Brown, C. Yorio, and R. Crymes, (eds.), *On TESOL '77*, (pp. 278–93). Washington, DC: TESOL.

Long, M. and Porter, P. (1985) Group work, interlanguage talk, and second language acquisition. *TESOL Quarterly*, 19, 207–228.

McLaughlin, B., Rossman, T., and McLeod, B. (1983) Second language learning: an information processing perspective. *Language Learning*, 33, 135–158.

Roberts, M. (1995) Awareness and the efficacy of error correction. In R. Schmidt (ed.), *Attention and Awareness in Foreign Language Learning* (pp. 163–182). University of Hawai'i at Manoa: Second Language Teaching and Curriculum Centre.

Rubin, J. (1975) What the "good language learner" can teach us. *TESOL Quarterly*, 9(1), 41–51.

Schmidt, R. (1990) The role of consciousness in second language learning. *Applied Linguistics*, 11(2), 129–158.

Schmidt, R. and Frota, S. (1986) Developing basic conversational ability in a second language: a case study of an adult learner of Portuguese. In R. Day (ed.), *Talking to Learn: Conversation in Second Language Acquisition* (pp. 237–326). Rowley, MA: Newbury House.

Selinker, L. (1972) Interlanguage. *International Review of Applied Linguistics*, 10, 209–230.

Skinner, B. (1957) *Verbal Behavior*. New York: Appleton-Century-Crofts.

Tomasello, M. and Herron, C. (1989) Feedback for language transfer errors: the Garden Path technique. *Studies in Second Language Learning*, 11, 385–395.

Truscott, J. (1996) The case against grammar correction in L2 writing classes. *Language Learning*, 46, 327–369.

Ur, P. (1996) *A Course in Language Teaching*. Cambridge: Cambridge University Press.

Ur, P. (2000) Teaching grammar: what can we learn from research. *The TESOLANZ Journal*, 8, 14–22.

Vigil, F. and Oller, J. (1976) Rule fossilization: a tentative model. *Language Learning*, 26, 281–295.

Wode, H., Bahns, J., Bedey, H., and Frank, W. (1978) Developmental sequence: an alternative approach to morpheme order. *Language Learning*, 28, 175–185.

Wren, D. (1982) A case study in the treatment of oral errors. *Selected papers in TESOL*, 1, 90–103. Monterey, CA: Monterey Institute of International Studies.

23 Tasks and good language learners*

Joan Rubin and Patricia McCoy

In recent years there has been a great deal of interest in task-based language teaching and learning (for instance, Ellis, 2003, 2005; Nunan, 2004), as well as a considerable amount of research into issues related to the use of tasks (for instance, Cohen, 2003; Skehan and Foster, 1997). According to Skehan (1998), a language task is meaningful in its own right and linked to the real world, although it may also be focused on a particular language goal. Task-based language teaching does not begin with an ordered list of linguistic items (Nunan, 1999), but with a series of tasks which are intended to develop learners' communicative skills and contribute incidentally to their linguistic development (Ellis, 1997). Advantages of task-based language learning over other approaches (such as grammar-based) are that students are likely to be more motivated if they see an activity as meaningful and as having some relevance to authentic activities which they may be called on to perform outside class (Ur, 1996).

How do good language learners manage language tasks? One of the most important procedures in learner self-management (LSM) that expert learners use to be successful in their language learning is planning, which involves defining/selecting goals, setting criteria to measure goal achievement, task analysis, and setting a time line. Task analysis, while frequently cited, has not been extensively researched. This chapter will detail and then illustrate our development of Wenden's (1995) tripartite task analysis procedure (defining task purpose, task classification, and identifying task demands) and conclude with the results of a study to determine the effects of promoting detailed task analysis on learners' language performance.

Task analysis

In order to understand the role of task analysis, it is important to understand its place in the entire set of metacognitive procedures. Following Rubin (2001 and 2005), there are five major procedures: planning, moni-

*Our sincere thanks to Joie Starr for the statistical analysis, and to Pilar Caamano and Vicky de la Garza for serving as teachers of the two control groups.

toring, evaluating, identifying problem and solution, and implementing solution. Task analysis (TA) is part of planning.

Planning usually begins with a task (that is, some activity the teacher assigns or learners assign themselves). Based on their understanding of the task, learners establish goals, that is, what they want to learn. At this point, the learner is ready to carry out task analysis (TA). Wenden (1995) suggested that there were three parts to task analysis:

1 Task Purpose answers the question: "Why bother?" This provides the motivation for carrying out the task. Many academic learners only consider pedagogical reasons such as "to pass the course" or "to get a good grade" but when learners are able to associate a task with one of their life purposes, their motivation is much stronger.

2 Task classification asks three questions: "What kind of task is this?" "What do I know about the task?" and "How do I feel about the task?" Task classification is dependent on learners' goals (what they want to learn) and purpose (why they want to learn). For instance, if a listening task is to act as the basis for a subsequent debate, the listener will need to consider the characteristics of a debate as well as of the listening task itself.

3 The Task demand stage uses the results of task classification to consider the following questions: "How do I feel about the task?" and "What strategies and actions could I use?"

Table 1 (see p. 296) is an example of a listening task analysis based on these steps:

1 The learner is given a task: To listen to an interview.

2 The learner decides what to listen to: "A discussion about immigration". Then, the learner determines *what* it is they want to learn from the interview, in this case some positions on Mexican–American immigration.

3 The learner may at the same time consider the purpose (*why*) for doing this task, or for having chosen this topic: because they had a good reason for learning about the topic.

4 The learner then starts to do some task classification, possibly at the same time thinking about the task demands (that is, *how* the task will be accomplished).

5 In this example, the learner considers seven aspects of the task:
   a Skill: the nature of listening
   b Genre: that is, the type of text, basic structure or organization of the text
   c Rhetorical style: the ways ideas are organized
   d Language: characteristics of the language (formal/informal; planned/unplanned; level of syntactic complexity)
   e Vocabulary: kinds of words or phrases related to the topic

Table 1 Listening task analysis

Task: To listen to an interview	
Task goal (what I want to learn): Positions on Mexican–American immigration	
Task purpose (why I want to learn): Because I have relatives in the United States	

Task classification	Task demands
Listening skills: No word boundaries, Importance of intonation in English	Think about rising and falling intonation
Genre: An interview consists of questions and answers	Try to predict questions and answers
Rhetorical style: Expository or persuasive	If it is persuasive, I should listen for reasons or propositions or maybe some sort of support for the propositions.
Language: Fairly formal (hence more complex), might be planned (hence little slang)	1. Consider connectors that make language more formal. 2. Consider whether there are any "compare and contrast" examples or any "cause and effect" arguments. 3. Look for what is topicalized and what is put in the background.
Vocabulary: Words or phrases relating to immigration, border problems, benefits, liabilities	1. Migrant labor, illegal, green card 2. Coyote, vigilante groups. 3. Willing and available labor, direct aid 4. Cost of patrolling, English classes, health care and education.
Background Knowledge: 1. Know a little about immigration but not much about the contributions or liabilities. 2. Don't know much about the interviewer.	1. Read reports about the topic. 2. Read an article about the latest the speaker has said about this topic, or what the interviewer's opinion is about the topic.
Feelings about the topic and task: 1. I am a little familiar with interviews so I think I can do the task. 2. I am very interested in the topic so I will work hard.	1. I think I have enough time to do a good job. 2. I am not worried about listening but I need to pay attention. 3. I need to find time to do the reading. 4. I need to clear my mind so I can attend to the task.

f Knowledge about topic and personages
g Feelings about the topic and the task.

6 While or after doing task classification, learners use the information to consider how they will accomplish the task. Learners may come up with a large number of possible strategies to deal with aspects of the task classification. Only when an action plan has been created will learners be able to make the final determination regarding how they are going to proceed.

Clearly, this example is only illustrative of how a learner, following the categories given, might classify elements of this particular task and identify possible strategies to address aspects of this classification. Every individual learner may bring different background knowledge or feelings about the topic and task and may choose to consider different vocabulary, structure, rhetorical style, or genre. In short, a task analysis is a highly individual procedure which may vary greatly from learner to learner.

With the information gleaned from the task analysis, the learner is ready to establish an action plan. Without adequate task analysis procedures, the way learners approach tasks is very much "hit and miss" and does not allow them to take charge of their learning. The question, however, is: to what extent can the ability to do task analysis be successfully promoted by teachers and does this knowledge and skill have an effect on learner performance?

The study

A study was conducted in the language department at a major private university in Mexico. Four sections of the same English language course participated. Pat McCoy taught the two treatment groups, and two colleagues, both highly evaluated instructors, each taught a control group. The course used for the study, called LE 102, is primarily a reading and writing course at intermediate level. There is a unique aspect to this course: it was designed to give students who need it an extra semester at intermediate level before going on to a much tougher reading and writing course at a low advanced level, called LE 201. Thus, the learning objectives of course LE 102 are very similar to the previous course, LE 101. The text is different, and there is more reading and writing, but grammatical structures are recycled, not new. About 90% of the previous LE 101 students take it. Table 2 shows how these courses fit together.

Table 2 Required English courses

Course title	TOEFL range	Course type	Placement criteria
101	400–459	Four skills course	Students placed into this course
102	430–459	Emphasis on reading and writing	Students with grades of 89% or lower in 101
201	460–499	Reading and writing	Students with 90% and above in 101 or passing 102

Participants

The number of students per class was similar but not identical, as indicated in Table 3.

Table 3 Participant groups

Control Group 1 N = 17	Treatment Group 1 N = 19
Control Group 2 N = 21	Treatment Group 2 N = 20
Total = 38	**Total = 39**

We were keen to try out task analysis at this level because of the challenge of this student population. Most of the students viewed their English classes as a burdensome requirement, and not a tool for future endeavors. General characteristics of the LE 102 population included:

1   A 30–40% failure rate, both for this course (102) and for the previous English course (101) taken at this university.
2   Ten % of the students in the sample had taken this course, or the previous one, several times before, either because they failed it or because they dropped it.
3   Motivation was low: students would often suggest to the teacher that they go eat breakfast rather than stay in class, and would start getting ready to leave about ten minutes before the class was over.
4   Absenteeism and failure to turn in assignments were high.
5   Students often used inappropriate study strategies; for example, they would limit their studying to reading textbook pages without engaging in productive tasks.

6 Student learning behaviors were not consistent with stated beliefs. For example, one student stated that it was very important to create a system to identify one's own errors but seldom did it.

Intervention, data collection and analysis

Our treatment used task analysis instruction in the expectation that it would contribute to a difference between success and failure at this level through the use of appropriate planning procedures. In the two treatment groups, task analysis was regularly presented throughout the semester, while this was not routinely provided in the control groups. The following is an example of how task analysis was presented to the treatment groups. In this case, the task assigned was a writing task, and the first step was to establish SMART goals for the task:

S	= specific
M	= measurable
A	= attainable
R	= relevant
T	= time based

Much scaffolding was required throughout the process to get learners to state their SMART goals. After goal setting, and clarification of purpose, task classification was undertaken. Since this was new to the students, the larger categories of what was involved in a writing task (for instance genre, rhetorical style, audience, informational content, and different aspects of language) were provided as part of the scaffolding. A table design was used so that students could write down their task demands directly to the right of the task classification (as an example, see Table 1). This visual scheme made sense for the students, and resulted in a long list of choices for creating the action plan, which was developed using the "Action Plan" on p. 300.

Particularly challenging for learners was establishing criteria for evaluation, for which a checklist was jointly constructed by both student and instructor. On page 301 is an example of criteria for evaluation.

The complete task analysis procedure was available on McCoy's web page for students to consult. It was constantly updated as the semester progressed. McCoy's class presentations, linked to her web page using PowerPoint included task classification and demands in order to model them for different skills. The students then followed their own action plan for the assigned writing task. The control group was not

Action plan

Given everything you have considered above, what will you do to write this composition?

Think of possibly doing it in parts (body, introduction, conclusion, revision, and editing).

First I will . . .

Then I will . . .

Next I will . . .

Finally, I will use the checklist to verify I have reached my goal.

taught task analysis. However, the teacher in Control Group 2, recommended McCoy's web page to her students, thus, those students who used McCoy's web page to complement their instruction had some exposure to task analysis. Also, all foreign language learners were expected to complete weekly tasks in the Self-Access Center that foster learner self-management. Two different measures, of task analysis and exam results, were used to determine if there were any differences between the control and the treatment groups:

Measure of task analysis

This consisted of a composite of the learners' scores on five items: goal, purpose, task classification/task demands, action plan, and evaluation criteria. Both the control and the treatment groups carried out this

Criteria for evaluation

Introduction

- The text begins with an introduction.
- The introduction begins with an interest technique.
- The topic is stated.
- The author's point of view is stated.

Body

- Each paragraph begins with a topic sentence.
- The topic of the paragraph is explained or supported by four or five sentences that provide information.
- The text has anecdotes and uses evocative words such as *imagine, consider, this could happen to you,* that relate the information directly to the reader.
- The text uses adjectives, descriptions, and details that make the information interesting.

Language

- The vocabulary employed is correct for the sentence context.
- Sentences are varied in length.
- When a peer reads my work, he or she can readily understand it.
- Connecting words are used where ideas change in order to make the relationship among ideas clearer, for example: *However . . ., although . . ., if so . . ., and so . . ., but . . ., clearly . . .*

Conclusion

- The conclusion is short, no longer than 10% of the length of the text.
- The conclusion uses specific concluding techniques such as a quote, a summary, a concluding story, a dramatic statement.
- My view is emphasized or restated.
- The peer who read my text can restate my viewpoint from reading the conclusion.
- If necessary, my conclusion is emotional.

Mechanics

- Subject–verb agreement = the subject and the verb agree in number, or the subject is written.
- Verb tense = the verb tense used is correct for the context of the sentence.
- Active/passive = check active/passive usage.
- Verb Form = check for the correct verb form.

exercise at the beginning and end of the semester. The pre-course task was different from the post-course task. After the end-of-semester analysis, the difference between the scores was calculated and averaged.

Exam results

This was measured by the departmental final exam which all students at a particular level take. It should be noted that the evaluation of academic performance was based solely on the final exam. Additional correlations could be made with other indicators of academic performance (for instance, mid-term tests or a series of quizzes) but time did not permit this in this course. After the exam, the number and percentage of students who passed the exam were calculated. Differences were examined for significance using a non-pooled T-test.

Findings

The study used two groups of language students; a control group consisting of 38 students who were not given specialized task analysis training (although indirect training and exposure exist as part of the syllabus) and a treatment group consisting of 39 students who received additional specialized instruction and practice in the fundamentals of task analysis. The primary variables considered were task analysis score and the final exam score, as set out in Tables 4 and 5.

In comparing the pre-course scores on task analysis (Table 4), there was

Table 4 Task analysis scores

Class	Number of students doing task analysis	Total pre-course TA core	Total post-course TA score	Difference between TA scores	Average loss/gain on TA score
Control Group 1	12	41	36	−05	5/12 = −0.41
Control Group 2	19	53	61	+08	8/19 = +0.42
Total	**31**	**94**	**97**	**+3**	**3/31 = +0.96**
Treatment Group 2	15	44	61	+17	17/15 = +1.13
Treatment Group 1	14	50	75	+25	25/14 = +1.79
Total	**29**	**94**	**136**	**+42**	**42/29 = +1.44**

Table 5 Final exam scores

Class	Number of Students	Passed Final Exam (75% or higher)	% Pass
Control Group 1	17	8	47
Control Group 2	21	12	57
Total	**38**	**20**	**52.6**
Treatment Group 2	20	12	60
Treatment Group 1	19	12	63
Total	**39**	**24**	**61.5**

no difference in total TA score between the groups. That is, both groups started with about the same amount of task analysis knowledge. After instruction in task analysis, the difference between the pre-course and post-course scores of the combined treatment groups and the combined control groups was significant at the .01 level (non-pooled T test). The treatment groups improved their task analysis scores by +1.44 on average whereas the average change in the control groups was only +0.96.

On the final exam, the treatment groups considerably outperformed the control groups. Of the treatment groups, 61.5% compared with only 52.6% of the control groups got a passing grade of 75% or higher.

Implications for the teaching/learning situation

The results of this study indicate that learners can improve their ability to do task analysis with intensive instruction. Furthermore, this appears to be related to higher final exam scores.

We might also note that there was some evidence that students did continue to use task analysis after this course: in one case, a student who had taken LE 102 five times took the next course in the summer and passed it; another learner reported that he had begun to apply task analysis to his architecture classes.

On the other hand, there are some things that appear to be hard to change. These include the following:

1 Even though we provided instruction to be able to state SMART goals, learners found this difficult to do and evidently, needed more scaffolding.
2 Learners had difficulty distinguishing between a goal (that is, what you want to learn) and a purpose (that is, why you want to learn it). More targeted instruction may be needed to help learners clarify this distinction.

3   The part of task analysis that probably requires the most instruction and is most critical for a learner to be able to self-manage, is the ability to state criteria for success. That means that when tackling a task the learner can state in advance some observable measure that indicates what has been learned. This measure needs to be the learner's, not the teacher's grade on a quiz or a final exam. Learners need to independently measure their own success.

Although expert learners used their knowledge to do task analysis and are continually revising their planning skills, for most novice learners, TA is new and requires lots of scaffolding. With instruction it can enable learners to gain control of the learning process. With adequate planning, learners are able to select "appropriate" strategies for a task, for their learning style, for their own purpose, and not just use strategies in a random fashion.

Questions for ongoing research

We believe this is the first experiment testing the effect of TA instruction and considering its impact on language performance. Given that this was a highly unmotivated group of students, we feel the instruction should be even more effective with language classes where the course is not a required one with a record of lots of failure. Further research is needed to determine whether there is a direct relationship between TA training and improved language scores.

The results of the study described in this chapter suggest that, as part of the process of effective task management, expert (good) language learners use task analysis. Other components of planning, such as defining goals, setting criteria to measure achievement, and time management may well also contribute to successful language learning, along with other procedures such as monitoring, evaluating, identifying problems, and implementing solutions. The study reported in this chapter did not investigate these aspects of procedures, which all remain fruitful areas for further research.

Conclusion

In order to plan, learners need knowledge, and the more knowledge they have the more skilled they can be at planning. The relationship of knowledge to procedures was clearly and repeatedly outlined by Wenden (1995) and elaborated by Rubin (2001, 2005). Task analysis requires that learners bring all of their knowledge to the process. In addition, they need to be ready to develop new knowledge to accomplish the task.

Our work on task analysis builds on Wenden's (1995) tri-partite description of task analysis by spelling out more detailed task classification, by linking task demands directly to task classification and task purpose, and by separating goal (*what* is learnt) from task purpose (*why* it is learnt). Unlike good language learners, less expert learners often do little or no planning before beginning a task. Extensive instruction in task analysis can help learners select "appropriate" strategies for a task and for their learning style, and help them to not just use strategies in a random fashion.

References

Cohen, A.D. (2003) The learner's side of foreign language learning: where do styles, strategies and tasks meet? *IRAL*, 41, 279–291.

Ellis, R. (1997) *SLA Research and Language Teaching*. Oxford: Oxford University Press.

Ellis, R. (2003) *Task-based Language Teaching and Learning*. Oxford: Oxford University Press.

Ellis, R. (ed.) (2005) *Planning and Task Performance in a Second Language*. Philadelphia, PA: John Benjamins.

Nunan, D. (1999) *Second Language Teaching and Learning*. Boston, MA: Heinle & Heinle.

Nunan, D. (2004) *Task-based Language Teaching*. Cambridge: Cambridge University Press.

Rubin, J. (2001) Language learner self-management. *Journal of Asian Pacific Communication*, 11(1), 25–37.

Rubin, J. (2005) The expert language learner: a review of good language learner studies and learner strategies. In K. Johnson (ed.), *Expertise in Second Language Learning and Teaching*. Basingstoke, Hants, England: Palgrave Macmillan, pp. 37–63.

Skehan, P. (1998) Task-based instruction. *Annual Review of Applied Linguistics*, 18, 268–286.

Skehan, P. and Foster, P. (1997) Task type and task processing conditions as influences on foreign language performance. *Language Teaching Research*, 1(3), 185–211.

Ur, P. (1996) *A Course in Language Teaching*. Cambridge: Cambridge University Press.

Wenden, A.L. (1995) Learner training in context: a knowledge-based approach. In L. Dickinson and A.L. Wenden (eds.), *Special Issue on Autonomy*, System 23(2), 183–194.

The learners' landscape and journey: a summary

Rebecca L. Oxford and Kyoung Rang Lee

Thirty years ago, researchers passionately wanted to find out what characteristics constituted *the* good language learner (Naiman, Fröhlich and Todesco, 1975; Rubin, 1975, Stern, 1975). The research aim was to unearth the secrets of such learners, with the implicit assumption that if these secrets became more widely known, they could be shared with or transplanted to less successful language learners. The assumption of identifiability of a single set of characteristics possessed by the good language learner, and possible transferability of these characteristics to less fortunate learners gradually gave way to the realization that no single ideal set of characteristics existed. Instead, researchers (such as Stevick, 1990) showed that many different kinds of successful language learners ply their varied talents in a wide range of settings. This chapter describes the landscape of language learning and the journey that good language learners take.

Learner identity

In recent years, the important role played by learner identity in language learning has been increasingly recognized (for instance, Norton, 1997, 2000). A learner's identity is built up of a vast number of variables, many of which are dealt with in this volume. One of the most important is motivation. It is difficult to disagree with Ushioda's (this volume) suggestion that good language learners are motivated. Motivation is the spark which ignites the bonfire of action. Without motivation (be it intrinsic, extrinsic, instrumental, or integrative) little is likely to be achieved by way of language learning. An important question, however, is: What makes good language learners *good*? It is important to remember that the construct of *good* is, in fact, a value judgment related to purposes for language learning, and values and goals are approved by the society in which the learner operates. The learner therefore tends to be motivated to learn what is most socially valued: it is that which is usually considered *good*.

Intricately interwoven with motivation is language aptitude, often considered to be a relatively stable learner characteristic (Carroll,

306

1962), which is used to select or stream students for particular language courses (Ranta, this volume). Motivation, however, can compensate for aptitude deficiencies. The concept of aptitude is, in some senses, a little dangerous or perhaps even fallacious, especially when interpreted as implying that each person has a static, unchanging degree of aptitude for language learning and that some people, compared with others, possess more of "it." Feuerstein and his colleagues (Feuerstein, Klein, and Tannenbaum, 1991) demonstrate that teachers can literally increase students' intelligence or aptitude through teaching students to use more effective metacognitive and cognitive strategies. In other words, aptitude is dynamic, not static. Moreover, Carroll (1962) shows that no matter what the person's so-called aptitude, any person can learn any subject if given enough time and assistance. Aptitude is best treated as a shifting indicator, rather than a determiner, of the upper limit of learners' potential ability.

Of all a learner's identifying characteristics, none is more stable than age. It is possible, for instance, that a good program or an excellent teacher might effect changes in level of motivation. Nothing anyone can do, however, can change how old a learner is: we are as old as we are, and there is nothing we or anybody else can do about that. As Griffiths notes in Chapter 2 on age, although older students can be very effective language learners, most research shows that younger is generally better. The advantages of younger learners are well known, including ease of acquiring native-like pronunciation, stress, and fluency. These advantages have been variously attributed to (a) critical and sensitive periods for language learning, (b) age-related general cognitive differences, (c) language shock and culture shock, (d) lower expectations and fewer pressures for children, and (e) differences in learning situations. Though most advantages seem to rest with the young, adults are favored in terms of metacognition, strategy awareness and use, and explicit grammatical understanding. Some older learners can make significant progress in language learning by accentuating positive features and disregarding, to the extent possible, fear and social comparison.

Another identifying characteristic which tends to be somewhat resistant to change is learning style. Nel (this volume), contends that there is no one style typical of good language learners: various learning styles can contribute to success. Although there are some theoretical difficulties inherent in Curry's (1991) onion model, the three layers are often used to organize the discussion of learning style factors: (a) instructional and environmental, (b) information processing, and (c) personality.

Although personality may affect style, it is also an important variable in its own right. According to Ehrman (this volume), a specific personality combination (introversion–intuition–thinking–judging, or

The learners' landscape and journey

INTJ) is significantly over-represented among the top language learners at the Foreign Service Institute (FSI), where she worked. It is possible that any given individual can become a good language learner through style flexing or through strategies that take advantage of strengths. The immediate question raised by Ehrman's study is naturally whether the key finding – that INTJ learners are the top learners at a particular institution – would be replicated in other settings. It might well be that the successful personality at the FSI might be very different from the successful personalities in less intensive settings, in study-abroad environments, or in immigrant or refugee situations. The most important message from Ehrman's work may not be that INTJ's are the best learners everywhere, but instead, that it is valuable to identify the personality features, styles, and strategies that are most functional in any given setting.

Although gender might at one time have been considered immutable as far as the question of identity was concerned, contemporary views are rather less rigid. As Nyikos (this volume) explains, many investigations into gender-related differences in language learning depict women as slightly more successful than men, partly due to their flexibility in use of strategies for learning and communication. Nyikos also mentions neurological studies showing that, although women utilize the same area of the brain as men to process language, women often use both sides of the brain and activate more areas in their brain than men do. We might add that the "both sides now" theory, as we might call it, has been supported in a variety of studies showing that the corpus callosum (the fibrous band connecting the two hemispheres) is larger in women than in men. Social factors also play a role in gender differences in language learning (see Oxford, 1993, 1994, 1995; Oxford, Nyikos, and Ehrman, 1988).

Identity relates to learners' beliefs. According to Cynthia White (this volume), good language learners possess positive beliefs about the language they are learning and about themselves as language learners. Beliefs are the basis of how learners approach their learning, the strategies they employ, their motivation, their attitudes, and their success in language learning. Beliefs, in turn, are influenced by culture (Finkbeiner, this volume). During any given day, learners can live in multiple, intersecting cultures related to the particular situations they inhabit: home, work, classroom, cafeteria, mosque, store, or freeway. These environments vary dramatically in their constraints and affordances: they can be exciting, enriching, enlightening, encouraging, confirming, supportive, indifferent, confusing, repressive, stultifying, or dangerous. Sometimes the goals of the individual clash with the goals of the "large culture" or the "small culture" (as in the classroom) creating identity conflicts which can be difficult to resolve since learners' motivation toward/investment

308

in/resistance to language learning is often influenced by issues of cultural/linguistic identity.

In order to attain advanced levels of proficiency in a language other than the first, learners almost certainly undergo some degree of identity change related to pragmatics, semantics, and spoken communication. Some learners believe that any identity change might be a threat to their view of themselves, and they resist such change. Canagarajah (1999) shows how learners strategically resist the forms of cultural and linguistic domination viewed (by some learners) as inherent in many textbooks and cooperative learning techniques. For instance, he found that learners of English in Sri Lanka used highly creative strategies to resist domination: writing graffiti in margins of their textbooks to highlight their own cultural values and denigrate Western values, learning only enough basic English grammar to pass standardized tests, and not participating in activities that might commit them emotionally or socially to the new language.

Identity-related issues are important in language learning and include strategies for cultural acclimatization, identity-stretching, managing power relationships, and resistance that learners use at different proficiency levels, in different learning situations, and for target languages that have different levels of social prestige. These issues have yet to be researched in a systematic way. Identity issues could be introduced more widely into research on good language learners by using mixed methods (Creswell, 2002; Tashakkori and Teddlie, 2003), that is, combining quantitative research methods with qualitative research methods. Many of the identity issues are not captured by traditional quantitative formats but only emerge through more intensive, ethnographic, qualitative methodologies, or through mixed methods.

Learner self-regulation

Good language learners have often been described as self-regulated learners, either in the Vygotskian (1978) sense (McCaslin and Hickey, 2001) or in an information-processing mode (O'Malley and Chamot, 1990; Winne, 2001, 2005). Self-regulation refers to how learners manage their own learning (Dörnyei, 2005) and involves strategies, metacognition, and autonomy (see Oxford and Schramm, 2007).

Learners need to know that there are strategies available for them to use to help them traverse the language learning landscape. Learners use learning strategies for certain tasks based on their decision about the purpose of each task. Griffiths (this volume) presents several definitions of strategies throughout the last 30 years and comes to a succinct definition: "activities consciously chosen by learners for the purpose of regulating their own language learning". Metacognition serves as a guide for choosing, monitoring, combining and evaluating approaches for learning languages (Anderson, this volume), without which learners have no direction. Without the metacognitive compass, learners cannot decide what strategies to use and when to use them. Metacognition is also an essential element of autonomy, or the ability to take charge of one's own learning. Cotterall (this volume) describes a very interesting study of two students learning Spanish in a course devoted to learning grammatical structures. Of these two students (Simon and Harry), only one obtained a good grade, though they both passed. Perhaps, however, we should be careful about identifying Simon as a good language learner and Harry as not a good language learner. Perhaps Harry, who rebelled against – or at least heartily disagreed with – the very limited structural agenda put forth in the course, was actually a better learner than Simon, who agreed with the course goal and performed well according to that circumscribed standard, but who may not have done so well in a different situation.

The learning situation

There has recently been a great deal of interest in issues related to the learning situation (for instance Norton and Toohey, 2001). It is the situation in which learners find themselves which provides the opportunity for learning, the third variable on which good language learning depends, as identified by Rubin (1975). It would be possible to enumerate a great many situational variables which might have an effect on learning outcomes. Although methodologists can be very emphatic about the advantages or disadvantages of particular methods, Griffiths (this volume) discovered that good language learners are very eclectic in their preferences, suggesting that there is more than one way to learn language well, and that good language learners can flexibly employ the methods which best suit themselves and/or their situations in order to achieve their learning goals. We also need to ask how less successful language learners – that is, learners who are less deliberate, less self-aware, and often more desperate (Reiss, 1981) – can deal with methods. Although we would like to believe that learners, if they figure out they are on the wrong mountain entirely, or the wrong path on the right mountain, can try a different way, it is not that simple in reality. Many less effective learners do not realize they are on the wrong mountain or do not recognize many possible paths they might take on the mountain where they are.

Perhaps strategy instruction might help these kinds of learners. Chamot (this volume) stresses the importance of culture and context on strategy instruction, which can be seen as a tool to provide learners with a means of achieving success in language learning. Holliday (2003), however, describes learner training as an attempt by a dominant culture to suppress the values of a less dominant culture. Even the best-devised strategy instruction can give that impression if learners' own existing cultural values and experiences are not dealt with directly, and if the value of the new strategies is not clearly enough explained by instructors/researchers or accepted by learners. Error correction (Roberts and Griffiths, this volume) and task-based learning (Rubin and McCoy, this volume) are other areas which require cultural sensitivity, and consideration of the situation where they are employed, if they are to be effective.

The learning destination

In order to achieve proficiency in a target language, learners are faced with a sometimes daunting landscape dotted with a variety of destinations in the form of knowledge (vocabulary, grammar, pronunciation, function) and skills (listening, speaking, reading, writing). In the minds of many learners, these language goals are a wilderness, vast, perilous, and inaccessible. The learner's task is to tame the wilderness by understanding it, identifying landmarks, and charting a path within it.

The study of vocabulary learning (Moir and Nation, this volume) showed that the poorer learners were not interested in taking charge of their own learning by using in-depth, personalized learning techniques as required by their program. Their learning agenda (memorizing words for tests) differed greatly from the researchers' plans. Perhaps a video such as Cynthia White (this volume) describes might have helped to shift learners' beliefs towards new strategies. Bade's chapter on grammar (this volume) underscores the importance of grammatical knowledge for good language learners. Although research has not definitively shown the most effective ways to teach grammar, good language learners employ strategies for using the grammar system to communicate, and to exploit language functions (Tajeddin, this volume). Also important for communication is pronunciation, as noted by Brown (this volume) who presents key issues in pronunciation learning.

Developing the skills to use linguistic knowledge is also an important part of language learning. Although knowledge of vocabulary, grammar, and pronunciation is essential for effective listening, empathy is also vital for understanding spoken messages (Goodith White, this volume). Good language learners are able to use a number of listening strategies, with strategy use varying according to learning style, task, and type of listening. In real life, of course, listening and speaking often go hand-in-hand.

In order to develop speaking skills, Kawai (this volume) used an electronic chat program which resulted in a mild increase in speaking participation. Kawai also reported on a retrospective case study of two
Japanese women who used English professionally. For these successful
speakers, making a deliberate effort to interact in English seemed to be
the most important strategy. The development of reading skills involves
meaning construction (Schramm, this volume), whereby readers construct mental models using linguistic and topic-specific background
knowledge, as well as a propositional textbase which they construct as
they process the visual information of the text surface. And, according to
Gordon (this volume), reading in the target language is a characteristic of
good writers, who also attend to vocabulary, meaning, and grammar
while developing strategies to manage uncertainty. Good writers independently revise their writing for relevance, clarity, and coherence, are
self-motivated, and create outside-of-class opportunities to write.

Implications for the teaching/learning situation

This book has many implications for teaching. In particular:

1 Teachers must understand the crucial roots of language learning,
such as age, gender, personality, and aptitude. It is especially important for teachers to remember that a slightly lower aptitude can be
balanced by strong motivation and positive use of strategies. Teachers
should never assume that a given learner lacks the aptitude to learn a
language.
2 Teachers need to recognize that just as there is no single good language learner model, there is no single perfect instructional method
or error correction technique that works for all students in all settings. Learners are different, every single one, even though some
general categories can be identified. In response to learner diversity,
principled eclecticism is required.
3 Because motivation is the fire that creates action, it is crucial for
teachers to tend the fire. If learners are intrinsically motivated by challenge, personal satisfaction, and interest, they will be active and
involved. Learners must, however, possess beliefs that foster motivation. If they believe that language learning is unimportant, that they
have no talent for learning languages, or that their cultural values and
personal identity are about to be subverted, they will not have the
motivation to learn the language.
4 Teachers must realize that they can provide strategy instruction that
empowers and strengthens their students. Strategy instruction can

occur in the four skills of reading, writing, listening, and speaking, as well as in vocabulary, grammar, and pronunciation. Through strategy instruction, teachers can help learners discover how to identify strategies that meet task demands and that relate to learners' styles. In doing so, teachers can become catalysts in the growth of culturally appropriate patterns of learner autonomy. However, strategy instruction must take into account learners' cultural expectations and beliefs; otherwise it will fail. If a shift in beliefs is essential in order for a student to learn certain new strategies, the teacher must first think carefully whether such a change in beliefs and strategies is necessary, worthwhile, culturally respectful, and linguistically appropriate. Only then should strategy instruction take place, and communication during and around it should be as open as possible. Understanding the cultural context is crucial for strategy instruction, just as it is for any other aspect of language learning and teaching.

Questions for future research

How do students keep themselves going when the going gets tough? To say that good language learners are motivated is really to do little more than state the obvious. How do they maintain their motivation? Volitional strategies are widely known in the self-regulation literature but are rarely, if ever, explained in the language learning literature. Exciting work has recently been done on volitional strategies (for instance, Corno, 2001; Oxford and Schramm, 2007; Rheinberg, Vollmeyer, and Rollett, 2000), which take up where motivational strategies leave off, that is, when learners encounter problems and feel that there is no further they can go. If motivational strategies provide the "pull" toward a goal, volitional strategies offer the brute-force "push" that learners sometimes need to employ in difficult learning situations. Volition is distinct from motivation. The term *volition* simply means the capability of making a conscious choice or decision, but as *volitional strategies* or *volitional control strategies*, the concept of volition has taken on two different meanings in self-regulated learning:

1 Strategies for exerting massive amounts of control over virtually all aspects of learning, such as cognition (attention, encoding, processing), emotion, motivation, task, setting, and even peers and teacher.
2 A more delimited set of strategies designed to help the learner keep learning despite many kinds of difficulties.

Rheinberg *et al.* (2000) present the most relevant volition-related model of self-regulation: the *expectancy-value model*. This model involves:

1 *Expectancy* that the learning activities will improve the outcome and that the outcome will actually have the desired consequences (e.g., contentment, pride, praise, instrumental use of the knowledge, decreased need to study).
2 *Incentive value* of having a good result.

Both expectancy and value must be present. However, sometimes students face aversive or difficult situations, so the model includes volitional strategies to help the learner continue working toward the desired outcome even in the face of serious problems. Examples of volitional strategies in the expectancy-value model are:

1 Pay attention to why the learning is important.
2 Try to block emotions that undermine volition.
3 Manipulate the environment to help control emotion and motivation (for instance, make social commitments that might help maintain an intention).
4 Halt any thought that would undermine the power of the intention.

Given that many leisure activities are usually more appealing than studying, students often have to use such volitional control strategies until more positive incentives (such as enjoyment of the activity) arise. If no positive incentives emerge, that is, if there is no more motivation-fuel forthcoming, "the learning activity has to be maintained continually with volitional control strategies" (Rheinberg *et al.*, 2000, p. 517). These strategies can be taught and learned and therefore have strong elements of consciousness. Individuals are not born with ideal strategies to extricate them from difficulties in language learning, although some individuals are probably born with greater general resiliency in difficult situations. These strategies await discovery.

Conclusion

The chapters of this book have painted a very complicated picture of what is involved in learning language, which might be conceived as a metaphorical landscape whose features include vocabulary, grammar, pronunciation, function, and language skills, or a complex mixture of any or all of these. In the process of trying to situate good language learners within this landscape, we must consider a dizzying array of variables, including individual characteristics such as age, aptitude, gender, personality, culture, style, beliefs, and motivation. This complex individual must employ appropriate behaviors (for instance strategies, metacognition, or autonomy), and utilize available facilitating opportunities afforded by the learning situation (for example teaching/learning method, strategy instruction, error correction, or task) in order to traverse the learning landscape and arrive at the desired learning destination. Good language learners are those who manage this difficult journey successfully.

Although we have learnt a lot about how language is learnt in the last 30 years since Rubin's (1975) article was published, many questions remain, some of which have been highlighted in this volume. Language learning is a difficult journey across a demanding landscape by extremely complex beings who behave in complicated ways. Ongoing research on a number of fronts is essential if we are to help our learners traverse this landscape successfully, no matter how they do it.

References

Anderson, N. (this volume) Chapter 7: Metacognition and good language learners.

Bade, M. (this volume) Chapter 13: Grammar and good language learners.

Brown, A. (this volume) Chapter 15: Pronunciation and good language learners.

Canagarajah, A.S. (1999) *Resisting Linguistic Imperialism in English Teaching*. Oxford: Oxford University Press.

Carroll, J.B. (1962) The prediction of success in intensive language training. In R. Glaser (ed.), *Training research and education*. Pittsburgh: University of Pittsburgh Press.

Chamot, A.U. (this volume) Chapter 21: Strategy instruction and good language learners.

Corno, L. (2001) Volitional aspects of self-regulated learning. In B.J. Zimmerman and D.H. Schunk (eds.), *Self-regulated Learning and Academic Achievement: Theoretical Perspectives*. Mahwah, NJ: Erlbaum, 191–225.

Cotterall, S. (this volume) Chapter 8: Autonomy and good language learning.

Creswell, J.W. (2002) *Research Design: Qualitative, Quantitative, and Mixed Methods Approaches*. Thousand Oaks, CA: Sage.

Curry, L. (1991) Patterns of learning style across selected medical specialities. *Educational Psychology*, 11(3), 247–277.

Ehrman, M.E. (this volume) Chapter 4: Personality and good language learners.

Finkbeiner, C. (this volume) Chapter 10: Culture and good language learners.

Feuerstein, K., Klein, P.S., and Tannenbaum, A.J. (1991) *Mediated Learning Experience: Theoretical, Psychological, and Learning Implications*. London: Freund.

Gordon, L. (this volume) Chapter 19: Writing and good language learners.

Griffiths, C. (this volume) Chapter 2: Age and good language learners.

Griffiths, C. (this volume) Chapter 6: Strategies and good language learners.

Griffiths, C. (this volume) Chapter 20: Teaching/learning method and good language learners.

315

The learners' landscape and journey

Holliday, A. (2003) Social autonomy: Addressing the dangers of culturism in TESOL. In D. Palfreyman, and R.C. Smith (eds.), *Learner autonomy across cultures: Language education perspectives*. London: Palgrave Macmillan, 110–126.

Kawai, Y. (this volume) Chapter 17: Speaking and good language learners.

McCaslin, M. and Hickey, D.T. (2001) Self-regulated learning and academic achievement: A Vygotskian view. In B.J. Zimmerman and D.H. Schunk (eds.), *Self-regulated Learning and Academic Achievement: Theoretical Perspectives*. Mahwah, NJ: Erlbaum, 227–252.

Moir, J. and Nation, P. (this volume) Chapter 12: Vocabulary and good language learners.

Naiman, N., Fröhlich, M., and Todesco, A. (1975) The good second language learner. *TESL Talk*, 6, 68–75.

Nel, C. (this volume) Chapter 3: Learning style and good language learners.

Norton, B. (1997) Language, identity and the ownership of English. *TESOL Quarterly*, 31(3), 409–427.

Norton, B. (2000) *Identity and Language Learning: Gender, Ethnicity and Educational Change*. Harlow: Longman.

Norton, B. and Toohey, K. (2001). Changing perspectives on good language learners. *TESOL Quarterly*, 35(2), 307–322.

Nyikos, M. (this volume) Chapter 5: Gender and good language learners.

O'Malley, J.M. and Chamot, A.U. (1990) *Learning Strategies in Second Language Acquisition*. Cambridge: Cambridge University Press.

Oxford, R.L. (1993) Instructional implications of gender differences in language learning styles and strategies. *Applied Language Learning* 4(1–2), 65–94.

Oxford, R.L. (1994) Gender differences in strategies and styles for L2 learning: What is the significance? Should we pay attention? In J.E. Alatis (ed.), *Theory and Practice of Strategies in Second Language Acquisition*. Washington, DC: Georgetown University Press, 541–557.

Oxford, R.L. (1995) Gender differences in language learning styles: what do they mean? In J.M. Reid (ed.), *Using Learning Styles in the ESL Classroom*. Boston, MA: Heinle & Heinle, 34–46.

Oxford, R.L. and Schramm, K. (2007) Bridging the gap between psychological and sociocultural perspectives on language learning strategies. In A.D. Cohen and E. Macaro (eds.), *Language Learner Strategies: 30 Years of Research and Practice*. Oxford: Oxford University Press.

Oxford, R.L., Nyikos, M., and Ehrman, M.E. (1988) Vive la différence? Reflections on sex differences in use of language learning strategies. *Foreign Language Annals*, 21(4), 321–329.

Ranta, L. (this volume) Chapter 11: Aptitude and good language learners.

Reiss, M.A. (1981) Helping the unsuccessful language learner. *Modern Language Journal*, 65(2), 1.

Rheinberg, F., Vollmeyer, R., and Rollett, W. (2000) Motivation and action in self-regulated learning. In M. Boekaerts, P.R. Pintrich and M. Zeidner (eds.), *Handbook of Self-regulation*. San Diego: Academic Press, 503–529.

Roberts, M. and Griffiths, C. (this volume) Chapter 22: Error correction and good language learners.

316

Rubin, J. (1975) What the "good language learner" can teach us. *TESOL Quarterly*, 9(1), 41–51.

Rubin, J. and McCoy, P. (this volume) Chapter 23: Tasks and good language learners.

Schramm, K. (this volume) Chapter 18: Reading and good language learners.

Stern, H.H. (1975) What can we learn from the good language learner? *Canadian Modern Language Review*, 34, 304–318.

Stevick, E. (1990) *Success with Foreign Languages: Seven Who Achieved it and What Worked for Them*. Englewood Cliffs, NJ: Prentice-Hall International.

Tajeddin, L. (this volume) Chapter 14: Function and good language learners.

Tashakkori, A. and Teddlie, C. (2003) *Handbook of Mixed Methods in Social and Behavioral Research*. Thousand Oaks, CA: Sage.

Ushioda, E. (this volume) Chapter 7: Motivation and good language learners.

Vygotsky, L.S. (1978) *Mind in Society*. Cambridge, MA: Harvard University Press.

White, C. (this volume) Chapter 9: Beliefs and good language learners.

White, G. (this volume) Chapter 16: Listening and good language learners.

Winne, P.H. (2001) Self-regulated learning viewed from models of information processing. In B.J. Zimmerman and D.H. Schunk (eds.), *Self-regulated Learning and Academic Achievement: Theoretical Perspectives*. Mahwah, NJ: Erlbaum, 153–189.

Winne, P.H. (2005) Key issues in modeling and applying research on self-regulated learning. *Applied Psychology: An International Review*, 54, 232–238.

Index

Index

Index

Index

teaching/learning methods 40, 146, 255–63
  audiolingual method 175, 218, 256
  cognitive view 256–7
  communicative language teaching 142,
   146–7, 176, 258–9
  direct method 259
  grammar–translation method 175,
   255–6
  Krashen's hypotheses 257–8
  natural method 259, 284, 285–6
  postmethod 259
  research study 259–61, 261t
  silent way 259
  situational language teaching 259
  suggestopedia 259
terminology 3–5
Terrell, T. 40, 284
think-aloud protocols 83, 106, 211, 235,
  268–9
third culture 135–6
Thompson, I. 10, 220
Thornbury, S. 180
Tomasello, M. 287
Toohey, K. 23–5, 26, 29, 40, 78, 121, 124,
  127, 258
Torres, E. 102
total physical response method 259
Transformational-Generative Grammar
  257
Tremblay, P.F. 20
Trosborg, A. 187, 190
Truscott, J. 286
Tyre, P. 74, 77–8, 80

Uhrig, K. 11
Universal Grammar (UG) 257, 283, 285
Ur, P. 174, 181, 290, 294
Ushioda, E. 25, 26, 27

Van Dijk, T.A. 234
Van Houtte, M. 77, 80
Van Naerssen, M. 219
Vandergrift, L. 103, 211
Vann, R. 11, 104, 122–3
Varela, E. 219–20
Victori, M. 123
videos for self-evaluation 103–4, 105–6
Vigil, F. 286, 290
vocabulary 91, 159–73
  aspects of word knowledge 164–5,
   167–8
  beliefs 162–3
  language awareness 169–70
  learning and memorizing words 165–6,
   168
  learning strategies 159, 170, 171–2
  notebooks 160

  personal approaches: study 160–71,
   161t, 311
  revision 166, 168
  selection of words 163–4, 167
  self-evaluation and monitoring 166–7,
   168–9
  teacher/course expectations 170–1
  for writing 249
volitional strategies 313–14
Vygotsky, L.S. 25, 136

Weaver, G.R. 131
Weaver, S.J. et al. 220
Weinbach, L. 189
Wells, C.G. 144
Wenden, A.L. 10, 11, 83, 104, 114, 122,
  125, 294, 295, 304, 305
Wenger, J. 126
Wesche, M.B. 84, 146, 147, 149
Wharton, G. 272
White, C. 124–5, 127
White, J. 148
Widdowson, H. 259
Wilkins, D.A. 186–7, 189, 258
Williams, J. 182
Williams, M. 23
Willing, K. 10, 53
Winne, P. 85, 86
Witkin, H.A. 51
Wode, H. et al. 284
Wolfersberger, M. 102–3
Wong Fillmore, L. 83
Woods, D. 125
Wren, D. 287
writing 244–53
  feedback 245, 287–8
  functional approach 246–7
  genre approach 245–6, 249
  goals 251
  grammar 245, 250
  meaning 249–50
  motivation 250, 251
  opportunities 251, 252
  process approach 245–6, 250
  and reading 248
  revising 245, 250
  skills development: study 247–51
  strategies for uncertainty 249
  task analysis 297–303, 298t, 302–3t
  theories 244–7
  vocabulary 249

Yalden, J. 175
Yang, N.-D. 123
Yoshimura, Y. 143
Young, R. 132
Yule, G. 175, 202, 262

324